CODE OF ALABAMA
1975

With Provision for Subsequent Pocket Parts

Prepared Under the Supervision of

The Code Revision Subcommittee of
The Legislative Council

Robert H. Harris, Chairman

by

The Editorial Staff of the Publishers

Under the Direction of

A. D. Kowalsky, S. C. Willard, W. L. Jackson,
M. A. Sancilio, and T. R. Troxell

VOLUME 15A

1992 REPLACEMENT VOLUME

---

*Including Acts through the 1992 Regular and First Special Sessions
and annotations taken through Southern Reporter,
Second Series, Volume 595, page 856*

THE MICHIE COMPANY
Law Publishers
Charlottesville, Virginia
1992

Table of Titles

In Addition, This Publication Contains

Table of Contents

VOLUME 15A

User's Guide

In order to assist both the legal profession and the layman in obtaining the maximum benefit from the Code of Alabama, a User's Guide has been included in Volume 1. This guide contains comments and information on the many features found within the Code of Alabama intended to increase the usefulness of this set of laws to the user. See Volume 1 of this set for the complete User's Guide.

Scope of Annotations

The annotations contained in this volume are derived from the following sources:

Southern Reporter, Second Series, through volume 580, p. 566.
Federal Reporter, Second Series, through volume 934, p. 1266.
Federal Supplement, through volume 764, p. 193.
Federal Rules Decisions, through volume 136, p. 231.
Bankruptcy Reporter, through volume 127, p. 500.
Supreme Court Reporter, through volume 111, p. 2280.
Opinions of the Clerk of the Supreme Court of Alabama.

CODE OF ALABAMA

TITLE 26.

INFANTS AND INCOMPETENTS.

TABLE OF CONTENTS

Cross references. — As to accounts of minors in savings and loan associations, see § 5-16-43. As to actions for furnishing liquor to minors, see § 6-5-70. As to liability of parents for intentional, wilful or malicious destruction of property by minor, see § 6-5-380. As to actions for injuries to minor child, see § 6-5-390. As to actions for wrongful death of minor, see § 6-5-391. As to contracts of insane persons, see § 8-1-170. As to ownership of securities by minors, see § 8-6-90 et seq. As to infant stockholders, see § 10-6-1 et seq. As to employing, harboring, procuring or using girls between ages of ten and eighteen years for purpose of prostitution, see §§ 13A-12-111, 13A-12-112. As to betting with minors, see §§ 13A-12-21, 13A-12-22. As to child labor generally, see § 25-8-1 et seq. As to purchase of insurance by or for minors, see § 27-14-5. As to minimum age for contracting marriage, see § 30-1-4. As to consent of parents for marriage of persons under eighteen years of age, see § 30-1-5. As to power of minor veterans to contract liability for repayment of certain loans, see § 31-1-2. As to prohibition against minors playing billiards, see § 34-6-9. As to permitting minors to play billiards or pool, see § 34-6-10. As to Uniform Transfers to Minors Act, see § 35-5A-1 et seq. As to aid to dependent children, see § 38-1-1 et seq. As to time limitation for infants and persons of unsound mind to contest validity of wills, see § 43-8-201.

CHAPTER 1.

GENERAL PROVISIONS.

Collateral references. — Judgment in guardian's final accounting proceedings as res judicata in ward's subsequent action against guardian. 34 ALR4th 1121.

§ 26-1-1. Age of majority designated as 19 years.

(a) Any person in this state, at the arrival at the age of 19 years, shall be relieved of his disabilities of minority and thereafter shall have the same legal rights and abilities as persons over 21 years of age. No law of this state shall discriminate for or against any person between and including the ages of 19 and 21 years solely on the basis of age.

(b) This section shall also apply to any person who arrived at the age of 19 and 20 years before July 22, 1975, but shall not abrogate any defense or abridge any remedy available to him prior to such date.

(c) All laws or parts of laws which read "under the age of 21 years" hereafter shall read "under the age of 19 years." Wherever the words "under the age of 21 years" appear in any law limiting the legal rights and abilities of persons under such age, such words shall be construed to mean under the age of 19 years.

(d) Notwithstanding the provisions of subsection (c) of this section, nothing in this section shall be deemed to repeal any provision of Chapter 19 of Title 15 of this Code. (Acts 1975, No. 77.)

Cross references. — As to relief from disabilities of minority for married women and widows 18 years of age and over, see § 30-4-15. As to relief from disabilities of minority for married men and widowers 18 years of age and over, see § 30-4-16.

Persons not exempted from mandates of section due to status on effective date of law. — This section was not intended to exempt persons from the responsibilities of adulthood merely because they were the beneficiaries of child support payments on the date that the act became law, nor was any group of persons to be exempted from its mandates, nor was the statutory change in adulthood to apply to the future only or to the past. Davenport v. Davenport, 356 So. 2d 205 (Ala. Civ. App. 1978).

The rule in Alabama is that minority is a status, rather than a fixed or vested right. Davenport v. Davenport, 356 So. 2d 205 (Ala. Civ. App. 1978).

Minority is not a vested right. — Minority is a status rather than a vested right, and a new age of majority applies to a plaintiff even if his cause of action accrued before the statute creating the new age of majority was enacted. Garner v. Hunt, 577 So. 2d 898 (Ala. 1991).

Removal of disabilities of nonage does not create new rights nor abrogate existing ones. — The removal of the disabilities of nonage does not create new rights nor abrogate existing ones. It merely extends new privileges to a class of persons to whom these privileges were formerly unavailable. Davenport v. Davenport, 356 So. 2d 205 (Ala. Civ. App. 1978).

But may terminate certain privileges of minors. — A change in the age of adulthood may terminate certain privileges, one of which is the receipt of child support by a child who previously would have been deemed a minor. Davenport v. Davenport, 356 So. 2d 205 (Ala. Civ. App. 1978).

This section, as applied to former § 12-16-43 (qualifications of jurors), was not retrospective. For present provisions or qualifications of jurors, see § 12-16-55, et seq. Hurley v. State, 335 So. 2d 183 (Ala. Crim. App.), cert. denied, 335 So. 2d 188 (Ala. 1976).

The Youthful Offender Act is clearly applicable to a person charged with driving under the influence of alcohol, provided that the offense "was committed in his minority but was not disposed of in juvenile court." King v. Wooldridge, 547 So. 2d 579 (Ala. 1989).

Age of rape victim is relevant in analysis of forcible compulsion. — The age of a rape victim is very relevant in an analysis of forcible compulsion. Therefore, there was no error in the trial court's charge that the victim had not yet reached the age of majority. Parks v. State, 587 So. 2d 1015 (Ala. Crim. App. 1991).

Cited in Godec v. Godec, 346 So. 2d 459 (Ala. Civ. App. 1977); Thornton v. Badger Northland, Inc., 346 So. 2d 944 (Ala. 1977); Campbell v. Campbell, 426 So. 2d 848 (Ala. Civ. App. 1983); Wynn v. State, 480 So. 2d 1 (Ala. Civ. App. 1983).

Collateral references. — Statutory change of age of majority as affecting preexisting status or rights. 75 ALR3d 228.

Witnesses: child competency statutes. 60 ALR4th 369.

§ 26-1-2. Creation of durable power of attorney; effect of acts performed pursuant to durable power of attorney during period of disability, etc., of principal; appointment by court of guardian, etc., subsequent to execution of durable power of attorney; effect of death of principal upon agency relationship and validity of acts of person acting under power of attorney; execution, etc., of affidavit by person exercising power of attorney as to lack of knowledge of revocation, etc., of power of attorney.

(a) A durable power of attorney is a power of attorney by which a principal designates another his attorney in fact or agent in writing and the writing contains the words "This power of attorney shall not be affected by disability, incompetency, or incapacity of the principal" or "This power of attorney shall become effective upon the disability, incompetency, or incapacity of the principal" or similar words showing the intent of the principal that the authority conferred shall be exercisable notwithstanding the principal's subsequent disability, incompetency or incapacity.

(b) All acts done by an attorney in fact pursuant to a durable power of attorney during any period of disability, incompetency or incapacity of the principal have the same effect and inure to the benefit of and bind the principal and his successors in interest as if the principal were competent, not disabled and not incapacitated.

(c)(1) If, following execution of a durable power of attorney, a court of the principal's domicile appoints a guardian, curator or other fiduciary charged with the management of all the principal's property or all of his property except specified exclusions, the attorney in fact is accountable to the fiduciary as well as to the principal. The fiduciary has the same power to revoke or amend the power of attorney that the principal would have had if he were not disabled, incompetent or incapacitated.

(2) A principal may nominate, by a durable power of attorney, the guardian, curator or other fiduciary for consideration by the court if proceedings to appoint a fiduciary for the principal are thereafter commenced. The court shall make its appointment in accordance with the principal's most recent nomination in a durable power of attorney except for good cause or disqualification.

(d)(1) The death of a principal who has executed a written power of attorney, durable or otherwise, does not revoke or terminate the agency as to the attorney in fact or other person who, without actual knowledge of the death of the principal, acts in good faith under the power. Any action so taken, unless otherwise invalid or unenforceable, binds the successors in interest of the principal.

(2) The disability, incompetency or incapacity of a principal who has previously executed a written power of attorney that is not a durable power does not revoke or terminate the agency as to the attorney in fact or other person who, without actual knowledge of the disability, incompetency or incapacity of the principal, acts in good faith under the power. Any action so taken, unless otherwise invalid or unenforceable, binds the principal and his successors in interest.

(e) As to acts undertaken in good faith reliance thereon, an affidavit executed by the attorney in fact under a power of attorney, durable or otherwise, stating that he did not have, at the time of the exercise of the power, actual knowledge of the termination of the power by revocation or of the principal's death, disability, incompetency or incapacity is conclusive proof of the nonrevocation or nontermination of the power at that time. If the exercise of the power of attorney requires execution and delivery of any instrument that is recordable, the affidavit, when authenticated for record, is likewise recordable.

(f) This section shall not affect any provision in a power of attorney for its termination by expiration of time or occurrence of an event other than express revocation or a change in the principal's capacity. (Acts 1981, No. 81-98, p. 117.)

Collateral references. — 3 C.J.S., Agency, §§ 150-152.
3 Am. Jur. 2d, Agency, §§ 34, 51, 55, 60.

§ 26-1-3. Blood donations by persons 17 or older.

Any person who is 17 years of age or older shall be eligible to donate blood without the necessity of obtaining parental permission or authorization. (Acts 1984, 1st Ex. Sess., No. 84-763, p. 134.)

Collateral references. — Discovery of identity of blood donor. 56 ALR4th 755.

§ 26-1-4. Department of Public Safety to provide criminal conviction information on applicants for positions involving child care and treatment; such information to be confidential; applicant to be denied status if has felony conviction; children may be removed from home.

(a) Notwithstanding any other provisions of law to the contrary, upon request to the Department of Public Safety, by the Department of Human Resources, or by any other youth service agency approved by the department, such center shall provide information to the department or an approved agency concerning the felony criminal conviction record in this or another state of an applicant for a paid or voluntary position, including one established by contract, whose primary duty is the care or treatment of children, including applicants for adoption or foster parents. All information, including any criminal conviction record, procured by the department or an approved agency shall be confidential and shall not be further disclosed by such agencies or their representatives. The applicant may be denied an adoptive or foster parent status if he or she has a felony conviction, and if a foster parent is subsequently convicted of a felony the child or children may be removed from that home and relocated with another foster parent. This determination shall be made by the court handling the matter, giving primary consideration to the best interests of the child.

(b) The Department of Public Safety shall provide appropriate forms and shall create a procedure for the application for such information.

(c) Any violation of the provisions of this section relative to the confidentiality of information received by the department or other approved agency shall be punishable by a fine of not more than $1,000.00. (Acts 1985, No. 85-537, p. 651.)

§ 26-1-5. Age of majority for purposes of contracting for college level education and above.

Notwithstanding any other law to the contrary, the age of majority for the purposes of contracting for educational loans for college level education and above, within the State of Alabama, shall be 17 years of age. (Acts 1987, No. 87-801, p. 1574.)

CHAPTER 2.

APPOINTMENT OF GUARDIANS.

ARTICLE 1.

GENERAL PROVISIONS.

Cross references. — As to actions for appointment of trustees to preserve estates of intemperates or inebriates, see § 6-6-520 et seq. As to substitution of guardian for next friend in actions other than those for personal injury, see § 6-7-100. As to action for improper appointment of guardians ad litem, see § 6-7-103. As to appointment of guardians ad litem for infants or incompetents in eminent domain proceedings, see § 18-1A-275.

§ 26-2-1. "Person of unsound mind" and "partially disabled person" defined; application of provisions to partially disabled persons. Repealed by Acts 1987, No. 87-590, p. 975, § 2-333(a), effective January 1, 1988.

§ 26-2-2. Removal of guardianship or conservatorship from probate to circuit court.

The administration or conduct of any guardianship or conservatorship of a minor or incapacitated person may be removed from the probate court to the circuit court, at any time before the final settlement thereof by the guardian or conservator of any such guardianship or conservatorship or guardian ad litem or next friend of such ward or anyone entitled to support out of the estate of such ward without assigning any special equity, and an order of removal must be made by the court or judge upon the filing of a sworn petition by any such guardian or conservator or guardian ad litem or next friend for the ward or such person entitled to support out of the estate of such ward, reciting in what capacity the petitioner acts and that in the opinion of the petitioner such guardianship or conservatorship can be better administered in the circuit court than in the probate court. (Code 1923, § 8102; Acts 1939, No. 125, p. 168; Code 1940, T. 21, § 26; Acts 1987, No. 87-590, p. 975, § 2-333(b).)

Removal under this section invokes ordinary powers of court. — The removal of administration of guardianship of insane person from probate court to circuit court invokes ordinary powers of court. Evans v. Crump, 232 Ala. 521, 168 So. 879 (1936); Montgomery v. Montgomery, 236 Ala. 33, 180 So. 709 (1938); Ex parte Garrison, 260 Ala. 379, 71 So. 2d 33 (1954).

Where a case is removed from a probate court into a circuit court the proceeding had and the rules and practice that prevail are the general jurisdiction and procedure of the circuit court and the powers conferred by law. The jurisdiction of the probate court over final settlements of guardians being statutory and limited, must be exercised strictly according to such statutes. However, since the jurisdiction of the circuit court is original and general, such statutes should be applied in the light of the practice and procedure of the circuit court but without abuse of judicial discretion. Ex parte Garrison, 260 Ala. 379, 71 So. 2d 33 (1954).

And court may adjust all equities between the parties. Ex parte Garrison, 260 Ala. 379, 71 So. 2d 33 (1954).

Next of kin of deceased ward have no right under this section to remove a guardianship administration to the circuit court without assigning any special equity. Smith v. Smith, 248 Ala. 49, 26 So. 2d 571 (1946).

"Grandmother and next friend" within class of persons authorized to remove guardianship of minor. — Where in her petition for the removal of the guardianship petitioner described herself as "the grandmother and next friend," she came within the class of persons designated in this section as authorized to remove the administration or conduct of any guardianship of a minor before the final settlement by the guardian. Fuller v. Jackson, 519 So. 2d 936 (Ala. 1988).

Effect of decree of foreign court restoring sanity. — A Florida decree that Florida resident had been restored to sanity made it duty of Alabama ancillary guardian to make a final settlement of his guardianship, but did not ipso facto remove or discharge him. Ward v. Stallworth, 243 Ala. 651, 11 So. 2d 374 (1942).

Case properly remanded to probate court. — Where decedent's estate was removed from probate court to the circuit court at a time when probate court had entered upon the exercise of its jurisdiction of settlement of special administration and before expiration of the time within which settlement had been ordered, the case was properly remanded to the probate court. Gardner v. Gardner, 244 Ala. 107, 11 So. 2d 852 (1943).

Court has power to authorize guardian to mortgage estate regardless of section. — As to the power of court to authorize a guardian of a non compos mentis to mortgage the ward's real estate, it has been said that the power exists, irrespective of this section, by which the guardianship may be removed to circuit court and there administered. The power was upheld in the case of Montgomery v. Perryman & Co., 147 Ala. 207, 41 So. 838 (1906), provided it be reported to and confirmed by that court, since the mortgage is by the court, not the guardian, except as the agent of the court, the title standing in the ward. Wilson v. McKleroy, 206 Ala. 342, 89 So. 584 (1921); Evans v. Crump, 232 Ala. 521, 168 So. 879 (1936).

On the same principle a court has like power in respect to the guardianship of a minor (Warren v. Southall, 224 Ala. 653, 141 So. 632 (1932)) and to the administration of the estate of a decedent (First Nat'l Bank v. De Jernett, 229 Ala. 564, 159 So. 73 (1935)). Evans v. Crump, 232 Ala. 521, 168 So. 879 (1936).

Having acted to remove entire guardianship to circuit court, petitioner has waived any right of appeal from probate court's order on motion to remove another as guardian. Indeed, a party cannot by his own volition choose two distinct jurisdictional forums in which to litigate the same issue; such an election is tantamount to appealing from an order to which he has consented. Fuller v. Jackson, 519 So. 2d 936 (Ala. 1988).

Cited in Pierce v. Barbaree, 238 Aia. 676, 193 So. 115 (1939); Priest v. Chenault, 239 Ala. 209, 194 So. 651 (1940); McNairy v. McNairy, 416 So. 2d 735 (Ala. 1982).

Collateral references. — 21 C.J.S., Courts, § 502. 39 C.J.S., Guardian & Ward, § 4.

Validity of appointment of guardian for infant without service of process upon, or notice to, latter. 1 ALR 919.

Minority of parent as affecting right to guardianship or custody of person or state of child. 19 ALR 1043.

Appointment of guardian for infant as affecting rights and duties of parents. 63 ALR 1147.

Right of parent to notice and hearing before being deprived of custody of child. 76 ALR 242.

Necessity and sufficiency of notice of appointment of successor to guardian to ward. 138 ALR 1364.

Nonresidence as affecting one's right to award of custody of child. 15 ALR2d 432.

Consideration and weight of religious affiliations in appointment of guardian for minor child. 22 ALR2d 696.

Function, power, and discretion of court where there is testamentary appointment of guardian of minor. 67 ALR2d 803.

ARTICLE 2.

GENERAL CONSERVATOR FOR COUNTY; GUARDIANS OF MINORS.

Cross references. — As to appointment of guardians ad litem for infants in partition proceeding, see § 35-6-60. As to sale of land of minors for distribution among joint owners, see § 35-6-80 et seq.

§§ 26-2-20 through 26-2-25. Repealed by Acts 1987, No. 87-590, p. 975, § 2-333(a), effective January 1, 1988.

Code commissioner's note. — Section 2-334 of Acts 1987, No. 87-590 provides: "Guardianships created prior to the effective date of this Act, and continuing in effect on the date this Act becomes effective, are not terminated, even though the statute under which the appointment was made may be repealed by this Act. Those guardianships continue in effect as they existed prior to this Act with all the powers and duties of the guardianship, except that the guardian previously appointed in addition will have the powers and duties of a guardian and a conservator under this Act to the extent that the powers and duties under this Act may be broader or more clearly expressed." See § 26-2A-8.

Cross references. — As to application of Chapter 2A to guardianships created prior to January 1, 1988, and continuing in effect on January 1, 1988, see § 26-2A-8.

§ 26-2-26. General conservator for county.

The judge of probate may appoint a general conservator for the county who must be appointed and act as a conservator when no other fit person applies for appointment and qualifies. The term of office of such general conservator shall continue during the term of the judge by whom he is appointed, unless he is reappointed. If he is reappointed, his bond, if deemed sufficient, shall remain as a continuing security, or he may be required to execute a new bond. (Code 1867, § 2423, Code 1876, § 2765; Code 1886, § 2376; Code 1896, § 2253; Code 1907, § 4343; Code 1923, § 8100; Code 1940, T. 21, § 7; Acts 1987, No. 87-590, p. 975, § 2-333(b).)

§ 26-2-27. Appointment of sheriff as guardian.

If no fit person is appointed and qualifies as guardian of a minor and there be no general guardian for the county, the sheriff must be appointed guardian and the guardianship attaches to the office of sheriff. (Code 1852, § 2017; Code 1867, § 2416; Code 1876, § 2767; Code 1886, § 2377; Code 1896, § 2254; Code 1907, § 4344; Code 1923, § 8101; Code 1940, T. 21, § 8.)

Sheriff and his sureties become liable when he is appointed guardian. — When the sheriff is appointed guardian, by virtue of this section and the condition of his bond, the sheriff and his sureties become bound, in all respects, so long as his guardianship continues, as if the bond had been specially executed by him as guardian. Pearce v. Hall, 113 Ala. 245, 21 So. 250 (1896).

His responsibility does not cease upon termination of his office. — The termination of the sheriff's official office and of his guardianship does not relieve the officer from liability for money received as guardian, and for failure to account therefor his sureties are liable. Pearce v. Hall, 113 Ala. 245, 21 So. 250 (1896). Whether or not the sureties would be liable where the money was received after the expiration of the officer's term is left undecided, but under the authority of Gravett v. Malone, 54 Ala. 19 (1875), it would seem that they could be relieved.

Cited in Lee v. Lee, 67 Ala. 406 (1880); Hamilton v. James, 231 Ala. 668, 166 So. 425 (1936).

ARTICLE 3.

GUARDIANS OF INCAPACITATED PERSONS.

Cross references. — As to actions against guardians of persons of unsound mind, see § 6-7-102. As to appointment of guardians ad litem for persons of unsound mind in partition proceedings, see § 35-6-60. As to sale of land of insane persons for distribution among joint owners, see § 35-6-80 et seq.

Probate court's authority to appoint guardian must be exercised only as prescribed by statute. Fowler v. Nash, 225 Ala. 613, 144 So. 831 (1932).

Validity of appointment depends on incompetent being declared insane. — The validity of appointment of guardian for incompetent person and guardian's authority to bring action depends on record showing of a legal declaration that incompetent was of unsound mind. Montgomery v. Montgomery, 236 Ala. 33, 180 So. 709 (1938).

Where the decree declaring a person of unsound mind is not void, the subsequent proceedings in the guardianship, including partial settlement, are not void. Riley v. Smyer, 265 Ala. 475, 91 So. 2d 820 (1956).

The property rights of the adjudged incompetent are not affected by an adjudication of insanity. On the contrary the very purpose of the inquisition proceeding is ultimately to appoint a guardian to preserve the property of the incompetent. Smith v. Smith, 254 Ala. 404, 48 So. 2d 546 (1950).

Evidence sufficient to show proceedings to adjudge man insane were fraudulent. — Averment in motion to set aside proceedings adjudging property owner insane and appointing guardian, that proceedings were fraudulent scheme to deprive owner of his property, held sustained by evidence. Fowler v. Nash, 225 Ala. 613, 144 So. 831 (1932).

Proceedings adjudging property owner insane and appointing guardian without giving him required notice of proceedings held void as denial of due process of law. Fowler v. Nash, 225 Ala. 613, 144 So. 831 (1932).

Cited in Whetstone v. Whetstone, 75 Ala. 495 (1883); Patterson v. Downs, 255 Ala. 197, 50 So. 2d 408 (1951).

Collateral references. — Mental condition which will justify the appointment of guardian, committee, or conservator of the estate for an incompetent or spendthrift. 9 ALR3d 774.

Priority and preference in appointing conservator or guardian for an incompetent. 65 ALR3d 991.

§ 26-2-40. Authorization generally. Repealed by Acts 1987, No. 87-590, p. 975, § 2-333(a), effective January 1, 1988.

Code commissioner's note. — Section 2-334 of Acts 1987, No. 87-590 provides: "Guardianships created prior to the effective date of this Act, and continuing in effect on the date this Act becomes effective, are not terminated, even though the statute under which the appointment was made may be repealed by this Act. Those guardianships continue in effect as they existed prior to this Act with all of the powers and duties of the guardianship, except that the guardian previously appointed in addition will have the powers and duties of a guardian and a conservator under this Act to the extent that the powers and duties under this Act may be broader or more clearly expressed. See § 26-2A-8.

Cross references. — As to application of Chapter 2A to guardianships created prior to January 1, 1988, and continuing in effect on January 1, 1988, see § 26-2A-8.

§§ 26-2-41, 26-2-42. Repealed by Acts 1987, No. 87-590, p. 975, § 2-333(a), effective January 1, 1988.

§ 26-2-43. Procedure generally — Summoning, etc., of jurors, witnesses and person alleged to be incapacitated.

The judge of probate must issue a writ directed to the sheriff commanding him to summon six disinterested persons of the neighborhood for the trial thereof and also issue subpoenas for witnesses, as the parties may require, returnable to the time of trial. The probate judge must also issue a writ directed to the sheriff to take the person alleged to be incapacitated and, if consistent with his health or safety, have him present at the place of the trial. (Code 1852, § 2751; Code 1867, § 3190; Code 1876, § 2758; Code 1886, § 3393; Code 1896, § 2258; Code 1907, § 4348; Code 1923, § 8106; Code 1940, T. 21, § 12; Acts 1945, No. 468, p. 704; Acts 1987, No. 87-590, p. 975, § 2-333(b).)

Section does not violate constitutional right of trial by jury. — This section providing for a six-man jury in an insanity inquisition is not in conflict with the Constitution, § 11, for, even though such an inquisition partakes of the nature of a civil action, it is a proceeding sui generis. Smith v. Smith, 254 Ala. 404, 48 So. 2d 546 (1950).

Technical error in writ does not void it. — The writ of the judge issued to the sheriff will not be held void because not technically correct, where its meaning is evident and the person is before the court. Craft v. Simon, 118 Ala. 625, 24 So. 380 (1898), aff'd, 182 U.S. 427, 21 S. Ct. 836, 45 L. Ed. 1165 (1901).

Where the process fails to specify that the jury were to be summoned "of the neighborhood," but no objection to venire is made in probate court, and by recital in decree it appears that the jurors resided in the neighborhood of the insane person, it is harmless error. Benton v. Benton, 211 Ala. 43, 99 So. 300

(1924). See also, Craft v. Simon, 118 Ala. 625, 24 So. 380 (1898), aff'd, 182 U.S. 427, 21 S. Ct. 836, 45 L. Ed. 1165 (1901).

Alleged lunatic must have notice, and one method of bringing notice home to him is by restraining him of his liberty. Prestwood v. Prestwood, 395 So. 2d 8 (Ala. 1981).

Decree must affirmatively show that sheriff took person allegedly of unsound mind into custody. — Where decree adjudging person of unsound mind failed to affirmatively show that sheriff executed writ by taking person allegedly of unsound mind into his custody, as required by this section, and showed that writ was executed only by summoning the jurors for trial, the proceedings were void. Fowler v. Fowler, 219 Ala. 453, 122 So. 440 (1929).

In order to sustain the decree adjudging the complainant a person of unsound mind, it must affirmatively appear on the face of the record that all of the necessary jurisdictional steps were taken to complete the court's jurisdiction, and the record cannot be aided by intendment, even on collateral attack. Prestwood v. Prestwood, 395 So. 2d 8 (Ala. 1981).

Sufficiency of motion to set aside proceedings. — Averments of motion to set aside lunacy proceedings held to sufficiently show that writ was not executed in accordance with this section and that complainant was deceived as to nature of proceedings and had perfect defense thereto by reason of want of jurisdiction. Fowler v. Fowler, 219 Ala. 453, 122 So. 440 (1929).

Cited in Fore v. Fore, 44 Ala. 478 (1870); Montgomery v. Montgomery, 236 Ala. 33, 180 So. 709 (1938); Hornaday v. Hornaday, 254 Ala. 267, 48 So. 2d 207 (1950); Walker v. Elrod, 284 Ala. 32, 221 So. 2d 391 (1969); Nigg v. Smith, 415 So. 2d 1082 (Ala. 1982).

Collateral references. — 44 C.J.S., Insane Persons, § 20.

§ 26-2-44. Procedure generally — Impaneling and swearing in of jury; filling of vacancies on jury.

(a) At the time set for the trial, if good cause be not shown for continuance, the jury must be impaneled and sworn well and truly to make inquisition of the facts alleged in the petition, and render a true verdict according to the evidence.

(b) If any of the jurors are excused from serving, fail to attend or are set aside for any cause, their places may be supplied from the bystanders. (Code 1852, § 2752; Code 1867, § 3191; Code 1876, § 2759; Code 1886, § 2394; Code 1896, § 2259; Code 1907, § 4349; Code 1923, § 8107; Code 1940, T. 21, § 13.)

This section sets forth the procedures to be followed by the probate judge in selecting a jury in matters of this nature. Walker v. Elrod, 284 Ala. 32, 221 So. 2d 391 (1969).

The probate court has unlimited authority to replace a juror provided the proceedings are started anew. Walker v. Elrod, 284 Ala. 32, 221 So. 2d 391 (1969).

In the absence of a summoned juror, a qualified bystander may be substituted. Sorter v. Austen, 221 Ala. 481, 129 So. 51 (1930); Walker v. Elrod, 284 Ala. 32, 221 So. 2d 391 (1969).

But this is applicable only before impanelment. Once the list is made up for the trial of a case, it is error to allow a juror to refuse to serve without being discharged by the court. Walker v. Elrod, 284 Ala. 32, 221 So. 2d 391 (1969).

Discharge of juror after selection. — The court may discharge a juror after his selection if he becomes sick or if, for other cause, it becomes necessary, in the opinion of the court, to discharge him. Walker v. Elrod, 284 Ala. 32, 221 So. 2d 391 (1969).

Right of parties to challenge members of jury for cause. — This section contains no specific procedures for striking jurors, nevertheless, the statute does authorize the setting aside of jurors for cause, thereby recognizing the right of the parties to challenge a member of the proposed jury for cause. Prestwood v. Prestwood, 395 So. 2d 8 (Ala. 1981).

Selection of another juror without consent of accused. — Where, after being selected and accepted by both parties, a juror was permitted to leave the court and another juror was selected in his place, without the consent of the accused, this was error. Walker v. Elrod, 284 Ala. 32, 221 So. 2d 391 (1969).

Cited in Montgomery v. Montgomery, 236 Ala. 33, 180 So. 709 (1938).

Collateral references. — 44 C.J.S., Insane Persons, § 21.

§ 26-2-45. Procedure generally — Entry of decree, recordation of proceedings and appointment of conservator by court upon rendition of verdict of jury.

If the jury find by their verdict that the facts alleged in the petition are true and that such person is incapacitated, the court shall enter a decree accordingly, and must cause the petition and all the proceedings thereon to be recorded and appoint a suitable conservator of such person. (Code 1852, § 2753; Code 1867, § 3192; Code 1876, § 2760; Code 1886, § 2395; Code 1896, § 2260; Code 1907, § 4350; Code 1923, § 8108; Code 1940, T. 21, § 14; Acts 1982, No. 82-384, p. 561, § 2; Acts 1987, No. 87-590, p. 975, § 2-333(b).)

The word "qualified" might be construed to include "suitable." Richards v. Elrod, 284 Ala. 19, 221 So. 2d 378 (1969).

Contents of decree. — A decree adjudging a person of unsound mind, which omitted the affirmation of the jurisdictional facts set forth in the petition, was not therefore rendered void, since omission did not affect the regularity or validity of the decree. Riley v. Smyer, 265 Ala. 475, 91 So. 2d 820 (1956).

Cited in In re Carmichael, 36 Ala. 514 (1860); Craft v. Simon, 118 Ala. 625, 24 So. 380 (1898), aff'd, 182 U.S. 427, 21 S. Ct. 836, 45 L. Ed. 1165 (1901); Montgomery v. Montgomery, 236 Ala. 33, 180 So. 709 (1938).

Collateral references. — 44 C.J.S., Insane Persons, §§ 26, 37.

Effect of death of appellant upon appeal from judgment of mental incompetence against him. 54 ALR2d 1161.

§ 26-2-46. Procedure where person alleged to be of unsound mind confined in hospital or asylum.

If the person alleged to be of unsound mind is a resident of the county and is at the time of the application confined in a hospital or asylum within or without the state, inquisition may be had and taken without notice to him, but, on the filing of the application, the court must appoint a guardian ad litem to represent and defend for him. It shall be the duty of such guardian by answer to put in issue the facts stated in the application and to employ counsel at the expense of such person of unsound mind to appear and defend him. (Code 1876, § 2761; Code 1886, § 2396; Code 1896, § 2261; Code 1907, § 4351; Code 1923, § 8109; Code 1940, T. 21, § 15.)

Proceedings not void for lack of notice. — Proceedings to declare a person of unsound mind, who was a resident of the state and who was confined in a sanitarium outside the state were not void for lack of notice, where the court appointed a competent attorney as guardian ad litem to represent and defend the person alleged of unsound mind, and the attorney put in issue the facts stated in the application. Riley v. Smyer, 265 Ala. 475, 91 So. 2d 820 (1956).

Cited in Montgomery v. Montgomery, 236 Ala. 33, 180 So. 709 (1938); Ex parte Herrin, 257 Ala. 392, 60 So. 2d 56 (1952).

§ 26-2-47. Appointment of guardian for nonresident incapacitated person having property within state — Authorization.

The court of probate of a county in which an incapacitated person residing without the state may have property, real or personal, requiring the care of a conservator, may appoint a conservator for the property of such person which may be within this state if such person has been declared an incapacitated person by a court having jurisdiction in the state of his residence. (Code 1867, § 2415; Code 1876, § 2755; Code 1886, § 2402; Code 1896, § 2267; Code 1907, § 4357; Code 1923, § 8115; Code 1940, T. 21, § 21; Acts 1987, No. 87-590, p. 975, § 2-333(b)).)

§ 26-2-48. Appointment of guardian for nonresident incapacitated person having property within state — Procedure.

The application for the appointment of a conservator for such person must be in writing, must be verified by affidavit and must state the name, sex, age and residence of such person, the court by which he was declared incapacitated and the property requiring the care of a conservator.

On the filing of such application, the court must appoint a day for the hearing thereof, notice of which must be given for three successive weeks by publication in some newspaper published in the county or, if there is no such paper published in the county, by publication in a paper published in an adjoining county, and a copy of such paper must be mailed by the probate judge to such person at the post office nearest his residence. The court must appoint a guardian ad litem to represent and defend for such person and it shall be the duty of such guardian ad litem to put in issue the facts stated in the application. If, on the hearing the application is not granted, the court must render a decree against the applicant for all the costs of the proceedings, including the reasonable compensation of the guardian ad litem. (Code 1867, § 2415; Code 1876, § 2755; Code 1886, § 2403; Code 1896, § 2268; Code 1907, § 4358; Code 1923, § 8116; Code 1940, T. 21, § 22; Acts 1987, No. 87-590, p. 975, § 2-333(b)).)

Cited in Armstrong v. Robertson, 2 Ala. 164 (1841).

§ 26-2-49. Selection of guardian where two or more applicants. Repealed by Acts 1987, No. 87-590, p. 975, § 2-333(a), effective January 1, 1988.

§ 26-2-50. Appointment of general conservator of county or sheriff as guardian.

The general conservator of the county must be appointed conservator of an incapacitated person if no other suitable person applies for appointment and qualifies and if there be no general conservator, the sheriff must be appointed. (Code 1852, § 2017; Code 1867, §§ 2416, 2423; Code 1876, §§ 2765, 2767; Code 1886, § 2405; Code 1896, § 2270; Code 1907, § 4360; Code 1923, § 8118; Code 1940, T. 21, § 24; Acts 1987, No. 87-590, p. 975, § 2-333(b)).)

Cited in Lee v. Lee, 67 Ala. 406 (1880); Duke v. Duke, 522 So. 2d 258 (Ala. 1988).
Collateral references. — Validity of guardianship proceeding based on brainwashing of subject by religious, political or social organization. 44 ALR4th 1207.

§ 26-2-51. Revocation of guardianship or conservatorship — Upon application by person ascertained to be incapacitated — Contents of application, etc.

At any time after the inquisition, the person ascertained to be incapacitated, by himself or by next friend, may apply in writing to the court of probate for a revocation of the proceedings against him and of the letters of guardianship or conservatorship, the application to be accompanied by the certificate in writing of two physicians or of two other competent persons stating that, after examination of such person, they believe the person's incapacity has terminated. (Code 1852, § 2758; Code 1867, § 2197; Code 1876, § 2804; Code 1886, § 2397; Code 1896, § 2262; Code 1907, § 4352; Code 1923, § 8110; Code 1940, T. 21, § 16; Acts 1987, No. 87-590, p. 975, § 2-333(b).)

Court is one of limited and statutory jurisdiction. — The court in proceedings for revocation of insanity proceedings against petitioner and for revocation of the letters of guardianship acts as a court of limited and statutory jurisdiction. Patterson v. Downs, 255 Ala. 197, 50 So. 2d 408 (1951).

Thus, the requirements of this section must be strictly complied with, and compliance must affirmatively appear from the record. Patterson v. Downs, 255 Ala. 197, 50 So. 2d 408 (1951).

And where court lacks jurisdiction its finding is void. — Where proceedings for revocation of insanity proceedings and letters of guardianship showed on their face that the court lacked jurisdiction, the court's finding was void and subject to collateral attack. Patterson v. Downs, 255 Ala. 197, 50 So. 2d 408 (1951).

Proceedings to revoke inquisition is a continuance of original. — As regards guardianship, proceeding to revoke inquisition may be considered part of and in nature of continuance of original proceeding. Pope v. Bolin, 224 Ala. 322, 140 So. 382 (1932).

Sufficiency of petition. — Under this section, petition reciting fact of former inquisition, appointment of qualified guardian and averring petitioner is now of sound mind, accompanied with required certificates, presents proper issue. Pope v. Bolin, 224 Ala. 322, 140 So. 382 (1932).

Decree in proceedings under this section is res judicata. — A decree in proceedings instituted under this section, declaring a person to be of sound mind, is res judicata, and a subsequent inquisition cannot be sustained if the evidence discloses no change of mental status. Jones v. Jones, 275 Ala. 678, 158 So. 2d 481 (1963).

The adjudication of unsoundness of mind made in January, 1964, is conclusive of that status at that time. The adjudication is res judicata and a further proceeding of like kind cannot be successfully presented if the evidence discloses no change of mental status. Sewall v. Fincher, 277 Ala. 152, 167 So. 2d 719 (1964).

The proceeding for revocation cannot be employed to retry the issue adjudicated on the inquisition. Sewall v. Fincher, 277 Ala. 152, 167 So. 2d 719 (1964).

Conflicting evidence. — Where there is a conflict in the evidence the jury should be left to find the facts without interference by the court, and if there is any evidence tending to prove a fact, no matter how slight, the court has no right to take such question from the consideration of the jury. It is the province of the jury and not of the court to find from the evidence the truth of a disputed fact. Roberson v. Roberson, 284 Ala. 5, 221 So. 2d 122 (1969).

Where evidence was presented that mental condition of the person involved had improved since the granting of the letters of the guardianship and though there was conflict in the evidence, it was sufficient to submit to the jury. This disputed fact of the change in the mental status of ward was properly submitted to the jury for determination. That verdict of the jury is presumed to be correct. Roberson v. Roberson, 284 Ala. 5, 221 So. 2d 122 (1969).

Burden of proof is on petitioner. — On petition to revoke inquisition, burden is on petitioner to establish averments of petition. Pope v. Bolin, 224 Ala. 322, 140 So. 382 (1932).

The burden is upon the petitioner for revocation to prove a changed mental condition since the decree adjudicating him of unsound mind. The issue is essentially one of presumption as to mental status and burden of proof as to showing a change therein. Sewall v. Fincher, 277 Ala. 152, 167 So. 2d 719 (1964).

After an inquisition declaring a person non compos mentis, the burden shifts to that person to prove he is of sound mind in a revocation proceeding. Nigg v. Smith, 395 So. 2d 47 (Ala. 1981).

The evidence is directed to present mental status. Pope v. Bolin, 224 Ala. 322, 140 So. 382 (1932).

Cited in Robinson v. Richards, 45 Ala. 354 (1871); Nigg v. Smith, 415 So. 2d 1082 (Ala. 1982).

Collateral references. — 44 C.J.S., Insane Persons, §§ 32, 33.

§ 26-2-52. Revocation of guardianship or conservatorship — Upon application by person ascertained to be incapacitated — Appointment of date for hearing on application; notice to guardian or conservator, etc.

On the filing of such application, the court must appoint a day for the hearing thereof, not more than 10 days thereafter, and the guardian or conservator and the person at whose instance the inquisition was had and taken must be cited to appear and show cause against it. (Code 1852, § 2758; Code 1867, § 3197; Code 1876, § 2804; Code 1886, § 2398; Code 1896, § 2263; Code 1907, § 4353; Code 1923, § 8111; Code 1940, T. 21, § 17; Acts 1987, No. 87-590, p. 975, § 2-333(b).)

Jurisdiction lacking where no citation was served. — Where the record of proceedings for revocation of an inquisition of insanity disclosed no citation served on the person who instituted the inquisition, the proceedings showed on their face that the court lacked jurisdiction, and the court's findings were void. Patterson v. Downs, 255 Ala. 197, 50 So. 2d 408 (1951).

§ 26-2-53. Revocation of guardianship or conservatorship — Upon application by person ascertained to be incapacitated — Conduct of hearing or trial upon contested application; entry of decree revoking guardianship or conservatorship, etc., where application not contested.

If the guardian or conservator or the person at whose instance the inquisition was had and taken appears and, in writing, denies the allegations of the application, the court must appoint a day for the trial of such contest, not more than 10 days thereafter, and must cause a jury to be summoned in the manner provided by Section 12-16-78 for the trial thereof, and proceedings must be had as upon the original inquisition.

If there be no contest of the allegations of the application and the court is satisfied of the truth thereof, a decree must be entered revoking the proceedings on the inquisition and the guardianship or conservatorship and declaring that the ward must be restored to the custody and management of his estate. (Code 1852, §§ 2759, 2760; Code 1867, §§ 3198, 3199; Code 1876, §§ 2805, 2806; Code 1886, § 2399; Code 1896, § 2264; Code 1907, § 4354; Code 1923, § 8112; Code 1940, T. 21, § 18; Acts 1987, No. 87-590, p. 975, § 2-333(b).)

This section does not intend annulment of former adjudication ab initio, but as revocation of same as evidence of continuing mental incapacity. Pope v. Bolin, 224 Ala. 322, 140 So. 382 (1932).

Adversary proceeding. — It clearly ap- pears from this section that the contest of the application here provided for contemplates an adversary proceeding. Patterson v. Downs, 255 Ala. 197, 50 So. 2d 408 (1951).

Cited in Simon v. Craft, 182 U.S. 427, 434, 21 S. Ct. 836, 45 L. Ed. 1165 (1901).

§ 26-2-54. Revocation of guardianship or conservatorship — Upon application by person ascertained to be incapacitated — Entry of decree or judgment as to contested application upon rendition of verdict of jury.

If, on the trial of the contest, the jury finds the facts stated in the application to be true, the court must enter a decree revoking the proceedings on the inquisition and the guardianship or conservatorship, and declaring that the ward must be restored to the custody and management of his estate and must adjudge the costs as is just and equitable, but if the verdict of the jury negatives the facts stated in the application, a judgment of dismissal at the cost of the applicant or of the next friend must be entered. (Code 1852, § 2761; Code 1867, § 3200; Code 1876, § 2807; Code 1886, § 2400; Code 1896, § 2265; Code 1907, § 4355; Code 1923, § 8113; Code 1940, T. 21, § 19; Acts 1987, No. 87-590, p. 975, § 2-333(b).)

Cited in Penney v. Pritchard & McCall, 255 Ala. 13, 49 So. 2d 782 (1950).

§ 26-2-55. Revocation of guardianship or conservatorship — Upon application by guardian or conservator.

If, at any time after his appointment, the guardian or conservator becomes satisfied that the incapacity of the ward has terminated, and is capable of managing his estate and the judge of probate is of the opinion, from the proof and the facts stated, that such representation is correct, the judge of probate must make an order that the guardian or conservator be discharged and that the estate of the ward be restored to him. (Code 1852, § 2757; Code 1867, § 3196; Code 1876, § 2803; Code 1886, § 2401; Code 1896, § 2266; Code 1907, § 4356; Code 1923, § 8114; Code 1940, T. 21, § 20; Acts 1987, No. 87-590, p. 975, § 2-333(b).)

Determination of adversary rights. — Since a proceeding under this section is an adversary proceeding, it is elementary that adversary rights cannot be determined without affording the opportunity to be heard by the party or parties who may be affected, these being the parties expressly set forth in this section. Patterson v. Downs, 255 Ala. 197, 50 So. 2d 408 (1951).

CHAPTER 2A.

ALABAMA UNIFORM GUARDIANSHIP AND PROTECTIVE PROCEEDINGS ACT.

ARTICLE 1.

GENERAL PROVISIONS, DEFINITIONS AND JURISDICTION OF COURT.

Division 1.

Short Title, Construction, General Provisions.

§ 26-2A-1. Short title.

This chapter may be cited as the Alabama Uniform Guardianship and Protective Proceedings Act. (Acts 1987, No. 87-590, p. 975, § 1-101.)

Comment

This Alabama Uniform Guardianship and Protective Proceedings Act is the product of the Alabama Law Institute and the work of a committee appointed by the ALI, which included attorneys, probate judges, law teachers and a representative of the Alabama department of pensions and security. This chapter is substantially based on the Uniform Guardianship and Protective Proceedings Act, which is contained in the Uniform Probate Code, Article V, Parts 1, 2, 3, and 4

(1982 edition). While there are changes in this chapter as compared with the Uniform Guardianship and Protective Proceedings Act, this chapter nevertheless is designated a "Uniform" Act for the purpose of aiding courts and other individuals, in construing this chapter, to find similar statutes in other states and court decisions construing those statutes in developing a general body of law to carry out the purpose of this and similar acts. The general policy supporting "uniformity" is that uniformity of these acts among the various enacting states will enhance the probability that the purposes of these acts will be achieved in our mobile society.

This chapter embodies separate systems of guardianship to protect persons of minors and persons otherwise incapacitated. An "incapacitated person" is defined in this chapter to include not only persons who are non compos mentis and who have been covered by guardianship statutes historically, but in a broader sense it also includes persons "who lack sufficient understanding or capacity to make or communicate responsible decisions concerning his person." The broader definition permits legal protection, commensurate with the person's capacity, without the stigma sometimes attached to a judicial decision of non compos mentis. This chapter also complements Durable Power of Attorney Acts [(see, Ala. Code section 26-1-2 (1975, as amended by Act No. 81-98))], which may be used by adults approaching senility or incompetence to avoid the necessity for other kinds of protective regimes.

This chapter also offers a system of protective proceedings principally based on conservatorships to provide for the management of substantial aggregations of property of persons who are, for one reason or another including minority and incapacity, unable to manage their property. In short, this chapter recognizes two fiduciary capacities — i.e., a "guardian" who is "of the person" and analogous to the role of the parent, and a "conservator" who is "of the property" and more closely analogous to the role of a trustee. Historically, in many states, including Alabama, the term "guardian" covered both of these capacities and for that reason has been a source of confusion not only as to the capacity of the fiduciary, but also as to his or her duties and responsibilities. Because this chapter, distinguishes between the two capacities, the duties and responsibilities may be separated by two appointments or one person may serve in both capacities (and with both titles) as the circumstances seem to dictate. For example, a corporate fiduciary cannot be appointed "guardian" of a person, but the court may be well advised to appoint a corporate fiduciary as "conservator" of the property when a natural person has been appointed guardian.

This chapter contains a variety of provisions designed to minimize or avoid the necessity of guardianship and protective proceedings, as well as provisions designed to simplify and minimize arrangements which become necessary to care for persons or their property. One example is a facility of payment provision which permits relatively small sums owed to a minor to be paid whether or not there is a guardian or other official who has been designated to act for the minor. Another example is the provisions which permit a judge to make appropriate orders concerning the property of a disabled person without appointing a fiduciary. Probably the principal example is the concept of "limited guardianship" included in this chapter.

The concept of "limited guardianship" is an attempt to avoid an asserted "overkill" implicit in "standard" or "historical" guardianship proceedings. It has been asserted that the "overkill" occurred because a finding of non compos mentis or incompetence has been the traditional threshold (including Alabama) for the appointment of a guardian. As a result, in consequence of the appointment of a guardian, all personal and legal autonomy is stripped from the ward and vested in the appointing court and guardian. The impetus for "limited guardianship" has been a call for more sensitive procedures and for appointments fashioned so that the authority of the protector will intrude only to the degree necessary on the liberties and prerogatives of the protected person. In short, rather than permitting an all-or-none status, there should be an intermediate status available to the courts through which the protected person will have personal liberties and prerogatives restricted only to the extent necessary under the circumstances. The court should be admonished to look for a least-restrictive protection approach. This philosophy of a least-intrusive approach to guardianships and protective proceedings is stated in various provisions through this chapter.

The purpose of this chapter is to permit greater flexibility for courts in providing the legal protection necessary for an individual who needs legal protection for some or all of his or her acts. A major contribution of this chapter also is its attempt to give definition to the powers and duties of the court, guardians, and conservators, which powers and duties prior to this chapter in Alabama were only defined to a very limited extent in the statutes and more vaguely defined perhaps in those "inherent powers of equity" in the court or "powers inherent in the office" of a guardian.

This chapter is generally consistent with the Alabama Uniform Veterans' Guardianship Act. Ala. Code, sections 26-9-1 through 26-9-19 (1975). The Alabama Uniform Veterans' Guardianship Act is not repealed by this chapter and for sections of this chapter where the wording might be different enough that a guardian or conservator should be alert to provisions in the other act, the difference is noted in the Comments to this chapter. It should be noted here, however, that the "guardian" referred to in the Uniform Veterans' Guardianship Act is primarily a "conservator" under this chapter, based on their comparable duties and responsibilities. If a ward receives benefits from the United States through the veterans' administration, the guardian or conservator must realize that both the Alabama Uniform Veterans' Guardianship Act and this chapter may have applicability.

Collateral references. — Alcoholism or intoxication as ground for discharge justifying denial of unemployment compensation. 64 ALR4th 1151.

Validity of inter vivos gift by ward to guardian or conservator. 70 ALR4th 499.

§ 26-2A-2. Rule of construction; purposes.

(a) This chapter shall be liberally construed and applied to promote its underlying purposes and policies.

(b) The underlying purposes and policies of this chapter are to:

(1) Simplify and clarify the law concerning the affairs of minors, missing or disappeared persons, protected persons, and incapacitated persons;

(2) Promote a speedy and efficient system for managing and protecting the estates of protected persons so that assets may be preserved for application to the needs of protected persons and their dependents;

(3) Provide a system of general and limited guardianships for minors and incapacitated persons and to coordinate guardianships and protective proceedings concerned with management and protection of estates of incapacitated persons; and

(4) Make uniform the law among the various jurisdictions. (Acts 1987, No. 87-590, p. 975, § 1-102.)

Comment

This section generally follows Uniform Guardianship and Protective Proceedings Act (hereafter abbreviated "UGPPA") Section 1-102. In this chapter, the term "missing or disappeared persons" is used instead of "missing persons" as used in the UGPPA, although there is no intended change in meaning. The term is intended to refer to individuals who are not present and cannot be reached through reasonable locating efforts. The individual's absence may be unexplained in that reasonable efforts to locate the individual are unsuccessful, or absence may be explainable in that the individual's location is known or approximately known, but the individual cannot be reached through legal processes (e.g., the individual may be a prisoner of war).

Subsection (b)(3) of this section refers to the feature in this chapter of distinguishing between a "guardian," who is "of the person" and like a parent in role, and a "conservator," who is "of the property" and like a trustee in role. These fiduciary capacities may be separated in different persons, or one person may serve in both capacities and have both titles. The reason for distinguishing between "guardians" and "conservators" is an effort to clearly recognize that the two roles are quite different and the qualities a fiduciary needs may be quite different depending upon which fiduciary capacity the person fills. Prior to this chapter Alabama (like a number of other states) used one term, i.e., "guardian," to identify fiduciaries in both capacities. This single-term identification led to a great deal of confusion on the part of third parties dealing with the "guardian" and to much uncertainty on the part of "guardians" as to their powers and duties. The restrictive use of "guardians" in Alabama also has limited the use of this fiduciary office in providing protection for certain types of individuals. By distinguishing between "guardians" and "conservators," the title of the fiduciary will identify the role of the fiduciary and the identity will be indicative also of powers and duties of the fiduciary. In this chapter, article 2, divisions 1 and 2, treat the role of "guardians," and article 2, division 3, treats the office of "conservator."

Subsection (b)(4) of this section refers to one purpose of this chapter as being to "make uniform the law among the various jurisdictions." It is recognized that in our modern society people are quite mobile and often cross state lines in their activities. The ideal of "uniformity" is that where various states enact statutes similar to this chapter, similarity or "uniformity" of application and construction (e.g., access to the courts, jurisdiction, powers and duties of fiduciaries, etc.) will tend to give greater assurance of achieving the general goals of this and similar Acts. Not only will "uniformity of construction" reduce problems with conflicts of laws, but it will facilitate the development of a larger body of case law construing similar provisions. Statutes should *not* tend to encourage guardians, conservators, or even wards to attempt to get into another jurisdiction seeking a different court or statutory construction. The basic policy of this chapter is to achieve "the best interest of the ward" and uniformity of construction tends to promote that policy.

§ 26-2A-3. Supplementary general principles of law applicable.

Unless displaced by the particular provisions of this chapter, the principles of law and equity supplement its provisions. (Acts 1987, No. 87-590, p. 975, § 1-103.)

§ 26-2A-4. Severability.

If any provision of this chapter or its application to any person or circumstances is held invalid, the invalidity does not affect other provisions or applications of the chapter which can be given effect without the invalid provision or application, and to this end the provisions of this chapter are severable. (Acts 1987, No. 87-590, p. 975, § 1-104.)

§ 26-2A-5. Construction against implied repeal.

This chapter is a general act intended as a unified coverage of its subject matter and no subsequent legislation shall be construed to repeal by implication any part of this chapter if that construction reasonably can be avoided. (Acts 1987, No. 87-590, p. 975, § 1-105.)

§ 26-2A-6. Facility of payment or delivery; notice of payment.

(a) Any person under a duty to pay or deliver money or personal property to a minor may perform the duty, in amounts as provided in this subsection, by paying or delivering the money or personal property to:

(1) Any person having the care and custody of the minor and with whom the minor resides;

(2) A guardian of the minor; or

(3) The judge of probate of the county in which the minor resides, if a resident of this state, or, if a nonresident, to the judge of probate or like officer of the county in which the debtor or creditor resides.

Payments under this subsection must not exceed $5,000.00 if paid in a single payment, or $3,000.00 a year if paid in a series of payments, and payments, by any person other than a conservator or judge, must not exceed a maximum of $25,000.00 during the minority of the minor ward. The person obligated to make payment is discharged of that duty or obligation by making the payment or delivery and filing a notice of such payment with the probate judge of the county in which the minor resides, if a resident of this state, or, if a nonresident, with the judge of probate or like officer of the county in which the debtor or creditor resides.

(b) This section does not apply if the person making payment or delivery has actual knowledge that a conservator has been appointed or proceedings for appointment of a conservator of the estate of the minor are pending.

(c) Persons, receiving money or personal property for a minor, are obligated to apply the money to the health, support, education or maintenance of the minor, but may not pay themselves except by way of reimbursement for out-of-pocket expenses for goods and services necessary for the minor's support. A person who receives money or personal property for a minor is obligated to preserve the money and personal property, except to the extent necessary for the health, support, education or maintenance of the minor, and any balance not so used and any personal property received for the minor must be turned over to the minor when majority is attained. A person who pays or delivers money or property in accordance with provisions of this section is not responsible for the proper application thereof. (Acts 1987, No. 87-590, p. 975, § 1-106; Acts 1988, 1st Ex. Sess., No. 88-898, p. 455, § 1.)

Comment

Where a minor has only a small amount of property, it would be wasteful to require protective proceedings to deal with the property. This section makes it possible for other persons, possibly including a guardian, to handle the less complicated property affairs of the ward. "Person," whether referring to the obligor or to the recipient, includes a judge. As contrasted with the Uniform Act, this chapter limits application to personal property. The Uniform Act provides in subsection (a) for payments "not exceeding $5,000.00 a year ...." Subsection (a) of this section provides a variation on the amounts that can be paid, but retains the $5,000.00 amount if the payment is in a single payment. The $25,000.00 maximum-during-minority is new in this chapter and the safeguards on that limitation are not perfect. The safeguards are dependent on an obligor knowing that a payment will exceed the limit or the guardian, at the risk of otherwise being charged with a breach of duty, refusing to accept payments that will exceed the limit. Protective proceedings, including the possible establishment of a conservatorship, should be sought where substantial property is involved.

This section does not go as far as many facility-of-payment provisions found in trust instruments, which usually permit application of sums due a minor beneficiary to any expense or charge for the minor. This section does not supersede nor should it affect the application of a facility-of-payment provision in a trust instrument where a trust exists. However, it was considered that such a broad facility-of-payment provision with so large an area of discretion to any category of persons who might owe funds to a minor would be unwise. Nonetheless, this section as drafted should reduce the need for trust facility-of-payment provisions somewhat, while extending opportunities to insurance companies and other debtors to minors for relatively simple methods of gaining discharge.

The protection afforded by the section is unavailable if the person making payment or delivery has actual knowledge that a conservator has been appointed for the minor's estate or knows that a proceeding seeking appointment of a conservator is pending. By way of contrast, the protection is available in spite of a payor's knowledge that a guardian for the minor has been appointed or may be appointed as a result of a pending proceeding. Guardianship proceedings affecting minors are described in article 2, division 1 of this chapter. A conservator for a minor comes into existence, if at all, incident to a protective proceeding as described in article 2, division 3. A guardian's powers, described in section 26-2A-78, do not include the authority to compel payment of money due the ward, but include authority to receive payments made under the protection of this section. In contrast, a conservator has title to all assets of the minor's estate, except as otherwise provided in the case of a limited conservator. See section 26-2A-148.

Subdivision (3) is a retention in substance of Ala. Code (1975) section 26-7-2.

Statute to be repealed: Ala. Code (1975) § 26-7-2.

§ 26-2A-7. Delegation of powers by parent or guardian; parental authority.

(a) A parent who has custody, or a guardian, of a minor or incapacitated person, by a properly executed power of attorney, may delegate to another person, for a period not exceeding one year, any power regarding health, support, education or maintenance of the person or property of the minor child or ward, except the power to consent to marriage or adoption of a minor ward. Temporary "delegation" of parental powers does not relieve the parent or guardian of the primary responsibility for the minor or incapacitated person.

(b) The provisions of subsection (a) of this section shall not be used or construed to allow a parent or guardian to thwart or circumvent provisions of Chapter 15 of Title 12 and Article 2 of Chapter 2 of Title 44. (Acts 1987, No. 87-590, p. 975, § 1-107; Acts 1988, 1st Ex. Sess., No. 88-898, p. 455, § 1.)

Comment

This section permits a temporary delegation of parental powers. For example, parents who have custody (or a guardian) of a minor may plan to be where they are not accessible immediately for some extended period of time, such as an extended business trip, hunting trip, or vacation. They may wish to empower a close relative (e.g., brother or uncle) to take any necessary action regarding the child while they are away. Using this section, they could execute an appropriate power of attorney giving the attorney-in-fact (e.g., brother or uncle) custody and power to consent. Then, if an emergency operation were required, the attorney-in-fact could consent on behalf of the child; as a practical matter he or she of course would attempt to communicate with the parents before acting. The section is designed to reduce problems relating to consents for emergency treatment.

A "parent" has the power to delegate his or her authority as described in this section without the benefit of this section. The effect of this section is therefore to extend similar powers of delegation to a "guardian," who by virtue of being a fiduciary cannot delegate his or her duties absent a granting of such authority in a creating instrument or statute. If a "parent" anticipates that she or he will be inaccessible for emergency contact for some period of time, she or he can (and probably should) execute a power of attorney giving powers of care, custody and control over property of the child to a trusted person who will be accessible during the period of time. This section adopts the position that a "guardian" acting in the role of a substitute parent should be extended the same power to delegate.

The delegation of powers under this section can be for a "period not exceeding one year ...." (the Uniform Act is for six months). The section does not preclude immediate renewals of the delegation for another temporary period, but the section contemplates "temporary" delegations of powers and is not intended to permit an abrogation of the primary responsibilities of the parent or guardian.

A guardian's authority over a ward, described in section 26-2A-78 (guardians of minors) and section 26-2A-108 (guardians of incapacitated persons), includes authority regarding the health, support, education, or maintenance of the person or property of the ward that goes well beyond consenting to health care.

In contrast to section 26-2A-75, which relates only to certain business affairs of minors, this section is pertinent to the affairs of minors and incapacitated persons for whom guardians have been appointed.

§ 26-2A-8. Application to existing relationships.

Guardianships created prior to January 1, 1988, and continuing in effect on January 1, 1988, are not terminated, even though the statute under which the appointment was made may be repealed by this chapter. Those guardianships continue in effect as they existed prior to this chapter with all of the powers and duties of the guardianship, except that the guardian previously appointed in addition will have the powers and duties of a guardian and a conservator under this chapter to the extent that the powers and duties under this chapter may be broader or more clearly expressed. (Acts 1987, No. 87-590, p. 975, § 2-334.)

Division 2.

Definitions.

§ 26-2A-20. General definitions.

As used in this chapter the following terms shall have the following meanings, respectively, unless the context clearly indicates otherwise:

(1) CLAIMS. In respect of a protected person, includes liabilities of the protected person, whether arising in contract, tort, or otherwise, and liabilities of the estate which arise at or after the appointment of a conservator, including expenses of administration.

(2) CONSERVATOR. A person who is appointed by a court to manage the estate of a protected person and includes a limited conservator described in Section 26-2A-148(a).

(3) COURT. A probate court of this state.

(4) COURT REPRESENTATIVE. A person appointed in a guardianship or protective proceeding who is trained in law, nursing, or social work, is an officer, employee, or special appointee of the court, and has no personal interest in the proceeding.

(5) DISABILITY. Cause for a protective order as described in Section 26-2A-130.

(6) ESTATE. Includes the property of the person whose affairs are subject to this chapter.

(7) GUARDIAN. A person who has qualified as a guardian of a minor or incapacitated person pursuant to parental or spousal nomination or court appointment and includes a limited guardian as described in Sections 26-2A-78(e) and 26-2A-105(c), but excludes one who is merely a guardian ad litem.

(8) INCAPACITATED PERSON. Any person who is impaired by reason of mental illness, mental deficiency, physical illness or disability, physical or mental infirmities accompanying advanced age, chronic use of drugs, chronic intoxication, or other cause (except minority) to the extent of lacking sufficient understanding or capacity to make or communicate responsible decisions.

(9) LEASE. Includes an oil, gas, or other mineral lease.

(10) LETTERS. Includes letters of guardianships and letters of conservatorship.

(11) MINOR. A person who is under 19 years of age and has not otherwise had the disabilities of minority removed.

(12) MORTGAGE. Any conveyance, agreement, or arrangement in which property is used as collateral.

(13) ORGANIZATION. Includes a corporation, business trust, estate, trust, partnership, association, two or more persons having a joint or common interest, government, governmental subdivision or agency, or any other legal entity.

(14) PARENT. Includes any person entitled to take, or who would be entitled to take if the child died without a will, as a parent by intestate succession from the child whose relationship is in question and excludes any person who is only a stepparent, foster parent, or grandparent.

(15) PERSON. An individual or an organization, unless the context otherwise requires.

(16) PETITION. A written request to the court for an order after notice.

(17) PROCEEDING. Includes action at law and suit in equity.

(18) PROPERTY. Includes both real and personal property or any interest therein and means anything that may be the subject of ownership.

(19) PROTECTED PERSON. A minor or other person for whom a conservator has been appointed or other protective order has been made as provided in Sections 26-2A-136 and 26-2A-137.

(20) PROTECTIVE PROCEEDING. A proceeding under the provisions of Article 2, Division 3.

(21) SECURITY. Includes any note, stock, treasury stock, bond, debenture, evidence of indebtedess, certificate of interest or participation in an oil, gas, or mining title or lease or in payments out of production under such a title or lease, collateral trust certificate, transferable share, voting trust certificate or, in general, any interest or instrument commonly known as a security, or any certificate of interest or participation, any temporary or interim certificate, receipt or certificate of deposit for, or any warrant or right to subscribe to or purchase any of the foregoing.

(22) WARD. A person for whom a guardian has been appointed. A "minor ward" is a minor for whom a guardian has been appointed solely because of minority. (Acts 1987, No. 87-590, p. 975, § 1-201.)

Comment

The probate court retains under this chapter the initial jurisdiction to handle matters involving minors and incapacitated persons. Proceedings seeking appointment of a personal guardian for a minor without other disability as described in section 26-2A-73 et seq. are somewhat less complicated, though formal in the sense that adjudications following notice and hearings are involved. The chapter does not contemplate use in connection with guardianships and other protective proceedings of "summary" or "informal" proceedings of the sort utilized in some states in decedent estate settlements for nonadjudicated probate of wills and appointment of personal representatives.

The designation of "court representative" in subdivision (4) of this section identifies the same person as the person designated as a "visitor" under the Uniform Act. The functions of the person are not changed in this chapter and for purposes of comparing statutes of other jurisdictions, the terms should be treated as being synonymous.

When read with section 26-2A-136(d), the defined term "disability" plainly does not refer to lack of legal capacity, but only to the grounds described in warranting a protective proceeding as described in section 26-2A-130.

The definition of "incapacitated person" supplies the substantive grounds for appointment of a guardian for reasons other than minority. See section 26-2A-105(b). The Alabama Uniform Veterans' Guardianship Act refers to guardians for "incompetents," which was consistent with Alabama law prior to this chapter. Ala. Code § 26-9-7 (1975).

The definition of "minor" in subdivision (11) takes into account that an individual may have the disabilities of minority removed otherwise than by reaching the nineteenth birthday, such as by emancipation under Ala. Code sections 26-13-1 through 26-13-8 (1975) (petition to juvenile court), and Ala. Code sections 30-4-15 and 30-4-16 (1975) (individuals who are 18 years of age and married).

The definition of "parent" is intended to include an adoptive parent, because an adoptive parent is eligible to inherit as a parent in intestate succession under the Alabama Probate Code and most statutes governing adoptions. The defined meaning of "parent" is especially significant when read with sections 26-2A-71 and 26-2A-72 which prevent the appointment of a guardian of a minor, other than a temporary guardian under section 26-2A-73(b), has custodial rights.

The terms "ward" and "protected person" help distinguish persons over whom another holds personal, custodial authority from those whose property, or some part thereof, has been ordered into a statutory trusteeship or otherwise subjected to a protective court order. A person for whom a guardian has been named and whose property is the subject of a conservatorship or other protective order is both a ward and a protected person. In this connection, note that section 26-2A-152(a) gives a conservator of a minor for whom no parent or guardian has parental rights of custody and control the duties and powers of a guardian. This section also specifies that the parental authority thus conferred on a conservator of a minor does not prevent appointment of another as guardian. In contrast, the existence of any other person having the custodial authority of a parent, a guardian by appointment of any court, or a guardian arising by parental appointment under section 26-2A-71 or as a result of parental or spousal appointment under section 26-2A-100, blocks any court appointment of a guardian.

Division 3.

Scope, Jurisdiction and Courts.

§ 26-2A-30. Territorial application.

Except as otherwise provided in this chapter, it applies to:

(1) Affairs and estates of disappeared persons, and persons to be protected, domiciled in this state;

(2) Property located in this state of nondomiciliaries who are disappeared persons or persons to be protected, or property coming into the control of a guardian or conservator who is subject to the laws of this state; and

(3) Incapacitated persons and minors in this state. (Acts 1987, No. 87-590, p. 975, § 1-301.)

Comment

This section covers the territorial authority of an Alabama probate court in matters involving minors and protected individuals which were previously covered in Ala. Code (1975) sections 26-2-24, 26-2-47, 26-4-1, 26-5-1 and 26-8-40. Although the wording of the section is somewhat different, the territorial authority is essentially unchanged by this chapter.

Statutes to be repealed: Ala. Code (1975) sections 26-2-24 and 26-4-1.

Statutes to be modified: Ala. Code (1975) sections 26-8-40, 26-2-47, and 26-5-1.

§ 26-2A-31. Subject matter jurisdiction.

(a) To the full extent permitted by the constitution, the court has jurisdiction over all subject matter relating to estates of protected persons and protection of minors and incapacitated persons.

(b) The court has full power to make order, judgments, and decrees and take all other action necessary and proper to administer justice in the matters that come before it.

(c) The court has jurisdiction over protective proceedings and guardianship proceedings.

(d) If both guardianship and protective proceedings as to the same person are commenced or pending in the same court, the proceedings may be consolidated.

(e) No provision of this chapter shall be construed to void, abate, or diminish, the powers or equity jurisdiction, when invoked, heretofore or hereafter granted by statute to certain probate courts. (Acts 1987, No. 87-590, p. 975, § 1-302.)

Comment

The "court" referred to in this section is the probate court. See section 26-2A-20(3). The subject matter jurisdiction stated herein will continue essentially the jurisdiction of the probate court as provided previously in Ala. Code (1975) sections 26-4-1, 26-5-1, and 26-8-40. Ala. Code (1975) section 26-4-46 provides that the circuit court has the same jurisdiction when matters involving guardianship are removed to circuit court. Subject matter jurisdiction granted in this section is not exclusive jurisdiction. When matters have been initiated in the probate court, but subsequently removed to the circuit court, the circuit court has coextensive jurisdiction by virtue of Ala. Code (1975) section 26-4-46 and to that extent subject matter jurisdiction in guardianship and protective proceedings is concurrent. This section shall not be construed to alter or affect the jurisdiction of the circuit court under the Adult Protective Services Act, Ala. Code (1975) sections 38-9-1 through 38-9-11, which continues in effect and will apply for petitions pertaining to adults in need of protective services. See Comment to section 26-2A-102 as to the jurisdiction of circuit courts under the Adult Protective Services Act of 1976. Ala. Code sections 38-9-1 through 38-9-11 (1975, as amended by Acts 1977, No. 780).

The subject matter jurisdiction described in this section affects the jurisdiction of the probate court only insofar as it applies to proceedings under this chapter and it does not purport to otherwise expand the jurisdiction of probate courts as established in other law.

Subsection (e) preserves the general equity jurisdiction that the legislature may have granted to certain probate courts or may hereafter grant to some probate courts. Prior granting of general equity powers to certain probate courts has been limited to the probate courts in Jefferson and Mobile counties.

Statute to be repealed: Ala. Code (1975) section 26-4-1.

Statutes to be modified: Ala. Code (1975) sections 26-8-40 and 26-5-1.

§ 26-2A-32. Venue; multiple proceedings; transfer.

(a) If a proceeding under this chapter could be maintained in more than one place in this state, the court in which the proceeding is first commenced has the exclusive right to proceed.

(b) If proceedings concerning the same estate, protected person, or ward are commenced in more than one court of this state, the court in which a proceeding was first commenced shall continue to hear the matter and determine venue. Any other court shall hold the matter in abeyance until the question of venue is decided. If the ruling court determines that venue is properly in another court, it shall transfer the proceeding to the other court.

(c) If the court finds that in the interest of justice a proceeding or a file should be located in another court of this state, the court may transfer the proceeding or file to the other court. (Acts 1987, No. 87-590, p. 975, § 1-303.)

Comment

Venue and the authority to remove to a more convenient forum have been provided for in Ala. Code (1975) sections 26-8-20 and 26-8-22. The right to remove from probate court to circuit court is provided in Ala. Code (1975) section 26-2-2. The use of the term "exclusive right" in subsection (a) is intended to clarify the question of venue particularly when the minor or incapacitated person is located in a county other than the individual's county of residence. Venue will remain unchanged by this chapter.

Statute to be modified and retained: Ala. Code (1975) section 26-2-2.

Statutes to be retained: Ala. Code (1975) sections 26-8-20 and 26-8-22.

§ 26-2A-33. Practice in court.

Unless specifically provided to the contrary in this chapter or inconsistent with its provisions, the rules of civil procedure including the rules concerning vacation of orders and appellate review govern proceedings under this chapter. (Acts 1987, No. 87-590, p. 975, § 1-304.)

Comment

This section adopts, for matters involving minors and incapacitated persons in the probate court, the Alabama Rules of Civil Procedure except where those rules are inconsistent with provisions of this chapter. The Alabama Rules of Civil Procedure otherwise are not applicable in probate courts. See A.R.C.P., Rule 1.

§ 26-2A-34. Records and certified copies.

The clerk of court shall keep a record for each ward or protected person involved in any document that may be filed with the court under this chapter, including petitions, requests, and any orders or responses by the court relating thereto, and establish and maintain a system for indexing, filing, or recording which is sufficient to enable users of the records to obtain adequate information. Upon payment of the required fees, the clerk shall issue certified copies of any letters issued to any guardian or conservator or of any other document filed or recorded. Certificates relating to letters must show the date of appointment. (Acts 1987, No. 87-590, p. 975, § 1-305.)

Comment

This chapter mandates a filing and indexing system for all documents involving protected persons. Prior law did not require expressly a subject-related filing of documents relating to wards. However Ala. Code (1975) section 26-8-23 does refer to a requirement that a transcript of the record of the proceedings be made and certified to the probate court to which a guardianship is removed. See also, Ala. Code (1975) section 26-8-24.

§ 26-2A-35. Jury trial.

(a) Except for proceedings in a court having general equity jurisdiction, a party is entitled to a trial by a jury of six disinterested persons in any proceeding to determine the incapacity of the individual and in other proceedings as to which a party has a constitutional right or a right under this chapter to a trial by jury. In any proceeding in a court having general equity jurisdiction, the right to trial by jury shall be determined under Alabama Rules of Civil Procedure, Rule 38.

(b) If there is no right to trial by jury under subsection (a) or the right is waived, the court in its discretion may call a jury to decide any issue of fact, in which case the verdict is advisory only. (Acts 1987, No. 87-590, p. 975, § 1-306.)

Comment

A party's right to a jury trial in a conservatorship or guardianship proceeding is granted by this chapter whenever there is a hearing to determine the need for a guardian or conservator, or in an appointment proceeding for a guardian or conservator. Under prior law the probate judge was required to impanel a jury of six disinterested persons. Ala. Code (1975) sections 26-2-43 and 26-2-44. The practice in the probate court of Jefferson county does not include the use of a six-person jury and that practice can be continued under this chapter pursuant to section 26-2A-31(e). In a hearing on a petition for removal of a guardian, the court is the fact finder, but if the controversy involves an issue of a party's imbecility, habitual inebriety, continual sickness, waste of property, or neglect of his affairs, either party is entitled to a trial of the issues of fact by a jury. Ala. Code (1975) section 26-6-4.

Statute to be repealed: Ala. Code (1975) section 26-6-4.
Statute to be modified: Ala. Code (1975) section 26-2-43.

Statute to be retained: Ala. Code (1975) section 26-2-44.

§ 26-2A-36. Appeals.

Appellate review, including the right to appellate review, interlocutory appeal, provisions as to time, manner, notice, appeal bond, stays, scope of review, record on appeal, briefs, arguments, and power of the appellate court, is governed by Title 12, Chapter 22, and the Alabama Rules of Appellate Procedure, as applicable, but in proceedings in which jury trial has been had as a matter of right the rules applicable to the scope of review in jury cases apply. (Acts 1987, No. 87-590, p. 975, § 1-307.)

Comment

This section preserves the right of appeal granted under Ala. Code (1975) sections 26-7A-16 and 26-5-53. Ala. Code (1975) section 26-4-143, relating to preservation of evidence received at a hearing, is not carried forward. Appellate procedures in Alabama generally are contained in Title 12, chapter 22, of the Code of Alabama (1975, as amended) and in the Alabama Rules of Appellate Procedure. Special procedures applicable to appeals from probate court are principally in Ala. Code, sections 12-22-20 through 12-22-27 (1975). Appellate procedures have been adopted in this chapter without any attempt to change them.

Statute to be repealed: Ala. Code (1975) section 26-4-143.

Division 4.

Notice, Parties and Representation in Guardianship and Protective Proceedings.

§ 26-2A-50. Notice; method and time of giving.

(a) If notice of a hearing on any petition is required, other than a notice meeting specific notice requirements otherwise provided, the petitioner shall cause notice of the time and place of hearing of any petition to be given to the person to be notified or to the attorney if the person has appeared by attorney or requested that notice be sent to an attorney.

(b) Notice must be given:

(1) By mailing a copy of the notice at least 14 days before the time set for the hearing by certified, registered, or ordinary first-class mail addressed to the person being notified using the post office address given in the request for notice, if any, or to the person's office or place of residence, if known;

(2) By delivering a copy thereof to the person being notified personally at least 14 days before the time set for the hearing; or

(3) If the address or identity of any person is not known and cannot be ascertained with reasonable diligence, by publishing, at least once a week for three consecutive weeks, a copy of the notice in a newspaper having general circulation in the county in which the hearing is to be held, the last publication of which is to be at least 10 days before the time set for the hearing.

(c) The court for good cause shown may provide for a different method or time of giving notice for any hearing.

(d) Proof of the giving of notice must be made not later than the hearing and filed in the proceeding. (Acts 1987, No. 87-590, p. 975, § 1-401.)

Comment

This section replaces eight Alabama statutes relating to notice of hearings involving appointment, leasing, sales, removal and settlements. This chapter provides a single set of notice requirements applicable generally to all petitions. Specific notice requirements that supersede the general requirements are described in section 26-2A-103 (notice by personal service required for the alleged incapacitated person in proceedings seeking appointment of a guardian for reasons other than minority) and section 26-2A-134 (notice by personal service required for the person for whom a protective order under section 26-2A-130 is sought, unless the person in question has disappeared or is otherwise situated so as to make personal service impractical). Section 26-2A-51 states that the notices by personal service required by sections 26-2A-103 and 26-2A-134 may not be waived.

Also, though this section explicitly covers only notices of hearings on petitions, the methods of giving notice described here may be used for the notices required before a guardian appointed by a parent or spouse under section 26-2A-100 can gain authority, [or, under (3), for any notice required prior to the sale or lease of a ward's property]. Note, however, that the notices required by section 26-2A-100 need to be given only seven, rather than 14, days prior to the appointment.

Statutes to be repealed: Ala. Code (1975) sections 26-4-44, 26-4-142, 26-4-145.

Statutes to be modified: Ala. Code (1975) sections 26-2-52, 26-5-9, 26-5-15, and 26-8-21.

§ 26-2A-51. Notice; waiver.

A person, including a guardian, guardian ad litem, conservator, or other fiduciary, may waive notice by a signed writing. A person for whom a guardianship or other protective order is sought, a ward, or a protected person may not waive notice. (Acts 1987, No. 87-590, p. 975, § 1-402.)

Comment

The subject of appearance is covered by section 26-2A-33.

A waiver of notice by a person who is the subject of a guardianship or protective proceeding is ineffective. In consequence, a period of not less than 14 days must elapse between the time when the respondent is personally served with notice of the proceeding as required by sections 26-2A-105 and 26-2A-134 and the earliest time when the matter may be heard. The required delay may serve to deter efforts to secure quick court orders having very serious consequences for a respondent's independence and property rights. In addition, a waiver of notice by one in need of a guardian or protective order would be suspect in many cases.

Under section 26-2A-133 and related sections, a competent spendthrift may petition for court intercession regarding property matters. The requirement of a nonwaivable notice by personal service as provided in section 26-2A-134 and this section still applies. If the rule were otherwise, persons interested in hurried court orders would be tempted to persuade the would-be respondent to serve as petitioner, thus compromising the purpose of the section to inject significant delay periods into every proceeding under sections 26-2A-105 and 26-2A-134.

Section 26-2A-75 requires that notice of a guardianship proceeding based on minority be given to the minor "if more than 14 years of age and not the petitioner." Unlike the notice required in other guardianship proceedings and in protective proceedings, the section 26-2A-6 notice to the respondent need not be by personal service. Further, if the respondent minor is under 14 or is 14 or older and acts as the petitioner in the proceeding, all required notices may be waived as provided in this section, thus eliminating the delay period that cannot be avoided in other guardianship and protective proceedings. Under section 26-2A-134(a), the same pattern applies to a protective proceeding instituted on account of an owner's minority.

In emergencies, a guardianship proceeding may be used to obtain a court order regarding the custody or well-being of a minor or incapacitated adult. Sections 26-2A-73(b) and 26-2A-107(a) are pertinent. Under section 26-2A-20(7), the term "guardian" as used throughout the chapter does not include a guardian ad litem.

The section overlaps a provision in section 26-2A-102(b) requiring the court in a guardianship proceeding to appoint an attorney for an unrepresented incapacitated person who may be granted the powers and duties of a guardian ad litem. Also, in section 26-2A-135(a) dealing with protective proceedings involving an inadequately represented minor, the court may appoint an attorney to represent the minor who may receive the powers and duties of a guardian ad litem. And under section 26-2A-135(b) the court is required to appoint an attorney who may be granted the powers and duties of a guardian ad litem to represent an allegedly disabled person who does not have "chosen counsel."

Current law does not explicitly permit a waiver of notice similar to that available under section 26-2A-51, nor does it protect potential wards by prohibiting their waiver of notice.

§ 26-2A-52. Guardian ad litem.

At any point in a proceeding, a court may appoint a guardian ad litem to represent the interest of a minor or other person if the court determines that representation of the interest otherwise would be inadequate. If not precluded by conflict of interests, a guardian ad litem may be appointed to represent several persons or interests. (Acts 1987, No. 87-590, p. 975, § 1-403.)

Comment

This section provides a comprehensive grant of power to the court to appoint guardians ad litem when necessary, consolidating similar provisions found in eight Alabama Code sections, which refer to the appointment of guardians ad litem in particular types of hearings such as appointment, compromise of debts, sales of property, accountings, settlements, and removal.

The court, under this section, has very broad discretion in appointing a guardian ad litem to represent the interest of any party before the court. Appointment can be made at any time and for virtually any reason. The court is not required to set out its reasons for appointing a guardian ad litem as a part of the record, but the court is encouraged to do so when such statement will be helpful to identify and to focus on particular concerns the court may have. For example, the court may be uncertain as to whether the interest of a particular person is coextensive with other persons before the court; or the court may be uncertain what the interest of the particular person is in certain property; or the court may be uncertain whether a particular order that has been requested is within the power of the court; or the court may wish to assure that the particular person has been adequately advised with regard to any consents the person is contemplating; etc.

Statutes to be modified: Ala. Code (1975) sections 26-5-2, 26-5-8, and 26-8-21.
Statutes to be repealed: Ala. Code (1975) sections 26-2-42, 26-4-81, and 26-4-142.

Attorney appointed under the Parental Consent Act is to be a guardian ad litem, and future appointments should be so designated and shall entail the responsibilities attendant to such appointments. In re Anonymous, 531 So. 2d 901 (Ala. 1988).

Right to counsel for minor seeking abortion. — Minor's conditional right to exercise her constitutional choice to have an abortion is protected by her right to legal counsel, and although the Parental Consent Act does not specifically provide for a guardian ad litem, the prerogative of the trial court to make such an appointment is provided, e.g., in this section and in § 12-15-8. In re Anonymous, 531 So. 2d 901 (Ala. 1988).

§ 26-2A-53. Request for notice; interested person.

Upon payment of any required fee, an interested person who desires to be notified before any order is made in a guardianship proceeding, including any proceeding subsequent to the appointment of a guardian under Section 26-2A-111, or in a protective proceeding under Section 26-2A-130, may file a request for notice with the clerk of the court in which the proceeding is pending. The clerk shall mail a copy of the request to the guardian and to the conservator if one has been appointed. A request is not effective unless it contains a statement showing the interest of the person making it and the address of that person or an attorney to whom notice is to be given. The request is effective only as to proceedings occurring after the filing. Any governmental agency paying or planning to pay benefits to the person to be protected is an interested person in protective proceedings. (Acts 1987, No. 87-590, p. 975, § 1-404.)

Comment

This chapter does not define "interest" or "interested person" as used in this section. The definition of "interested person" in § 1-201(20) of the Uniform Probate Code and in probate codes generally is too narrow as a test of would-be participants in guardian-ship and protective proceedings for it points only to persons having a property interest in the estate of the respondent or a claim against the estate. If extended to guardianship proceedings, this test would preclude nonowner children from participating in a proceeding concerning their parent. "Interested persons" may vary under this chapter depending on the type of proceeding, and therefore whether a person is an "interested person" should be determined by the type of proceeding involved.

This section contains special provisions, differing somewhat as between the three types of court proceedings it describes, regarding persons entitled to initiate a proceeding, persons entitled to notice of a proceeding, and persons who may intervene. Sections 26-2A-6(a), 26-2A-102(a), and 26-2A-133(a), respectively, control the identity of petitioners in a guardianship-for-a-minor proceeding, a guardianship proceeding for an incapacitated person, and a protective proceeding. The notice provisions applicable to the three proceedings are in sections 26-2A-6(b), 26-2A-103(a), and 26-2A-134(a). Provisions governing intervenors in guardianships for incapacitated persons and protective proceedings are in sections 26-2A-102(d) and 26-2A-135(e).

There were no comparable provisions in Alabama law prior to this section.

ARTICLE 2.

PROTECTION OF PERSONS UNDER DISABILITY AND THEIR PROPERTY.

Division 1.

Guardians of Minors.

§ 26-2A-70. Appointment and status of guardian of minor.

A person may become a guardian of a minor by parental appointment or upon appointment by the court. The guardianship status continues until terminated, without regard to the location from time to time of the guardian or minor ward. (Acts 1987, No. 87-590, p. 975, § 2-101.)

Comment

This section replaces Ala. Code (1975) sections 26-2-20 and 26-2-23. One of its purposes is to establish that a guardian created by parental appointment under sections 26-2A-71 and 26-2A-72 of this chapter has the same legal status as a guardian by court appointment under section 26-2A-73 and following sections. Further, "parental appointment" is not limited in this chapter to appointment by will, as it was under Ala. Code (1975) section 26-2-23. (See commentary to section 26-2A-71).

Another purpose is to declare that the relationship of guardian and ward continues even though both persons involved may move to another jurisdiction. Thus, this chapter makes the guardian and ward status more like the parent/child status it replaces. This is in contrast to the older concept embodied in prior Alabama law (e.g. Ala. Code (1975) section 26-2-20) that the court of guardianship, acting through the guardian as its appointee, carries the principal responsibility for wards under its jurisdiction. The older concept is not satisfactory as applied to instances where the persons involved leave the jurisdiction of the appointing court.

Statutes to be repealed: Ala. Code (1975) sections 26-2-20 and 26-2-23.

Code commissioner's note. — The cases cited below were decided under prior law.

Residence means legal domicile. — Under this section the minor's "residence" is his legal domicile, which is the domicile of his parents at the time of his death. Allgood v. Williams, 92 Ala. 551, 8 So. 722 (1891).

The removal of an infant of two years of age to the county where its parents were buried, and kept there, constitutes the establishment of the infant's residence in that county and the court of probate thereof has the authority to appoint the guardian. Loftin v. Carden, 203 Ala. 405, 83 So. 174 (1919).

Widow may not change infant's domicile after guardian is appointed. — The removal of domicile by the wife upon the death of her husband raises the question as to what court of probate is authorized to appoint a guardian for the minor child. The determination depends upon the general rule that the domicile of the father at the time of his death is the domicile of his infant child; and if a guardian has been appointed the mother cannot change the domicile without his consent. But she may change it during her widowhood if the child be of tender age, and there is no guardian. And where a change is made in such case the court of probate of the new county is authorized to appoint a guardian, this section furnishing the only basis for one probate court to supersede a valid appointing of another by the appointment of a new guardian. Moses v. Faber, 81 Ala. 445, 1 So. 587 (1887).

Collateral references. — 39 C.J.S., Guardian & Ward, §§ 8, 10.

§ 26-2A-71. Parental appointment of guardian for minor.

(a) The parent of an unmarried minor may appoint a guardian for the minor by will, or other writing signed by the parent and attested by at least two witnesses or acknowledged.

(b) Subject to the right of the minor under Section 26-2A-72, if both parents are dead or incapacitated or the surviving parent has no parental rights or has been adjudged to be incapacitated, a parental appointment becomes effective when the guardian seasonably files an acceptance in the court in which a nominating instrument is probated, or, in the case of a nontestamentary nominating instrument, in the court at the place where the minor resides or is present. If two or more appointments are made, the latter in time has priority, and if both parents are dead or incapacitated, an effective appointment by the parent, who was eligible to make the appointment and who dies or became incapacitated later in time, has priority.

(c) A parental appointment effected by filing the guardian's acceptance under a will probated in the state of the testator's domicile is effective in this state.

(d) Upon acceptance of appointment, the guardian shall give written notice as to when the appointment is effective to the minor and to the person having the minor's care or the minor's nearest adult relative. (Acts 1987, No. 87-590, p. 975, § 2-102.)

Comment

Replacing Ala. Code (1975) section 26-2-23, this section confers authority on a parent to appoint a guardian; no action by a court is required, as under prior law. In addition to the right to appoint a guardian by will, which was previously conferred upon parents in Ala. Code (1975) section 26-2-23, the chapter enables a parent to exercise the appointing authority by deed as well as by will. The instrument appointing the guardian may be executed like a will with two witnesses (cf., Ala. Code, section 43-8-131 (1975, as amended in 1982)) or it may be acknowledged (i.e. an authentication of the signature under oath) like a deed (cf., Ala. Code, section 35-4-23 (1975)). Both forms of appointment become effective only when the appointee files an acceptance in the appropriate court and the other conditions of the statute are met. These conditions are: (1) the minor involved has not previously filed an unwithdrawn written objection to the appointment as provided in section 26-2A-3; and (2) both parents are dead or incapacitated as defined in section 26-2A-20(8), or the surviving parent has been adjudged incapacitated or has surrendered or been deprived of parental rights. Section 26-2A-6(c) of this chapter authorizes the court to issue letters of guardianship if all requirements are met. Under subsection (b) of this section, all requirements for the issuance of the letters of guardianship are met "when the guardian seasonably files an acceptance in the court in which a nominating instrument is probated" and the guardian is entitled to issuance of letters of guardianship.

The existence of a guardian who has gained authority from a parental appointment precludes any other appointment of another guardian for the same minor, except after the removal of the guardian appointed by the parent and settlement of accounts. This results follows from section 26-2A-78(a) which confers the powers and responsibilities of a parent on a guardian, and from section 26-2A-73(a) which prevents appointment of a guardian for a minor over whom another has parental rights of custody. However, the authority of a guardian arising by parental authority may be terminated by objection of the ward who is 14 or more years old as provided by section 26-2A-72 or section 26-2A-79.

The ability of a single custodial parent to appoint a guardian by deed as well as by will is especially important where local procedures for the probate of a will require advance notice to all interested persons and representation of all interested persons who are minors. The document making the appointment is not required to be filed in a public office but it would be desirable practice for it, or a conformed copy, to be attached to the written acceptance by the nominee when the latter document is filed in order to complete the appointment. Also, in cases where there is a prospect that the authority of the parental nominee may be challenged, it might be desirable to attach other documentation to the filed acceptance, including copies of death certificates or other documents tending to show that all parental rights of custody have been terminated. In this connection, it should be noted that guardians for minors, whether created by parental or court appointment, lack authority to sell or mortgage real or personal assets of the ward. See section 26-2A-78. Hence, the tendency of title examiners and insurers to insist on public record documentation regarding every possible question concerning title may be disregarded as one considers the extent and form of documentation to accompany a guardian's acceptance under this section. Notice, however, that a conservator arising by court appointment in protective proceedings as provided in article 2, division 3, of this chapter has full authority as a statutory trustee of all assets transferred by the appointment. Also, under section 26-2A-152(a), a conservator of the estate of an unmarried minor as to whom no one has parental rights has the authority of a guardian. However, a parent is not empowered (given a "right") to appoint a conservator by deed or will as this section gives with regard to a guardian. However, a parent or spouse of a minor or incapacitated person can "nominate" to the court a person to be the conservator and that nomination is given a priority in the selection as a substitute for the priority of the parent or spouse making the nomination. See, section 26-2A-138, infra, and the Comment to that section. In addition, a parent with assets to use for the purpose may, of course, establish a trust for a minor or anyone else, but a trustee's authority would not include authority over the person of the beneficiary like that available to a guardian.

Section 26-2A-50 of this chapter governs the method and time requirements of a notice as required in this section.

Statute to be repealed: Ala. Code (1975) section 26-2-23.

Code commissioner's note. — The case cited below was decided under prior law.

Section 26-2-22 distinguished. — This section authorizes a testator parent to appoint whomever he or she chooses as the guardian of the estate of a minor child, while § 26-2-22 applies in those instances when no guardian is mentioned in the will or when the deceased dies intestate. Smith v. Tribble, 485 So. 2d 1083 (Ala. 1986).

Collateral references. — 39 C.J.S., Guardian & Ward, §§ 13, 68.

39 Am. Jur. 2d, Guardian & Ward, §§ 11-16.

Power of parent to appoint testamentary guardian for adult imbecile child. 24 ALR 1458.

Domicile of infant on death of both parents: doctrine of natural guardianship. 32 ALR2d 863.

Function, power, and discretion of court where there is testamentary appointment of guardian of minor. 67 ALR2d 803.

§ 26-2A-72. Objection by minor of 14 or older to parental appointment.

A minor 14 or more years of age who is the subject of a parental appointment may prevent the appointment or cause it to terminate by filing in the court in which the nominating instrument is filed a written objection to the appointment before it is accepted or within 30 days after receiving notice of its acceptance. An objection may be withdrawn. An objection does not preclude appointment by the court in a proper proceeding of the parental nominee or any other suitable person. (Acts 1987, No. 87-590, p. 975, § 2-103.)

Comment

Ala. Code (1975) section 26-2-21, previously permitted a minor "over 14 years of age" to "nominate" to the court a person as the person's guardian. However, prior law did not permit a minor to block or terminate his or her guardian's appointment. Under this chapter, a written objection of the minor to a parental appointment prevents a later accepted appointment from becoming effective. However, if the objection is withdrawn before the filing of the guardian's acceptance, the effect of the objection is cancelled. An objection filed within 30 days following the filing of an acceptance terminates the appointment but does not invalidate acts done previously in reliance on the guardian's authority. See section 26-2A-79. It may be questioned, however, whether a post-acceptance objection that serves to terminate the authority of a parental guardian may be withdrawn so as to reinstate the guardian's authority. Safe practice in such a case would dictate that those interested in establishing a legal guardianship petition the court for an appointment under section 26-2A-73.

The final sentence in the section is not intended to imply that a court proceeding for appointment of a guardian is necessary or appropriate when there has been an effective parental appointment. It was inserted to indicate that a minor age 14 or more may not block a court appointment of one nominated as guardian by a parent even though the prospective ward is able to block or terminate a parental appointment that does not involve action by the court. In this connection, note that section 26-2A-76, applicable to an appointment by the court, directs the court to respect the nomination of the prospective ward if 14 or more years of age. But, the court may conclude that appointment of the minor's nominee would be contrary to the best interest of the minor, clearing the way for appointment of a parental nominee or some other suitable person.

Statute to be repealed: Ala. Code (1975) section 26-2-21.

§ 26-2A-73. Court appointment of guardian of minor; conditions for appointment.

(a) The court may appoint a guardian for an unmarried minor if all parental rights have been terminated or suspended by circumstances or prior order of a court having jurisdiction; unless a custodian has been appointed under Section 26-18-8, or otherwise by the juvenile court when parental rights have been terminated or suspended. A guardian appointed pursuant to Section 26-2A-71 whose appointment has not been prevented or nullified under Section 26-2A-72 has priority over any guardian who may be appointed by the court, but the court may proceed with another appointment upon a finding that the parental nominee has failed to accept the appointment within 30 days after notice of the guardianship proceeding.

(b) If necessary, and on appropriate petition or application, the court may appoint a temporary guardian who shall have the full authority of a general guardian of a minor, but the authority of a temporary guardian may not last longer than six months. The appointment of a temporary guardian for a minor may occur even though the conditions described in subsection (a) have not been established. (Acts 1987, No. 87-590, p. 975, § 2-104; Acts 1988, 1st Ex. Sess., No. 88-898, p. 455, § 1.)

Comment

This section and sections 26-2A-74 through 26-2A-76 following cover proceedings to secure a court-appointed guardian of a minor. Sections 26-2A-77 through 26-2A-81 are applicable to all guardians of minors who derive authority from parental appointment or court appointment as contemplated in this division. Nothing in this chapter is intended to deal with the status of a so-called natural guardian, with the authority of a parent over a child, or with authority over a child or children that may be conferred by other state laws.

The court is not authorized to appoint a guardian for one for whom a parent has custodial rights or for one who has a parental guardian. Two purposes are served by this restriction. First, it prevents use of guardianship proceedings as a weapon or tactic in a squabble between parents concerning child custody, thereby forcing these disputes to the court having jurisdiction over marital matters. Second, it establishes that a guardian by parental appointment is as completely endowed with authority as a guardian as one appointed by court order. A guardian by parental appointment may be replaced by one appointed by the court following removal in proceedings under section 26-2A-81. If a court-appointed guardian comes into existence before a parental nomination is discovered or implemented by acceptance, it will be necessary to terminate the authority of the court-appointed guardian in order to clear the way for the parental nominee. See section 26-2A-70. In this connection, the second sentence of subsection (a) may be revoked in appropriate cases by the proponent of the parental nomination. This question would arise in proceedings incident to an application to the court for an order correcting the original appointment. Alternatively, the parental nominee may urge removal of the court-appointed guardian on the ground that the best interest of the minor as contemplated in section 26-2A-81 would be served by termination of the prior appointment.

Subsection (b) gives the court having jurisdiction of guardianship matters important power regarding the welfare of a minor in the form of authority to appoint a temporary guardian in cases of necessity. The authority permits appointment of a temporary guardian even though one or both parents have parental authority. It is to be noted, however, that the appointment of a temporary guardian must be preceded by notice and hearing as required for appointment of any court appointed guardian. The authority might be particularly useful in a case where both parents have disappeared or simply departed without making adequate arrangements for their children. If the needs of minor children require the creation of guardianships before it is possible to prove the death of the parents, the subsection opens the way to appointment of one having parental authority for up to six months that does not require proof of the requirement of subsection (a) that "all parental rights of custody have been terminated or suspended by circumstances ...."

In addition to guardians by parental appointment and court-appointed guardians, section 26-2A-152(a) of this chapter grants a conservator of the estate of a minor for whom no guardian or parent holds parental rights the powers of a guardian. The same section makes it clear that appointment of a conservator for the estate of a minor, even though it may create a form of guardianship authority over the minor, does not preclude court appointment of a guardian nor acceptance of a parental nomination. Thus, the statute enables persons interested in the affairs and welfare of a minor to secure a single authority competent to handle the personal and business needs of the minor. Alternatively, for cases in which circumstances suggest that one person should be in charge of decisions regarding the minor's living conditions, health care, and education, and another in charge of management of the minor's property interests, two appointments may be made.

This section expressly provides powers which may only have been implied under prior Alabama law by providing for the parental circumstances under which the court may appoint a guardian, and for the appointment of a temporary guardian under any circumstances the court deems appropriate.

Statutes to be repealed: Ala. Code (1975) sections 26-2-20 and 26-2-25.

§ 26-2A-74. Venue.

The venue for guardianship proceedings for a minor pursuant to Section 26-2A-73 is in the court at the place where the minor resides or is present at the time the proceedings are commenced. (Acts 1987, No. 87-590, p. 975, § 2-105.)

Comment

This chapter permits guardianship proceedings to be held in the county where the minor is present, as well as where the minor resides. Ala. Code (1975) section 26-2-20 previously provided for venue only in the county where the minor resides.

This section should be read with section 26-2A-32 dealing with multiple venue proceedings and transfer of venue.

Statute to be repealed: Ala. Code (1975) section 26-2-20.

§ 26-2A-75. Procedure for court-appointment of guardian of minor.

(a) A minor or any person interested in the welfare of the minor may petition for appointment of a guardian.

(b) After the filing of a petition, the court shall set a date for hearing, and the petitioner shall give notice of the time and place of hearing the petition in the manner prescribed by Section 26-2A-50 to:

(1) The minor, if 14 or more years of age and not the petitioner;

(2) Any person alleged to have had the principal care and custody of the minor during the 60 days preceding the filing of the petition; and

(3) Any living parent of the minor.

(c) Upon hearing, if the court finds that a suitable person seeks appointment, venue is proper, the required notices have been given, the conditions of Section 26-2A-73(a) have been met, and the welfare and best interest of the minor will be served by the requested appointment, it shall make the appointment and issue letters. In other cases, the court may dismiss the proceedings or make any other disposition of the matter that will serve the best interest of the minor.

(d) If the court determines at any time in the proceeding that the interests of the minor are or may be inadequately represented, it may appoint an attorney to represent the minor, giving consideration to the preference of the minor if the minor is 14 or more years of age. (Acts 1987, No. 87-590, p. 975, § 2-106.)

Comment

Subsection (a) is new to this chapter. It is intended to qualify as a potential petitioner any person with a serious interest or concern for a minor's welfare, including a relative or a non-relative having knowledge of the circumstances who completes a petition to the court, and any public official having official or personal concerns for the minor's welfare. If the court determines that the petitioner's concerns in the matter stem from interests that may not serve the welfare and best interest of the minor, it may dismiss the proceeding on the ground that the conditions for appointment as specified in subsection (b) have not been met.

The second sentence of subsection (b) may be interpreted to authorize an order directing that the petition be recast as a petition for a protective order under section 26-2A-130. That authority is expressly conferred on the court by section 26-2A-105 relating to a guardianship proceeding based on incapacity. The authority would be useful, for example, if the court determines that asset management is likely to be involved and that the person seeking appointment as guardian would be an appropriate person to serve as conservator with the power of a guardian. In these circumstances, two appointments could be avoided if the petitioner were willing to recast the petition as required by section 26-2A-130.

Alabama law did not previously have a statute expressing the details of this section.

§ 26-2A-76. Court appointment of guardian of minor; qualifications; priority of minor's nominee.

The court may appoint as guardian any person whose appointment would be in the best interest of the minor. The court shall appoint a person nominated by the minor, if the minor is 14 or more years of age, unless the court finds the appointment contrary to the best interest of the minor. (Acts 1987, No. 87-590, p. 975, § 2-107.)

Comment

While prior law provided for the nomination of a guardian by a minor over 14 years of age, it did not give priority to that nomination. Rather, the probate judge had to prefer the person of nearest relationship who will best manage the estate of the ward. See, Ala. Code (1975) sections 26-2-21 and 26-2-25.

The approach of this chapter is, rather than to provide priorities among various classes of relatives, to give priority only to the person nominated by the minor. The important point is to locate someone whose appointment will be in the best interest of the minor. If there is contention among relatives over who should be named, it is not likely that a statutory priority keyed to degrees of kinship would help resolve the matter. For example, if the argument involved a squabble between relatives of the child's father and relatives of its mother, priority in terms of degrees of kinship would be useless. Guardianships under this chapter are not likely to be attractive positions for persons who are more interested in handling a minor's estate than in his or her personal well being. An order of a court having equity power is necessary if the guardian is to receive payment for services where there is no conservator for the minor's estate. Also, the powers of management of a ward's estate conferred on a guardian are restricted so that if a substantial estate is involved, a conservator will be needed to handle the financial matters.

Compare section 26-2A-72, above, under which there is a similar priority as guardian given to the person appointed by the parent. Under that section, the minor may object to the parental appointee, thereby preventing the appointment without a court proceeding. Unless there is an objection, however, the appointment of the guardian under section 26-2A-3 is not a court appointment as provided in this section.

Statutes to be repealed: Ala. Code (1975) sections 26-2-21 and 26-2-25.

§ 26-2A-77. Consent to service by acceptance of appointment; notice.

By accepting a parental or court appointment as guardian, a guardian submits personally to the jurisdiction of the court in any proceeding relating to the guardianship that may be instituted by any interested person. The petitioner shall cause notice of any proceeding to be delivered or mailed to the guardian at the guardian's address listed in the court records and to the address then known to the petitioner. Letters of guardianship must indicate whether the guardian was appointed by court order or parental appointment. (Acts 1987, No. 87-590, p. 975, § 2-108.)

Comment

The "long-arm" principle behind this section is well established, It seems desirable that the court in which acceptance is filed be able to serve its process on the guardian wherever he or she has moved. The continuing interest of that court in the welfare of the minor is ample to justify this provision. The consent to service is real rather than fictional in the guardianship situation, where the guardian acts voluntarily in filing acceptance. It is probable that the form of acceptance will expressly embody the provisions of this section, although the statute does not expressly require this.

Alabama previously did not have a comparable statute.

§ 26-2A-78. Powers and duties of guardian of minor.

(a) A guardian of a minor ward has the powers and responsibilities of a parent regarding the ward's health, support, education, or maintenance, but a guardian is not personally liable for the ward's expenses and is not liable to third persons by reason of the relationship for acts of the ward.

(b) In particular and without qualifying the foregoing, a guardian shall:

(1) Become or remain personally acquainted with the ward and maintain sufficient contact with the ward to know of the ward's capacities, limitations, needs, opportunities, and physical and mental health;

(2) Take reasonable care of the ward's personal effects and commence protective proceedings if necessary to protect other property of the ward;

(3) Apply any available money of the ward to the ward's current needs for health, support, education, or maintenance;

(4) Conserve any excess money of the ward for the ward's future needs, but if a conservator has been appointed for the estate of the ward, the guardian, at least quarterly, shall pay to the conservator money of the ward to be conserved for the ward's future needs; and

(5) Report the condition of the ward and of the ward's estate that has been subject to the guardian's possession or control, as ordered by the court on petition of any person interested in the ward's welfare or as required by court rule.

(c) A guardian may:

(1) Receive money payable for the support of the ward to the ward's parent, guardian, or custodian under the terms of any statutory benefit or insurance system or any private contract, devise, trust, conservatorship, or custodianship, and money or property of the ward paid or delivered pursuant to Section 26-2A-6;

(2) If consistent with the terms of any order by a court of competent jurisdiction relating to detention or commitment of the ward, take custody of the person of the ward and establish the ward's place of abode within or without this state;

(3) If no conservator for the estate of the ward has been appointed, institute proceedings, including administrative proceedings, or take other appropriate action to compel the performance by any person of a duty to support the ward or to pay sums for the welfare of the ward;

(4) Consent to medical or other professional care, treatment, or advice for the ward without liability by reason of the consent for injury to the ward resulting from the negligence or acts of third persons unless a parent would have been liable in the circumstances;

(5) Consent to the marriage or adoption of the ward; and

(6) If reasonable under all of the circumstances, delegate to the ward certain responsibilities for decisions affecting the ward's well-being.

(d) A guardian is entitled to reasonable compensation for services as guardian and to reimbursement for room, board and clothing personally provided to the ward, but only as approved by order of the court. If a conservator, other than the guardian or one who is affiliated with the guardian, has been appointed for the estate of the ward, reasonable compensation and reimbursement to the guardian may be approved and paid by the conservator without order of the court controlling the guardian.

(e) In the interest of developing self-reliance on the part of a ward or for other good cause, the court, at the time of appointment or later, on its own motion or on appropriate petition or motion of the minor or other interested person, may limit the powers of a guardian otherwise conferred by this section and thereby create a limited guardianship. Any limitation on the statutory power of a guardian of a minor must be endorsed on the guardian's letters or, in the case of a guardian by parental appointment, must be reflected in letters that are issued at the time any limitation is imposed. Following the same procedure, a limitation may be removed and appropriate letters issued. (Acts 1987, No. 87-590, p. 975, § 2-109.)

Comment

This section exemplifies the difference between prior Alabama guardianship law and the system created by this chapter. While this chapter makes a clear distinction between a guardian of the person and one of his property (the latter denominated "conservator"), prior statutes were vague or imprecise as to the nature of the guardian's obligations with regard to the personal, as opposed to financial, needs of the protected person or minor. The bulk of the previously existing provisions related to settlement or to responsibilities indigenous to conservatorship under this chapter.

Subsection (a) specifies that the parental powers and responsibilities entailed in a guardianship are those concerned with the ward's "health, support, education, or maintenance." These terms, when read with subsection (b), obviously refer to all kinds of considerations that should be weighed and implemented on behalf of the ward by one invested with legal authority to control the ward's activities.

Subdivision (b)(1) reflects a belief that a person who accepts a guardianship for a minor should be forewarned by explicit statutory language that the position entails responsibilities to make and maintain personal contact with the ward.

The basic duties of a guardian are described in the mandates of subsection (b). Subsection (c) outlines optional authority that is extended to every guardian by the statute. Subsection (d), dealing with the delicate question of compensation for a guardian, requires that a guardian obtain approval from an independent conservator of the minor's estate or from the court before taking sums as compensation from funds of the minor that have been received by the guardian. In short, this section requires court approval before any guardian's claim for reimbursement can be satisfied otherwise than through a conservator. Note, however, that no advance court approval is required in order to permit a guardian to use available funds of the ward for the ward's current needs as provided in subsection (b)(3).

The amount of the guardian's compensation is set by the standard of "reasonableness," to be determined by the court or conservator, rather than by the percentage of disbursements and receipts as previously provided under Alabama law. See, Ala. Code (1975) section 26-5-16. The percentage compensation may be more suited to the guardian of property than to a guardian of the person.

The powers of a guardian regarding property of the ward are quite limited. Note also that the section does not encourage a guardian to apply to the appointing court for additional property power. Rather, the Act is designed to encourage use of a protective proceeding under section 26-2A-130 if property powers beyond those statutorily available to a guardian are needed. In this connection, it may be observed that subsection (c)(3), which contains one of the section's few references to use of the courts by a guardian, authorizes a guardian to institute proceedings to enforce a duty to support or pay money only if there is no conservator for the estate of the ward.

If the circumstances of a minor dictate that authority to control both person and property be obtained, protective proceedings under sections 26-2A-130 et seq. of this chapter are indicated. Section 26-2A-152(a) provides that a conservator for a minor as to whom no one has parental authority has the powers of a guardian as well as plenary power as a statutory trustee over the assets of the minor. In addition, as noted in the comment to section 26-2A-73, the Act enables interested persons to obtain appointment of the same or different persons as guardian and conservator for a minor even though section 26-2A-152(a) makes it patently unnecessary to obtain two appointments in a case where a single person is to serve in both capacities.

Subsection (e) extends the limited guardianship concept to guardians of minors by encouraging court orders limiting the already limited authority of a guardian. Using this provision, a court, at the time of appointment or on petition thereafter, might limit the authority of a guardian so that, for example, the guardian would not be able to direct the ward's religious training, or so that the guardian would be restricted in controlling the ward's place of abode by a condition that the ward's consent to any change of abode be given. The section provides that special restrictions of this sort may be removed or altered by further court order. Obviously, the drafters did not intend that the procedure for contracting and expanding special limitations on a guardian's power should be used to grant a guardian greater powers than are described in the section. Prior Alabama law did not contain a limited guardianship provision.

Statutes to be repealed: Ala. Code (1975) sections 26-4-60, 26-4-61, and 26-4-66.

Statutes to be modified: Ala. Code (1975) sections 26-5-2, 26-5-7, 26-5-16, and 26-5-30.

§ 26-2A-79. Termination of appointment of guardian; general.

A guardian's authority and responsibility terminate upon the death, resignation, or removal of the guardian or upon the minor's death, adoption, marriage, or attainment of majority, but termination does not affect the guardian's liability for prior acts or the obligation to account for funds and assets of the ward. Resignation of a guardian does not terminate the guardianship until it has been approved by the court. (Acts 1987, No. 87-590, p. 975, § 2-110.)

Comment

The position taken in this section that termination of a guardian's authority and responsibility does not apply retroactively to nullify prior acts is intended to govern all forms of termination including termination by objection as described in section 26-2A-72.

Any of various events, which may or may not appear from the records of the court that appointed a guardian, may serve to terminate the guardian's authority and responsibility. The extremely limited authority of a guardian over the ward's money and property tends to reduce instances when third persons may be jeopardized by an unknown termination of a guardian's authority. Principles protecting third persons who rely to their detriment on an apparent authority that has been terminated without their knowledge should govern the occasional cases in which a prior, unknown termination clouds the legality of a guardian's act.

Prior Alabama law dealt with termination primarily in terms of a requirement of settlement (see, Ala. Code (1975) sections 26-5-7 and 26-5-33), but Alabama previously was in accord with this section relative to liability of the guardian and sureties. Ala. Code (1975) section 26-6-1.

Statute to be repealed: Ala. Code (1975) section 26-6-1.

Statutes to be modified: Ala. Code (1975) sections 26-5-7 and 26-5-33.

§ 26-2A-80. Proceedings subsequent to appointment; venue.

(a) The court at the place where the ward resides has concurrent jurisdiction with the court that appointed the guardian or in which acceptance of a parental appointment was filed over resignation, removal, accounting, and other proceedings relating to the guardianship.

(b) If the court at the place where the ward resides is neither the appointing court nor the court in which acceptance of appointment is filed, the court in which proceedings subsequent to appointment are commenced in all appropriate cases shall notify the other court, in this or another state, and after consultation with that court determine whether to retain jurisdiction or transfer the proceedings to the other court, whichever is in the best interest of the ward. A copy of any order accepting a resignation or removing a guardian must be sent to the appointing court or the court in which acceptance of appointment is filed. (Acts 1987, No. 87-590, p. 975, § 2-111.)

Comment

Under sections 26-2A-20(3) and 26-2A-31, the court is designated as the proper court to handle matters relating to guardianship. The instant section is intended to give jurisdiction to the forum where the ward resides as well as to the one where appointment initiated. This provision has primary importance where the ward's residence has been moved from the appointing state. Because the court where acceptance of appointment is filed may as a practical matter be the only forum in which jurisdiction over the person of the guardian may be obtained (by reason of section 26-2A-77), that court is given concurrent jurisdiction.

The concurrent jurisdiction and transfer provisions in this chapter facilitate proceedings by extending the jurisdictions granted in prior Ala. Code (1975) section 26-5-1, which gave jurisdiction only to the court from which the guardian's appointment was derived. The court in the county in which the ward resides often will have a better opportunity to observe the conditions of the guardianship and the welfare of the ward.

Statute to be modified: Ala. Code (1975) section 26-5-1.

§ 26-2A-81. Resignation, removal, and other post-appointment proceedings.

(a) Any person interested in the welfare of a ward or the ward, if 14 or more years of age, may petition for removal of a guardian on the ground that removal would be in the best interest of the ward or for any other order that is in the best interest of the ward. A guardian may petition for permission to resign. A petition for removal or for permission to resign may, but need not, include a request for appointment of a successor guardian.

(b) Notice of hearing on a petition for an order subsequent to appointment of a guardian must be given, as prescribed in Section 26-2A-50, to the ward, the guardian, and any other person as ordered by the court.

(c) After notice and hearing on a petition for removal or for permission to resign, the court may terminate the guardianship and make any further order that may be appropriate.

(d) If the court determines at any time in the proceeding that the interest of the ward is or may be inadequately represented, it may appoint an attorney to represent the minor, giving consideration to the preference of the minor if the minor is 14 or more years of age. (Acts 1987, No. 87-590, p. 975, § 2-112.)

Comment

Prior Ala. Code (1975) section 26-6-2 enumerated specific causes for which a guardian could be removed. Application for removal could be made by the ward, or next friend, or on the court's own motion. However, this chapter provides a general standard for removal stated as "the best interest of the ward," leaving the court broad discretion in the matter.

Subsection (b) of this section identifies who must be given notice of any post-appointment proceedings affecting a guardianship. Section 26-2A-50 describes methods and time requirements concerning notices required by this section. Section 26-2A-51, which controls waiver of required notices, prevents waiver of notice by the ward. It would seem that a ward who is the petitioner in a post-appointment proceeding would not need to receive notice. However, a ward should be given notice of a petition initiated in the ward's name by a next friend.

Statutes to be repealed: Ala. Code (1975) sections 26-6-1, 26-6-2, 26-6-3, 26-6-4, 26-6-5, and 26-6-6.

Statute to be modified: Ala. Code (1975) section 26-2-51.

Code commissioner's note. — The cases cited below were decided under prior law.

A guardian cannot be capriciously removed. Huie v. Nixon, 6 Port. 77 (1837).

Removal from state is ground for revoking appointment. — The removal of a guardian beyond the limits of the state is a sufficient reason for severing the relation of guardian and ward and revoking the appointment. Eidland v. Chandler, 8 Ala. 781 (1845); Speight v. Knight, 11 Ala. 461 (1847); Dupree v. Perry, 18 Ala. 34 (1850).

The removal of a guardian from the state is a sufficient reason for displacing him from the trust, whenever, in the discretion of the court, he, as a nonresident, would not have been appointed in the first instance. Speight v. Knight, 11 Ala. 461 (1847).

Under this section the appointment of a guardian who is a nonresident should be revoked, although the ward has reached the age of 14 years, and has nominated a guardian who refuses to accept the trust. Cockrell v. Cockrell, 36 Ala. 673 (1860).

Improper use of property may be cause for removal. — Where it appeared that a guardian failed to return his account, employed the slaves, etc., of his ward in his own service, kept his own stock on his ward's land, and fed them on the corn of his ward, it was held that this was sufficient cause of removal. Ripitoe v. Hall, 1 Stew. 166 (1827).

Next friend must petition in minor's name. — A petition for removal of minor's

guardian, which petition was filed in name of next friend of minor rather than in minor's name by his next friend, was an action by next friend as sole plaintiff and minor was not a party, and next friend had no standing as party plaintiff, and no amendment could be made since to do so would constitute complete change of parties. Ex parte Cabaniss, 235 Ala. 181, 178 So. 1 (1937).

Notice by publication, when the address of the person to be notified is known, is inadequate notification. Mullane v. Central Hanover Bank & Trust Co., 339 U.S. 306, 70 S. Ct. 652, 94 L. Ed. 865 (1950).

Court may proceed without application for removal. — Under this section the court may proceed, of its own motion, on any information at hand, without an application, giving notice and hearing to the guardian, and appointing a guardian ad litem to represent and protect the interest of the minor on such hearing. This section vests in the probate court jurisdiction quite analogous to that inherent in the (former) chancery court. Ex parte Cabaniss, 235 Ala. 181, 178 So. 1 (1937).

The court has the inherent power to remove a guardian, proceeding according to its own practices, always giving notice and opportunity for a hearing. Lee v. Lee, 55 Ala. 500 (1876); Murphree v. Hanson, 197 Ala. 246, 72 So. 437 (1916); Ward v. Jossen, 218 Ala. 530, 119 So. 220 (1928); First Nat'l Bank v. Robertson, 220 Ala. 654, 127 So. 221 (1930); Ex parte Cabaniss, 235 Ala. 181, 178 So. 1 (1937).

Collateral references. — 39 C.J.S., Guardian & Ward, §§ 44, 45.

39 Am. Jur. 2d, Guardian & Ward, §§ 57-59.

Resignation or removal of executor, administrator, guardian, or trustee, before final administration or before termination of trust, as affecting his compensation. 96 ALR3d 1102.

Improper handling of funds, investments, or assets as ground for removal of guardian. 128 ALR 535.

Division 2.

Guardians of Incapacitated Persons.

§ 26-2A-100. Appointment of guardian for incapacitated person by will or other writing.

(a) The parent of an unmarried incapacitated person may appoint by will, or other writing signed by the parent and attested by at least two witnesses or acknowledged, a guardian of the incapacitated person. If both parents are dead or the surviving parent is adjudged incapacitated, a parental appointment becomes effective when, after having given seven days prior written notice of intention to do so to the incapacitated person and to the person having the care of the person or to the nearest adult relative residing in this state, the guardian files acceptance of appointment in the court in which the will is probated, or in the case of a nontestamentary nominating instrument, in the court at the place where the incapacitated person resides or is present. If both parents are dead, an effective appointment by the parent who died later has priority.

(b) The spouse of a married incapacitated person may appoint by will, or other writing signed by the spouse and attested by at least two witnesses or acknowledged, a guardian of the incapacitated person. The appointment becomes effective when, after having given seven days prior written notice of intention to do so to the incapacitated person and to the person having care of the incapacitated person or to the nearest adult relative residing in this state, the guardian files acceptance of appointment in the court in which the will is probated or, in the case of nontestamentary nominating instrument, in the court at the place where the incapacitated person resides or is present. An effective appointment by a spouse has priority over an appointment by a parent.

(c) An appointment effected by filing the guardian's acceptance under a will probated in the state of the decedent's domicile is effective in this state.

(d) Upon the filing in the court in which the will was probated or, in the case of a nontestamentary nominating instrument, in the court at the place where the incapacitated person resides or is present, of written objection to the appointment by the incapacitated person for whom a parental or spousal appointment or guardian has been made, the appointment is terminated. An objection does not prevent appointment by the court in a proper proceeding of the parental or spousal nominee or any other suitable person upon an adjudication of incapacity in proceedings under the succeeding sections of this division. (Acts 1987, No. 87-590, p. 975, § 2-201.)

Comment

This section confers upon a spouse or a parent authority to appoint a guardian for an incapacitated person. The instrument appointing the guardian may be executed like a will with two witnesses (cf., Ala. Code, section 43-8-131 (1975, as amended in 1982)) or it may be acknowledged (i.e., an authentication of the signature under oath) like a deed (cf., Ala. Code, section 35-4-23 (1975)). Unlike the prior Alabama law, which conferred the authority to appoint a guardian for a person of "unsound mind" only on the probate court (see, Ala. Code (1975) section 26-2-40), the procedure in this chapter initially requires no action by any court. However, a condition of an effective parental or spousal appointment is that the appointee file an acceptance in an appropriate court. Such a filing does not initiate a court proceeding or require any response from the court. A parental or spousal guardian is entitled to a writing (letters) from the court showing that an acceptance has been filed and that a guardian's authority as provided by the statute (see section 26-2A-34) appears to have been conferred.

The authority to appoint a guardian under this section also is not premised on whether the person to be protected has an estate. The concern for property motivates guardianship proceedings for incompetents under prior Alabama law (see Ala. Code (1975) section 26-2-40); this difference relates back to the guardian/conservator dichotomy utilized in this chapter. (See Comment to section 26-2A-78.)

This section is modeled after section 26-2A-71, but it differs from section 26-2A-71 in several particulars. For one, it applies to guardians for persons who are incapacitated for reasons other than minority. See the definition of incapacity in section 26-2A-20(8). Also, no advance written notice of intention to accept a parental appointment as a guardian for a minor under section 26-2A-71 is required while seven days' advance notice is required for completion of a parental or spousal appointment under this section. Note, too, that termination by objection to an appointment under section 26-2A-71 can be effected by virtue of section 26-2A-72 only if the objection is filed within 30 days after the filing of the acceptance. In contrast, this section permits the ward to upset a parental or spousal appointment based on incapacity by written objection at any time.

Whether it is accomplished by deed or will, this section expressly provides that a parental appointment of a guardian based on the incapacity of a child cannot become effective until both parents are dead or the surviving parent has become incapacitated. Thus, a parent's appointing authority is limited to providing for a replacement of whatever authority might have been attached to the status of parent. A spousal appointment by will would be ambulatory and could not become effective until after the spouse's death. However, a spousal appointment by deed may become effective before the appointing spouse's death if the appointing instrument so provides and all other conditions of an effective appointment are met. Thus, a spouse of an incapacitated person is enabled to confer a guardian's authority over an incapacitated mate. The authority arising by spousal appointment may be helpful in cases where the appointing spouse plans to be absent, or in situations where some third person hesitates to respect the directions of an incompetent's spouse and insists on some form of guardianship paper.

The section provides several safeguards that attend the procedure. The case with which the authority available under this section may be ended by objection of the ward provides a safeguard against abuse of the procedure. For another safeguard, the absence of any adjudication of incapacity incident to a conferral of authority under the section means that a purported appointment is effective only if, upon challenge, it is determined by a court that the essential condition of incapacity existed when the appointment was accepted. Also, as noted earlier, the ward of a guardian who claims authority by virtue of the procedure described in this section may cause the authority to terminate by filing a written objection at any time.

It may be questioned whether a legislature should bother to provide for an authority as fragile as that contemplated by the section. It is believed that the procedure will be particularly helpful to parents of children suffering from congenital or other defects who require some lifetime care arrangements. These parents may desire some legal assurance that persons of their choice will be able to continue monitoring the care arrangements for their children when they become unable to do so. Since the role to be played calls principally for personal concern for the welfare of the incapacitated person, a prima facie showing of legal authority will suffice in many cases, and it will be unimportant that the overseer's legal authority is not impregnable.

See the Comment following section 26-2A-71 for additional observations regarding the utility of appointments of guardians by deed.

Statute to be repealed: Ala. Code (1975) section 26-2-40.

§ 26-2A-101. Venue.

The venue for guardianship proceedings for an incapacitated person is in the place where the incapacitated person resides or is present at the time the proceedings are commenced. If the incapacitated person is admitted to an institution pursuant to order of a court of competent jurisdiction, venue is also in the county in which that court is located. (Acts 1987, No. 87-590, p. 975, § 2-202.)

Comment

This section introduces the procedure for securing a court appointment of a guardian for an incapacitated person described in sections 26-2A-101 through 26-2A-107.

Except for the case in which the authority of a parental or spousal guardian for an incapacitated person may be question or ended, the powers of a court-appointed guardian are the same as those of a spousal or parental guardian. Section 26-2A-108 describes the powers. Perusal of section 26-2A-108, of section 26-2A-78 on which it is based, and of the Comment following section 26-2A-78, is recommended. From these materials, it will be seen that most of the more traditional purposes of guardianships will not be served by the guardian's position described in this chapter. Rather, a conservator, as described in division 3 of article 2, will be much better equipped than a guardian to handle financial affairs of an incapacitated person. Consequently, the new guardianship as described in this chapter is likely to be much less widely used than traditional guardianship procedures. Counselors will be well advised to determine, in all cases where a guardianship may be suggested whether a guardianship, as distinguished from a conservatorship, will serve any useful purpose. Alternative methods of obtaining health and care services, including consents to medical treatment and authority for voluntary or involuntary diagnostic or protective custodies, should be given careful consideration. Also, volunteer or paid companions, or placements with public or private nursing homes or other limited or total care providers, may be possible without the interposition of a court-appointed guardian.

Prior Alabama law provided for venue only in the county where the person of unsound mind resides (Ala. Code (1975) section 26-2-40) even though the person may be confined to a hospital in another county or state. Ala. Code (1975) section

26-2-46. This chapter extends venue also to the county where the incapacitated person is present and in a county where the person is institutionalized.

Statute to be repealed: Ala. Code (1975) section 26-2-40.

Cited in Martin v. Clark, 554 So. 2d 1030 (Ala. 1989).

§ 26-2A-102. Procedure for court-appointment of a guardian of an incapacitated person.

(a) An incapacitated person or any person interested in the welfare of the incapacitated person may petition for appointment of a guardian, limited or general.

(b) After the filing of a petition, the court shall set a date for hearing on the issue of incapacity so that notices may be given as required by Section 26-2A-103, and, unless the allegedly incapacitated person is represented by counsel, appoint an attorney to represent the person in the proceeding. The person so appointed may be granted the powers and duties of a guardian ad litem. The person alleged to be incapacitated must be examined by a physician or other qualified person appointed by the court who shall submit a report in writing to the court. The person alleged to be incapacitated also must be interviewed by a court representative sent by the court. The court representative also shall interview the person who appears to have caused the petition to be filed and any person who is nominated to serve as guardian and visit the present place of abode of the person alleged to be incapacitated and the place it is proposed that the person will be detained or reside if the appointment is made and submit a report in writing to the court. The court may utilize the service of any public or charitable agency as an additional court representative to evaluate the condition of the allegedly incapacitated person and to make appropriate recommendations to the court.

(c) A person alleged to be incapacitated is entitled to be present at the hearing in person. The person is entitled to be represented by counsel, to present evidence, to cross-examine witnesses, including the court-appointed physician or other qualified person and any court representative, and upon demand to trial by jury as provided in Section 26-2A-35. The issue may be determined at a closed hearing if the person alleged to be incapacitated or counsel for the person so requests.

(d) Any person may apply for permission to participate in the proceeding, and the court may grant the request, with or without hearing, upon determining that the best interest of the alleged incapacitated person will be served thereby. The court may attach appropriate conditions to the permission. (Acts 1987, No. 87-590, p. 975, § 2-203.)

Comment

The procedure described in this section involves three designations or appointments of persons as mandatory participants in a court-appointed guardianship proceeding based on incapacity. First, the respondent must be represented by counsel who also may be granted the powers and duties of a guardian ad litem and who may represent the respondent in all cases in which he or she lacks adequate counsel of choice. In context, the court probably should determine not only that private counsel is in the case, but that such counsel has been engaged by the respondent acting without undue pressure from others having some possible personal interest in the proceeding. Also, the court is required to designate a physician and a court representative to function as described. The roles of physician and court representative may be filled by a single person, provided the person has the requisite qualifications.

Mandatory participation by a court representative and physician (or other qualified person) is not mentioned in connection with guardianship proceedings based on minority. See section 26-2A-75. "Other qualified person" permits, for example, the court to appoint a psychologist or clinical psychologist. These officials are mentioned in section 26-2A-135 covering court proceedings seeking what has sometimes been called a "guardian of the estate" and is referred to in this chapter as a conservator.

Underlying the guardian ad litem, court representative, and physician requirements in this section is the belief that an individual's liberty to select an abode and to receive or to refuse medical, psychiatric, vocational, or other therapy or attention should not be displaced by appointment of a guardian unless the appointment is clearly necessary. In order to evaluate properly the merits of a petition seeking appointment of a guardian, the court should have access to information regarding the respondent other than as provided by the petitioner and associated counsel. The precautionary procedures tend to reduce the risk that relatives of the respondent may use guardianship procedures to relieve themselves of burdensome but bearable responsibilities for care, or to prevent the respondent from dissipating assets they would like to inherit, or for other reasons that are not in the best interest of the respondent. Also, they are designed to increase the perceptions of the respondent available to the court and lessen the risk that honestly held but overly-narrow judgments regarding tolerable limits of eccentricity may cause the loss of an individual's liberty.

The mandatory features of a guardianship proceeding make the procedure somewhat more complex than a protective proceeding under section 26-2A-130 et seq. seeking the appointment of a conservator. The differences may tend to discourage use of guardianships and so reduce the instances in which persons may be declared to be without legal capacity. Loss of control over one's property is serious, to be sure, but there are reasons why it may be viewed as less serious than suffering a judgment that one is legally incapacitated and must be placed under the care of a guardian. First, one's property can and should be made available for support of legal dependents. Also, court-directed management of one's property does not impede the personal liberty of the protected person nor prevent the acquisition and enjoyment of assets that may be acquired thereafter. Finally, the interposition of another's control of one's personal freedom is rarely necessary or justified in noncriminal settings. Alternative methods of protecting persons with little ability to care for themselves should be encouraged.

Except for this chapter's expressed more stringent precautions against unnecessary appointments, this chapter generally parallels prior Alabama procedural requirements. Ala. Code (1975) sections 26-2-40 through 26-2-46.

This chapter does not expressly repeal, nor is it intended to repeal by implication, the Adult Protective Services Act of 1976, Ala. Code, sections 38-9-1 through 38-9-11 (1975, as amended by Acts 1977, No. 780). The Adult Protective Services Act is principally an act to provide protective services (i.e., "services whose objective is to protect an incapacitated person from himself and from others") and placement to prevent abuse, neglect, and exploitation of adults. The act authorizes the department of human services, in an emergency, and any "interested person" (which presumably includes the department of human services), to petition the circuit court for protective services or placement, when the adult is unable or unwilling to consent to services or placement. The Adult Protective Services Act provides [Ala. Code section 38-9-6(g) (1975, as amended by Acts 1977, No. 780)] that the circuit court "may" appoint a "guardian," but "the department [of human services] shall not be appointed as guardian." In appointing the "guardian," the act refers to this chapter for the powers of the guardian and procedures in the appointment. Both that act and this chapter are consistent in that both acts provide for the use of a six-person jury to determine some facts and both acts permit the use of a court representative to evaluate the needs of the allegedly incapacitated person. In addition, both acts adopt the policy of placing the "least possible restriction on personal liberty and exercise of constitutional rights consistent with due process and protection ...." of the protected person. See particularly, Ala. Code, section 38-9-3 (1975, as amended by Acts 1977, No. 780) and, for example, section 26-2A-105 of this chapter.

Statutes to be repealed: Ala. Code (1975) sections 26-2-40, 26-2-41, and 26-2-42.

Statute to be modified: Ala. Code (1975) section 26-2-45.

Code commissioner's note. — The cases cited below were decided under prior law.

Authority and jurisdiction of court. — Although former section provided that a guardian shall not be appointed "until an inquisition has been had and taken as directed," the proceedings were, nevertheless, before the probate court as a court, and the issues were determinable in that court. The jurisdiction attached both as to the subject matter and the person upon the filing of a proper petition. Craft v. Simon, 118 Ala. 625, 24 So. 380 (1898), aff'd, 182 U.S. 427, 21 S. Ct. 836, 45 L. Ed. 1165 (1901).

In order to sustain a decree adjudging person of unsound mind, it must affirmatively appear on face of record that all necessary jurisdictional steps, were taken to complete the court's jurisdiction. Fowler v. Fowler, 219 Ala. 453, 122 So. 440 (1929).

Proceedings under this section are inquiries on behalf of society to determine the subject's present mental condition. The object is not to punish or to determine definitely any property rights, but to fix the mental status of the subject at the time of the proceeding, and to determine for the time being the propriety of appointing a guardian to preserve his property, both for his own protection and that he may not become a charge upon society. Hornaday v. Hornaday, 254 Ala. 267, 48 So. 2d 207 (1950).

The jurisdiction of cases for the inquiry into lunacies and idiocies, and into such mental incapacity as renders a party incompetent to manage his own affairs, and requires the assistance of a guardian, has been transferred from the chancellor to the judge of probate. This latter officer exercises the same jurisdiction that the chancellor did before this change, but in the manner prescribed by statute, and the proceedings before the judge of probate must have the same effect, that the like proceedings would have had before the chancellor. Fore v. Fore, 44 Ala. 478 (1870).

Probate court acts as court of limited and special jurisdiction. — In proceedings to declare a person non compos mentis, a probate court acts as a court of limited and special jurisdiction. In such case the jurisdictional facts must affirmatively appear from the face of the record. Riley v. Smyer, 265 Ala. 475, 91 So. 2d 820 (1956).

Hearing on issue of incapacity cannot be tried before sheriff. — An inquisition of lunacy (now hearing on issue of incapacity) must be tried before the probate judge, and he must administer the oath to the jury and receive their verdict when rendered; and, if tried before a sheriff in the absence of the probate judge, the entire proceedings are void. Laughinghouse v. Laughinghouse, 38 Ala. 257 (1862).

Jurisdictional averment in petition. — Under this section providing that on petition of any relative or friend of any person alleged to be of unsound mind, setting forth the facts, name, age, sex and residence of such person, the probate court shall name a day for the hearing thereof, a petition reciting that petitioner is a friend of one S., a female, 49 years of age, residing at Mobile, and a person of unsound mind, is sufficient to give the court jurisdiction. Craft v. Simon, 118 Ala. 625, 24 So. 380 (1898), aff'd, 182 U.S. 427, 21 S. Ct. 836, 45 L. Ed. 1165 (1901); Riley v. Smyer, 265 Ala. 475, 91 So. 2d 820 (1956). See Fowler v. Nash, 225 Ala. 613, 144 So. 831 (1932).

Proceedings should be conducted with reasonable dispatch. Prestwood v. Prestwood, 395 So. 2d 8 (Ala. 1981).

When guardian ad litem must be appointed. — Ordinarily one adjudged a non compos mentis can only act through a recognized representative, but this is not the case where the very object of the action is to determine whether the person alleged to be of unsound mind is in fact a person of unsound mind. Smith v. Smith, 254 Ala. 404, 48 So. 2d 546 (1950).

It is only when an alleged non compos mentis is not represented by counsel that the court is obligated under this section to appoint a guardian ad litem to represent and defend such person. Smith v. Smith, 254 Ala. 404, 48 So. 2d 546 (1950).

Appeal may be taken by counsel on behalf of alleged incompetent. — When this section is taken in connection with § 12-22-25, it is clear that an appeal may be taken by counsel on behalf of an alleged non compos mentis respondent by giving security for the costs of the appeal to be approved as provided in § 12-22-25. Smith v. Smith, 254 Ala. 404, 48 So. 2d 546 (1950).

The allowance of attorney's fees from the incompetent's estate to counsel for the petitioner in a proceeding under this section was sustained on the theory that the appointment of a guardian was "necessary" to the interest of the non compos mentis, and also that it created a trust fund and brought it into court for administration under the common benefit principle of § 34-3-60. Penney v. Pritchard & McCall, 255 Ala. 13, 49 So. 2d 782 (1950).

Insanity may be shown by proof of acts and conduct of the alleged incompetent inconsistent with his character and previous conduct. Hornaday v. Hornaday, 254 Ala. 267, 48 So. 2d 207 (1950).

Evidence of prior conduct. — The question for decision is the condition of the mind of the alleged incompetent at the time of the trial. But prior conduct which tends to throw some light upon that inquiry is admissible, and the trial court erred in limiting such conduct to a period of 30 days immediately preceding the trial. Hornaday v. Hornaday, 254 Ala. 267, 48 So. 2d 207 (1950).

Question whether the alleged incompetent must testify when present in court and when called by the person or persons asserting his incompetency is left to trial court's discretion, for the reason that conditions may exist which would make it injurious or detrimental to him. Hornaday v. Hornaday, 254 Ala. 267, 48 So. 2d 207 (1950).

Collateral references. — 44 C.J.S., Insane Persons, §§ 8-10, 14-19.

Necessity and sufficiency of notice to alleged incompetent of application for appointment of guardian. 23 ALR 594.

Notice to incompetent of application for appointment of successor to guardian. 138 ALR 1364.

Waiver of notice of proceeding for appointment of guardian by alleged incompetent. 152 ALR 1247.

Foundation or predicate to permit nonexpert witness to give opinion, in a civil action, as to sanity, mental competency, or mental condition. 40 ALR2d 15.

Right to counsel in insanity or incompetency adjudication proceedings. 87 ALR2d 950.

Recognition of foreign guardian as next friend or guardian ad litem. 94 ALR2d 162.

Physician-patient privilege: testimony as to communications or observations as to mental condition of patient treated for other condition. 100 ALR2d 648.

False imprisonment and malicious prosecution: liability for false imprisonment and/or malicious prosecution predicated upon institution of, or conduct in connection with, insanity proceedings. 30 ALR3d 523.

§ 26-2A-103. Notice in guardianship proceeding.

(a) In a proceeding for the appointment of a guardian of an incapacitated person, and, if notice is required in a proceeding for appointment of a temporary guardian, notice of hearing must be given to each of the following:

    (1) The person alleged to be incapacitated, her or his spouse (if any), and adult children, or if none, parents;

    (2) Any person who is serving as guardian, conservator, or who has the care and custody of the person alleged to be incapacitated;

(3) In case no other person is notified under paragraph (1), at least one of the nearest adult relatives residing in this state, if any can be found; and

(4) Any other person as directed by the court.

(b) Notice of hearing on a petition for an order subsequent to appointment of a guardian must be given to the ward, the guardian, and any other person as ordered by the court.

(c) Notice must be served personally on the alleged incapacitated person. Notices to other persons as required by subsection (a)(1) must be served personally if the person to be notified can be found within the state. In all other cases, required notices must be given as provided in Section 26-2A-50.

(d) The person alleged to be incapacitated may not waive notice. (Acts 1987, No. 87-590, p. 975, § 2-204.)

Comment

This section requires notice of the proceeding to be served personally on the person alleged to be incapacitated. This requirement appears in subsection (c), which qualifies both subsections (a) and (b). Subsection (b) applies to proceedings subsequent to the institution of a guardianship as covered in section 26-2A-111.

Prior law required personal service only in the appointment of a curator (Ala. Code (1975) section 26-7A-3), a position established in chapter 7A of Title 26 which roughly approximated that of the conservator. Also, in comparison with the previous notice requirements for appointment of a curator, this chapter requires that acting caretakers (if any) and at least one adult relative must be given notice. Alabama previously required other notice only to the spouse. Ala. Code (1975) section 26-7A-3.

This chapter calls for notice of the ward and guardian in proceedings subsequent to the guardianship appointment. Previously Alabama procedure only required notice by publication with a copy of the paper mailed by the probate judge to the person alleged to be of unsound mind and appointment of a guardian ad litem when a guardian is appointed over in-state property of a non-resident ward. Ala. Code (1975) section 26-2-48.

It may be noted that personal service is not necessary for the required notice to a minor age 14 or over under section 26-2A-75 governing proceedings seeking a court-appointed guardian for a minor. In this connection, it should be observed that the instant section, rather than section 26-2A-75, governs if the petition seeks to establish that a minor is incapacitated for reasons other than minority and so is in need of a guardian who will continue to serve in spite of the respondent's attainment of majority. See section 26-2A-79 and compare section 26-2A-109.

Statutes to be modified: Ala. Code (1975) sections 26-2-43, 26-2-47 and 26-2-48.

§ 26-2A-104. Who may be guardian; priorities.

(a) Any qualified person may be appointed guardian of an incapacitated person.

(b) Unless lack of qualification or other good cause dictates the contrary, the court shall appoint a guardian in accordance with the incapacitated person's most recent nomination in a durable power of attorney.

(c) Except as provided in subsection (b), the following are entitled to consideration for appointment in the order listed:

(1) The spouse of the incapacitated person or a person nominated by will of a deceased spouse or by other writing signed by the spouse and attested by at least two witnesses or acknowledged;

(2) An adult child of the incapacitated person;

(3) A parent of the incapacitated person, or a person nominated by will of a deceased parent or by other writing signed by a parent and attested by at least two witnesses or acknowledged;

(4) Any relative of the incapacitated person with whom the person has resided for more than six months prior to the filing of the petition; and

(5) A person nominated by the person who is caring for or paying for the care of the incapacitated person.

(d) With respect to persons having equal priority, the court shall select the one it deems best suited to serve. The court, acting in the best interest of the incapacitated person may pass over a person having priority and appoint a person having a lower priority or no priority. (Acts 1987, No. 87-590, p. 975, § 2-205.)

Comment

Subsection (a) limits those who may act as guardians for incapacitated persons to "suitable" persons. "Suitable" in its application to "persons" is not defined in this chapter, meaning that an appointing court has considerable discretion regarding the suitability of an individual to serve as guardian for a particular ward. In exercising this discretion, the court shall give careful consideration to the needs of the ward and to the experience or other qualifications of the applicant to react sensitively and positively to the ward's needs. In comparison, prior Alabama law emphasized the degree of kinship and the prospective guardian's ability to manage the ward's estate. Ala. Code (1975) section 26-2-49. Perhaps this difference in the statutes is explained by the role of the guardian under the Act and under prior law.

Subsections (b) and (c) govern priorities among persons who may seek appointment. Unless good cause or lack of qualification dictates otherwise, priority is with one nominated in an unrevoked power of attorney of the ward that remains effective though the ward has become incompetent since executing the power of attorney. Previously, only the nearest of kin received any priority in appointment.

It has been suggested that provision should be made for a "suitable institution" to be appointed guardian. The suggestion was discussed thoroughly for this chapter and rejected. The reasoning for limiting appointments to "suitable persons" is that for a guardianship of the person, the needs, duties and responsibilities are so personal that they should only be delegated to a natural person and not to an institution.

Statute to be repealed: Ala. Code (1975) section 26-2-49.

Code commissioner's note. — The cases cited below were decided under prior law.

The paramount consideration is the best interests of the ward and his estate. Boylan v. Kohn, 172 Ala. 275, 55 So. 127 (1911). And this overshadows any claim of relatives. Broxson v. Spears, 216 Ala. 385, 113 So. 248 (1927). Hence, an applicant of a more remote relationship will be appointed where the inter- ests of the ward will be best subserved, Boylan v. Kohn, supra, because the section is not mandatory in favor of the next of kin. Broxson v. Spears, 216 Ala. 385, 113 So. 248 (1927).

The paramount consideration of the law has always been the best interests of the ward and of his estate, and this is peculiarly the case in the selection of his guardian. Richards v. Elrod, 284 Ala. 19, 221 So. 2d 378 (1969);

Starnes v. Brassell, 286 Ala. 437, 241 So. 2d 109 (1970).

All relatives rejected if they are not suitable. — If none of the relatives applying is suitable, the court should reject them all, and appoint a general guardian under this section. Boylan v. Kohn, 172 Ala. 275, 55 So. 127 (1911).

Contest between applicants. — When there is a contest between applicants, there must be some affirmative evidence in the record on appeal to show that the applicant appointed by the probate court is a suitable

person for such appointment. Richards v. Elrod, 284 Ala. 19, 221 So. 2d 378 (1969).

Presumption on appeal is that finding in lower court is correct. — The court on appeal will presume that the finding of the lower court, where all the parties and witnesses are present, is correct. Broxson v. Spears, 216 Ala. 385, 113 So. 248 (1927), containing considerations in selecting a proper guardian.

Collateral references. — 39 Am. Jur. 2d, Guardian & Ward, §§ 27-36.

Priority and preference in appointment of conservator or guardian for an incompetent. 65 ALR3d 991.

§ 26-2A-104.1. Corporations as guardians for developmentally disabled.

(a) The term "developmentally disabled" means a person whose impairment of general intellectual functioning or adaptive behavior which is manifested before the person attains the age of 22 and results in mental retardation, cerebral palsy, epilepsy or autism and as defined in Public Law 98-527, the Developmental Disabilities Assistance and Bill of Rights Act (Section 102(7)).

(b) A private non-profit corporation organized under the laws of Alabama and qualified under the Internal Revenue Code as a 501(c)(3) tax exempt corporation as described herein is qualified for designation as guardian for persons with developmental disabilities and who has been determined by the probate court to need some degree of guardianship; provided that those corporations qualifying under this section shall be governed by a board of directors which shall have no fewer than 35 percent of its membership representing parents or siblings of persons with developmental disabilities. Further such corporation shall be established in perpetuity to provide a lifetime of service to those persons placed under their care. In no case shall a corporation appointed under this section engage in providing direct or indirect services to the wards/protective persons under its care or take any other action that could be considered a conflict of interest.

(c) The Alabama Department of Mental Health and Mental Retardation shall assist the courts in their implementation of this section and shall develop guidelines for the provision of guardianship services by corporations appointed under this section. (Acts 1991, No. 91-547, p. 1009, §§ 1-3.)

Effective date. — The act which added this section became effective July 29, 1991.

U.S. Code. — The federal Developmental

Disabilities Assistance and Bill of Rights Act, referred to in subsection (a), is codified as 42 U.S.C., § 6000 et seq.

§ 26-2A-105. Findings; order of appointment.

(a) The court shall exercise the authority conferred in this division so as to encourage the development of maximum self-reliance and independence of the incapacitated person and make appointive and other orders only to the extent necessitated by the incapacitated person's mental and adaptive limitations or other conditions warranting the procedure.

(b) The court may appoint a guardian as requested if it is satisfied that the person for whom a guardian is sought is incapacitated and that the appointment is necessary or desirable as a means of providing continuing care and supervision of the person of the incapacitated person. The court, on appropriate findings, may (i) treat the petition as one for a protective order under Section 26-2A-130 and proceed accordingly, (ii) enter any other appropriate order, or (iii) dismiss the proceedings.

(c) The court, at the time of appointment or later, on its own motion or on appropriate petition or motion of the incapacitated person or other interested person, may limit the powers of a guardian otherwise conferred by this chapter and thereby create a limited guardianship. Any limitation on the statutory power of a guardian of an incapacitated person must be endorsed on the guardian's letters or, in the case of a guardian by parental or spousal appointment, must be reflected in letters issued at the time any limitation is imposed. Following the same procedure, a limitation may be removed or modified and appropriate letters issued. (Acts 1987, No. 87-590, p. 975, § 2-206.)

Comment

The purpose of subsections (a) and (c) is to remind an appointing court that a guardianship under this legislation should not confer more authority over the person of the ward than appears necessary to alleviate the problems caused by the ward's incapacity. This is a statement of the general principle underlying a "limited guardianship" concept. For example, if the principal reason for the guardianship is the ward's inability to comprehend a personal medical problem, the guardian's authority could be limited to making a judgment, after evaluation of all circumstances, concerning the advisability and form of treatment and to authorize actions necessary to carry out the decision. Or, if the ward's principal problem stems from memory lapses and associated wanderings, a guardian with authority limited to making arrangements for suitable security against this risk might be indicated. Alabama adopted the concept of limited guardianship by a 1982 amendment to the Alabama law. Ala. Code (1975, as amended by Act No. 82-384) section 26-2-45. This chapter proposes to give body and detail to that skeleton principle.

Subsection (c) facilitates use by the appointing court of a trial-and-error method to achieve a tailoring of the guardian's authority to changing needs and circumstances. Read with the last sentence of section 26-2A-102(b) and with subsection (d) of section 26-2A-102, the instant section authorizes use of any public or charitable agency that demonstrates interest and competence in evaluating the condition and needs of the ward in arriving at a decision regarding the appropriate powers of the guardian.

The section does not authorize enlargement of the powers of a guardian beyond those described in section 26-2A-108 and related sections. Rather, limitations on a guardian's section 26-2A-108 powers and duties may be imposed and removed.

As with prior Alabama law, the partially incapacitated person retains all legal rights which the court has not seen fit to delegate to the limited guardian. Thus, if the court determines that most of a respondent's demonstrated problems probably could be alleviated by the institution of an appropriate authority to manage the ward's property and make appropriate expenditures for the ward's well-being, the court should utilize subsection (b) to recast the proceedings so that a conservator, rather than a guardian, would be appointed. If the respondent's problems call for both a guardian and a conservator, subsection (b) authorizes the court to direct that the proceedings be recast to seek both forms of relief. In this connection, the case of an incapacitated person differs from that of a minor who needs both a personal guardian and a conservator. This difference is recognized in that the second sentence of section 26-2A-152(a), which applies only to conservators of estates of unmarried minors, enables a minor's conservator, but not a conservator for an incapacitated person, to exercise the powers of a personal guardian.

Statute to be modified: Ala. Code (1975) section 26-2-45.

§ 26-2A-106. Acceptance of appointment; consent to jurisdiction.

By accepting appointment, a guardian submits personally to the jurisdiction of the court in any proceeding relating to the guardianship that may be instituted by any interested person. Notice of any proceeding must be delivered or mailed to the guardian at the address listed in the court records and at the address as then known to the petitioner. (Acts 1987, No. 87-590, p. 975, § 2-207.)

Comment

This section is comparable to sections 26-2A-77 and 26-2A-141.

The "long-arm" principle behind this section is well established. It seems desirable that the court in which acceptance is filed be able to serve its process on the guardian wherever he or she has moved. The continuing interest of that court in the welfare of the minor is ample to justify this provision. The consent to service is real rather than fictional in the guardianship situation, where the guardian acts voluntarily in filing acceptance. It is probable that the form of acceptance will expressly embody the provisions of this section, although the statute does not expressly require this.

The proceedings in this chapter are flexible. The court should not appoint a guardian unless one is necessary or desirable for the care of the person. If it develops that the needs of the person who is alleged to be incapacitated are not those which would call for a guardian, the court may adjust the proceeding accordingly. By acceptance of the appointment, the guardian submits to the court's jurisdiction in much the same way as a personal representative.

Alabama previously did not have a comparable statute.

§ 26-2A-107. Emergency orders; temporary guardians.

(a) If an incapacitated person has no guardian, an emergency exists, and no other person appears to have authority to act in the circumstances, on appropriate petition the court, without notice, may appoint a temporary guardian whose authority may not extend beyond 15 days and who may exercise those powers granted in the order.

(b) If the appointed guardian is not effectively performing duties and the court further finds that the welfare of the incapacitated person requires immediate action, it may appoint, with or without notice, a temporary guardian for the incapacitated person having the powers of a general guardian for a specified period not to exceed six months. The authority of any permanent guardian previously appointed by the court is suspended as long as a temporary guardian has authority.

(c) The court may remove a temporary guardian at any time. A temporary guardian shall make any report and comply with any conditions the court imposes or requires. In other respects the provisions of this chapter concerning guardians apply to temporary guardians. (Acts 1987, No. 87-590, p. 975, § 2-208.)

Comment

Subsection (a) requires an "emergency" situation for its application. Various suggestions were discussed of permissible periods for appointment of "temporary guardians" in "emergencies." Ultimately the chapter provides a period of 15 days. Of course, it is recognized in providing for a short period of appointment that a court can renew the appointment for an additional period or additional periods according to the exigencies of the emergency.

The language "and no other person appears to have authority to act in the circumstances" has been added to subsection (a) of this section. The added language should aid in preventing the mere institution of a guardianship proceeding from upsetting an arrangement for care under a durable power of attorney, or for nullifying an opportunity to use legislation like the Model Health Care Consent Act to resolve a problem involving the care of a person who is unable to care for himself or herself.

Under subsection (b), the appointing court retains authority to act on petition or on its own motion to suspend a guardian's authority by appointing a temporary guardian. The necessary finding, which need not follow notice to interested persons, is that the welfare of the incapacitated person requires action and the appointed guardian is not acting effectively.

Previously, Alabama law permitted use of a general guardian for the county or the sheriff to act as guardian where no other guardian has been appointed. Ala. Code (1975) sections 26-2-26, 26-2-27 and 26-2-50. However, guardians under these statutory authorities were not designed nor well suited to act in the emergencies contemplated by this section. Therefore, it can be stated that Alabama did not have a comparable statute.

§ 26-2A-108. General powers and duties of guardian.

Except as limited pursuant to Section 26-2A-105(c), a guardian of an incapacitated person is responsible for health, support, education, or maintenance of the ward, but is not liable to third persons by reason of that responsibility for acts of the ward. In particular and without qualifying the foregoing, a guardian has the same duties, powers and responsibilities as a guardian for a minor as described in Section 26-2A-78(b), (c) and (d). (Acts 1987, No. 87-590, p. 975, § 2-209.)

Comment

The reference to section 26-2A-105(c) coordinates this section with the limited guardianship concept. All guardians, however appointed, have the powers and duties of a guardian of a minor as provided in section 26-2A-78, subsections (b), (c), and (d). As discussed in the Comment to section 26-2A-78, these powers do not enable a guardian to deal with property matters of the ward, as do the powers granted by the prior Alabama law. Instead, a protective order under section 26-2A-130 et seq. is indicated when property management is needed. Though the legislation does not contemplate that the statutory authority of a guardian may be increased by court order, the court, at the time of appointment or on motion or petition thereafter, may limit the power of a guardian in any respect. The provisions of section 26-2A-103(b) requiring advance notice of a proceeding regarding a guardian's power instituted subsequent to appointment would apply to a post-appointment proceeding to impose or remove restrictions on a guardian's authority.

The standard of care adopted in this section is slightly different in description from the Uniform Act section 26-2A-108. However, the standard adopted here (i.e., "health, support, education or maintenance") reflects the change in and parallels section 26-2A-76 of this chapter. The language regarding a guardian's liability to third persons for acts of the ward is intended to prevent attribution of liability to a guardian on account of a ward's acts that might be thought to follow from the guardian's legal control of the ward. The provision is not intended to exonerate the guardian from the consequences of his or her own negligence.

There was not any comparable prior Alabama statute.

§ 26-2A-109. Termination of guardianship for incapacitated person.

The authority and responsibility of a guardian of an incapacitated person terminates upon the death of the guardian or ward, the determination of incapacity of the guardian, or upon removal or resignation as provided in Section 26-2A-110. Termination does not affect a guardian's liability for prior acts or the obligation to account for funds and assets of the ward. (Acts 1987, No. 87-590, p. 975, § 2-210.)

Comment

The comparable section of this chapter, section 26-2A-79, dealing with termination of the authority of a guardian whose authority derives solely from a ward's minority, differs from the instant section in that a guardian of a minor automatically loses authority when the minor attains the age of majority. Under the instant section, an adjudication is necessary to establish that a ward's incapacity has ended otherwise than upon the ward's death. Prior Ala. Code (1975) section 26-2-55, under which an acting guardian could ask the court for an order restoring the ward's estate to him and discharging the guardian, was in accord.

The concept that a guardian's authority may be terminated even though the guardian remains liable for prior acts or unaccounted funds is a corollary of the proposition that a guardian's authority to act for the ward should end automatically and without court order in certain circumstances. Alabama previously had the concept on resignation of a guardian. Ala. Code (1975) section 26-6-1. A more primitive concept to the effect that a guardian's authority derived from a court order continues until the court orders otherwise generates unnecessary and excessive use of the courts. Nonetheless, the question of whether a person's incapacity exists or continues and whether a guardian is necessary to provide continuing care and supervision of the ward is too complex to be resolved automatically save in the instances enumerated in this section. If a court determines that a ward's incapacity or need for a guardian has ended, it may terminate the authority and make an appropriate, additional order regarding the guardian's liabilities for acts done or funds for which there has not been any accounting. The additional order might defer the determination regarding liabilities to a later time.

Statute to be repealed: Ala. Code (1975) section 26-6-1.

Statutes to be modified: Ala. Code (1975) sections 26-2-55 and 26-5-33.

§ 26-2A-110. Removal or resignation of guardian; termination of incapacity.

(a) On petition of the ward or any person interested in the ward's welfare, or on its own motion, the court, after hearing, may remove a guardian if to do so is in the best interest of the ward. On petition of the guardian, the court, after hearing, may accept a resignation.

(b) An order adjudicating incapacity may specify a minimum period, not exceeding one year, during which a petition for an adjudication that the ward is no longer incapacitated may not be filed without special leave. Subject to that restriction, the ward or any person interested in the welfare of the ward may petition for an order that the ward is no longer incapacitated and for termination of the guardianship. A request for an order may also be made informally to the court and any person who knowingly interferes with transmission of the request may be adjudged guilty of contempt of court.

(c) Upon removal, resignation, or death of the guardian, or if the guardian is determined to be incapacitated, the court may appoint a successor guardian and make any other appropriate order. Before appointing a successor guardian, or ordering that a ward's incapacity has terminated, the court shall follow the same procedures to safeguard the rights of the ward that apply to a petition for appointment of a guardian. (Acts 1987, No. 87-590, p. 975, § 2-211.)

Comment

The ward's incapacity is a question that usually may be reviewed at any time. However, this chapter provides for a discretionary restriction on review. In all review proceedings, the welfare of the ward is paramount. While such restriction was not found previously in the Alabama law, this chapter lends more priority to the welfare of the ward in that it removes the requirement that a petitioning ward must be examined by and produce certificates from two professionals in order to prove his capacity. Prior law favored the judgment of the guardian in determining competency or capacity. Compare Ala. Code (1975) section 26-2-51 with section 26-2-55 and section 26-6-3.

The provisions of subsection (b) were designed to provide another protection against use of guardianship proceedings to secure a lock-up of a person who is not capable of looking out for his or her personal needs. If the safeguards imposed at the time of appointment fail to prevent an unnecessary guardianship, subsection (b) is intended to facilitate a ward's unaided or unassisted efforts to inform the court that an injustice has occurred as a result of the guardianship.

Statutes to be repealed: Ala. Code (1975) sections 26-6-1, 26-6-2, 26-6-3, and 26-6-6.

Statutes to be modified: Ala. Code (1975) sections 26-2-51 and 26-2-55.

§ 26-2A-111. Proceedings subsequent to appointment; venue.

(a) The court at the place where the ward resides has concurrent jurisdiction with the court that appointed the guardian or in which acceptance of a parental or spousal appointment was filed over resignation, removal, accounting, and other proceedings relating to the guardianship, including proceedings to limit the authority previously conferred on a guardian or to remove limitations previously imposed.

(b) If the court at the place where the ward resides is not the court in which acceptance of appointment is filed, the court in which proceedings subsequent to appointment are commenced, in all appropriate cases, shall notify the other court, in this or another state, and after consultation with that court determine whether to retain jurisdiction or transfer the proceedings to the other court, whichever may be in the best interest of the ward. A copy of any order accepting a resignation, removing a guardian, or altering authority must be sent to the court in which acceptance of appointment is filed. (Acts 1987, No. 87-590, p. 975, § 2-212.)

Comment

The language in subsection (a) specifies that proceedings to alter the authority of the guardian, which may occur at any time subsequent to the original appointment of the guardian as provided in section 26-2A-105(c), are included in the described concurrent jurisdiction. Previously Alabama law granted jurisdiction only to the appointing court. Ala. Code (1975) section 26-5-1.

The section also includes recognition of appointments of guardians by nontestmentary written instruments executed by a parent or spouse.

Statute to be modified: Ala. Code (1975) section 26-5-1.

Cited in Martin v. Clark, 554 So. 2d 1030 (Ala. 1989).

Division 3.

Protection of Property of Persons Under Disability and Minors.

§ 26-2A-130. Protective proceedings.

(a) Upon petition and after notice and hearing in accordance with the provisions of this division, the court may appoint a conservator or make any other protective order for cause as provided in this section.

(b) Appointment of a conservator or other protective order may be made in relation to the estate and affairs of a minor if the court determines that a minor owns funds or property requiring management or protection that cannot otherwise be provided or has or may have business affairs that may be jeopardized or prevented by minority, or that funds are needed for health, support, education, or maintenance and that protection is necessary or desirable to obtain or provide funds.

(c) Appointment of a conservator or other protective order may be made in relation to the estate and affairs of a person if the court determines that (i) the person is unable to manage property and business affairs effectively for such reasons as mental illness, mental deficiency, physical illness or disability, physical or mental infirmities accompanying advanced age, chronic use of drugs, chronic intoxication, confinement, detention by a foreign power, or disappearance; and that (ii) (aa) the person has property that will be wasted or dissipated unless property management is provided, or that (bb) funds are needed for the health, support, education, or maintenance of the person or of those entitled to the person's support and that protection is necessary or desirable to obtain or provide the funds. (Acts 1987, No. 87-590, p. 975, § 2-301.)

Comment

This is the basic section of this division providing for protective proceedings for minors and disabled persons. "Protective proceeding" is a generic term used to describe proceedings to establish conservatorships and obtain protective orders. Persons who may be subjected to the proceedings described here include a broad category of persons who, for a variety of different reasons, may be unable to manage their own property.

Since the problems of property management are generally the same for minors and disabled persons, it was considered undesirable to treat these problems in two separate parts. Where there are differences, these have been separately treated in specific sections.

The Comment to section 26-2A-105, supra, points up the different meanings of "incapacity" (warranting guardianship) and "disability."

Under subsection (c)(i) the court has the power to determine whether a person detained by a foreign power, or who has disappeared, is a "missing or disappeared person" as referred to in section 26-2A-2(b)(1) and whether a conservator is needed to manage the property and business affairs of the person. Note also that subsection (c)(ii) allows for protective proceedings not only for the purpose of conserving the disabled person's property, but also to assure that the property is managed in such a way that she or he may obtain needed income.

Alabama law previously was somewhat confused as to the responsibilities of a guardian and of a curator. An adult individual unable to take care of his or her property could have been a curator, almost identical to the conservator described in this chapter, without an adjudication of incompetency. Ala. Code (1975, as amended by Act No. 79-101) section 26-7A-1. However, Ala. Code (1975) section 26-2-40, also provided for guardians for persons of unsound mind, yet the court's authority to appoint such guardians was premised on the ward's "having an estate." Part of the problem arises because prior Alabama law through the use of the single term "guardian" rarely made a clear distinction between a guardian of the person and a guardian of property. Most of the time it was relatively clear that legislation is more concerned about property.

Property management for minors was also handled differently under prior law. In Alabama, the guardian of a minor accepted the responsibility of caring for the minor's property; in fact, many statutes implied that the property, not the person, was to be the guardian's primary concern. Under this chapter, a conservator need not be appointed for the minor unless the standard set forth in section 26-2A-130(b) is met, and the minor's guardian need not take responsibility for significant financial management needs of the ward unless the person also is concurrently serving as conservator.

Statutes to be repealed: Ala. Code (1975) sections 26-2-20, 26-2-40, and 26-4-1.

§ 26-2A-131. Protective proceedings; jurisdiction of business affairs of protected persons.

After the service of notice in a proceeding seeking the appointment of a conservator or other protective order and until termination of the proceeding, the court in which the petition is filed has:

(1) Exclusive jurisdiction to determine the need for a conservator or other protective order until the proceedings are terminated; and

(2) Exclusive jurisdiction to determine how the estate of the protected person which is subject to the laws of this state must be managed, expended, or distributed to or for the use of the protected person, the protected person's dependents, or other claimants. (Acts 1987, No. 87-590, p. 975, § 2-302.)

Comment

While the bulk of all judicial proceedings involving the conservator will be in the court supervising the conservatorship, third parties may bring suit against the conservator or the protected person on some matters in other courts. Claims against the conservator after appointment are dealt with by section 26-2A-156.

Prior Alabama law essentially was in accord in granting jurisdiction over conservatorship proceedings to the court from which the appointment derives. Ala. Code (1975) section 26-5-1. Jurisdiction over curators in Alabama was coextensive with the provisions of this chapter. Ala. Code (1975), as amended by Act No. 79-701) section 26-7A-1. This chapter, however, more clearly defines the extent of jurisdiction.

Statutes to be modified: Ala. Code (1975) sections 26-5-1, 26-5-30 and 26-5-31.

§ 26-2A-132. Venue.

Venue for proceedings under this division is:

(1) In the court at the place in this state where the person to be protected resides whether or not a guardian has been appointed in another place; or

(2) If the person to be protected does not reside in this state, in the court at any place where property of the person is located. (Acts 1987, No. 87-590, p. 975, § 2-203.)

Comment

Venue for protective proceedings lies in the county of residence (rather than domicile) or, in the case of a nonresident, where property of the protected person is located. "Resides" or "residence" as used in this section is not used in a strict sense, but it includes a temporary, permanent, or transient place of abode. The purpose in this broad use of the term is to make courts easily and readily accessible for the protection of persons covered in this chapter. It is expected also that a court, having taken jurisdiction over the person, can and will transfer the proceedings, under forum non conveniens considerations, to a court in a more convenient forum if there is one. Power to remove the proceedings to a more convenient forum is provided for in section 26-2A-32, above. Unitary management of the property is obtainable through easy transfer of proceedings (section 26-2A-32[b]) and easy collection of assets by foreign conservators (section 26-2A-159).

Prior Alabama law did not make specific provision for venue for all conservatorship proceedings. Code of Ala. (1975, as amended by Act No. 79-701) section 26-7A-2 provided that the jurisdiction of a court to appoint a curator lay with the court at the place of the curator's residence. However, other Alabama statutes implied that venue remained with the appointing court. See, Ala. Code (1975) sections 26-2-20, 26-2-40, and 26-2-47. The chapter clarifies the importance of the place where the protected person resides (or has property, if a nonresident) as the place of proper venue.

Statutes to be repealed: Ala. Code (1975) sections 26-2-20 and 26-2-40.

Statute to be modified: Ala. Code (1975) section 26-2-47.

§ 26-2A-133. Original petition for appointment or protective order.

(a) The person to be protected or any person who is interested in the estate, affairs, or welfare of the person, including a parent, child, guardian, custodian, or any person who would be adversely affected by lack of effective management of the person's property and business affairs may petition for the appointment of a conservator or for other appropriate protective order.

(b) The petition must set forth to the the extent known the interest of the petitioner; the name, age, residence, and address of the person to be protected; the names and addresses of all persons, known to the petitioner, who must be given notice, a general statement of the person's property with an estimate of the value thereof, including any compensation, insurance, pension, or allowance to which the person is entitled; the reason why appointment of a conservator or other protective order is necessary, and whether bond has been relieved. If the appointment of a conservator is requested, the petition must also set forth the name and address of the person whose appointment is sought and the basis of the claim to priority for appointment. (Acts 1987, No. 87-590, p. 975, § 2-304.)

Comment

Previously in Alabama, a successful petition for the determination that a person is of unsound mind (and thus in need of a guardian for his or her estate) and a petition for the appointment of a curator differed somewhat. "Any of the friends or relatives" of a person alleged to be of unsound mind could petition to have the person so declared. Ala. Code (1975) section 26-2-42. However, the appointment of a curator required the person, his or her next of kin, or one of a list of relatives, or the sheriff to file the petition. Ala. Code (1975, as amended by Act. No. 79-701) section 26-7A-2. Both provisions may have been narrower than this chapter's recognition of a petition by any person related to the protected person or who is interested in the estate to be protected. Also, neither Alabama provision required that the petitioner give an estimate of the property value held by the person to be protected. Although it seems apparent that a "child" of the person to be protected would be an individual encompassed in the terms "or any person who is interested in the estate. ..." of the person, this section adds "child" to the enumerated list of such persons as contained in the Uniform Act.

Subsection (b) has been changed, as compared to the Uniform Act, in respect to what the petition must state regarding bond. The change is made to be consistent with the policy of requiring a bond adopted in this chapter in section 26-2A-139.

Another difference between this chapter and previous law, which is inherent in the conceptual distinction between a guardian under prior Alabama law and a conservator, is that the appointment of a guardian of one of unsound mind required two distinct judicial acts: a determination of incompetency, and the appointment of a guardian following a separate application. Under this chapter, only one petition, requesting an appropriate protective order or appointment, is necessary.

Statutes to be repealed: Ala. Code (1975) sections 26-2-23 and 26-2-42.

Statute to be modified: Ala. Code (1975) section 26-2-48.

§ 26-2A-134. Notice.

(a) On a petition for appointment of a conservator or other protective order, the requirements for notice described in Section 26-2A-103 apply, but (i) if the person to be protected has disappeared or is otherwise situated so as to make personal service of notice impracticable, notice to the person must be given by publication as provided in Section 26-2A-50, and (ii) if the person to be protected is a minor, the provisions of Section 26-2A-75 also apply.

(b) Notice, as described in Section 26-2A-103, of any hearing on a petition for an order subsequent to appointment of a conservator or other protective order must be given to the protected person, any conservator of the protected person's estate, and any other person as ordered by the court. (Acts 1987, No. 87-590, p. 975, § 2-305.)

Comment

The primary sections providing for notice in this chapter are sections 26-2A-50 and 26-2A-103. These provisions merely make reference back to the primary notice provisions rather than repeating the requirements here. The substituted service by publication referred to in subsection (a)(i) is a substitute only for the personal service required in section 26-2A-103 (a)(1) when those individuals have disappeared and are missing. This alternative method of giving notice is not intended to relieve the notice requirements as otherwise stated in sections 26-2A-50 and 26-2A-103.

The provision relative to responding to requests for notice is in section 26-2A-53. This section intends to include responses to requests for notice through the provision for giving notice to other persons as ordered by the court in subsection (b).

Previously Alabama law provided no alternative form of notice for cases in which personal service to the potential protected person is impracticable. Neither did it require service of process on the primary interested parties in proceedings following the appointment of a conservator. For example, in proceedings regarding settlements of accounts, Alabama law previously required only notice by publication. See Ala. Code (1975) sections 26-5-3, 26-4-145 and 26-5-15. Personal service, as in this chapter, was required where a curator was involved. Ala. Code (1975, as amended by Act No. 79-701) section 26-7A-3.

Statute to be repealed: Ala. Code (1975) section 26-4-145.

Statute to be modified: Ala. Code (1975) section 26-5-15.

§ 26-2A-135. Procedure concerning hearing and order on original petition.

(a) Upon receipt of a petition for appointment of a conservator or other protective order because of minority, the court shall set a date for hearing. If the court determines at any time in the proceeding that the interests of the minor are or may be inadequately represented, it may appoint an attorney to represent the minor, giving consideration to the choice of the minor if 14 or more years of age. An attorney appointed by the court to represent a minor may be granted the powers and duties of a guardian ad litem.

(b) Upon receipt of a petition for appointment of a conservator or other protective order for reasons other than minority, the court shall set a date for hearing. Unless the person to be protected has chosen counsel, the court shall appoint an attorney to represent the person who may be granted the powers and duties of a guardian ad litem. If the alleged disability is mental illness, mental deficiency, physical illness or disability, physical or mental infirmities accompanying advanced age, chronic use of drugs, or chronic intoxication, the court must direct that the person to be protected be examined by a physician or other qualified person designated by the court, preferably one who is not connected with any institution in which the person is a patient or is detained. The court may send a court representative to interview the person to be protected. The court representative may be a guardian ad litem or an officer or employee of the court.

(c) The court may utilize, as an additional court representative, the service of any public or charitable agency to evaluate the condition of the person to be protected and make appropriate recommendations to the court.

(d) The person to be protected is entitled to be present at the hearing in person. When the person to be protected is not present in person at the hearing, the court, before proceeding at the hearing in the person's absence, must determine that the person's absence is in the best interest of the person to be protected. At the request of the person to be protected, the person is entitled to be represented by counsel, at the person's expense, to present evidence, to cross-examine witnesses, including any court-appointed physician or other qualified person and any court representative, and upon demand to trial by jury as provided in Section 26-2A-35. The issue may be determined at a closed hearing if the person to be protected or counsel for the person so requests.

(e) Any person may apply for permission to participate in the proceeding and the court may grant the request, with or without hearing, upon determining that the best interest of the person to be protected will be served thereby. The court may attach appropriate conditions to the permission.

(f) After hearing, upon finding that a basis for the appointment of a conservator or other protective order has been established, the court shall make an appointment or other appropriate protective order. (Acts 1987, No. 87-590, p. 975, § 2-306.)

Comment

The section establishes a framework within which professionals, including the judge, attorney, and physician, if any, may be expected to exercise good judgment in regard to the minor or disabled person who is the subject of the proceeding. The premise is accepted that it is desirable to rely on professionals rather than to attempt to draft detailed standards of conditions for appointment. Under prior Alabama law relating to the appointment of a curator, professional input on the question of disability was mandated only after the conclusion of proceedings and the issuance of the court's findings. (See Ala. Code [1975, as amended by Act No. 79-701] sections 26-7A-4 and 26-7A-6). The concept of getting a comprehensive evaluation of the need for protective orders, like the use of the court representative in subsections (b) and (c), is adopted also in Alabama's Adult Protective Services Act. See, Ala. Code, section 38-9-6(c) (1975, as amended by Acts 1977, No. 780). Subsection (c) of this section permits, but does not require, the court to utilize agencies, who may have a particular expertise, to aid in evaluating the person's condition when a protective order is sought.

In subsection (b), this section requires ("must") the court to direct that the person to be protected be examined. This provision differs from the Uniform Act section 26-2A-135, which makes the direction discretionary with the court. In exercising this direction, this subsection also permits the examination to be by "other qualified person", which is an addition that is not in the Uniform Act section 26-2A-135. The Alabama committee made this addition based on the belief that the procedures under sections 26-2A-102 and 26-2A-135 should be parallel in this regard. As in section 26-2A-102, "other qualified person " will include perhaps psychologists and clinical psychologists if the court so determines.

Since there has not been any prior determination of incapacity, the person, for whom a protective order is sought, should be extended the same rights as any other person whose personal freedom may be restricted as a result of the proceedings. Subsection (d) expressly recognizes those rights. The Uniform Act (§ 2-306[d]) takes cognizance that requiring the presence in court of a very young child does not provide any greater protection for the child, but in the absence of the minor, the court is required to determine whether the absence of the child is in minor's best interest. The second sentence of subsection (d) of this section adopts the same rationale and extends its applicability also to all "persons to be protected," but retains the same safeguards at the hearing. The hearing will be an open hearing, unless the protected person or counsel for the person requests a closed hearing.

Subsection (e) permits a person, who might not otherwise be an "interested person," to request permission to participate in the proceeding. The court may or may not grant the permission and may attach conditions to the permission when granted. The court is given broad latitude in using public-interest agencies and in permitting persons, who do not otherwise qualify as "interested persons," in aiding the court to evaluate the case and in determining measures that will be in the best interest of the person for whom a protective order is sought. Prior Alabama law did not so contemplate the court's use of disinterested outside sources. There are not any rights for these groups to participate in the proceedings — their involvement initially and the extent of their involvement are within the discretionary control of the court.

Statutes to be repealed: Ala. Code (1975) sections 26-2-21, 26-2-41 and 26-2-42.

Statutes to be modified: Ala. Code (1975) sections 26-2-43 and 26-2-45 through 26-7A-6.

§ 26-2A-136. Permissible court orders.

(a) The court shall exercise the authority conferred in this division to encourage the development of maximum self-reliance and independence of a protected person and make protective orders only to the extent necessitated by the protected person's mental and adaptive limitations and other conditions warranting the procedure.

(b) The court has the following powers that may be exercised directly or through a conservator in respect to the estate and business affairs of a protected person:

(1) While a petition for appointment of a conservator or other protective order is pending and after preliminary hearing and without notice, the court may preserve and apply the property of the person to be protected as may be required for the support of the person or dependents of the person.

(2) After hearing and upon determining that a basis for an appointment or other protective order exists with respect to a minor without other disability, the court has all those powers over the estate and business affairs of the minor which are or may be necessary for the best interest of the minor and members of minor's immediate family.

(3) After hearing and upon determining that a basis for an appointment or other protective order exists with respect to a person for reasons other than minority, the court, for the benefit of the person and members of the person's immediate family, has all the powers over the estate and business affairs which the person could exercise if present and not under disability, except the power to make a will. Subject to subsection (c), those powers include, but are not limited to, power to make gifts; to convey or release contingent and expectant interests in property, including marital property rights and any right of survivorship incident to joint tenancy or tenancy by

the entirety; to exercise or release powers held by the protected person as trustee, personal representative, custodian for minors, conservator, or donee of a power of appointment; to enter into contracts; to create revocable or irrevocable trusts of property of the estate which may extend beyond the disability or life of the protected person; to exercise options of the protected person to purchase securities or other property; to exercise rights to elect options and change beneficiaries under insurance and annuity policies and to surrender the policies for their cash value; to exercise any right to an elective share in the state of the person's deceased spouse and to renounce or disclaim any interest by testate or intestate succession or by inter vivos transfer.

(c) The court may exercise or direct the exercise of the following powers only if satisfied, after notice and hearing, that it is in the best interest of the protected person, and that the person either is incapable of consenting or has consented to the proposed exercise of power:

(1) To exercise or release powers of appointments of which the protected person is done;

(2) To renounce or disclaim interests;

(3) To make gifts in trust or otherwise exceeding in the aggregate 20 percent of the year's income of the estate; and

(4) To change beneficiaries under insurance and annuity policies.

(d) Except for the disability necessitating the appointment, a determination that a basis for appointment of a conservator or other protective order exists has no effect otherwise on the capacity of the protected person. A conservator has all the powers granted by this section, unless specifically limited by the court. A protected person does not have or possess powers granted to the conservator. (Acts 1987, No. 87-590, p. 975, § 2-307.)

Comment

The court which is supervising a conservatorship is given all the powers that the individual would have if the person were of full capacity. These powers are given to the court managing the protected person's property, because their exercise has important consequences with respect to that property.

Subsection (a) is a general admonition against an overly intrusive exercise of its authority by the court adopting the concept of a limited guardianship. The court should not assume any greater authority over the protected person than the capacity and ability of that person necessitates.

Subsection (d) expressly states a necessary conclusion and for clarity it states the conclusion from two opposite approaches. Following the concept that under this chapter a court should exercise its power in a manner to place the least possible restriction on the personal liberty and exercise of constitutional rights consistent with due process and the desired protection, the subsection provides that the protected person retains all rights and powers, except to the extent those rights and powers are restricted by the court. After admonishing the court that it should not restrict the protected person to any greater extent than is necessitated by the circumstances, the subsection provides that the conservator has all of the powers granted to conservators by this section, unless specifically limited by the court. For further clarity, it provides that the protected person does not have any powers granted by the court to the conservator.

This chapter clarifies the status of the law on limited guardianship as it relates to protection of property. Under prior Alabama statutes, the definition given in Ala. Code (1975, as amended by Act No. 82-384) section 26-2-45, a limited guardianship, while contextually aimed at protection of the person, could conceivably have been used as the equivalent of a limited conservatorship. This conclusion could have inferred from Ala. Code (1975) section 26-4-140, which gave the court authority to direct investment or sale of the ward's property. However, the conclusion was not entirely clear from the statute, particularly when read with Ala. Code (1975, as amended by Act No. 82-384) section 26-7A-7. The latter section specified that a person requiring a curator for his or her property would lose his or her ability to contract. The provision seemed to negate the possibility of any limited guardianship over the property, but it was also unclear from the statutes. Alabama previously accepted the skeleton principle of "limited guardianship". This chapter provides definition for that principle.

Statutes to be repealed: Ala. Code (1975) sections 26-4-140, 26-4-144, 26-4-150, 26-7-1, 26-7-2 and 26-7-4.

Statute to be modified: Ala. Code (1975) section 26-2-45.

§ 26-2A-137. Protective arrangements and single transactions authorized.

(a) If it is established in a proper proceeding that a basis exists for the appointment of a conservator or protective order as described in Section 26-2A-130, the court, without appointing a conservator, may authorize, direct, or ratify any transaction necessary or desirable to achieve any security, service, or care arrangement meeting the foreseeable needs of the protected person. Protective arrangements include payment, delivery, deposit, or retention of funds or property; sale, mortgage, lease, or other transfer of property; entry into an annuity contract, a contract for life care, a deposit contract, or a contract for training and education; or addition to or establishment of a suitable trust.

(b) If it is established in a proper proceeding that a basis exists for the appointment of a conservator or protective order as described in Section 26-2A-130, the court, without appointing a conservator, may authorize, direct, or ratify any contract, trust, or other transaction relating to the protected person's property and business affairs if the court determines that the transaction is in the best interest of the protected person.

(c) Before approving a protective arrangement or other transaction under this section, the court shall consider the interests of creditors and dependents of the protected person and, in view of the disability, whether the protected person needs the continuing protection of a conservator. The court may appoint a special conservator to assist in the accomplishment of any protective arrangement or other transaction authorized under this section who shall have the authority conferred by the order and serve until discharged by order after report to the court of all matters done pursuant to the order of appointment. (Acts 1987, No. 87-590, p. 975, § 2-308.)

Comment

It is important that the provision be made for the approval of single transactions or the establishment of protective arrangements as alternatives to full conservatorship. Under prior law, a guardianship often had to be established simply to make possible a valid transfer of land or securities. This section, consistent with the concept of a limited conservatorship, eliminates the necessity of the establishment of long-term arrangements in this situation.

A court appointing a curator under prior Alabama law had power to regulate the ward's business affairs and to appoint a special curator, which authority closely approximates that given by section 26-2A-137. However, there are two important differences between prior Ala. Code (1975, as amended by Act No. 79-701) section 26-7A-10 and this section. First, the court's ability to exercise power over the estate previously was contingent upon the appointment of a curator; under the Act, the court need only determine that a basis exists under section 26-2A-130 for affecting a person's property or business affairs. Second, the standards for court action differ. This chapter requires that court-made protective arrangements follow a determination that the transaction is in the best interest of the protected person. Prior Alabama law was narrower in scope and applied only to the curator's power to sell, mortgage or lease property, but it only required a finding that a mortgage, sale or lease, whether for the protection of the estate or of the person, was "reasonably necessary or expedient." Ala. Code (1975, as amended by Act No. 79-701) section 26-7A-9.

Statutes to be repealed: Ala. Code (1975) sections 26-7-1 through 26-7-5.

§ 26-2A-138. Who may be appointed conservator; priorities.

(a) The court may appoint an individual or a corporation with general power to serve as trustee or conservator of the estate of a protected person. The following are entitled to consideration for appointment in the order listed:

(1) A conservator, guardian of property, or other like fiduciary appointed or recognized by an appropriate court of any other jurisdiction in which the protected person resides;

(2) An individual or corporation nominated by the protected person who is 14 or more years of age and of sufficient mental capacity to make an intelligent choice;

(3) An attorney-in-fact under a valid durable power of attorney previously executed by the protected person and giving the attorney-in-fact reasonably broad powers over the property of the protected person;

(4) The spouse of the protected person, or a person nominated by the will of a deceased spouse to whom the protected person was married at the decedent's death and the protected person has not remarried;

(5) An adult child of the protected person;

(6) A parent of the protected person, or a person nominated by the will of a deceased parent;

(7) Any relative of the protected person who has resided with the protected person for more than six months before the filing of the petition;

(8) A person nominated by one who is caring for or paying benefits to the protected person; and

(9) A general guardian or sheriff for the county who must be appointed and act as conservator when no other fit person applies for appointment and qualifies.

(b) A person in priorities (1), (4), (5), (6), or (7) may designate in writing a substitute to serve instead and thereby transfer the priority to the substitute. With respect to persons having equal priority, the court shall select the one it deems best suited to serve. The court, acting in the best interest of the protected person, may pass over a person having priority and appoint a person having a lower priority or no priority. (Acts 1987, No. 87-590, p. 975, § 2-309; Acts 1988, 1st Ex. Sess., No. 88-898, p. 455, § 1.)

Comment

A flexible system of priorities for appointment as conservator has been provided. Unlike sections 26-2A-71 and 26-2A-100, which give a parent or spouse a right to appoint a guardian, which becomes effective on the filing of an acceptance by the guardian, this section provides that conservators will be appointed only by the court. However, a parent or guardian may make a nomination of a conservator to the court and the nomination by the parent or spouse is substituted in priority for the parent or spouse who made the nomination. The "nomination" can be by a will under subsection (b) or by a "writing" addressed to the court, under subsection (b), if the parent or spouse is living. The addition in the line of priorities of a "general conservator" for the county is an addition to the Uniform Act, but it retains the office of "general conservator of the county." Ala. Code section 26-2-26 (1975).

Prior Alabama law did not contain a provision for priorities to be given prospective curators. The statute relative to selection of a guardian for a person of unsound mind mandated a preference for the person of nearest relation whom the judge believes would best manage the ward's estate, rather than establishing a hierarchy of preferences. Ala. Code (1975) sections 26-2-25 and 26-2-49. Previously under Ala. Code (1975) section 26-2-23 a parent could "appoint" a guardian by a will. In addition, a minor "over 14 years of age" could nominate a person as a guardian in Alabama previously, but that person did not have a priority to appointment. Ala. Code (1975) section 26-2-21.

Statutes to be repealed: Ala. Code (1975) sections 26-2-21, 26-2-23, 26-2-25, and 26-2-49.

§ 26-2A-139. Bond.

(a) The court must require a conservator to furnish a bond payable to the judge of probate conditioned upon faithful discharge of all duties of the trust according to law, with sureties as it shall specify. Unless otherwise directed, the bond must be in the amount of the aggregate capital value of the property of the estate in the conservator's control, plus one year's estimated income, and minus the value of securities deposited under arrangements requiring an order of the court for their removal and the value of any land which the fiduciary, pursuant to Section 26-2A-152(d), lacks power to sell or convey without court authorization. The court, in lieu of sureties on a bond, may accept other collateral for the performance of the bond, including a pledge of securities or any other assets or a mortgage of land.

(b) The court may at any time reduce the bond of the conservator or require the conservator to provide additional or larger bond as may seem to be proper or necessary to protect the interests of the protected person.

(c) Any individual, who is authorized under this chapter to nominate a conservator by will or other writing, may, by express provision in the will or other writing nominating the conservator, exempt the conservator from giving bond; and when a provision to that effect is made, the bond must not be required except in the following cases:

(1) When any guardian, conservator, guardian ad litem, other fiduciary, or any person interested in the ward or the estate of the protected person makes affidavit, showing the affiant's interest and alleging that the interest is, or will be, endangered for want of security; or

(2) When, in the opinion of the court, the estate is likely to be wasted, to the prejudice of any person interested therein.

(d) In the cases provided for by subsection (c), upon application for the conservator to give bond, the conservator may show cause against applications of the exceptions and must have notice as the judge may deem reasonable; but if the conservator is not in the state, the application may be heard and determined without notice. (Acts 1987, No. 87-590, p. 975, § 2-310.)

Comment

The bond requirements for conservators are somewhat more strict than the requirements for personal representatives generally. This section follows prior Alabama law in that the judge "must" require a bond. Ala. Code (1975) section 26-3-1. The term was "shall" for curators. Ala. Code (1975, as amended by Act No. 79-701) section 26-7A-8. The formula for the amount differs in that guardians, under prior law, had to furnish bond in the sum prescribed by the judge, which could not be less than double the estimated value of both the personal property and rental value of real estate of the ward, for three years. Ala. Code (1975) section 26-3-1. This section prescribes a formula for determining the amount of the bond, which will provide a sum less than prior Alabama law, but perhaps different from the bond of a curator, which had to be "good and sufficient." Ala. Code (1975, as amended by Act No. 79-701) section 26-7A-8. If the protected person is receiving benefits from the United States through the veterans' administration, the court also must consider Ala. Code section 26-9-9 (1975) in setting the bond, but that section and this section are consistent.

Since subsection (a) of this section adopts the policy of requiring a bond for the conservator (as contrasted with the Uniform Act and other modern probate revisions which make the presumption that a bond will not be required, unless some person interested in the estate so requests), it seemed advisable to also adopt a provision whereby an individual, who has the authority to nominate a conservator, can also avoid an unnecessary cost to the estate by relieving the conservator from the requirement of providing bond. Subsections (c) and (d) permit the relief from providing bond and still provide safeguards under circumstances when it seems apparent that the relief was given unwisely. Subsections (c) and (d) follow Ala. Code section 43-2-81 (1975), which permits exemption from the requirement to provide bond for personal representatives.

Statute to be repealed: Ala. Code (1975) section 26-3-2.

Statutes to be modified: Ala. Code (1975) sections 26-3-1, 26-3-3, 26-3-4 and 26-3-5.

§ 26-2A-140. Terms and requirements of bonds.

(a) The following requirements and provisions apply to any bond required under Section 26-2A-139.

(1) Sureties are jointly and severally liable with the conservator and with each other.

(2) By executing an approved bond of a conservator, the surety consents to the jurisdiction of the court that issued letters to the primary obligor in any proceeding pertaining to the fiduciary duties of the conservator and naming the surety as a party respondent. Notice of any proceeding must be delivered to the surety or mailed by registered or certified mail to the address listed with the court at the place where the bond is filed and to the address as then known to the petitioner.

(3) On petition of a successor conservator or any interested person, a proceeding may be initiated against a surety for breach of the obligation of the bond of the conservator.

(4) The bond of the conservator is not void after the first recovery but may be proceeded against from time to time until the whole penalty is exhausted.

(b) No proceeding may be commenced against the surety on any matter as to which an action or proceeding against the primary obligor is barred by adjudication or limitation. (Acts 1987, No. 87-590, p. 975, § 2-311.)

Comment

This section codifies five provisions for conservatorship bonds. These provisions did not appear previously in Alabama statutes, which dealt primarily with the continuity of guardianship bonds, rather than liability thereon. However, these "requirements and provisions" of this section are common provisions in bonds and may be in Alabama bonds even though they previously have not been expressly required.

Statutes to be repealed: Ala. Code (1975) sections 26-3-2 and 23-3-6.

Statutes to be modified: Ala. Code (1975) sections 26-3-3, 26-3-4, 26-3-5, 26-3-7, 26-3-8, 26-3-10, 26-3-11 through 26-3-14 and 26-5-52.

§ 26-2A-141. Effect of acceptance of appointment.

By accepting appointment, a conservator submits personally to the jurisdiction of the court in any proceeding relating to the estate which may be instituted by any interested person. Notice of any proceeding must be delivered to the conservator or mailed by registered or certified mail to the address as listed in the petition for appointment or as thereafter reported to the court and to the address as then known to the petitioner. (Acts 1987, No. 87-590, p. 975, § 2-312.)

Comment

This section states directly a fact which was only implied under the prior Alabama law. A conservator personally submits to the court's jurisdiction in relation to the conservatorship. Prior Alabama guardianship and curatorship statutes referred frequently to the court's power over the guardian, etc., and although the statutes were worded differently from this section, the reference was to the appointing court. See, Ala. Code (1975) sections 26-4-1 and 26-5-1.

Statute to be repealed: Ala. Code (1975) section 26-4-1.

Statute to be modified: Ala. Code (1975) section 26-5-1.

§ 26-2A-142. Compensation; eligibility; reimbursement.

(a) If not otherwise reasonably compensated for services rendered, any court representative, attorney, physician, conservator, or special conservator appointed in a protective proceeding and any attorney whose services resulted in a protective order or in an order that was beneficial to a protected person's estate is entitled to reasonable compensation from the estate. The conservator shall be allowed from the estate of the protective person all reasonable premiums paid on his bond and reimbursement of any court costs paid.

(b) If not otherwise reasonably compensated for services rendered, any court representative, attorney, physician appointed in a guardianship and any attorney whose services resulted in a guardianship order or in an order that was beneficial to a ward is entitled to reasonable compensation from the estate. The guardian may be reimbursed from the estate of the ward for any court costs paid. (Acts 1987, No. 87-590, p. 975, § 2-313; Acts 1988, 1st Ex. Sess., No. 88-898, p. 455, § 1.)

Comment

This chapter abandons percentage formulae of former Ala. Code (1975) section 26-5-16 and other rules regarding compensation, set forth previously in several sections of the Code, in favor of an objective but discretionary "reasonable" fee from the estate. Ala. Code (1975) section 26-5-17 previously referred to "reasonable commissions" not to exceed the formula.

This chapter does not repeal the provisions of the Alabama Uniform Veteran's Guardianship Act under which there remains a formula of compensation "not to exceed five percent of the income of the ward during any year." Ala. Code section 26-9-17 (1975). If the estate of the protected person includes benefits received from the United States through the veterans' administration, this formula will be applicable to those funds.

Statutes to be modified: Ala. Code (1975) sections 26-5-13, 26-5-14, 26-5-16, and 26-5-18.

§ 26-2A-143. Death, resignation, or removal of conservator.

The court, on petition or on its own motion, may remove a conservator for good cause, upon notice and hearing, or accept the resignation of a conservator. Upon the conservator's death, resignation, or removal, the court may appoint another conservator. A conservator so appointed succeeds to the title and powers of the predecessor. (Acts 1987, No. 87-590, p. 975, § 2-314.)

This section consolidates six Alabama statutes dealing with resignation and removal of guardians and curators. In lieu of the statutory grounds for removal of a guardian enumerated previously in Ala. Code (1975) section 26-6-2, this chapter utilizes a "good cause" standard, giving the court more flexibility in dealing with dismissals and replacements. An Alabama court under the prior statute could act on its own motion to remove a guardian [Ala. Code (1975) section 26-6-6] which power this chapter continues.

Notice, as required by this section, is given in accordance with section 26-2A-134(b).

Statutes to be repealed: Ala. Code (1975) sections 26-6-1, 26-6-2, 26-6-3 and 26-6-6.

§ 26-2A-144. Petitions for orders subsequent to appointment.

(a) Any person interested in the welfare of a person for whom a conservator has been appointed, any person interested in the proper administration of the estate, or the court on its own motion, may file a petition in the appointing court or the court to which the conservatorship has been transferred for an order:

(1) Requiring bond or collateral or additional bond or collateral, or reducing bond;

(2) Requiring an accounting for the administration of the trust;

(3) Directing distribution;

(4) Removing the conservator and appointing a temporary or successor conservator; or

(5) Granting other appropriate relief.

(b) A conservator may petition the appointing court or the court to which the conservatorship has been transferred for instructions concerning fiduciary responsibility.

(c) Upon notice and hearing, the court may give appropriate instructions or make any appropriate order.

(d) If, on the hearing, it should appear that there is no satisfactory cause for the petition, the petition must be dismissed at costs of the petitioner. (Acts 1987, No. 87-590, p. 975, § 2-315.)

Once a conservator has been appointed, the court supervising the trust acts only upon the request of some moving party. This section is in accord with prior Alabama law that was contained in several separate sections of the Alabama Code. See, former Ala. Code (1975) sections 26-3-8, 26-6-3, 26-5-31, 26-8-21, and 26-8-41. See also, former Ala. Code (1975, as amended by Act No. 79-701) section 26-7A-10. Although section (b), relating to fiduciary advice, is a codification of historic equity practice, Alabama has not had the practice codified prior to this chapter.

Subsection (d) does not appear in the Uniform Guardianship and Protective Proceedings Act and it has been added in this chapter, but it is a direct carry-over of the provision previously stated in Ala. Code, section 26-5-31 (1975).

Statute to be repealed: Ala. Code (1975) section 26-6-3.

Statute to be modified: Ala. Code (1975) sections 26-3-8, 26-5-31, 26-8-21 and 26-8-41.

§ 26-2A-145. Conservator's standard of care and performance.

A conservator, in relation to powers conferred by this division, or implicit in the title acquired by virtue of the proceeding, shall observe the standards in dealing with the estate of the protected person that would be observed by a prudent person dealing with the property of another, and if the conservator has special skills or is appointed conservator on the basis of representations of special skills or expertise, the conservator is under a duty to use those skills. (Acts 1987, No. 87-590, p. 975, § 2-316.)

Comment

The intent of this section is to adopt for conservators the standard of care and performance otherwise applicable to trustees in Alabama. Generally, this standard is that of a "prudent person," although it is not generally codified and is modified by statute in some instances. This section codifies for conservators the standard of care and performance of a prudent person. Previously, for both guardians and curators appointed under existing Alabama law, there was a very narrowly stated duty to manage the estate "frugally and to improve it to the best of his skill and ability" (Ala. Code [1975] section 26-4-3), and it has been held that that statute establishes a prudent person standard of care. See, Gordon v. Brunson, 287 Ala. 535, 253 So. 2d 183 (1971). At least, this section codified a much clearer statement of the standard.

A conservator must be aware that Ala. Const. art. IV, Section 74 (1901) prohibits the legislature from enacting any statute authorizing the investment of any trust fund by "guardians," etc., in the bonds or stock of any private corporation. This section is not intended to be in defiance of that prohibition by implication. The constitutional prohibition merely will remain as an additional restriction on the prudent-person standard. However, if the constitutional prohibition were repealed, a conservator, in exercising the care of a prudent person, could consider investments in the stocks and bonds of private corporations.

Statute to be repealed: Ala. Code (1975) section 26-4-3.

Code commissioner's note. — The cases cited below were decided under prior law.

Former §§ 26-4-3 and 26-4-120 are to be construed in pari materia. Sims v. Russell, 236 Ala. 562, 183 So. 862 (1938).

Guardian is responsible for ward's property. — It is the duty of the guardian, under former § 26-4-2, to collect and take into possession the assets of the ward. He is to discharge the duties of the trust in the same manner that a careful and prudent businessman manages his like personal affairs. And it follows from this general rule that the guardian is responsible for the properties of the ward coming into his hands, or that should have been reduced to his possession. Ramsey v. McMillan, 214 Ala. 185, 106 So. 848 (1925); Kelly v. Wilson, 234 Ala. 455, 175 So. 551 (1937).

A successor guardian should, in exercise of required diligence in obtaining possession of ward's estate, obtain securities from former guardian, proceed with their collection and receive payment therefor when tendered. Kelly v. Wilson, 234 Ala. 455, 175 So. 551 (1937); Hines v. Dollar, 236 Ala. 329, 181 So. 748 (1938).

A guardian is chargeable with any property of the ward which could have been received or recovered by the use of reasonable diligence to that end — the diligence which a prudent man would exercise in the prosecution of his own like affairs. Hastings v. Huber, 241 Ala. 160, 1 So. 2d 749 (1941).

It is the duty of a guardian until his letters are revoked to manage the estate of the ward, and this duty applies to the estate of a non compos mentis. Ward v. Stallworth, 243 Ala. 651, 11 So. 2d 374 (1942).

And is liable for negligence in collecting assets. — A guardian who has notice of a debt due to his ward, and makes no attempt to collect it, is chargeable on final settlement with the amount of the debt, if it is lost through his negligence. Hughes v. Mitchell, 19 Ala. 268 (1851).

A guardian, on final settlement, is properly chargeable with the amount of a decree rendered by the probate court in favor of the ward against the administrator of the ward's father, when the same could have been collected by due diligence. Lane v. Mickle, 43 Ala. 109 (1869).

This property should be made to yield an income, if practical. — The policy, declared by this section, is that moneys of the ward shall be made to yield an income, if practical. Sims v. Russell, 236 Ala. 562, 183 So. 862 (1938).

This section is declaratory of the ordinary duty, of a guardian to make his ward's funds productive by investing the surplus so that it draws interest. Gordon v. Brunson, 287 Ala. 535, 253 So. 2d 183 (1971).

Independent of any statute upon the subject, it is one of the ordinary duties of a guardian to invest the surplus funds of his ward, and make interest thereon, whenever it is practicable to do so. Allen v. Martin, 36 Ala. 330 (1860); Owen v. Peebles, 42 Ala. 338 (1868).

This section defines and fixes the duty of the guardian as to the management and improvement of his ward's estate, and as to making the surplus money productive. He must, if practicable, lend out all surplus money of the ward. Gordon v. Brunson, 287 Ala. 535, 253 So. 2d 183 (1971).

It is the guardian's duty to keep his ward's moneys safely, without charge, if he cannot loan them out, or reinvest them, under order of the proper court. Hall v. Hall, 43 Ala. 488 (1869).

To this end the guardian is expressly empowered to take good personal security, as well as real estate security. Sims v. Russell, 236 Ala. 562, 183 So. 862 (1938).

A guardian is responsible for interest on his ward's estate where he through neglect fails to invest to earn such interest. However, it is equally clear that the rate to which the guardian should respond should be no more than the rate which the money could have earned had he discharged his duty to invest it. Gordon v. Brunson, 287 Ala. 535, 253 So. 2d 183 (1971).

As a general principle, a guardian is chargeable with interest whenever it appears that he has been guilty of neglect in failing to put out his ward's money at interest, and has not exercised the prudence and diligence which a discreet man would have exercised in respect to the management of his own surplus money under like circumstances. The applicability of this principle is necessarily dependent upon the particular circumstances of each case. Gordon v. Brunson, 287 Ala. 535, 253 So. 2d 183 (1971).

If a guardian suffers his ward's funds to remain unemployed, when, by the exercise of reasonable diligence, they would have been safely invested, he is responsible for at least simple interest. Gordon v. Brunson, 287 Ala. 535, 253 So. 2d 183 (1971).

This section restricts the discretion of the guardian as to the class or kinds of securities which may be taken, but does not constitute him the exclusive and final judge of the practicability of investing in such securities, or of their sufficiency. Gordon v. Brunson, 287 Ala. 535, 253 So. 2d 183 (1971).

Evil or corrupt intention of a guardian is a prerequisite to charging him compound interest on uninvested funds. Gordon v. Brunson, 287 Ala. 535, 253 So. 2d 183 (1971).

Where a guardian uses his ward's funds, or lends them to a firm of which he is a member, the interest must be compounded annually. Gordon v. Brunson, 287 Ala. 535, 253 So. 2d 183 (1971).

A guardian must be held to the same accountability as if he had personally made use of the ward's funds where he lends the ward's money to a corporation of which he is the managing officer. Gordon v. Brunson, 287 Ala. 535, 253 So. 2d 183 (1971).

Making a loan to a corporation of which the guardian is the managing officer, without security, outside the law and in breach of trust, the guardian must be regarded in the same position as if he had appropriated the money to his own use. While a severe rule, perhaps, it is sanctioned by experience and cannot be relaxed without exposing the helpless to the risk of losses which the law has expressly declared shall not be incurred. Gordon v. Brunson, 287 Ala. 535, 253 So. 2d 183 (1971).

Compound interest at the legal rate must be charged on money loaned to a corporation of which the guardian is the managing officer. Gordon v. Brunson, 287 Ala. 535, 253 So. 2d 183 (1971).

It is not imprudent to hold some of a ward's money in a checking account for contingencies. The fact that no contingencies calling for the expenditure of this amount arise should not be held against the guardian. Gordon v. Brunson, 287 Ala. 535, 253 So. 2d 183 (1971).

Title to real estate mortgage security is in guardian. — This section authorizes the loan of surplus money of the ward on mortgage security, and it appears to have been assumed, that such loans are made with title to the security in the guardian as such. Brewer v. Ernest, 81 Ala. 435, 2 So. 84 (1887). And in Kirsch v. Green, 232 Ala. 65, 166 So. 774 (1936), was the holding that the guardian had the right to sell and dispose of the mortgage security so executed to him as such guardian. Former §§ 26-4-120 and 26-4-121, dealing with the matter of investment of the funds of the ward in the purchase of real estate are inapplicable. Kelly v. Wilson, 234 Ala. 455, 175 So. 551 (1937).

Guardian must act with prudence of ordinary businessman. — A guardian making an investment for his ward is bound to act honestly and faithfully and exercise a sound discretion such as men of ordinary prudence and intelligence use in their own affairs, and if he is negligent in this respect he must answer for any resulting loss. He is not, however, an insurer, of the safety of the investments, and if he acts in good faith, using due care and prudence and having regard to the best pecuniary interest of the ward, he will not be liable for any loss arising out of the transaction, although he may have committed an error of judgment in respect to the transaction out of which the loss arose. Brewer v. Ernest, 81 Ala. 435, 2 So. 84 (1887); Hines v. Dollar, 236 Ala. 329, 181 So. 748 (1938); Hall v. Esslinger, 235 Ala. 451, 179 So. 639 (1938).

A guardian making investments for his ward is bound to act honestly and exercise a sound discretion such as men of ordinary prudence and intelligence use in their own affairs. Gordon v. Brunson, 287 Ala. 535, 253 So. 2d 183 (1971).

General principles regarding care and prudence. — The guardian in the exercise of his duties must use the care and diligence with which a careful and prudent businessman manages his like personal affairs. Ramsey v. McMillan, 214 Ala. 185, 106 So. 848 (1925). But if he hazards the money of the ward upon the credit of the borrower and neglects to take good personal security, he becomes an insurer against loss to the ward. And this is true no matter what is the credit or solvency of the borrower. Cunningham v. Cunningham, 215 Ala. 484, 111 So. 208 (1927). (Where the loan was made to corporation of which the guardian was stockholder and managing officer.) See also, Leach v. Gray, 201 Ala. 47, 77 So. 341 (1917) (where the unsecured loan was to the guardian's partner).

If the property of the ward is lost or injured through the negligence or misfeasance of the guardian, the latter is liable to the extent that any trustee would be liable under the same circumstances. Ramsey v. McMillan, 214 Ala. 185, 106 So. 848 (1925).

The guardian is liable for, at least, simple interest if in the exercise of reasonable diligence the ward's funds could have been invested in the recognized securities. But if it is not practicable to make such investments the guardian is not liable for any interest, Brand v. Abbott, 42 Ala. 499 (1868), the application of the rule as to interest depending on the particular facts of each case. And it should not be allowed where a partial settlement is made since by § 26-5-6 it is presumed that the failure to invest the surplus has been accounted for. And although it is incumbent on the guardian to show that he could not, using due diligence, safely lend the money, the question of practicability is one ultimately for the decision of the court. Thompson v. Thompson, 92 Ala. 545, 9 So. 465 (1891), modifying to this extent the ruling in Ashley v. Martin, 50 Ala. 537 (1874). See also, Westmoreland v. Birmingham Trust & Sav. Bank, 214 Ala. 593, 108 So. 536 (1926).

A guardian who has notice of debts due ward is chargeable with amount thereof if debt is lost through guardian's negligence. Kelly v. Wilson, 234 Ala. 455, 175 So. 551 (1937).

Guardian depositing trust funds in bank accounts showing trust character thereof, at interest, withdrawable at any time, held not liable for loss thereof on bank's failure. Barnes v. Clark, 227 Ala. 651, 151 So. 586 (1933).

Duty in seeing that loan is repaid is same as duty in making investment. — Clearly the duty of a guardian to exercise care and prudence in seeing that a loan is either paid or remains well secured is the same as the duty in making the loan in the first instance. Sims v. Russell, 236 Ala. 562, 183 So. 862 (1938).

Where guardian made loan, in 1926, of ward's funds secured by borrower's note, with pledge of stock in national bank of the face value equal to amount of loan as collateral security, interest payments were made regularly until 1930, and irregularly until October, 1931, when borrower became a bankrupt, stock was released to guardian and was sold in 1936 for less than one-third the amount of loan, and in October, 1931, full amount of loan could have been realized from sale of the stock, guardian was chargeable with loss of the funds. Sims v. Russell, 236 Ala. 562, 183 So. 862 (1938).

Burden is on guardian to show he acted with care. — When a guardian seeks to excuse himself for loss of his ward's money on a loan made by him the burden is on him to show such loss is due to no fault, want of reasonable vigilance and foresight on his part. Sims v. Russell, 236 Ala. 562, 183 So. 862 (1938).

Recovery of property from guardian. — Neither a ward restored to sanity nor her grantee can recover possession of ward's property from guardian at law until he shall make settlement required by law, since it is guardian's duty to collect and take into possession the ward's assets. Ward v. Stallworth, 243 Ala. 651, 11 So. 2d 374 (1942).

Where the ward has suffered no actual loss, he has no right to recover damages from the guardian because the latter has made an unauthorized loan on real estate. Hall v. Esslinger, 235 Ala. 451, 179 So. 639 (1938).

Purchase of notes on advice of bank officer. — Where guardian, on advice of bank trust officer, with incompetent's funds, purchased notes from bank, if notes were prohibited investment, right to maintain an action for money had and received arose in favor of the guardian upon receipt of money by bank. Spann v. First Nat'l Bank, 240 Ala. 539, 200 So. 554 (1941).

Investing in private corporation bonds. — Guardian of incompetent war veteran held not entitled to credit for money obtained under war risk insurance act which money guardian lost by investing in first mortgage bonds of private corporation with consent of regional attorney of veterans' bureau. White v. White, 230 Ala. 641, 162 So. 368 (1935).

Contract of ward who is sui juris. — A ward either a minor or a non compos mentis, having become sui juris, can make a binding contract as to his property rights then in the custody of the guardian, subject to the power of the court over the same necessary to a final settlement of the guardianship. Ward v. Stallworth, 243 Ala. 651, 11 So. 2d 374 (1942).

Liability of successor guardian. — Where successor guardian of a non compos was chargeable with amount of judgment against former guardian which had not been collected, the successor guardian was chargeable as of date of the judgment as for funds of his ward in his hands which he failed to invest. Cox v. Williams, 241 Ala. 427, 3 So. 2d 129 (1941).

The supreme court may render judgment on appeal in contest of a guardian's final settlement where the evidence is without substantial dispute. Gordon v. Brunson, 287 Ala. 535, 253 So. 2d 183 (1971).

Collateral references. — 39 C.J.S., Guardian & Ward, § 76.

39 Am. Jur. 2d, Guardian & Ward, §§ 73-96.

Power of court to authorize guardian to borrow ward's money. 30 ALR 461.

Care required of guardian with respect to retaining securities coming into his hands as assets of the estate. 77 ALR 505, 112 ALR 355.

Power of guardian in respect of insurance on ward's life, or a policy under which he has interest. 84 ALR 366.

Liability of guardian for loss of funds invested as affected by order of court authorizing the investment. 88 ALR 325.

Liability of guardian for loss of funds deposited in bank in form which discloses trust or fiduciary character. 90 ALR 641.

Effect of beneficiary's consent to, acquiescence in, or ratification of, improper investments or loans by guardian. 128 ALR 4.

Right of guardian to incur obligations so as to bind incompetent or his estate, or to make expenditures, without prior approval by court. 130 ALR 133.

Torts: liability of incompetent's estate for torts committed by guardian, committee, or trustee in managing estate. 40 ALR2d 1103.

Debts: power of guardian, committee, or trustee of mental incompetent, after latter's death, to pay debts and obligations. 60 ALR2d 963.

Bank deposits: rights and powers of guardian with reference to joint bank deposit in name of incompetent and another. 62 ALR2d 1091.

Interest: guardian's liability for interest on ward's funds. 72 ALR2d 757.

Charitable gifts: power to make charitable gifts from estate of incompetent. 99 ALR2d 946.

Lease: guardian's power to make lease for infant ward beyond minority or term of guardianship. 6 ALR3d 570.

Noncharitable gifts: power of court or guardian to make noncharitable gifts or allowances out of funds of incompetent ward. 24 ALR3d 863.

Right of guardian or committee of incompetent to incur obligations so as to bind incompetent or his estate, or to make expenditures, without prior approval by court. 63 ALR3d 780.

§ 26-2A-146. Inventory and records.

(a) Within 90 days after appointment, each conservator shall prepare and file with the appointing court a complete inventory of the estate subject to the conservatorship together with an oath or affirmation that the inventory is believed to be complete and accurate as far as information permits. The conservator shall provide a copy thereof to the protected person if practicable and the person has attained the age of 14 years. A copy also shall be provided to any guardian or parent with whom the protected person resides.

(b) The conservator shall keep suitable records of the administration and exhibit the same on request of any interested person. (Acts 1987, No. 87-590, p. 975, § 2-317.)

Comment

Like Ala. Code (1975) section 26-4-2 did previously, this section requires a conservator to make an inventory of the ward's property within 90 days (three months under the present Alabama statute) of appointment.

This chapter adds a requirement that the conservator must provide a copy of the inventory to a protected person. The general philosophy of this chapter makes this an important feature; a protected person may not always be incapacitated completely as would a ward under the current Alabama statutes, and may need to be kept informed in the event that he or she recovers from the disability. The Alabama statutes regarding curators did not have a provision on inventories.

Statute to be repealed: Ala. Code (1975) section 26-4-2.

Code commissioner's note. — The cases cited below were decided under prior law.

Where failure to comply does not merit removal. — The failure of the guardian to file an inventory under this section, if due to inadvertence, is not ground for removal in view of the provisions of former § 26-4-3. Willoughby v. Willoughby, 203 Ala. 138, 82 So. 168 (1919); Ramsey v. McMillan, 214 Ala. 185, 106 So. 848 (1925).

Guardian may obtain assistance in preparing inventory. — Although the filing of an inventory is a duty of the guardian, there is no rule of law that prevents a guardian from obtaining assistance in preparing this inventory and listing the cost of the assistance as an expense of the estate of the ward. Humphries v. Lynch, 579 So. 2d 612 (Ala. 1991).

Collateral references. — 39 C.J.S., Guardian & Child, § 77.

§ 26-2A-147. Accounts.

Each conservator shall account to the court for administration of the conservatorship upon resignation or removal and at other times as the court may direct, but if not otherwise directed, the conservator must, at least once in three years, account to the court. If the conservator shall die before making the accounting, the conservator's personal representative will make the accounting, or if no personal representative has been appointed, the sureties on the conservator's bond may proceed to make the accounting. On termination or removal of the protected person's minority or disability, a conservator shall account to the court or to the formerly protected person. An order after notice and hearing allowing an intermediate account of a conservator is a final adjudication as to liabilities concerning the matters considered in connection therewith. Thereafter, at any time prior to final settlement, the account may be reopened by the court on motion or petition of the conservator or ward or other party having an interest in the estate for amendment or revision if it later appears that the account is incorrect either because of fraud or mistake. An order, following notice and hearing, allowing a final account is a final adjudication as to all previously unsettled liabilities of the conservator to the protected person or the protected person's successors relating to the conservatorship. In connection with any account, the court may require a conservator to submit to a physical examination of the estate, to be made in any manner the court specifies. (Acts 1987, No. 87-590, p. 975, § 2-318.)

Comment

The persons who are to receive notice of intermediate and final accounts will be identified by court order as provided in section 26-2A-134. Notice is given as described in section 26-2A-50. In other respects, procedures applicable to accountings will be as provided by court rule.

Alabama previously had a number of statutes dealing with accounting, partial settlements and settlements. See, Ala. Code (1975) sections 26-4-8, 26-4-121, 26-5-1 through 26-5-18, 26-5-30 through 26-5-39, and 26-5-50 through 26-5-54. See also, Ala. Code (1975 as amended by Act No. 79-701) sections 26-7A-11 through 26-7A-13.

There are several technical differences between this chapter and prior Alabama statutes dealing with procedural aspects of settlements. First, prior law required a guardian to file an accounting at least once every three years (Ala. Code section 26-5-2 [1975]), and a curator to account yearly (Ala. Code section 26-7A-13 [1975, as amended by Acts 1979, No. 79-701, p. 1246]). The Alabama Uniform Veterans' Guardianship Act requires an annual accounting, but a continuance for filing an accounting may be extended by the court in its discretion and without formal proceedings for a period not to exceed three years. Ala. Code section 26-9-14 (1975). This chapter retains the requirement for at least a triennial accounting (as an addition to the Uniform Act) and otherwise only upon resignation, removal, or as the court directs.

Second, if the cause of the protected person's disability is terminated, the conservator may report his accounting either to the court or to the protected person. (There is not necessarily court supervision in the latter case.) While prior Alabama law required a curator to file a final settlement with the court (Ala. Code [1975, as amended by Act No. 79-701] section 26-7A-13), the guardian of a minor or a person of unsound mind could enter into a consent settlement as to the final accounting (Ala. Code [1975] section 26-5-12), subject to court approval.

An intermediate settlement under this chapter adjudicates the matters pertinent to that settlement. Likewise, under prior Alabama law, an intermediate settlement, which had been prefaced with the same notice as required on final settlements, was final as to all matters contained therein. The Alabama statute, however, tempered the finality with a provision for the reopening of accounts if there appeared to have been a fraud or mistake, as long as the reopening petition was filed before the final settlement. Ala. Code, section 26-5-15 (1975). For clarity, that express statement from the prior Alabama statute is added in this section.

The provision regarding the accounting by a conservator's personal representative or sureties on the bond is a carry-over from Ala. Code (1975) section 26-5-34 and 26-5-52 and added to this section for clarification.

Statutes to be repealed: Ala. Code (1975) sections 26-4-8, 26-4-121, 26-5-17 and 26-5-37.

Statutes to be modified: Ala. Code (1975) sections 26-5-1, 26-5-2, 26-5-4, 26-5-5, 26-5-7 through 26-5-10, 26-5-12 through 26-5-16, 26-5-18, 26-5-30 through 26-5-36, 26-5-38, 26-5-39, and 26-5-50 through 26-5-52.

Collateral references. — Validity of inter vivos gift by ward to guardian or conservator. 70 ALR4th 499.

§ 26-2A-148. Conservators; title by appointment.

(a) The appointment of a conservator vests in the conservator title as trustee to all property, or to the part thereof specified in the order, of the protected person, presently held or thereafter acquired, including title to any property theretofore held for the protected person. Appointment of a conservator does not terminate a custodianship created under a Uniform Gifts to Minors Act or a Uniform Transfers to Minors Act, or a valid durable power of attorney, except on order of the court. An order specifying that only a part of the property of the protected person vests in the conservator creates a limited conservatorship.

(b) Except as otherwise permitted herein, the interest of the protected person in property vested in a conservator by this section is not transferable or assignable by the protected person. An attempted transfer or assignment by the protected person, though ineffective to affect property rights, may generate a claim for restitution or damages which, subject to presentation and allowance, may be satisfied as provided in Section 26-2A-156. (Acts 1987, No. 87-590, p. 975, § 2-319.)

Comment

This section permits independent administration of the property of the protected person once the appointment of a conservator has been obtained. Any interested person may require the conservator to account in accordance with section 26-2A-147. As a trustee, a conservator holds title to the property of the protected person. In subsection (a), the Uniform Act provides that the appointment of a conservator vests title in that person to property "held for the protected person" and continues "by custodians or attorneys in fact." This chapter expressly provides for a different effect with respect to custodianships under either the Uniform Gifts to Minors Act or the Uniform Transfers to Minors Act and with respect to durable powers of attorney. Appointment of a conservator does not affect the legal relationship of a custodian for the minor created under a Uniform Gifts to Minors Act or a Uniform Transfers to Minors Act. Subsection (a) further expressly provides that a valid durable power of attorney is not terminated on the appointment of a conservator. In this regard, Ala. Code section 26-1-2(c)(1) (1975, as amended by Acts 1981, No. 81-98, p. 117) provides that if there is an appointment of a conservator, subsequent to execution of a durable power of attorney, the attorney in fact under the durable power of attorney "is accountable to the [conservator] as well as to the principal. The [conservator] has the same power to revoke or amend the power of attorney that the principal would have had if the principal were not disabled, incompetent or incapacitated." The statutes are compatible, but consistent application may require that the conservator know the termination provisions under the applicable durable power of attorney instrument and to exercise those termination powers through an order of court. However, a springing durable power of attorney, which is to become effective on the disability of the principal, may not come into effect because of the appointment of a conservator, but the attorney-in-fact under the durable power of attorney is given a priority in the appointment of the conservator under section 26-2A-138.

The appointment of a conservator is a serious matter and the court must select the fiduciary with great care. Once appointed, the conservator is free to carry on all fiduciary responsibilities. If the conservator defaults in these in any way, the conservator may be made to account to the court. Alabama statutes previously did not provide specifically regarding title. It is clear, particularly as to real property, that the guardian had powers to dispose of real property only with a prior court order. Ala. Code (1975) sections 26-4-140 through 26-4-155. Alabama law previously also did not specifically vest title in the curator as trustee, but gave the curator general powers, through the appointing court, over the sale, mortgage, or lease of the ward's property. Ala. Code (1975, as amended by Act No. 79-701) sections 26-7A-7 and 26-7A-9.

Unlike a situation involving appointment of a guardian, the appointment of a conservator has no bearing on the capacity of the disabled person to contract or engage in other transactions except insofar as the spendthrift provisions of subsection (b) of this section apply to property transactions. This provision is in contrast to Ala. Code (1975, as amended by Act No. 79-701) section 26-7A-7 of the prior law, whereby the appointment of a curator "wholly" deprived the protected person of the right to contract unless he or she had the prior approval of the court.

The phrase "or to the part thereof specified in the order," in the first sentence and the second sentence of subsection (a) are necessary in the adoption of the concept of a limited guardianship.

Subsection (b) provides a spendthrift effect for property of the protected person vested in the conservator. An attempt by the protected person to transfer or alienate property may, nevertheless, generate a claim for restitution. Under prior law, the ward's lack of power to execute an effective writing would negate the possibility of such a claim against the estate. Several suggestions were made that the spendthrift provisions should be incorporated in the Act. The concept is analogous to spendthrift trust provisions often included when the beneficiary is incapable of managing his or her own property. The concept is also consistent with a conservatorship arrangement for protecting the estate of an incapacitated person. Alabama presently has a statute permitting spendthrift trusts (Ala. Code [1975] section 19-3-1), but the concept has not been extended previously to guardianships or conservatorships as this chapter does.

§ 26-2A-149. Recording of conservator's letters.

(a) Except for property unaffected by the appointment of a conservator specified in Section 26-2A-148(a), letters of conservatorship are evidence of transfer of all assets, or the part thereof specified in the letters, of a protected person to the conservator. An order terminating a conservatorship is evidence of transfer of all assets subject to the conservatorship from the conservator to the protected person, or to successors of the person.

(b) Subject to the requirements of general statutes governing the filing or recordation of documents of title to land or other property, letters of conservatorship and orders terminating conservatorships may be filed or recorded to give record notice of title as between the conservator and the protected person. For the filing and recordation of letters of conservatorship and orders terminating conservatorships, the probate judge shall receive the same compensation (fees of registration) therefor as for recording deeds to land, but no tax levied upon the recordation of mortgages, deeds, and instruments of like character shall be levied upon or collected. (Acts 1987, No. 87-590, p. 975, § 2-320.)

Comment

The phrases "or the part thereof specified in the letters" in the first sentence and "subjected to the conservatorship" in the second sentence are included here to recognize the concept of a limited conservatorship.

There is not a similar or parallel provision identifying the significance of guardianship or curatorship documents under the prior Alabama law. Since the concept of title to property being in the conservator is new in Alabama, a provision like this section has not been needed previously.

Fees of registration for recording deeds are generally covered in Ala. Code, sections 12-19-90 (1975, as amended) and 35-4-58 (1975) and the tax levied upon the recordation of deeds is covered in Ala. Code, section 40-22-1 (1975).

§ 26-2A-150. Sale, encumbrance, or transaction involving conflict of interest; voidable; exceptions.

Any sale or encumbrance to or purchase from a conservator, the spouse, agent, attorney of a conservator, any person related to the conservator by blood or marriage within the fourth degree, or any corporation, trust, or other organization in which the conservator has a substantial beneficial interest, or any other transaction involving the estate being administered by the conservator which is affected by a substantial conflict between fiduciary and personal interests is voidable unless the transaction is approved by the court after notice as directed by the court. (Acts 1987, No. 87-590, p. 975, § 2-321.)

Comment

This section is without counterpart in the prior Alabama statutes, as it relates to the more stringent fiduciary responsibilities placed upon a conservator under this chapter. The language in this section is designed to preclude conflicts of interest in transactions where independence of the fiduciary/conservator might be compromised. The phrase "any person related to the conservator by blood or marriage within the fourth degree" has been added in Alabama to further identify relationships where the potential for conflict of interests seems very great. The civil-law method for computing degrees of kinship is used in Alabama. Historically, the prohibition against fiduciaries entering into transactions involving a conflict of interests has been very strong if not absolute.

§ 26-2A-151. Persons dealing with conservators; protection.

(a) A person who in good faith either assists or deals with a conservator for value in any transaction other than those requiring a court order as provided in Section 26-2A-136 is protected as if the conservator properly exercised the power. The fact that a person knowingly deals with a conservator does not alone require the person to inquire into the existence of a power or the propriety of its exercise, but restrictions on powers of conservators which are endorsed on letters as provided in Section 26-2A-154 are effective as to third persons. A person is not bound to see to the proper application of estate assets paid or delivered to a conservator.

(b) The protection expressed in this section extends to any procedural irregularity or jurisdictional defect occurring in proceedings leading to the issuance of letters and is not a substitution for protection provided by comparable provisions of the law relating to commercial transactions or to simplify transfers of securities by fiduciaries. (Acts 1987, No. 87-590, p. 975, § 2-322.)

Comment

The section codifies the b.f.p. rule generally followed in transactions with fiduciaries, particularly trustees and personal representatives. Nevertheless, any person dealing with a known conservator for another should examine the letters of appointment of the conservator for any limitations on the conservator's authority endorsed on the letters pursuant to section 26-2A-154.

Since a guardian under Alabama law previously had few, if any, powers to deal with the ward's property without a court, there was not a provision in the statutes comparable to this provision; it was not needed.

The protection for b.f.p.'s provided in this section is a common protection designed to promote marketability of property and extended to persons dealing with fiduciaries. Alabama already has adopted this policy in analogous situations. See, Alabama's Uniform Fiduciaries Act, Ala. Code, sections 19-1-1 through 19-1-13 (1975) and particularly Ala. Code, section 19-1-3 (1975). See also, Ala. Code, section 35-4-254 (1975). While the protection is a limitation on parties against whom one may pursue a remedy, remedies that a person otherwise may have for a breach of fiduciary duty by a conservator are not affected by this section.

§ 26-2A-152. Powers of conservator in administration.

(a) Subject to limitation provided in Section 26-2A-154, a conservator shall have all of the powers conferred in this section and any additional powers now or hereafter conferred by law on trustees in this state. In addition, a conservator of the estate of an unmarried minor as to whom no one has parental rights, has the powers of a guardian of a minor described in Section 26-2A-78 until the minor attains the age of 19 years, or the disabilities of nonage have been removed, but the parental rights so conferred on a conservator do not preclude appointment of a guardian as provided in division 1 of this article.

(b) A conservator without court authorization or confirmation may invest and reinvest funds of the estate as would a trustee.

(c) A conservator, acting as a fiduciary in efforts to accomplish the purpose of the appointment, may act without court authorization or confirmation, to

(1) Collect, hold, and retain assets of the estate including land in another state and stocks of private corporations, until determining that disposition of the assets should be made, and the assets may be retained even though they include an asset in which the conservator is personally interested;

(2) Receive additions to the estate;

(3) Acquire an undivided interest in an asset of the estate that is otherwise an investment authorized for the conservator and in which the conservator, in any fiduciary capacity, holds an undivided interest;

(4) Invest and reinvest estate assets in accordance with subsection (b);

(5) Deposit estate funds to the extent insured in a state or federally insured financial institution, including one operated by the conservator;

(6) Acquire an asset for the estate that is an authorized investment for conservators, including land in another state, for cash or on credit, at public or private sale, and manage, develop, improve, partition, or change the character of an estate asset;

(7) Dispose of an asset, other than real property, of the estate for cash or on credit, at public or private sale, and manage or change the character of an estate asset;

(8) Make ordinary or extraordinary repairs or alterations in buildings or other structures;

(9) Enter for any purpose into a lease as lessor or lessee for a term not exceeding five years;

(10) Enter into a lease or arrangement for exploration and removal of minerals or other natural resources or enter into a pooling or unitization agreement;

(11) Grant an option for a period not exceeding one year involving disposition of an estate asset;

(12) Vote a security, in person or by general or limited proxy;

(13) Pay calls, assessments, and any other sums chargeable or accruing against or on account of securities;

(14) Sell or exercise stock-subscription or conversion rights;

(15) Deposit any stocks, bonds, or other securities at any time held in any pool or voting trust containing terms or provisions approved by the conservator;

(16) Consent, directly or through a committee or other agent, to the reorganization, consolidation, merger, dissolution, or liquidation of a corporation or other business enterprise;

(17) Insure the assets of the estate against damage or loss and the conservator against liability with respect to third persons;

(18) Borrow money for the protection of the estate to be repaid from estate assets or otherwise; advance money for the protection of the estate or the protected person and for all expenses, losses, and liability sustained in the administration of the estate or because of the holding or ownership of any estate assets, for which the conservator has a lien on the estate as against the protected person for advances so made;

(19) Pay or contest any claim; settle a claim by or against the estate or the protected person by compromise, arbitration, or otherwise; and release, in whole or in part, any claim belonging to the estate to the extent the claim is uncollectible;

(20) Pay reasonable annual compensation of the conservator, subject to final approval of the court in an accounting under Section 26-2A-147;

(21) Pay taxes, assessments, and other expenses incurred in the collection, care, administration, and protection of the estate;

(22) Allocate items of income or expense to either estate income or principal, as provided by the applicable principal and income act or other law, including creation of reserves out of income for depreciation, obsolescence, or amortization, or for depletion in mineral or timber properties;

(23) Pay any sum distributable to a protected person or dependent of the protected person by — (i) paying the sum to the distributee, (ii) applying the sum for the benefit of the distributee, or (iii) paying the sum for the use of the distributee to the guardian of the distributee, or, if none, to a relative or other person having custody of the distributee;

(24) Employ persons, including attorneys, auditors, investment advisors, or agents, even though they are associated with the conservator, to advise or assist in the performance of administrative duties;

(25) Prosecute or defend actions, claims, or proceedings in any jurisdiction for the protection of estate assets and of the conservator in the performance of fiduciary duties;

(26) Execute and deliver all instruments that will accomplish or facilitate the exercise of the powers vested in the conservator; and

(27) Hold a security in the name of a nominee or in other form without disclosure of the conservatorship so that title to the security may pass by delivery, but the conservator is liable for any act of the nominee in connection with the stock so held.

(d) A conservator, acting as a fiduciary in efforts to accomplish the purpose of the appointment, may act with prior court authorization, to

(1) Continue or participate in the operation of any business or other enterprise;

(2) Demolish any improvements and raze or erect new party walls or buildings;

(3) Dispose of any real property, including land in another state, for cash or on credit, at public or private sale, and manage, develop, improve, partition, or change the character of estate real property;

(4) Subdivide, develop, or dedicate land or easements to public use; make or obtain the vacation of plats and adjust boundaries;

(5) Enter for any purpose into a lease as lessor or lessee for a term of five or more years or extending beyond the term of the conservatorship;

(6) Grant an option for a term of more than one year involving disposition of an estate asset; and

(7) Take an option for the acquisition of any asset. (Acts 1987, No. 87-590, p. 975, § 2-323.)

Comment

Subsection (a) refers to the "removal of the disabilities of nonage." Removal of the disabilities of nonage is in the jurisdiction of the juvenile court in Alabama (Ala. Code, section 12-15-30 (1975)), applying Ala. Code, sections 26-13-1 through 26-13-8 (1975). The disabilities of nonage also are relieved for persons who are married and 18 or more years of age. Ala. Code, sections 30-4-15 and 30-4-16 (1975).

This section generally is designed to provide statutory powers for a conservator similar to powers usually contained in a trustees powers act or usually given to trustees by the scrivener in a trust instrument. The section is divided into those powers a conservator has without a prior court order in subsection (c) and powers for which the conservator needs a prior court order in subsection (d).

Subsection (b) merely provides that a conservator can invest funds of the estate with the same powers as a trustee in Alabama. Trustee investment powers are generally provided in Ala. Code sections 19-3-120 through 19-3-132 (1975). If veterans' benefits are part of the estate, Ala. Code section 26-9-10 (1975) is applicable, but these sections are consistent.

Subsection (c)(1) authorizes the conservator to "retain" (i.e., to continue to keep or hold) stocks in private corporations, when the stocks were investments received by the conservator as part of the estate of the protected person initially. Retention of investments that include stocks in private corporations does not violate Alabama's Constitutional prohibition (Ala. Const., art. IV, Section 74 (1901)) precluding the Legislature from passing an act permitting fiduciaries to invest in bonds and stocks of private corporations. See, Stovall, as Guardian v. Heid, 268 Ala. 656, 110 So. 2d 267 (1959). Since the conservator can only "retain" stocks in private corporations, the provisions in subsections (c)(12), (13), and (14) are applicable to rights derived from "retained" stocks in private corporations.

Any limitations or enlargements of the powers in this section for the conservator must be endorsed on the conservator's letters of appointment as provided in section 26-2A-154. Powers enumerated in subsection (d) may be endorsed on the conservator's letters of appointment at the time of initial appointment or subsequently either in a general order granting these powers or singularly in an order involving a particular transaction. In any event, a person dealing with a conservator should always request to see the conservator's letters of appointment for any endorsement limiting powers otherwise given in subsection (c). With respect to any transaction enumerated in subsection (d) or perhaps not enumerated in subsection (c) or subsection (d), a person dealing with the conservator should request to see the conservator's letters of appointment endorsed to include the power or other court order authorizing the action. An enlargement of powers of the conservator, if not enumerated in subsection (d), can only be authorized by a court having general equity jurisdiction under section 26-2A-154.

Alabama previously did not have a general guardianship powers act. Most acts of a guardian required a prior court authorization. See, Ala. Code (1975) sections 26-4-1 through 26-4-155. The powers essentially concerned the compromise of debts and the leasing or sale of land.

In exercising the power under subsection (c)(23) to make payments out of the estate for the benefit of dependents of the protected person, the payments will require an order of court if the source of the funds is benefits received from the United States through the veterans' administration. Ala. Code section 26-9-11 (1975).

Statutes to be repealed: Ala. Code (1975) sections 26-4-1 through 26-4-104 and 26-4-140 through 26-4-155.

Code commissioner's note. — The cases cited below were decided under prior law.

Confirmation of lease by ward attaining full age. — A ward who demands, on attaining full age, the proceeds of a lease of his real estate executed by the guardian without the authority of the probate court, thereby ratifies and confirms the lease. Steinhart v. Gregory, 176 Ala. 368, 58 So. 266 (1912).

The word "claim," used in this section, includes a demand arising out of tort. Bishop v. Big Sandy Lumber Co., 199 Ala. 463, 74 So. 931 (1917).

Safety of reinvestment is controlling. — The probate court should exercise discretion in all cases under this section with a view to the safety of the reinvestment rather than to the mere enhancement of its income return. Fuller v. Vincentelli, 205 Ala. 262, 87 So. 335 (1921).

Decree of the probate court cannot be collaterally attacked. — The decree of the probate court cannot be collaterally attacked where the petition alleged sufficient facts to confer jurisdiction, and this is true even though errors intervene between acquiring jurisdiction and the decree of sale. Holton v. Rogers, 191 Ala. 48, 67 So. 1004 (1915).

Purchase of realty will not be authorized where funds insufficient to get unincumbered title. — If ward has neither funds on hand nor property subject to sale for reinvestment under this section sufficient to acquire an unincumbered title, probate court should not authorize purchase of realty. Ward v. Jossen, 218 Ala. 530, 119 So. 220 (1928).

Procedural steps for selling real estate. — See Wilson v. McKleroy, 206 Ala. 342, 89 So. 584 (1921).

Fraudulent procurement of sale. — A good action for recovery of property is shown where it is averred, among other things, that there existed a conspiracy and fraud to procure sale of infant's land, to which fraud the infant's representative was a party, and the persons acquiring the property through fraud are chargeable as trustees ex maleficio. Edmondson v. Jones, 204 Ala. 133, 85 So. 799 (1920).

An agreement made by a guardian to sell or exchange his ward's land in the future is not per se fraud on the probate court, and where it is beneficial, courts will sanction and confirm it. Roche v. Slocumb, 206 Ala. 223, 89 So. 491 (1921).

§ 26-2A-153. Distributive duties and powers of conservator.

(a) A conservator may expend or distribute income or principal of the estate without court authorization or confirmation for the health, support, education, or maintenance of the protected person and dependents in accordance with the following principles:

(1) The conservator shall consider recommendations relating to the appropriate standard of support, education, and benefit for the protected person or dependents made by a parent or guardian, if any. The conservator may not be surcharged for sums paid to persons or organizations furnishing support, education, or maintenance to the protected person or a dependent pursuant to the recommendations of a parent or guardian of the protected person unless the conservator knows that the parent or guardian derives personal financial benefit therefrom, including relief from any personal duty of support, or the recommendations are clearly not in the best interest of the protected person.

(2) The conservator shall expend or distribute sums reasonably necessary for the health, support, education, or maintenance of the protected person and dependents with due regard to (i) the size of the estate, the probable duration of the conservatorship, and the likelihood that the protected person, at some future time, may be fully able to be wholly self-sufficient and able to manage business affairs and the estate; (ii) the accustomed standard of living of the protected person and dependents; and (iii) other funds or sources used for the support of the protected person.

(3) The conservator may expend funds of the estate for the support of persons legally dependent on the protected person and others who are members of the protected person's household who are unable to support themselves, and who are in need of support. In expending funds under this division, the conservator shall consider and apply the criteria considered in subdivision (a)(2).

(4) Funds expended under this subsection may be paid by the conservator to any person, including the protected person, to reimburse for expenditures that the conservator might have made, or in advance for services to be rendered to the protected person if it is reasonable to expect the services will be performed and advance payments are customary or reasonably necessary under the circumstances.

(5) A conservator, in discharging the responsibilities conferred by court order and this division, shall implement the principles described in Section 26-2A-136(a) to the extent possible.

(b) If the estate is ample to provide for the purposes implicit in the distributions authorized by the preceding subsections, a conservator for a protected person other than a minor has power to make gifts to charity and other objects as the protected person might have been expected to make, in amounts that do not exceed in total for any year 20 percent of the income from the estate.

(c) When a minor who has not been adjudged disabled under Section 26-2A-130(c) attains majority, the conservator, after meeting all claims and expenses of administration, shall pay over and distribute all funds and properties to the formerly protected person as soon as possible.

(d) If satisfied that a protected person's disability, other than minority, has ceased, the conservator, after meeting all claims and expenses of administration, shall pay over and distribute all funds and properties to the formerly protected person as soon as possible and petition the court for a termination of the conservatorship in accordance with Section 26-2A-158.

(e) If a protected person dies, the conservator shall deliver to the court for safekeeping any will of the deceased protected person which may have come into the conservator's possession, inform the executor or beneficiary named therein of the delivery, and retain the estate for delivery to a duly appointed personal representative of the decedent or other persons entitled thereto. If, 40 days after the death of the protected person, no other person has been appointed personal representative and no application or petition for appointment is before the court, the conservator may apply to exercise the powers and duties of a personal representative in order to be able to proceed to administer and distribute the decedent's estate. Upon application for an order granting the powers of a personal representative to a conservator, after notice to any person nominated personal representative by any will of which the applicant is aware, the court may grant the application upon determining that there is no objection and endorse the letters of the conservator to note that the formerly protected person is deceased and that the conservator has acquired all of the powers and duties of a personal representative. The making and entry of an order under this section has the effect of an order of appointment of a personal representative, but the estate in the name of the conservator, after administration, may be distributed to the decedent's successors without prior re-transfer to the conservator as personal representative. (Acts 1987, No. 87-590, p. 975, § 2-324.)

Comment

This section sets out those situations wherein the conservator may distribute property or disburse funds during the continuance of or on termination of the trust. Section 26-2A-144(b) makes it clear that a conservator may seek instructions from the court on questions arising under this section. Subsection (e) is derived in part from § 11.80.150 Revised Code of Washington (RCWA 11.80.150).

The primary difference between this chapter and prior Alabama law is the discretion given the conservator. No court authorization or proceeding is required to appropriate any property of the incapacitated person to the care of the protected individual or his dependents. Under prior Alabama law, affidavits, applications and other procedural requirements complicated such distributions. See Ala. Code (1975) sections 26-4-60 through 26-4-68.

Paragraph (a)(5) is a cross-reference to the admonition in section 26-2A-136(a) reiterating the principle that the conservator should continually be conscious of the policies of this chapter against an overly intrusive exercise of control over property of the protected person.

Subsection (d) is similar to Ala. Code (1975, as amended by Act No. 79-701) section 26-7A-14 with regard to discharge of the curator or conservator following the cessation of the protected person's disability.

Subsection (e) permits the conservator to apply to the personal representative of the decedent's estate, if no other person has applied to be the personal representative within 40 days after the death of the protected person. This subsection does not supersede or give the conservator a priority over a county or general administrator, who may be appointed within the same time frame. See, Ala. Code, sections 43-2-170 through 43-2-175 (1975). This subsection merely gives the probate court an additional person who may be considered as a possible appointee as personal representative in determining the most efficient and effective way to administer the estate of a formerly protected person who is deceased.

Statutes to be repealed: Ala. Code (1975) sections 26-4-60 through 26-4-68.

Code commissioner's note. — The cases cited below were decided under prior law.

Determining proper amount to be appropriated for support. — In fixing the portion of the income or principal of the estate of an insane person to be appropriated to the support of the indigent father, the court should determine: Is the estate sufficiently able to do so? If so then the amount thereof should be suitable to the estate and the condition in life of all the parties to be supported from it. Gamble v. Leva, 212 Ala. 155, 102 So. 120 (1924).

This section is applicable to natural or foster father. — If natural or foster father is unable to maintain infant child who has an independent estate, court will, upon application by the father, make allowance to him for maintenance of such child. Law v. Bush, 239 Ala. 612, 195 So. 885 (1940).

Order from court necessary before tuition paid can be recovered. — Neither the guardian nor ward can recover money paid by guardian as tuition for ward's education without order of the probate court. Nolen v. Starke, 17 Ala. App. 244, 84 So. 398 (1919).

Money spent under section used as setoff in action against judge. — In view of this section authorizing probate judge to appropriate principal of estate of minors if necessary for maintenance and education, probate judge, in action against him and his surety for alleged negligence in failing to require guardian to make good and sufficient bond, is entitled to show what amount was used by guardian therefor, and what should have been credited to him on settlement, as showing what damages were sustained on account of insufficient bond. Rowe v. Johnson, 214 Ala. 510, 108 So. 604 (1926).

Sufficient allowance. — Under this section governing allowance to guardian for maintenance and education of minor, order authorizing guardian who had adopted child to use $15.00 per month out of corpus of minor's estate for support, maintenance and education, was proper. Law v. Bush, 239 Ala. 612, 195 So. 885 (1940).

Allowances from government life insurance. — This section conferred on the probate court jurisdiction to entertain application of the guardian for allowances to the minor for her support out of payments to the guardian by the government under war insurance policies on the life of the father, a deceased soldier. Maddox v. Elliott, 248 Ala. 271, 27 So. 2d 498 (1946).

Burden of proof on minor. — As respects settlement of guardianship account, a minor has burden of proving rendition of services to father, and value of such services as basis for claim of setoff against credit to father for expenses of maintenance. Law v. Bush, 239 Ala. 612, 195 So. 885 (1940).

Court has power, irrespective of this section to authorize guardian of an incompetent to sell or mortgage incompetent's realty and personalty, whenever necessary to pay estate's debts or to provide necessary maintenance and support for the incompetent and his family. Montgomery v. Montgomery, 236 Ala. 33, 180 So. 709 (1938).

Recovery of property bars guardian's liability. — Where the ward is entitled to recover property sought to be sold by his guardian without order of court, and has exercised the right, he cannot charge the guardian with its value. McGowan v. Milner, 195 Ala. 44, 70 So. 175 (1915).

Procedural steps for selling real estate. — When a necessity exists to sell the real estate of a ward, the order may be obtained from a court of competent jurisdiction, there must be a public sale, the sale reported to the court, the report confirmed, the purchase money paid and deed directed to be made by the court to the purchaser. Wilson v. McKleroy, 206 Ala. 342, 89 So. 584 (1921).

Reimbursement of guardian. — See Spidle v. Blakeney, 151 Ala. 194, 44 So. 62 (1907).

§ 26-2A-154. Enlargement or limitation of powers of conservator.

Subject to the restrictions in Section 26-2A-136(c), a court having equity jurisdiction may confer on a conservator at the time of appointment or later, in addition to the powers conferred by Sections 26-2A-152 and 26-2A-153, any power that the court itself could exercise under Sections 26-2A-136(b)(2) and 26-2A-136(b)(3). The court, at the time of appointment or later, may limit the powers of a conservator otherwise conferred by Sections 26-2A-152 and 26-2A-153 or previously conferred by the court and may at any time remove or modify any limitation. If the court limits any power conferred on the conservator by Section 26-2A-152 or Section 26-2A-153, or specifies, as provided in Section 26-2A-148(a), that title to some but not all assets of the protected person vests in the conservator, the limitation or specification of assets subject to the conservatorship must be endorsed upon the letters of appointment. (Acts 1987, No. 87-590, p. 975, § 2-325.)

Comment

This section makes it possible to appoint a fiduciary whose powers are limited to part of the estate or who may conduct important transactions, such as sales and mortgages of land, only with special court authorization. In the latter case, a conservator would be in much the same position as a guardian of property under the law currently in force in most states (including Alabama), but the conservator would have title to the property. The purpose of giving conservators title as trustees is to ensure that the provisions for protection of third parties have full effect. The Veterans Administration may insist, when it is paying benefits to a minor or disabled person, that the letters of conservatorship limit powers to those of a guardian under the Uniform Veteran's Guardianship Act and require the conservator to file annual accounts. See particularly, Ala. Code, section 26-9-14 (1975), which is part of Alabama's Uniform Veteran's Guardianship Act, Ala. Code, sections 26-9-1 through 26-9-19 (1975).

Not only may the court limit the powers of the conservator, but it may expand powers of the conservator so as to make it possible to act as the court itself might act.

Presently, only the probate courts of Jefferson and Mobile counties have general equity jurisdiction in matters involving estates of minors and incapacitated persons. The intent of this chapter to preserve the equity jurisdiction of those courts and not to limit the jurisdiction of those courts is expressly stated in section 26-2A-31(e), above.

Previously, there was no similar provision in Alabama law. This was due to the constant participation of the court in curatorship activities which was required under the present statutory scheme in effect.

§ 26-2A-155. Preservation of estate plan; right to examine.

In (i) investing the estate, (ii) selecting assets of the estate for distribution under subsections (a) and (b) of Section 26-2A-153, and (iii) utilizing powers of revocation or withdrawal available for the support of the protected person and exercisable by the conservator or the court, the conservator and the court shall take into account any estate plan of the protected person known to them, including a will, any revocable trust of which the person is settlor, and any contract, transfer, or joint ownership arrangement originated by the protected person with provisions for payment or transfer of benefits or interests at the person's death to another or others. The conservator may examine the will of the protected person. (Acts 1987, No. 87-590, p. 975, § 2-326.)

Comment

This concept or admonition is novel to Alabama law.

§ 26-2A-156. Claims against protected person; enforcement.

(a) A conservator may pay or secure from the estate claims against the estate or against the protected person arising before or after the conservatorship upon their presentation and allowance in accordance with the priorities stated in subsection (d). A claim may be presented by either of the following methods:

(1) The claimant may deliver or mail to the conservator a written statement of the claim indicating its basis, the name and mailing address of the claimant, and the amount claimed; or

(2) The claimant may file a written statement of the claim, in the form prescribed by rules of the court, with the clerk of court and deliver or mail a copy of the statement to the conservator.

(b) A claim is deemed presented on the first to occur of receipt of the written statement of claim by the conservator or the filing of the claim with the court. A presented claim is presumed to be disallowed if receipt of the claim is not acknowledged by written statement mailed by the conservator to the claimant within 60 days after its presentation. The presentation of a claim tolls any statute of limitation relating to the claim until 30 days after its disallowance. A creditor whose debt is secured by a lien on certain property is not required to file a claim under this subsection in order to preserve the creditor's priority to the extent of the security, but the creditor must file a claim under this subsection in order to acquire a priority for the debt to the extent it exceeds the value of the security.

(c) A claimant whose claim has not been paid may petition a court of general jurisdiction for determination of the claim at any time before it is barred by the applicable statute of limitation and, upon due proof, procure an order for its allowance, payment, or security from the estate. If a proceeding is pending against a protected person at the time of appointment of a conservator or is initiated against the protected person thereafter, the moving party shall give notice of the proceeding to the conservator if the proceeding could result in creating a claim against the estate.

(d) If it appears that the estate in conservatorship is likely to be exhausted before all existing claims are paid, the conservator shall distribute the estate in money or in kind in payment of unsecured claims in the following order:

(1) Costs and expenses of administration;

(2) Claims of the federal or state government having priority under other laws;

(3) Claims incurred by the conservator for care, maintenance, and education, previously provided to the protected person or the protected person's dependents;

(4) Claims arising prior to the conservatorship;

(5) All other claims.

(e) No preference may be given in the payment of any claim over any other claim of the same class, and a claim due and payable is not entitled to a preference over claims not due; but if it appears that the assets of the conservatorship are adequate to meet all existing claims, the court, acting in the best interest of the protected person, may order the conservator to give a mortgage or other security on the conservatorship estate to secure payment at some future date of any or all claims in class 5. (Acts 1987, No. 87-590, p. 975, § 2-327.)

Comment

The establishment of preferences by categories of claims for conservatorships is new in this chapter and was not previously provided for in the Alabama law, which provided only for the sale of property to satisfy claims incurred prior to the appointment of a guardian. Thereafter, only claims for maintenance or education of the ward and his family were to be paid. See Ala. Code (1975) sections 26-4-64 and 26-4-65. The last sentence of subsection (b) with regard to secured claims is not in the Uniform Act. It has been added in this chapter in order to make the handling of claims in conservatorships consistent with the handling of claims in decedents' estates, where the policy adopted here has been established for some time. See, e.g., Jones v. McLauchlin, 293 Ala. 31, 299 So.2d 723 (1974); and Rives v. Cabel, 213 Ala. 206, 104 So. 420 (1925).

A "receipt," signed by the conservator for having received goods or services represented, satisfies the presentation of the claim and acknowledgment required in subsection (b).

Statutes to be repealed: Ala. Code (1975) sections 26-4-64 and 26-4-65.

§ 26-2A-157. Personal liability of conservator.

(a) Unless otherwise provided in the contract, a conservator is not personally liable on a contract properly entered into in fiduciary capacity in the course of administration of the estate unless the conservator fails to reveal the representative capacity and identify the estate in the contract.

(b) The conservator is personally liable for obligations arising from ownership or control of property of the estate or for torts committed in the course of administration of the estate only if personally at fault.

(c) Claims based on (i) contracts entered into by a conservator in fiduciary capacity, (ii) obligations arising from ownership or control of the estate, or (iii) torts committed in the course of administration of the estate, may be asserted against the estate by proceeding against the conservator in fiduciary capacity, whether or not the conservator is personally liable therefor.

(d) Any question of liability between the estate and the conservator personally may be determined in a proceeding for accounting, surcharge, or indemnification, or other appropriate proceeding or action. (Acts 1987, No. 87-590, p. 975, § 2-328.)

Comment

Alabama previously did not have a comprehensive provision for conservator liability. The only liabilities specifically addressed by the Alabama statutes were those for defective title to land purchased for the ward (Ala. Code (1975) section 26-4-122) and for depreciation in the value of land purchased with a ward's money. Ala. Code (1975) section 26-4-120 (A guardian is liable for the former event, but not the latter.). Otherwise it must be assumed that only common-law principles controlled the liability of a guardian in Alabama.

Statutes to be repealed: Ala. Code (1975) sections 26-4-120 and 26-4-122.

Code commissioner's note. — The cases cited below were decided under prior law.

Former §§ 26-4-3 and 26-4-120 are to be construed in pari materia. Sims v. Russell, 236 Ala. 562, 183 So. 862 (1938).

A guardian making an investment for his ward is bound to act honestly and faithfully and exercise a sound discretion such as men of ordinary prudence and intelligence use in their own affairs, and if he is negligent in this respect he must answer for any resulting loss. He is not, however, an insurer of the safety of the investments, and if he acts in good faith, using due care and prudence and having regard to the best pecuniary interest of the ward, he will not be liable for any loss arising out of the transaction, although he may have committed an error of judgment in respect to the transaction out of which the loss arose. Brewer v. Ernest, 81 Ala. 435, 2 So. 84 (1887); Hall v. Esslinger, 235 Ala. 451, 179 So. 639 (1938).

Guardian has no authority to incur debt on behalf of ward in purchase of lands, and no power to give mortgage thereon, or to take bond for title leaving an unpaid balance as burden on ward's estate. Ward v. Jossen, 218 Ala. 530, 119 So. 220 (1928).

Former §§ 26-4-120 and 26-4-121 have no application to loan secured by real estate mortgage. — Former §§ 26-4-120 and § 26-4-121 which deal with the purchase of real estate by the guardian with funds of the ward, with title in the ward, have no application to a mere loan of money by the guardian secured by a mortgage on real estate. Such a transaction is not a purchase of real estate, which is the subject matter of former § 26-4-120. Kelly v. Wilson, 234 Ala. 455, 175 So. 551 (1937), overruling Howell v. Ward, 230 Ala. 379, 161 So. 487 (1935).

Collateral references. — 39 C.J.S., Guardian & Ward, § 84.

39 Am. Jur. 2d, Guardian & Ward, §§ 88-93.

Power of guardian after mortgaging infant's real property. 95 ALR 839.

§ 26-2A-158. Termination of proceedings.

(a) The protected person, conservator, or any other interested person may petition the court to terminate the conservatorship. A protected person seeking termination is entitled to the same rights and procedures as in an original proceeding for a protective order. If the conservator has accounted to the formerly protected person, no accounting is necessary. The court, upon determining after notice and hearing that the minority or disability of the protected person has ceased, shall terminate the conservatorship. Upon termination, title to assets of the estate passes to the formerly protected person or to successors. The order of termination must provide for expenses of administration and direct the conservator to execute appropriate instruments to evidence the transfer.

(b) A conservator appointed by any court of this state, on termination or removal of the protected person's minority or disability, may present a verified petition to the court in which the conservatorship is pending, praying for a final consent settlement by and between the conservator and the protected person. If the consent settlement is agreed to by the protected person in a written instrument signed by the protected person and acknowledged as conveyances of real estate are acknowledged, the court may approve the settlement without notice. The agreement of the protected person may be expressed by joining in the petition with the conservator or by a separate written instrument. Any final settlement so approved by the court shall have the same force and effect as settlements made in compliance with subsection (a). (Acts 1987, No. 87-590, p. 975, § 2-329.)

Comment

Persons entitled to notice of a petition to terminate a conservatorship are identified by section 26-2A-134.

Subsection (a) follows the Uniform Guardianship and Protective Proceedings Act in providing for final settlement by the conservator in court. Subsection (b) re-enacts in substance former Ala. Code, section 26-5-12 (1975) that provides for final settlements by consent in some situations. The consent settlement is a slightly different approach, but it is consistent in policy with approval of a kind of "consent accounting" to the formerly protected person under section 26-2A-147 and the last sentence added to subsection (a) further recognizes such accountings.

Any interested person may seek the termination of a conservatorship if there is some question as to whether the trust is still needed. In some situations (e.g., the individual who returns after being missing) it may be perfectly clear that the person is no longer in need of a conservatorship. By way of comparison, Alabama law previously required that the protected person, a next friend, or his guardian must petition the court and bring forth proof of his capabilities. See, Ala. Code (1975) sections 26-2-51 and 26-2-55. See also Ala. Code (1975, as amended by Act No. 79-701) section 26-7A-14.

An order terminating a conservatorship may be recorded as evidence of the transfer of title from the estate. See, section 26-2A-149.

Statutes to be modified: Ala. Code (1975) sections 26-2-51 and 26-2-55.

§ 26-2A-159. Payment of debt and delivery of property to foreign conservator without local proceedings.

(a) Any person indebted to a protected person or having possession of property or of an instrument evidencing a debt, stock, or chose in action belonging to a protected person may pay or deliver it to a conservator, guardian of the estate, or other like fiduciary appointed by a court of the state of residence of the protected person upon being presented with proof of appointment and an affidavit made by or on behalf of the fiduciary stating:

(1) That no protective proceeding relating to the protected person is pending in this state; and

(2) That the foreign fiduciary is entitled to payment or to receive delivery.

(b) If the person to whom the affidavit is presented is not aware of any protective proceeding pending in this state, payment or delivery in response to the demand and affidavit discharges the debtor or possessor. (Acts 1987, No. 87-590, p. 975, § 2-330.)

Comment

Section 26-2A-138(1) gives a foreign conservator or guardian of property, appointed in the jurisdiction in which the disabled person resides, first priority for appointment as conservator in this state. A foreign conservator may easily obtain any property in this state and take it to the residence of the protected person for management.

Alabama statutes previously dealt with the foreign guardian by authorizing an Alabama court to order removal of property to the state of residence of the guardian. Ala. Code (1975) sections 26-8-40 through 26-8-50. This chapter focuses on the residence of the protected person and authorizes discharge of liability through payment of a debt or delivery of property to the foreign conservator appointed where the protected person resides and without a court order.

Statutes to be modified: Ala. Code (1975) sections 26-8-40 through 26-8-46 and 26-8-48 through 26-8-50.

§ 26-2A-160. Foreign conservator; proof of authority; bond; powers.

If a conservator has not been appointed in this state and no petition in a protective proceeding is pending in this state, a conservator appointed in the state in which the protected person resides may file in a court of this state in a [county] in which property belonging to the protected person is located, authenticated copies of letters of appointment and of any bond. Thereafter, the domiciliary foreign conservator may exercise as to assets in this state all powers of a conservator appointed in this state and may maintain actions and proceedings in this state subject to any conditions imposed upon nonresident parties generally. (Acts 1987, No. 87-590, p. 975, § 2-331.)

Comment

The prior Alabama statute was much more restrictive than this chapter in that the foreign guardian "must produce a transcript from the records of a court of competent jurisdiction, certified according to the act of congress ...." to satisfy the credentials requirement. Ala. Code (1975) section 26-8-46. This chapter is much simpler in that "authenticated copies of letters of appointment and of any bond" will satisfy the credentials requirements for a foreign conservator.

Statute to be modified: Ala. Code (1975) section 26-8-46.

CHAPTER 3.

BONDS OF GUARDIANS.

Collateral references. — 39 C.J.S., Guardian & Ward, §§ 31-36.

Judgment in guardian's final accounting proceedings as res judicata in ward's subsequent action against guardian. 34 ALR4th 1121.

§ 26-3-1. Generally.

Before the issue of letters of conservatorship, other than letters to the general conservator or to the sheriff, the judge of probate must require the conservator appointed to enter into bond with sufficient sureties, payable to the judge of probate, in a penalty prescribed by him. (Code 1886, §§ 2378, 2406; Code 1896, § 2272; Code 1907, § 4362; Code 1923, § 8135; Code 1940, T. 21, § 27; Acts 1987, No. 87-590, p. 975, § 2-333(b).)

Cross references. — As to actions on official bonds of guardians, see § 6-5-30 et seq. As to liability of guardian (sheriff) upon termination of official office, see notes under § 26-2-27.

Cited in Donnell v. Jones, 17 Ala. 689 (1850); Pittman v. Pittman, 419 So. 2d 1376 (Ala. 1982); Duke v. Duke, 522 So. 2d 258 (Ala. 1988).

Collateral references. — 39 C.J.S., Guardian & Ward, § 32.

39 Am. Jur. 2d, Guardian & Ward, § 48.

Leave of court as prerequisite to action on statutory bond. 2 ALR 563.

Invalidity of designation of fiduciary as affecting liability on bond. 18 ALR 274.

Right of sureties on bond to take advantage of noncompliance with statutory requirement as to approval of bond. 77 ALR 1479.

Liability or sureties on bond of guardian for defalcation or deficit occurring before bond was given. 82 ALR 585.

Accounting by guardian as a necessary condition to action on his bond. 119 ALR 83.

Right of surety on bond of guardian to terminate liability as regards future defaults of principal. 150 ALR 485.

§ 26-3-2. Bonds of certain guardians for sale of lands of wards.

Repealed by Acts 1987, No. 87-590, p. 975, § 2-333(a), effective January 1, 1988.

§ 26-3-3. Relief of testamentary conservator of minor from requirement of giving bond and effect thereof.

A testator may by his last will relieve the conservator of his appointment for a minor child or children from giving bond and sureties for the faithful performance of his duties as conservator, but the authority of such conservator shall not extend to any other property or estate of such minor child or children than such as is derived by gift, devise, descent or distribution from the testator, unless he gives bond, with sufficient sureties, as is required of other conservators. (Code 1852, § 2018; Code 1867, § 2417; Code 1876, § 2762; Code 1886, § 2379; Code 1896, § 2274; Code 1907, § 4364; Code 1923, § 8137; Code 1940, T. 21, § 29; Acts 1987, No. 87-590, p. 975, § 2-333(b).)

Cited in Bank of Mobile v. Planters', etc., Bank, 9 Ala. 645 (1846); Walker v. Cuthbert, 10 Ala. 213 (1846); King v. Seals, 45 Ala. 415 (1871); Morrow v. Wood, 56 Ala. 1 (1876); Brunson v. Brooks, 68 Ala. 248 (1880).

Collateral references. — 39 C.J.S., Guardian & Ward, § 33.

§ 26-3-4. Requirement by probate court of bond from testamentary conservator of minor; effect of failure to give bond.

Before the issue of letters of conservatorship to a testamentary conservator relieved from giving bond and sureties or at any time thereafter, if the judge of probate deems it necessary for the safety of such minor child or children, he may require of such conservator bond with sufficient sureties, or, on the application of such minor child or children by next friend and for good cause shown, he may require of such conservator bond with sufficient sureties. In either case, if such conservator fails for 10 days after the requisition of such bond to give the same, the judge of probate must withhold from his letters of conservatorship or, if letters have issued, must remove him and recall and revoke such letters. (Code 1852, § 2018; Code 1867, § 2417; Code 1876, § 2762; Code 1886, § 2380; Code 1896, § 2275; Code 1907, § 4365; Code 1923, § 8138; Code 1940, T. 21, § 30; Acts 1987, No. 87-590, p. 975, § 2-333(b).)

Collateral references. — 39 C.J.S., Guardian & Ward, § 33.

§ 26-3-5. General conservator for county.

The general conservator of the county must give bond, with at least two good and sufficient sureties, in a penalty to be prescribed by the judge of probate and payable to him, with condition to faithfully perform all the duties which are or may be required of him by law during the time he acts as such conservator. (Code 1867, § 2424; Code 1876, § 2766; Code 1886, § 2381; Code

1896, § 2276; Code 1907, § 4366; Code 1923, § 8139; Code 1940, T. 21, § 31; Acts 1987, No. 87-590, p. 975, § 2-333(b).)

Cited in East v. East, 80 Ala. 199 (1885).

§ 26-3-6. Sheriff appointed as guardian; effect of failure to give bond.
Repealed by Acts 1987, No. 87-590, p. 975, § 2-333(a), effective January 1, 1988.

§ 26-3-7. Requirement of new or additional bond from conservator; effect of failure to give same.

The judge of probate shall have authority and it shall be his duty, whenever he deems it necessary for the safety of the ward, to require the conservator to give a new or additional bond. If, on notice of such requisition, such conservator fails for 10 days to give such new or additional bond, the judge is authorized to remove him and revoke his letters. (Code 1852, § 2019; Code 1867, § 2418; Code 1876, § 764; Code 1886, §§ 2384, 2408; Code 1896, § 2278; Code 1907, § 4368; Code 1923, § 8141; Code 1940, T. 21, § 33; Acts 1987, No. 87-590, p. 975, § 2-333(b).)

§ 26-3-8. Giving of new bond by conservator upon application for discharge from liability of surety — Required; effect of failure to give bond.

Upon the application in writing of any surety or sureties upon the bond of a conservator requesting to be discharged from future liability as such surety or sureties or upon the application in writing of the personal representative or of an heir or devisee of a deceased surety upon such bond requesting that the estate of such deceased surety be discharged from future liability by reason of such suretyship, it shall be the duty of the court to give such conservator notice of such application and to require him, within 15 days after the service of the notice, to make a new bond. Upon the failure to make such bond, such conservator shall be removed and his letters revoked and upon such removal he shall make settlement of his conservatorship. Any number of persons having the right to make application under this section may join in the application. (Code 1852, § 2019; Code 1867, § 2418; Code 1876, § 2764; Code 1886, §§ 2385, 2409; Code 1896, § 2279; Code 1907, § 4369; Code 1923, § 8142; Code 1940, T. 21, § 34; Acts 1987, No. 87-590, p. 975, § 2-333(b).)

§ 26-3-9. Giving of new bond by conservator upon application for discharge from liability of surety — Effect of giving of new bond upon liability of surety.

When a new bond is given under Section 26-3-8, the surety on whose application or the estate of the deceased surety on whose behalf the application was made, as the case may be, is discharged as to all breaches subsequent to the execution and approval of the new bond. (Code 1896, § 2280; Code 1907, § 4370; Code 1923, § 8143; Code 1940, T. 21, § 35.)

§ 26-3-10. Bonds of certain conservators to have force and effect of statutory bonds.

The bond of the general conservator of the county or of the conservator of a minor or of an incapacitated person is valid and operative as a statutory bond and is of the same obligation, force and effect as a statutory bond, though it may not be approved or in the penalty or payable or with the condition required by law. (Code 1886, § 2387; Code 1896, § 2281; Code 1907, § 4371; Code 1923, § 8144; Code 1940, T. 21, § 36; Acts 1987, No. 87-590, p. 975, § 2-333(b).)

§ 26-3-11. Liability of sureties upon certain conditionally executed bonds.

A surety on the bond of the general conservator of the county or on the bond of the conservator of a minor or an incapacitated person cannot avoid liability thereon on the ground that he signed or delivered it on condition that it should not be delivered to the judge of probate or should not become perfect unless it was executed by some other person who does not execute it. (Code 1886, § 2388; Code 1896, § 2282; Code 1907, § 4372; Code 1923, § 8145; Code 1940, T. 21, § 37; Acts 1987, No. 87-590, p. 975, § 2-333(b).)

Bonds otherwise invalid are made valid by this section. — Though the failure of the principal to execute the bond prevents it being good as a statutory bond, this section makes it good as a common-law bond. Matthews v. Mauldin, 142 Ala. 434, 38 So. 849 (1905).

Cited in Birmingham News Co. v. Moseley, 225 Ala. 45, 141 So. 689 (1932).

§ 26-3-12. Approval, filing and recordation of bonds.

All bonds given by conservators must be approved by the judge of probate issuing the letters of conservatorship and must be filed and recorded in his office. (Code 1852, § 2020; Code 1867, § 2419; Code 1876, § 2763; Code 1886, § 2386; Code 1896, § 2284; Code 1907, § 4374; Code 1923, § 8147; Code 1940, T. 21, § 39; Acts 1987, No. 87-590, p. 975, § 2-333(b).)

Cited in Noble & Bro. v. Cullom & Co., 44 Ala. 554 (1870).

§ 26-3-13. Liability of probate judge, etc., for neglect or omission in taking bonds.

The judge of probate and the sureties on his official bond are liable to any person injured for any neglect or omission of the judge in not taking from a conservator a good and sufficient bond or for taking thereon insufficient surety or for the neglect or omission to require the execution of a new or of an additional bond in the cases in which such bond is required by law, if he knows or has good cause to believe that the case exists in which such new or additional bond should be required. (Code 1886, § 2389; Code 1896, § 2283; Code 1907, § 4373; Code 1923, § 8146; Code 1940, T. 21, § 38; Acts 1987, No. 87-590, p. 975, § 2-333(b)).)

Judge's liability is independent of guardian's liability. — The liability of a judge of probate and sureties on his official bond are independent of that of a guardian dealing with and in the settlement of the estate of a ward. Wilbanks v. Mitchell, 237 Ala. 3, 184 So. 894 (1938).

The determination of the sufficiency of a proffered surety is a judicial act, "the result of judgment or discretion." Cole v. Hartford Accident & Indem. Co., 379 F. Supp. 1265 (M.D. Ala. 1974).

Cited in Rowe v. Johnson, 214 Ala. 510, 108 So. 604 (1926).

§ 26-3-14. Reduction of conservator's bond upon partial settlement of estate.

Upon the filing of any partial settlement by the conservator of a minor or an incapacitated person in the court in which such estate is pending, such conservator may pray for a reduction in the amount of his bond as such conservator. Thereupon, the court must set a day for the hearing of such partial settlement and must cause notices to be issued to all parties in interest as is now provided by law for final settlements of such estates and, on the day set for hearing, the court may fix the amount to which the bond shall be reduced, which shall be determined as now provided by law for such bonds. (Acts 1939, No. 560, p. 883; Code 1940, T. 21, § 40; Acts 1987, No. 87-590, p. 975, § 2-333(b)).)

CHAPTER 4.

POWERS AND DUTIES OF GUARDIANS GENERALLY.

REPEALED.

§§ 26-4-1 through 26-4-155. Repealed by Acts 1987, No. 87-590, p. 975, § 2-333(a), effective January 1, 1988.

Cross references. — For present provisions relating to powers and duties of guardians, see the Alabama Uniform Guardianship and Protective Proceedings Act, § 26-2A-1 et seq.

CHAPTER 5.

SETTLEMENTS OF ACCOUNTS OF CONSERVATORS.

ARTICLE 1.

IN GENERAL.

Cross references. — As to correction by circuit court of errors of law or fact in settlement of accounts of guardians in probate court, see § 12-11-60.

Collateral references. — 39 Am. Jur. 2d, Guardian & Ward, §§ 162-186.

§ 26-5-1. Jurisdiction.

The court of probate from which the appointment of a conservator is derived has jurisdiction of the settlement, partial or final, of the accounts of the conservator. (Code 1886, § 2453; Code 1896, § 2338; Code 1907, § 4428; Code 1923, § 8201; Code 1940, T. 21, § 128; Acts 1987, No. 87-590, p. 975, § 2-333(b).)

Jurisdiction of probate court is statutory. — The jurisdiction of the court of probate in the matter of the final settlement of the guardianship of minors is limited and statutory. Lewis v. Allred, 57 Ala. 628 (1877).

Ward's only remedy to prevent removal is mandamus. — Mandamus held ward's only remedy to prevent removal of guardianship from probate court after circuit court's void order directing removal. Ex parte Chapman, 225 Ala. 168, 142 So. 540 (1932).

Annual or semiannual settlements of accounts of a guardian may be opened or reconsidered before, during or after final settlement of the guardian's accounts, where proceedings are instituted within the time limits prescribed by statute. Hastings v. Huber, 241 Ala. 160, 1 So. 2d 749 (1941).

Cited in United States Fid. & Guar. Co. v. Pittman, 183 Ala. 602, 62 So. 784 (1913).

Collateral references. — 39 C.J.S., Guardian & Ward, §§ 46(f), 50(d), 153.

39 Am. Jur. 2d, Guardian & Ward, § 163.

Refusal or failure of guardian to pay over, or account for, funds, as contempt. 134 ALR 927.

§ 26-5-2. Partial settlement — When required; filing of account and vouchers by conservator; appointment of guardian ad litem for ward.

If not otherwise directed, the conservator must, at least once in three years, file in the court of probate an account of his guardianship, accompanied with the vouchers showing his receipts and disbursements, which must be verified by affidavit. Upon the filing of such account and vouchers the court must appoint a guardian ad litem to represent the ward. (Code 1852, § 2022; Code 1867, § 2421; Code 1876, § 2771; Code 1886, § 2454; Code 1896, § 2339; Code 1907, § 4429; Code 1923, § 8202; Code 1940, T. 21, § 129; Acts 1987, No. 87-590, p. 975, § 2-333(b).)

Award of commissions and attorney fees not set aside. — Award of guardian ad litem commissions and attorney fees in a partial settlement hearing was not set aside where, although there was no guardian ad litem appointed to represent the ward at the partial settlement hearing as required by this section, it was clear from the record that the probate judge, at the time of the final settlement hearing, examined each item of expense, cover-ing the period of the guardianship, as to which the executor raised an objection. Humphries v. Lynch, 579 So. 2d 612 (Ala. 1991).

Cited in Agee v. Williams, 30 Ala. 636 (1857); Childress v. Childress, 49 Ala. 237 (1873); Pittman v. Pittman, 419 So. 2d 1376 (Ala. 1982).

Collateral references. — 39 C.J.S., Guardian & Ward, § 143.

39 Am. Jur. 2d, Guardian & Ward, § 165.

§ 26-5-3. Partial settlement — Establishment of day for settlement; notice thereof.

The court must also appoint a day for the settlement, of which notice must be given, as the court may direct, either by advertisement for three successive weeks in a newspaper published in the county or for the same length of time by posting notice at the courthouse door and at three other public places in the county. (Code 1886, § 2455; Code 1896, § 2340; Code 1907, § 4430; Code 1923, § 8203; Code 1940, T. 21, § 130.)

Collateral references. — 39 C.J.S., Guardian & Ward, § 154.

§ 26-5-4. Partial settlement — Examination of vouchers and auditing and stating of account; taxing of costs for contest or examination where vouchers or items rejected.

On the day appointed or on any other day to which the settlement may be continued, the court must proceed to examine the vouchers and to audit and state the account, requiring evidence in support of all such vouchers or items of the account as may be contested or as may not on examination appear to the court to be just and proper, such evidence to be taken by affidavit or by any other legal mode. If any voucher or item be rejected, all costs accruing on the contest or examination thereof must be taxed against the conservator personally. (Code 1886, § 2456; Code 1896, § 2341; Code 1907, § 4431; Code 1923, § 8204; Code 1940, T. 21, § 131; Acts 1987, No. 87-590, p. 975, § 2-333(b).)

There is no fixed rule for keeping guardianship accounts, the purpose of which is to furnish evidence of the condition of the estate that the court may correctly adjudicate the rights of the parties. Hastings v. Huber, 241 Ala. 160, 1 So. 2d 749 (1941).

Where presumption that money spent is charge against wards' property. — Where mother, as guardian, had management of minor children's property, presumption on subsequent settlement upon mother's death was that support and education of minors were a charge upon minors' property, where mother possessed no property or income. Farmer v. Coleman, 231 Ala. 527, 165 So. 778 (1936).

Cited in McGowan v. Milner, 195 Ala. 44, 70 So. 175 (1915).

§ 26-5-5. Partial settlement — Rendition and recordation of decree as to vouchers and account; recordation of account and vouchers.

After the examination of the vouchers, and the audit and statement of the account, the court must render a decree passing the same and declaring the amount of the charge against the conservator and of the credits allowed, which must be entered of record. The account and vouchers must be recorded. (Code 1886, § 2457; Code 1896, § 2342; Code 1907, § 4432; Code 1923, § 8205; Code 1940, T. 21, § 132; Acts 1987, No. 87-590, p. 975, § 2-333(b).)

Collateral references. — 39 C.J.S., Guardian & Ward, § 157.

§ 26-5-6. Partial settlement — Presumption as to correctness upon final settlement; reexamination, etc., of items of account.

Upon the final settlement, a partial settlement must be taken and presumed as correct, but any item of the account may be reexamined and, if, on reexamination, it is found incorrect, the item must be disallowed or allowed only so far as its correctness may appear. (Code 1886, § 2458; Code 1896, § 2343; Code 1907, § 4433; Code 1923, § 8206; Code 1940, T. 21, § 133.)

Partial settlement not reviewable on appeal. — Partial settlements under this section are not reviewable by appeal except after final settlement in view of § 12-22-21. Cunningham v. Cunningham, 215 Ala. 484, 111 So. 208 (1927).

As to presumption that failure to invest surplus money of ward is accounted for in partial settlement, see Thompson v. Thompson, 92 Ala. 545, 9 So. 465 (1891).

Collateral references. — Conclusiveness and effect of settlement of annual or intermediate accounts of guardian of infant or incompetent. 99 ALR 996.

§ 26-5-7. Final settlement generally — When required.

On the death, resignation or removal of the conservator or on the expiration of his authority otherwise or on the arrival of the ward at full age or on termination of the ward's incapacity or on his death or on the marriage of the ward, if 18 years of age or older or upon the ward becoming 18 years of age after marriage or after becoming a widow or widower, a final settlement of the conservatorship must be made, such settlement in the event of the death of the conservator to be made by his personal representative. (Code 1886, § 2459; Code 1896, § 2344; Code 1907, § 4434; Code 1923, § 8207; Code 1940, T. 21, § 134; Acts 1951, No. 31, p. 241; Acts 1987, No. 87-590, p. 975, § 2-333(b).)

The final settlement is strictly a judicial proceeding, having all the elements of an action, and the decree rendered has the force, finality and dignity of a judgment. It ascertains and settles conclusively the extent of the liability of the guardian and the rights of the ward. Lee v. Lee, 55 Ala. 590 (1876); Randall v. Wadsworth, 130 Ala. 633, 31 So. 555 (1900).

Final settlement is not allowed during continuance of relationship. — The probate court has no jurisdiction to proceed to a final settlement of the guardianship of a female ward while the relation of guardian continues, the ward being a minor and unmarried; and consequently such a settlement cannot operate a bar to a filing for account and final settlement filed by the ward after her marriage. Lewis v. Allred, 57 Ala. 628 (1877).

A settlement of the guardian's accounts in the probate court, made during the minority of the ward, before resignation of the guardian, and without appointment of a guardian ad litem, is void for want of jurisdiction. Cox v. Johnson, 80 Ala. 22 (1885).

Sureties of deceased guardian not excused from liability. — Sureties of deceased guardian were not excused from liability by final settlement of administration of guardian's insolvent estate, on theory that this had effect of discharging estate from liability on decree on final settlement of guardianship. Warren v. Ellis, 227 Ala. 497, 150 So. 484 (1933).

Consideration of whole account. — In settlement of guardian's final account, court could look to the whole of the guardian's account to find the truth of challenged matters. Hastings v. Huber, 241 Ala. 160, 1 So. 2d 749 (1941).

Restoration of sanity does not remove guardian. — A Florida decree that Florida resident had been restored to sanity made it duty of Alabama ancillary guardian to make a final settlement of his guardianship, but did not ipso facto remove or discharge him. Ward v. Stallworth, 243 Ala. 651, 11 So. 2d 374 (1942).

But guardian should make final settlement. — Where ancillary guardian was appointed in Alabama for Florida resident adjudicated insane in Florida, adjudication that ward was restored to sanity, by a competent Florida court within its jurisdiction properly invoked, would not ipso facto serve to revoke letters of guardianship, discharge power of Alabama guardian or restore Alabama property to ward's custody, but would be ground for order of revocation and for requiring guardian to make settlement under this section. Ward v. Stallworth, 243 Ala. 651, 11 So. 2d 374 (1942).

Cited in Blue v. United States Fid. & Guar. Co., 228 Ala. 239, 153 So. 150 (1934); Howell v. Ward, 230 Ala. 379, 161 So. 487 (1935); Ex parte Garrison, 260 Ala. 379, 71 So. 2d 33 (1954); Pittman v. Pittman, 419 So. 2d 1376 (Ala. 1982).

Collateral references. — 39 C.J.S., Guardian & Ward, §§ 143, 146, 147, 160, 166.

39 Am. Jur. 2d, Guardian & Ward, §§ 172-175.

§ 26-5-8. Final settlement generally — Filing of account and vouchers by conservator; appointment of guardian ad litem for ward.

The conservator, or his personal representative, must file in the court of probate a full account of the conservatorship, accompanied by the vouchers and verified by affidavit. Upon the filing of such account and vouchers, the court must appoint a guardian ad litem to represent the ward if he be a minor or otherwise incapacitated. (Code 1886, § 2460; Code 1896, § 2345; Code 1907, § 4435; Code 1923, § 8208; Code 1940, T. 21, § 135; Acts 1987, No. 87-590, p. 975, § 2-333(b).)

Cited in Vreeland v. Marshall, 584 So. 2d 809 (Ala. 1991).

§ 26-5-9. Final settlement generally — Establishment of day for settlement; notice thereof.

The court must appoint a day for the settlement, of which 10 days' notice must be given to the succeeding conservator, if there is such conservator, or to the personal representative of the ward, if the ward is dead, or to the ward, if he is a resident of the state and has arrived at full age or has been relieved of the disability of nonage or incapacity has terminated, and to all sureties on the bond of such conservator, by the service of process, and notice must also be given, as the court may direct, either by advertisement for three successive weeks in some newspaper published in the county or for the same length of time by posting notice at the courthouse door and at three other public places in the county. (Code 1886, § 2461; Code 1896, § 2346; Code 1907, § 4436; Code 1923, § 8209; Acts 1931, No. 704, p. 829; Code 1940, T. 21, § 136; Acts 1987, No. 87-590, p. 975, § 2-333(b).)

Cited in Rittenberry v. Wharton, 176 Ala.
390, 58 So. 293 (1912).

§ 26-5-10. Final settlement generally — Examination of vouchers and auditing and stating of account; taxing of costs for contest or examination where voucher or items rejected.

On the day appointed or on any other day to which the settlement may be continued, the court must proceed to examine the vouchers and to audit and state the account, requiring evidence in support of all such vouchers or items of the account as may be contested or as may not on examination appear to the court to be just and proper, such evidence to be taken by affidavit or in any other legal mode. If any voucher or item be rejected, all costs accruing on the contest or examination thereof must be taxed against the conservator or his personal representative and not against the ward or his estate. (Code 1886, § 2462; Code 1896, § 2347; Code 1907, § 4437; Code 1923, § 8210; Code 1940, T. 21, § 137; Acts 1987, No. 87-590, p. 975, § 2-333(b).)

Cited in Vreeland v. Marshall, 584 So. 2d
809 (Ala. 1991).

§ 26-5-11. Final settlement generally — Rendition and recordation of decree as to vouchers and account; recordation of account and vouchers.

After the examination of the vouchers and the audit and statement of the account, the court must render a decree passing the same and declaring the amount due the ward, if there be any amount due him, which must be entered of record. The account and vouchers must be recorded. (Code 1886, § 2463; Code 1896, § 2348; Code 1907, § 4438; Code 1923, § 8211; Code 1940, T. 21, § 138.)

Cited in Chancy v. Thweatt, 91 Ala. 329, 8
So. 283 (1890).

§ 26-5-12. Final consent settlement between conservator and ward.

A conservator appointed by any court of this state for a minor or incapacitated person may, on the arrival of his ward at full age or on termination of the ward's incapacity or on removal of his ward's disabilities of nonage by a court of competent jurisdiction or, if the ward is married and has attained the age of 18 years, or if the ward has died, present a verified petition to the court in which the conservatorship is pending, praying for a final consent settlement by and between him and his ward, or the ward's personal representative, if the ward has died. If such consent settlement is agreed to by the ward, or the ward's personal representative, if the ward has died, by a written instrument, signed by him and acknowledged as conveyances of real estate are acknowledged, the court may approve such settlement without notice or publication or posting. The agreement of the ward, or the ward's personal representative, if the ward has died, may be expressed by joining in the petition with his conservator or by a separate written instrument.

Any final settlement, so approved by the court shall have the same force and effect as other settlements made in compliance with the requirements of this article. (Acts 1951, No. 769, p. 1339; Acts 1984, 2nd Ex. Sess., No. 85-49, p. 72, Acts 1987, No. 87-590, p. 975, § 2-333(b).)

§ 26-5-13. Determination, allowance, etc., of conservator's and attorney's fees generally — Annual, partial or final settlements generally.

Upon any annual, partial or final settlement made by any conservator, the court having jurisdiction thereof may fix, determine and allow the fees or other compensation to which such conservator is entitled from an estate up to the time of such settlement and may also fix, determine and allow an attorney's fee or compensation to be paid from such estate to attorneys representing such conservator for services rendered to the time of such settlement. (Acts 1936, Ex. Sess., No. 128, p. 90; Code 1940, T. 21, § 139; Acts 1987, No. 87-590, p. 975, § 2-333(b).)

Award of commissions and attorney fees not set aside although no guardian ad litem appointed. — Award of guardian ad litem commissions and attorney fees in a partial settlement hearing was not set aside where, although there was no guardian ad litem appointed to represent the ward at the partial settlement hearing as required by § 26-5-2, it was clear from the record that the probate judge, at the time of the final settlement hearing, examined each item of expense, covering the period of the guardianship, as to which the executor raised an objection. Humphries v. Lynch, 579 So. 2d 612 (Ala. 1991).

Collateral references. — 39 C.J.S., Guardian & Ward, § 163.

39 Am. Jur. 2d, Guardian & Ward, §§ 184-186.

Guardian's contract employing attorney as binding on ward or his estate. 171 ALR 468.

Amount of attorneys' compensation in matters involving guardianship and trusts. 57 ALR3d 550.

§ 26-5-14. Determination, allowance, etc., of conservator's and attorney's fees generally — Final settlements.

In the allowance of fees to conservators and their attorneys on final settlement the court shall take into consideration such fees as may have been allowed and paid to them prior to such final settlement, but such conservators shall be entitled to full credit for any fees allowed and paid on any annual or partial settlement after notice given as provided for in case of final settlements. (Acts 1936, Ex. Sess., No. 128, p. 90; Code 1940, T. 21, § 141; Acts 1987, No. 87-590, p. 975, § 2-333(b).)

§ 26-5-15. Notice of filing of annual, partial or final settlement; finality of orders or decrees of court as to such settlement, etc., generally; reopening of accounts.

Whenever any conservator shall file any annual, partial or final settlement in any court having jurisdiction thereof, the court shall, at the request of such conservator, require that notice thereof be given in the same manner as required by law in cases of final settlements. Any order or decree of the court on such settlement after such notice shall be final and conclusive as to all items of receipts and disbursements and other transactions and matters shown therein and as to all fees and compensation fixed or allowed to such conservator and attorney, and appeals therefrom shall and must be taken in the manner provided for from any other final decrees of such court. Thereafter, at any time prior to final settlement, the account may be reopened by the court on motion or petition of the conservator or ward or other party having an interest in the estate for amendment or revision if it later appears that the account is incorrect either because of fraud or mistake. (Acts 1936, Ex. Sess., No. 128, p. 90; Code 1940, T. 21, § 140; Acts 1987, No. 87-590, p. 975, § 2-333(b).)

Award of commissions and attorney fees not set aside. — Award of guardian ad litem commissions and attorney fees in a partial settlement hearing was not set aside where, although there was no guardian ad litem appointed to represent the ward at the partial settlement hearing as required by § 26-5-2, it was clear from the record that the probate judge, at the time of the final settlement hearing, examined each item of expense, covering the period of the guardianship, as to which the executor raised an objection. Humphries v. Lynch, 579 So. 2d 612 (Ala. 1991).

Collateral references. — Lapse of time after guardian settlement as affecting liability of guardian or his sureties. 50 ALR 61.

Failure of guardian to disclose self-dealing as ground for vacating order or decree settling account. 132 ALR 1522.

Settlement of account of guardian as precluding attack upon transaction involving self-dealing. 1 ALR2d 1060.

§ 26-5-16. Compensation of conservator — Commissions generally; allowances for actual expenses and for special or extraordinary services rendered; premiums on bond.

A conservator is entitled for his services to reasonable compensation.

On final settlement, an allowance must be made of actual expenses necessarily incurred by him and, for special or extraordinary services rendered, such compensation must be allowed the conservator as is just, but no allowance of actual expenses or for special or extraordinary services must be made except upon an itemized account, verified by affidavit, of such expenses or of such special or extraordinary services, and in its decree the court must state each item for such services for which compensation is allowed. The conservator shall be allowed all reasonable premiums paid on his bond as conservator. (Code 1886, § 2465; Code 1896, § 2350; Code 1907, § 4440; Code 1923, § 8213; Code 1940, T. 21, § 143; Acts 1987, No. 87-590, p. 975, § 2-333(b).)

The word "receipts" as used in this section should carry the same meaning as the word has been given in § 43-2-680, dealing with commissions to which executors and administrators are entitled. It has traditionally been defined to mean the value of the estate coming into the hands of the fiduciary. Gordon v. Brunson, 287 Ala. 535, 253 So. 2d 183 (1971).

This rule of allowance of commissions should be strictly observed by courts of probate. McGowan v. Milner, 195 Ala. 44, 70 So. 175 (1915).

And no sum should be deducted until allowed by a decree of the court. McGowan v. Milner, 195 Ala. 44, 70 So. 175 (1915).

A guardian has no right to deduct any sum for compensation until it has been allowed by a decree of the court. Gordon v. Brunson, 287 Ala. 535, 253 So. 2d 183 (1971).

Where such premature deduction did not forfeit the commissions, interest thereon should be charged. McGowan v. Milner, 195 Ala. 44, 70 So. 175 (1915).

Commissions on "receipts" and "disbursements" are compensation for discharge of ordinary duties incident to administration of ward's estate. McGowan v. Milner, 195 Ala. 44, 70 So. 175 (1915).

No commission for custody and safekeeping of either money or choses in action. — See Alexander v. Alexander, 8 Ala. 796 (1845).

Amount on hand at settlement is not a disbursement. — A guardian is not entitled to commissions on the amount on hand on final settlement, it not being a disbursement. Allen v. Martin, 34 Ala. 442 (1859).

Guardian is entitled to commissions on amount of his receipts and disbursements as shown by the record, and no voucher or proof aliunde is necessary to sustain the item for such credit. Newman v. Reed, 50 Ala. 297 (1874).

Entitled to actual expenses. — See Pinckard v. Pinckard, 24 Ala. 250 (1854).

This section contains no specific $100.00 limitation and such a limitation cannot be reasonably implied to support plaintiff's argument that a guardian's compensation is limited to $100.00, because of the provisions of § 43-2-681; therefore, the trial court's award of $81,630.70 for guardianship fees was authorized by this section, and it was, therefore, proper. Pate v. Bobo, 540 So. 2d 660 (Ala. 1988).

A claim for five dollars per day to cover expenses and loss of time in attending to business of ward is not unreasonable (but was here disallowed for failure to verify by affidavit). McGowan v. Milner, 195 Ala. 44, 70 So. 175 (1915).

Special or extraordinary services do not comprehend ordinary duties. McGowan v. Milner, 195 Ala. 44, 70 So. 175 (1915). See also, O'Neill v. Donnell, 9 Ala. 734 (1846).

Hence lending money is not special service. — Service performed by a guardian in lending his ward's money and compounding the interest thereon does not belong to the class of special or extraordinary services. Allen v. Martin, 36 Ala. 330 (1860). See also, Newberry v. Newberry, 28 Ala. 691 (1856).

Keeping the estate together and lending out money may be an extraordinary service for which compensation is allowable. Reese v. Gresham, 29 Ala. 91 (1856).

Nor is auditing claims against estate. — A guardian is not entitled to extra commissions, over and above those allowed him by law, for his services in auditing a claim presented against the estate of his ward; the claim presenting only the ordinary questions of fact as to whether it had been contracted, was just and reasonable. Brewer v. Ernest, 81 Ala. 435, 2 So. 84 (1887).

Nor is attendance in court on final settlement. — See McGowan v. Milner, 195 Ala. 44, 70 So. 175 (1915).

Facts considered in determining compensation. — In Gould v. Hays, 25 Ala. 426 (1854), it was declared that the court should look to the loss of time, trouble, risk and responsibility which are demanded by the nature of the trust, and actually incurred, and allow such a remuneration as a prudent and just man would under such circumstances consider a fair compensation. McGowan v. Milner, 195 Ala. 44, 70 So. 175 (1915).

Where no special or extraordinary services were shown, court was limited, in making allowance, to the percentage specified in former § 26-5-17, and could not be governed by the testimony of witness as to the value of the services. Neilson v. Cook, 40 Ala. 498 (1867).

Failure to file account does not deprive guardian of compensation. — Under this section, neither failure to file annual accounts nor negligence, which works no injury, and is not mala fides, can deprive a guardian of compensation. Ramsey v. McMillan, 214 Ala. 185, 106 So. 848 (1925).

Neither a failure to file annual accounts, nor negligence which works no injury, when there is no mala fides, can deprive a guardian of his compensation. Neilson v. Cook, 40 Ala. 498 (1867). See also, Powell v. Powell, 10 Ala. 900 (1846).

But no commission is allowed where guardian uses funds in own business. McGowan v. Milner, 195 Ala. 44, 70 So. 175 (1915).

The trial court's award of guardianship

fees in the amount of $81,630.70 was not excessive and inordinate where the record indicated that: defendant personally undertook to dispose of the property; from all indications, he accomplished that undertaking in a prudent and reasonable manner; and by his personal undertaking to dispose of the property, defendant obviated the need of subjecting the transaction to a real estate commission—a real estate commission could have ranged from approximately 3 percent to 10 percent of the sales price. Pate v. Bobo, 540 So. 2d 660 (Ala. 1988).

Collateral references. — 39 C.J.S., Guardian & Ward, § 162.

39 Am. Jur. 2d, Guardian & Ward, §§ 184-186.

Death of guardian as affecting right to compensation. 7 ALR 1595.

Fiduciary's compensation on estate assets distributed in kind. 32 ALR2d 778.

Resignation or removal of executor, administrator, guardian, or trustee, before final administration or before termination of trust, as affecting his compensation. 96 ALR3d 1102.

§ 26-5-17. Compensation of guardian — Commissions on money, personal property, etc., paid or surrendered to ward, etc.

Repealed by Acts 1987, No. 87-590, p. 975, § 2-333(a), effective January 1, 1988.

§ 26-5-18. Enforcement of orders or decrees of probate court against conservator, etc.

The court of probate may, by attachment, compel a conservator to obey its orders or decrees, and all final decrees rendered against a conservator or against the personal representative of the conservator on a final settlement have the force and effect of a judgement at law, on which execution may issue against the conservator or his personal representative and against the sureties of the conservator, whether the principal has signed the bond or not, whether such settlement is voluntary or involuntary and whether such settlement is made by the conservator while living or by his personal representative after his death. Process of garnishment may issue from the court of probate upon such decrees in like cases and manner as it may issue on judgments in courts of record and may, in like manner, be prosecuted to judgment against the garnishee. (Code 1886, § 2464; Code 1896, § 2349; Code 1907, § 4439; Code 1923, § 8212; Code 1940, T. 21, § 142; Acts 1987, No. 87-590, p. 975, § 2-333(b).)

Cross references. — As to attachment, see § 6-6-30 et seq.

Guardian's liability at settlement. — If guardian allowed ward's funds to remain in possession of corporation when he could have collected them, he violated duty involving devastavit, and he and surety were liable, regardless of solvency or insolvency of corporation at time of settlement. Dumas v. Hollins, 228 Ala. 644, 154 So. 781 (1934).

Guardian is chargeable with any property, whether principal or interest, which he could have received by use of reasonable diligence. Dumas v. Hollins, 228 Ala. 644, 154 So. 781 (1934).

Sureties are by section made parties to settlement with right to appear, and may

defend against any decree being rendered against principal or see that decree is rendered only for proper amount. Dumas v. Hollins, 228 Ala. 664, 154 So. 781 (1934).

Decree on final settlement by personal representative of deceased guardian held not conclusive but merely to shift to sureties desiring to resist enforcement of decree burden of asserting defense personal to sureties, since otherwise due process would be denied. Warren v. Ellis, 227 Ala. 497, 150 So. 484 (1933).

Such decree amounts to personal decree against guardian's sureties, though not parties to proceeding. Courson v. Tollison, 226 Ala. 530, 147 So. 635 (1933).

Liability of sureties. — A decree on final settlement of guardianship, lawfully made and without fraud, is conclusive upon and has the force and effect of a judgment against the surety on the guardian's bond. Bean v. Harrison, 213 Ala. 33, 104 So. 244 (1925). An execution may issue against the sureties whether their principal has signed the bond or not. Hannis Distilling Co. v. Lanning, 191 Ala. 280, 68 So. 137 (1915); Watson v. White, 216 Ala. 396, 113 So. 260 (1927). But they are not technically parties, and their liability seems predicated on the fact that the settlement is an act which their principal must perform. Hannis Distilling Co. v. Lanning, 191 Ala. 280, 68 So. 137 (1915). See also, United States Fid. & Guar. Co. v. Harton, 202 Ala. 134, 79 So. 600 (1918).

Liability of successor guardian for failure to collect judgment. — Where judgment against former guardian on final settlement of his guardianship of a non compos was not recorded, and execution was not issued thereon for period of more than six years, although successor guardian was present when the former guardian made his final settlement and knew of the existence of the judgment, all actions on the judgment were barred as to sureties on the former guardian's bonds by the six-year statute of limitations. The successor guardian was chargeable on his final settlement with the amount due on the judgment. Cox v. Williams, 241 Ala. 427, 3 So. 2d 129 (1941).

Execution against bonds of sheriff after expiration of office. — Where sheriff was appointed guardian of a non compos by virtue of his office, and sheriff's official bond served as a guardian's bond but a guardian's bond was subsequently executed, and on expiration of the sheriff's term of office an additional guardian's bond was executed, decree rendered against the guardian after expiration of his term of office as sheriff for funds belonging to the non compos had the effect of a judgment on which execution could have issued against sureties on any or all of the three bonds. Cox v. Williams, 241 Ala. 427, 3 So. 2d 129 (1941).

Cited in Ex parte Chapman, 225 Ala. 168, 142 So. 540 (1932); Blue v. United States Fid. & Guar. Co., 228 Ala. 239, 153 So. 150 (1934).

ARTICLE 2.

COMPULSION OF SETTLEMENT BY PROBATE COURT.

Collateral references. — 39 C.J.S., Guardian & Ward, § 143.

39 Am. Jur. 2d Guardian & Ward, §§ 166, 167.

§ 26-5-30. Partial settlement generally — Authorization and procedure generally.

The court of probate may, at any time it is deemed necessary for the safety of the ward, require a conservator to make partial settlement of his conservatorship. The conservator must have notice of such requirement 10 days before the day appointed for his appearance by service of process and may appear and show, if he can, that such settlement is not necessary. (Code 1886, § 2467; Code 1896, § 2352; Code 1907, § 4442; Code 1923, § 8215; Code 1940, T. 21, § 145; Acts 1987, No. 87-590, p. 975, § 2-333(b).)

§ 26-5-31. Partial settlement generally — Application of ward, etc., for partial settlement; issuance of process to conservator as to hearing thereupon; dismissal of application.

On the application of the ward by next friend or the sureties on the conservator's bond, showing satisfactory cause, the court may issue process to the conservator, requiring him to appear and show cause why he should not make a partial settlement of his conservatorship, of which process there must be service 10 days before the day appointed for the appearance of the conservator. If, on the hearing, it should appear that there is no satisfactory cause for ordering such settlement, the application must be dismissed at the costs of the next friend or the sureties on the conservator's bond, as the case may be. (Code 1886, § 2468; Code 1896, § 2353; Code 1907, § 4443; Code 1923, § 8216; Code 1940, T. 21, § 146; Acts 1987, No. 87-590, p. 975, § 2-333(b).)

§ 26-5-32. Partial settlement generally — Issuance of process requiring conservator to make partial settlement; taxing of costs.

If a conservator fails to make a partial settlement as often as such settlement is required of him, the court must issue process to him, requiring him to make such settlement, and all the costs thereof and of the process must be taxed against him personally and must not be charged against the ward or his estate, unless he appears in answer to the process and shows a satisfactory excuse for his failure and files his accounts and vouchers for such settlement. (Code 1886, § 2469; Code 1896, § 2354; Code 1907, § 4444; Code 1923, § 8217; Code 1940, T. 21, § 147; Acts 1987, No. 87-590, p. 975, § 2-333(b).)

§ 26-5-33. Final settlement generally — Authorization and procedure generally for compulsion of settlement by conservator.

On the termination of a conservatorship by the arrival of the ward at full age by termination of the ward's incapacity or on the expiration of his authority otherwise, the court of probate may issue process requiring the conservator to appear at any time within 10 days after the service thereof, on a day named therein, and file his accounts and vouchers for a final settlement. If the conservator resides without the state, the court of probate may appoint a day for him to appear and file his accounts and vouchers for a final settlement. (Code 1886, § 2470; Code 1896, § 2355; Code 1907, § 4445; Code 1923, § 8218; Code 1940, T. 21, § 148; Acts 1987, No. 87-590, p. 975, § 2-333(b).)

Cited in Vreeland v. Marshall, 584 So. 2d 809 (Ala. 1991).

Collateral references. — 39 C.J.S., Guardian & Ward, §§ 40-44, 47, 48.

§ 26-5-34. Final settlement generally — Authorization and procedure generally for compulsion of settlement by personal representative of conservator.

On the death of a conservator, at any time after the expiration of six months from the qualification of his personal representative, such representative may be required, on 10 days' notice, such notice to be given by the service of process, to appear and make settlement of the conservatorship of his testator or intestate. (Code 1886, § 2471; Code 1896, § 2356; Code 1907, § 4446; Code 1923, § 8219; Code 1940, T. 21, § 149; Acts 1987, No. 87-590, p. 975, § 2-333(b).)

Collateral references. — 39 C.J.S., Guardian & Ward, § 146.

§ 26-5-35. Proceedings upon failure of conservator to obey process to appear and file accounts and vouchers.

If a conservator fails to obey any process requiring him to appear and file his accounts and vouchers for a final or partial settlement, the court of probate may, by attachment, compel his appearance and may, if on appearance he refuses to file such accounts and vouchers or to show good cause for his omission, imprison him for a period not exceeding six months. (Code 1886, § 2472; Code 1896, § 2357; Code 1907, § 4447; Code 1923, § 8220; Code 1940, T. 21, § 150; Acts 1987, No. 87-590, p. 975, § 2-333(b).)

Cross references. — As to attachment, see § 6-6-30 et seq.

Collateral references. — 39 C.J.S., Guardian & Ward, § 145.

§ 26-5-36. Statement of account by court upon failure of conservator or personal representative to file accounts and vouchers after notice.

If a conservator, after notice, fails to file his accounts and vouchers for a final or partial settlement or if the personal representative of a conservator, after notice, fails to file the accounts and vouchers of his testator or intestate for final settlement, the court of probate has authority to state an account against the conservator or against his personal representative from the materials on file or of record in the court and from such evidence as may be adduced, charging such conservator with all wherewith he is by law chargeable and crediting him with all wherewith by law he ought to be credited. (Code 1886, § 2473; Code 1896, § 2358; Code 1907, § 4448; Code 1923, § 8221; Code 1940, T. 21, § 151; Acts 1987, No. 87-590, p. 975, § 2-333(b).)

§ 26-5-37. Notice of statement of account and of day appointed for passing same. Repealed by Acts 1987, No. 87-590, p. 975, § 2-333(a), effective January 1, 1988.

§ 26-5-38. Proceedings upon appearance; filing of accounts and vouchers, etc., by conservator or personal representative on appointed day.

If, on or before the day so appointed, the conservator, or the personal representative of the conservator, if the account is stated against such representative, appears and files his accounts and vouchers for settlement and pays such costs as have accrued under the proceedings, the court must set aside such proceedings and proceed to settlement in the manner prescribed by law on the accounts and vouchers so filed. (Code 1886, § 2475; Code 1896,

§ 2360; Code 1907, § 4450; Code 1923, § 8223; Code 1940, T. 21, § 153; Acts 1987, No. 87-590, p. 975, § 2-333(b).)

§ 26-5-39. Proceedings upon failure of conservator or personal representative to appear and file accounts and vouchers on appointed day.

If such conservator or personal representative fails to appear and file his accounts and vouchers for settlement, any person having an interest may appear and contest such account and the court must hear and determine such contest and, whether such contest be made or not, must render a decree on such account which has the force and effect of a decree rendered on a voluntary settlement by such conservator or personal representative. (Code 1886, § 2476; Code 1896, § 2361; Code 1907, § 4451; Code 1923, § 8224; Code 1940, T. 21, § 154; Acts 1987, No. 87-590, p. 975, § 2-333(b).)

ARTICLE 3.

SETTLEMENT UPON DEATH OF CONSERVATOR.

Collateral references. — 39 C.J.S., Guardian & Ward, § 40.

§ 26-5-50. Filing of account and vouchers for final settlement with succeeding conservator, etc., by sureties on bond of conservator.

In case of the death of a conservator who has not made a final settlement of his conservatorship and when there shall have not been granted letters of administration or testamentary on his estate, the sureties on his official bond may proceed to make settlement of his administration of said estate as conservator in the probate court having jurisdiction thereof by filing an account and vouchers for final settlement with the succeeding conservator or cestui que trust or minors and guardian ad litem where minors are interested. (Acts 1923, § 5935; Code 1940, T. 21, § 155; Acts 1987, No. 87-590, p. 975, § 2-333(b).)

Purpose of section. — The evident purpose of this section and § 26-5-52 is to provide a remedy where no personal representative of the deceased guardian has been appointed. Blue v. United States Fid. & Guar. Co., 228 Ala. 239, 153 So. 150 (1934).

§ 26-5-51. Personal representative of conservator may be made party to settlement proceedings.

Should a personal representative of such deceased conservator be appointed at any time before final decree, any party to the proceeding may on motion have such personal representative of such deceased conservator made a party to such settlement on 10 days' notice. (Code 1923, § 5936; Code 1940, T. 21, § 156; Acts 1987, No. 87-590, p. 975, § 2-333(b).)

§ 26-5-52. Succeeding conservator, etc., may secure order requiring sureties to make settlement in probate court.

In any case where a conservator shall die without having made a final settlement of his conservatorship and a successor is appointed, such succeeding conservator or ward or the cestui que trust may by petition to the court in which such estate is pending have an order requiring the sureties on such bond to make settlement of such estate in said court after 10 days' notice of the day fixed by the judge thereof. (Code 1923, § 5937; Code 1940, T. 21, § 157; Acts 1987, No. 87-590, p. 975, § 2-333(b).)

Purpose of section. — See Blue v. United States Fid. & Guar. Co., 228 Ala. 239, 153 So. 150 (1934).

§ 26-5-53. Settlement conclusive.

In all such cases provided for in Section 26-5-52, the settlement therein provided for shall be final and conclusive against such sureties, save the right of review by appeal or otherwise as now provided by law. (Code 1923, § 5938; Code 1940, T. 21, § 158.)

§ 26-5-54. Issuance of execution, etc., against sureties.

Execution and all other final process may issue against the said sureties on said bond to enforce said judgments. (Code 1923, § 5939; Code 1940, T. 21, § 159.)

CHAPTER 6.

RESIGNATION AND REMOVAL OF GUARDIANS.

REPEALED.

§§ 26-6-1 through 26-6-6. Repealed by Acts 1987, No. 87-590, p. 975, § 2-333(a), effective January 1, 1988.

CHAPTER 7.

CUSTODY OF FUNDS OF MINORS OR PERSONS OF UNSOUND MIND NOT HAVING GUARDIANS BY PROBATE JUDGE.

REPEALED.

§§ 26-7-1 through 26-7-5. Repealed by Acts 1987, No. 87-590, p. 975, § 2-333(a), effective January 1, 1988.

CHAPTER 7A.

APPOINTMENT OF CURATORS.

Cross references. — As to the appointment of guardians generally, see chapter 2 of this title. For provisions relating to the custody of funds of minors or persons of unsound mind not having guardians, see chapter 7 of this title. For provisions relating to the guardianship and commitment of incompetent veterans and their dependents, see chapter 9 of this title. As to intemperates and inebriates, see § 6-6-520, et seq.

Collateral references. — 1 C.J.S., Absentees, §§ 2, 7, 9. 9 C.J.S., Banks and Banking, § 338. 39 C.J.S., Guardian and Ward, § 3. 43 C.J.S., Infants, § 107.

39 Am. Jur. 2d, Guardian and Ward, §§ 1, 77. 63 Am. Jur. 2d, Property, § 37. 77 Am. Jur. 2d, Veterans and Veterans Laws, §§ 53 to 67.

§ 26-7A-1. Probate court; grounds.

Any probate court may appoint a curator to take charge of, manage and conserve the property of any person permanently or temporarily residing in this state, who shall become physically incapacitated, or feeble-minded or epileptic or so mentally or physically defective by reason of age, sickness, use of drugs, the excessive use of alcohol or for other causes that he or she is unable to take care of his or her property, and in consequence thereof, is liable to dissipate or lose the same, or to become the victim of designing persons. (Acts 1979, No. 79-701, p. 1246, § 1; Acts 1983, 2nd Ex. Sess., No. 83-153, p. 162, § 1.)

Code commissioner's note. — Acts 1983, 2nd Ex. Sess., No. 83-153, § 2, provides for the ratification of all curators previously appointed by any probate judge which otherwise qualify under this chapter and in existence on February 22, 1983.

Application of 1983 amendment. — Act 83-153 ratified all curators previously appointed by any probate judge who otherwise qualified under chapter 7A of Title 26. To hold that only the curatorships continuing into

1983 were ratified, while those created in the exact same manner, but which terminated at an earlier date were invalid, would unreasonably discriminate against a narrow class of curators. It would also cast a cloud of doubt on all acts done on behalf of their wards by curators appointed by probate courts pursuant to this section, unless the appointing probate court had been specifically granted general equity jurisdiction, or unless the ward survived to the effective date of the act. There is no rational basis for such a result. Baker v. Johnson, 448 So. 2d 355 (Ala. 1983).

Ward of the court, under this chapter, is someone unable to manage his or her own property, for either physical or mental reasons, and whose property, therefore, requires management by a court-appointed curator. Barnes v. Willis, 497 So. 2d 90 (Ala. 1986).

§ 26-7A-2. Petition; who may file; venue; contents.

The jurisdiction of the court shall be invoked by the filing of a petition in the probate court of the county of his or her residence by the person for whose property a curator is sought; or by either the father, mother, brother, sister, husband, wife or child, grandchild or next of kin of such person; and if any such relative fails to act, then by the sheriff of the county of the domicile or residence of such person, which petition shall set forth the facts and reasons why it is proper, appropriate or reasonably necessary for the best interest of such person that such appointment be made. The petition shall state names and addresses of all members of the immediate family and the names and addresses of husband or wife and next of kin, as particularly as is known to the petitioner. (Acts 1979, No. 79-701, p. 1246, § 2.)

§ 26-7A-3. Service of petition; citation; contents; notice of hearing.

The court shall upon filing of a petition issue a citation to the proposed ward setting forth the time and place of the hearing thereon, which said citation, together with a copy of the petition, shall be personally served upon the proposed ward in the manner provided in subdivision (3) of subsection (c) of Rule 4 and of Rule 4.1 of the Alabama Rules of Civil Procedure, at least 10 days before the hearing. The citation shall state the nature and purpose of the proceedings and specify the legal standard by which the need for a curator is adjudged, as set forth in Sections 26-7A-1 and 26-7A-4, and the legal consequences which may follow from such an appointment, including those set forth in Sections 26-7A-7 and 26-7A-15. The citation shall further inform the proposed ward that he or she will have an opportunity at the hearing to present evidence and to cross-examine adverse witnesses, and that the court will appoint an attorney to represent the proposed ward if he or she has no legal counsel of his or her own.

Notice of the nature of the hearing and of the time and place thereof shall also be mailed by the court, at least 10 days before the hearing, to the spouse of the proposed ward if there be one residing with the ward or known to be residing in the state. (Acts 1979, No. 79-701, p. 1246, § 3.)

§ 26-7A-4. Conduct of hearing; evidentiary standard; decree.

The proposed ward shall have the right to be present at the hearing unless he or she or the guardian ad litem waives such right in writing. At such hearing the court shall take testimony from all witnesses who shall appear for any party to the proceedings and shall have the power to summon any witness requested by any said party. The rules of evidence shall apply, and no hearsay evidence which is not otherwise admissible in a court of law shall be admitted or considered. In such proceedings there is a legal presumption of capacity and the burden of proof shall be on the petitioner to prove by a preponderance of the competent evidence that the proposed ward is incapacitated within the definition set forth in Section 26-7A-1.

If the court shall find by a preponderance of the competent evidence presented at the hearing that the proposed ward is legally incapacitated within the definition set forth in Section 26-7A-1, the court shall appoint a curator of the estate of such ward. Any interested person may intervene with leave of court in such proceedings. (Acts 1979, No. 79-701, p. 1246, § 4.)

Cited in Tillery v. State Dep't of Pensions & Sec., 481 So. 2d 386 (Ala. Civ. App. 1985).

§ 26-7A-5. Appointment of guardian ad litem.

The court shall appoint a guardian ad litem to represent at the hearing the person against whom the proceedings are taken. (Acts 1979, No. 79-701, p. 1246, § 5.)

§ 26-7A-6. Appointment of committee of inquiry.

The court shall appoint a committee consisting of two practicing physicians to inquire into the report of its findings upon the question of the disability of such person. (Acts 1979, No. 79-701, p. 1246, § 6.)

§ 26-7A-7. Effect of decree; ward's subsequent acts.

From and after the rendition of the decree appointing a curator, such person for whom appointed shall be a ward of the court appointing such curator, and the ward shall be wholly incapable of making any contract of gift whatever, or any instrument in writing, of legal force and effect, except after leave of court is granted upon a hearing after notice to the curator and such next of kin as the court shall order given notice of application. (Acts 1979, No. 79-701, p. 1246, § 7.)

Will is "instrument in writing" under this section. — The statutory phrase itself — "any instrument in writing" in this section — clearly includes a will, which is a common and traditional instrument for the disposition of property. Furthermore, when an incapacitated individual attempts to make a will, the situation presents a ripe opportunity for "designing persons" to take advantage of the individual, which the curatorship statutes are generally intended to prevent. The legislature is authorized to treat the act of making a will as one needing the protection of the court. Therefore, a will is an "instrument in writing" within the meaning of this section. If a ward desires to make a legally effective will, then notice and hearing must be provided, and the court's approval must be obtained in accordance with the statute. Barnes v. Willis, 497 So. 2d 90 (Ala. 1986).

Testamentary capacity determined at hearing under this section. — The "sound mind" test still remains the standard for determining testamentary capacity. This holding merely requires that the factual question of testamentary capacity be determined at the hearing under this section, rather than when the will is contested. It is possible that one who is sufficiently mentally incapacitated to require a curator may still possess mental capacity to make a will, because testamentary capacity may be less than the competency to transact the ordinary business of life. A determination to appoint a curator is not an adjudication of testamentary capacity. In regard to situations where the ward is physically incapacitated but mentally competent, the statute may still be applicable and provide a measure of protection. Barnes v. Willis, 497 So. 2d 90 (Ala. 1986).

Collateral references. — Ademption or revocation of specific devise or bequest by guardian, committee, conservator, or trustee of mentally or physically incompetent testator. 84 ALR4th 462.

§ 26-7A-8. Bonds.

(a) *Bond of curator.* — The curator so appointed shall, before entering upon his duties, file with the probate court a good and sufficient bond, approved by the probate judge, with such surety or sureties as required of a guardian's bond, payable to the judge of the probate court in such penal sum as the court shall determine by order and conditioned to faithfully perform his duties according to the requirements of law and orders of the court.

(b) *Additional bond.* — The court may at any time require of the said curator such additional or larger bond as may seem to be proper or necessary to protect the interests of the ward. (Acts 1979, No. 79-701, p. 1246, § 8.)

§ 26-7A-9. Appointing court's powers; allowances for ward; sale, mortgage and leasing of estate.

The court appointing such curator shall have full power over the estate of the ward and allowances to or for the said ward, and may allow and assess against the estate of the ward all reasonable costs incurred in procuring the appointment of said curator and during the curatorship; and shall have full power to enter a decree for the selling, mortgaging or leasing of the real or personal property of the said ward, after the court shall have made an affirmative finding that a mortgage, sale or lease for such purposes is reasonably necessary or expedient (a) for the maintenance and support of the ward or to secure advances for the same, or (b) to discharge existing liens or (c) to protect the ward's estate; such sale, mortgaging or leasing shall be upon such terms and rates as shall be approved by the court, but no property of the ward shall be mortgaged at a rate of interest greater than the legal rate of interest. (Acts 1979, No. 79-701, p. 1246, § 9.)

§ 26-7A-10. Special curator; appointment; duties; powers.

After a curator is appointed and qualified he may move the court for the appointment of a "special curator," to prosecute any causes of action, suits or claims or to recover any property or other assets of the ward or to establish any rights in respect to the ward's estate, and such appointee shall have such powers, duties and responsibilities in respect thereto as the court shall prescribe, to the same extent and with the same limitations as would the principal curator. (Acts 1979, No. 79-701, p. 1246, § 10.)

§ 26-7A-11. Curator's account; procedure for confirmation; hearing; notice.

Every curator shall file annually, and as often as otherwise ordered, in the court making said appointment, a full accounting of the administration of said trust. The curator shall present his accounts to the court in debit and credit form and shall petition the court to have them examined, approved and confirmed finally. The court shall by order direct to whom and what notice, if any, shall be given of the hearing of the petition or motion for approval. (Acts 1979, No. 79-701, p. 1246, § 11.)

§ 26-7A-12. Audit and examination of accounts — Approval; cost.

(a) After filing proof of the service of the notice, the court may thereupon examine or audit the accounts, or may appoint an examiner or auditor to examine and audit such accounts and report thereon to the court.

(b) After the examination or audit of any accounting is completed, the court shall approve or disapprove the same, or any item thereof; and the court may at any time before the curator has been finally discharged, after notice, enter judgment against the curator and his sureties for failing to comply with or abide by the terms and conditions of his bond.

(c) The cost of the audit or examination shall be paid out of the estate, or as the decree of the court shall otherwise direct. (Acts 1979, No. 79-701, p. 1246, § 12.)

§ 26-7A-13. Audit and examination of accounts — Final records.

Upon the death or restoration to legal capacity of the ward, the curator shall file in the office of the probate judge a full and complete account of such items and matters as were not included in any former account confirmed finally. (Acts 1979, No. 79-701, p. 1246, § 13.)

§ 26-7A-14. Ward's recovery; effect; hearing; discharge.

If, at any time the ward shall become able to properly care for himself or his property, he may petition the court, setting forth such fact; and after a hearing, of which due notice shall be given to the curator and some one or more of the family, next of kin or next friend of the said person, as the court shall order, and after the appearance of the ward before the court, if the court shall find that the said person has regained the ability to properly care for his property, the court shall decree accordingly, and shall thereafter discharge the curator upon the rendition of a proper accounting and after same has been confirmed after notice and hearing. (Acts 1979, No. 79-701, p. 1246, § 14.)

§ 26-7A-15. Curator's powers same as guardian's; court's powers.

Except as herein otherwise provided, a curator shall have the powers and be subject to the same duties over and concerning the property of a ward as may be by law had and exercised by the guardians of the property of infants, and the court shall have and exercise the same powers touching such curator and the property of such person as may be by law had and exercised touching the guardian of the property of infants. (Acts 1979, No. 79-701, p. 1246, § 15.)

§ 26-7A-16. Appeals; parties.

Any orders or decrees of the probate court relating to a curatorship may be reviewed as are other orders of such court, and such an appeal may be taken by any person as next friend of the ward or by the curator or by the petitioner. (Acts 1979, No. 79-701, p. 1246, § 16.)

§ 26-7A-17. Provisions cumulative.

The provisions of this chapter are cumulative and shall not be construed to repeal or supersede any laws or parts of laws not directly inconsistent herewith. (Acts 1979, No. 79-701, p. 1246, § 17.)

CHAPTER 8.

REMOVAL OF PERSON OR PROPERTY OF MINORS AND WARDS.

Cited in McConnico v. Stallworth, 43 Ala. 389 (1869); Mobile v. Squires, 49 Ala. 339 (1873); Lavange v. Burke, 50 Ala. 61 (1873); Moses v. Faber, 81 Ala. 445, 1 So. 587 (1887); Broaddus v. Johnson, 235 Ala. 314, 179 So. 215 (1938).

Collateral references. — 39 C.J.S., Guardian & Ward, § 193.
25 Am. Jur. 2d, Domicil, §§ 72, 83.

ARTICLE 1.

GENERAL PROVISIONS.

§ 26-8-1. Applicability of chapter.

The provisions of this chapter are applicable to minors and to incapacitated persons. (Acts 1977, No. 20, p. 28; Acts 1987, No. 87-590, p. 975, § 2-333(b).)

ARTICLE 2.

REMOVAL TO ANOTHER COUNTY.

§ 26-8-20. Authorization generally.

The court of probate or circuit court from which letters of guardianship or conservatorship have issued has authority to order the removal to another county of the person and property of a minor or ward if it is shown that such removal will advance the interests of the minor or ward. (Code 1842, § 2035; Code 1867, § 2445; Code 1876, § 2802; Code 1886, § 2483; Code 1896, § 2368; Code 1907, § 4458; Code 1923, § 8231; Code 1940, T. 21, § 103; Acts 1987, No. 87-590, p. 975, § 2-333(b).)

§ 26-8-21. Application for removal and notice of hearing thereon; appointment of guardian ad litem.

Authority for such removal may be obtained on the application in writing, verified by affidavit, of the guardian, or of the minor or ward by next friend, stating the facts which show that the removal will advance the interests of the minor or ward. If application is made by the minor or ward by next friend, a day must be appointed for the hearing, 10 days' notice of which must be given the guardian or conservator by the service of process. If application is made by the guardian or conservator, a day, not less than 10 days after the filing of the application, must be appointed for the hearing and a guardian ad litem appointed to represent the minor or ward, who must put in issue the facts stated in the application and require proof thereof. (Code 1852, §§ 2031, 2035; Code 1867, §§ 2441, 2445; Code 1876, §§ 2796, 2802; Code 1886, § 2484; Code 1896, § 2369; Code 1907, § 4459; Code 1923, § 8232; Code 1940, T. 21, § 104; Acts 1987, No. 87-590, p. 975, § 2-333(b).)

Cited in Cook v. Wimberly, 24 Ala. 486 (1854); Desribes v. Wilmer, 69 Ala. 25 (1881).

§ 26-8-22. Hearing; entry of order authorizing removal or dismissal of application and taxing of costs against applicant.

If, on the hearing, the court is satisfied that the removal will advance the interests of the minor or ward, an order authorizing it shall be made and entered; otherwise, the application shall be dismissed and the guardian or conservator or the next friend, as the application may be made by the one or the other, must be taxed with the costs. (Code 1852, § 2031; Code 1867, § 2441; Code 1876, § 2796; Code 1886, § 2485; Code 1896, § 2370; Code 1907, § 4460; Code 1923, § 8233; Code 1940, T. 21, § 105; Acts 1987, No. 87-590, p. 975, § 2-333(b).)

§ 26-8-23. Preparation, certification and filing of record of proceedings; grant of guardianship or conservatorship and filing of transcript thereof; removal; powers of guardian or conservator as to recovery, receipt, etc., of property of minor or ward.

If the removal authorized is of the person and property of the minor or ward, a transcript of the record of the proceedings must be made and certified and filed in the court of probate of the county to which the removal is to be made. Upon the filing of such transcript, such court has jurisdiction to grant guardianship or conservatorship of the person or conservatorship of property of the minor or ward, and on such grant being made and a transcript thereof, duly certified, being filed in the court of probate authorizing the removal, such removal may be made. The conservator so appointed has full authority to demand, recover and receive the property of the minor or ward from and after the making of the removal. (Code 1886, § 2486; Code 1896, § 2371; Code 1907, § 4461; Code 1923, § 8234; Code 1940, T. 21, § 106; Acts 1987, No. 87-590, p. 975, § 2-333(b).)

§ 26-8-24. Settlement of conservatorship of former conservator and certification of transcript thereof to probate court of county to which removal authorized.

On the filing of such transcript, the court must require the conservator of its appointment to make a final settlement of his conservatorship; and when such settlement is made, the court must certify a transcript thereof to the court of probate of the county to which the removal was authorized. (Code 1886, § 2487; Code 1896, § 2372; Code 1907, § 4462; Code 1923, § 8235; Code 1940, T. 21, § 107; Acts 1987, No. 87-590, p. 975, § 2-333(b).)

§ 26-8-25. Jurisdiction of guardianship not affected where removal of property only authorized.

If the removal authorized is of the property only of the minor or ward, the jurisdiction of the court authorizing the removal is not affected, and it must retain jurisdiction of the guardianship as if such removal had not been authorized. (Code 1886, § 2488; Code 1896, § 2373; Code 1907, § 4463; Code 1923, § 8236; Code 1940, T. 21, § 108.)

ARTICLE 3.

REMOVAL TO ANOTHER STATE.

§ 26-8-40. Removal of property of minor or ward whose parent, etc., resides without state or removes minor or ward from state — Authorization generally.

When the parent, guardian or other person having legal custody of a minor child or incapacitated person resides without the state or removed with such child from the state, becoming a resident of another state, the court of probate or the circuit court, having jurisdiction of the estate of the minor or ward has authority to order the removal of the property of the minor or ward to a conservator in the state of the residence of the parent, guardian or other person having legal custody of the minor or ward. (Code 1876, § 2800; Code 1886, § 2489; Code 1896, § 2374; Code 1907, § 4464; Code 1923, § 8237; Code 1940, T. 21, § 109; Acts 1949, No. 128, p. 154; Acts 1987, No. 87-590, p. 975, § 2-333(b).)

Corporation stocks received from grandfather's estate. — The laws of state of domicile of minor child of testator's surviving daughter, who died before his widow's death, should control disposition of corporation stocks received by such minor's guardian as his distributive share of testator's estate under will bequeathing testator's property remaining at widow's death to his children or their heirs in equal shares, so that circuit court, to which guardianship was removed from probate court, erred in refusing to authorize removal of minor's property to such state and receipt thereof by minor's father appointed therein as minor's guardian. George v. Widemire, 242 Ala. 579, 7 So. 2d 269 (1942).

Cited in Desribes v. Wilmer, 69 Ala. 25 (1881); Moses v. Faber, 81 Ala. 445, 1 So. 587 (1887); Wright v. Martin, 214 Ala. 334, 107 So. 818 (1926); Broaddus v. Johnson, 235 Ala. 314, 179 So. 215 (1938).

Collateral references. — 25 Am. Jur. 2d, Domicil, §§ 72, 83.

§ 26-8-41. Removal of property of minor or ward whose parent, etc., resides without state or removes minor or ward from state — Application, etc., for order of removal.

The application for the order of removal must be made in writing, signed by the parent, guardian or other person having legal custody of the minor or ward, verified by affidavit and accompanied by a transcript, duly certified, of the appointment of a conservator for such minor or ward by a court of competent jurisdiction in the state of the residence of the parent, guardian or other person having legal custody of the minor and of the bond of such conservator with sureties approved by such court; provided, that if the conservator so appointed is a corporate fiduciary which, under the laws of the state wherein appointed, is not required to make bond, a certificate from the appointing authority stating this may be filed in lieu of a copy of the conservator's bond. (Code 1886, § 2490; Code 1896, § 2375; Code 1907, § 4465; Code 1923, § 8238; Code 1940, T. 21, § 110; Acts 1949, No. 140, p. 166; Acts 1987, No. 87-590, p. 975, § 2-333(b).)

Cited in Broaddus v. Johnson, 235 Ala. 314, 179 So. 215 (1938).

§ 26-8-42. Removal of property of minor or ward whose parent, etc., resides without state or removes minor or ward from state — Entry of order of removal.

The court, if satisfied of the truth of the application and that the transcript of the appointment of the conservator in the state of the residence of the parent or conservator is in due form and properly certified and that the court making the appointment has jurisdiction, must make an order authorizing the removal of the property of the minor or ward and authorizing such conservator to receive the same. (Code 1886, § 2491; Code 1896, § 2376; Code 1907, § 4466; Code 1923, § 8239; Code 1940, T. 21, § 111; Acts 1987, No. 87-590, p. 975, § 2-333(b).)

Cited in Broaddus v. Johnson, 235 Ala. 314, 179 So. 215 (1938).

§ 26-8-43. Removal of property of minor or ward whose parent, etc., resides without state or removes minor or ward from state — Settlement of conservatorship of conservator within state.

If such minor or ward has a conservator in this state appointed by the court or subject to the jurisdiction of the court, an order must be made and entered requiring such conservator to make a final settlement of this conservatorship. (Code 1876, § 2801; Code 1886, § 2492; Code 1896, § 2377; Code 1907, § 4467; Code 1923, § 8240; Code 1940, T. 21, § 112; Acts 1987, No. 87-590, p. 975, § 2-333(b).)

Effect on guardian of removal of ward's property to another state. — The Alabama guardian of minor, whose property is ordered removed to another state in which ward resides, should not be removed from office, but should be required to make final settlement of guardianship. George v. Widemire, 242 Ala. 579, 7 So. 2d 269 (1942).

Cited in Broaddus v. Johnson, 235 Ala. 314, 179 So. 215 (1938).

§ 26-8-44. Removal of property or money when minor or ward and conservator nonresidents — Authorization generally.

When the conservator and the minor or ward are both nonresidents and the minor or ward is entitled to any property in this state or is or will be entitled to any money from any estate, the administration of which is pending in this state, whether such estate shall or shall not have been finally settled, and the money or property may be removed to another state without conflict with any restriction or limitation thereupon and without impairing the right of the minor or ward thereto, such money and property may be received and removed to the state of the residence of the minor or ward upon application of the conservator to the judge of probate of the county in which the property of the minor or ward or the principal part thereof may be or in which such administration may be pending in the manner following. (Code 1852, § 2032; Code 1867, § 2442; Code 1876, § 2797; Code 1886, § 2494; Code 1896, § 2378; Code 1907, § 4468; Code 1923, § 8241; Code 1940, T. 21, § 113; Acts 1987, No. 87-590, p. 975, § 2-333(b).)

Cited in Saltmarsh v. Planters', etc., Bank, 17 Ala. 761 (1850); Dupree v. Perry, 18 Ala. 34 (1850); Carlisle v. Tuttle, 30 Ala. 613 (1857); Larry v. Craig, 30 Ala. 631 (1857); Broaddus v. Johnson, 235 Ala. 314, 179 So. 215 (1938).

Collateral references. — 39 C.J.S., Guardian & Ward, § 188.

§ 26-8-45. Removal of property or money when minor or ward and conservator nonresidents — When removal of person and estate of minor or ward permitted.

The guardian may remove the person or the conservator may remove the estate of a minor or ward to another state by making a full settlement with the judge of the probate court where his letters were granted of his conservator accounts and by procuring a transcript of the record of a court of competent jurisdiction of such other state, certified according to the act of congress, showing the appointment of such person as guardian or conservator of the minor or ward, the execution of bond by the conservator with surety for the performance of the trust. Thereupon, the judge of probate must make an order authorizing such removal. (Code 1852, § 2031; Code 1867, § 2441; Code 1876, § 2796; Code 1886, § 2493; Code 1896, § 2379; Code 1907, § 4469; Code 1923, § 8242; Code 1940, T. 21, § 114; Acts 1987, No. 87-590, p. 975, § 2-333(b).)

U.S. Constitution. — As to requirement that each state give full faith and credit to judicial proceedings of other states, see U.S. Const., art. IV, § 1.

U.S. Code. — For act of congress requiring courts of all states, territories and possessions to give full faith and credit to records and judicial proceedings of other states, territories and possessions, see 28 U.S.C., § 1738.

Cited in Broaddus v. Johnson, 235 Ala. 314, 179 So. 215 (1938).

Collateral references. — 39 C.J.S., Guardian & Ward, § 193.

§ 26-8-46. Removal of property or money when minor or ward and conservator nonresidents — Transcript showing appointment as conservator of minor or ward in state of residence, etc.; notice to resident administrator, guardian, etc.; entry of order authorizing removal of property to state of residence.

The conservator must produce a transcript from the records of a court of competent jurisdiction, certified according to the act of congress, showing that he has been appointed conservator of the minor or ward in the state in which he and the minor or ward reside and has duly qualified as such according to the laws thereof and given bond, with surety, for the performance of his trust; and must also give 10 days' notice to the resident executor, administrator or conservator, if there is such, of the intended application. Thereupon, if good cause is not shown to the contrary and the judge of probate shall be satisfied, upon proof being made, that it will be for the interest of the minor or ward, such judge of probate shall make an order granting such conservator leave to remove the property of the minor or ward to the state or place of his residence, which shall be an authority to him to sue for and recover the same in his own name for the use of the minor or ward. (Code 1852, § 2033; Code 1867, § 2443; Code 1876, § 2798; Code 1886, § 2495; Code 1896, § 2380; Code 1907, § 4470; Code 1923, § 8243; Code 1940, T. 21, § 115; Acts 1987, No. 87-590, p. 975, § 2-333(b).)

U.S. Constitution. — As to requirement that each state give full faith and credit to judicial proceedings of other states, see U.S. Const., art. IV, § 1.

U.S. Code. — For act of congress requiring courts of all states, territories and possessions to give full faith and credit to records and judicial proceedings of other states, territories and possessions, see 28 U.S.C., § 1738.

Cited in Carlisle v. Tuttle, 30 Ala. 613 (1857).

§ 26-8-47. Removal of property or money when minor or ward and conservator nonresidents — Discharge of resident administrator, etc.

Such order is a discharge of the executor, administrator or other person in whose possession such property may be at the time of the order made. (Code 1852, § 2034; Code 1867, § 2444; Code 1876, § 2799; Code 1886, § 2496; Code 1896, § 2381; Code 1907, § 4471; Code 1923, § 8244; Code 1940, T. 21, § 116.)

Cited in Kirksey v. Friend, 48 Ala. 276 (1872); Broaddus v. Johnson, 235 Ala. 314, 179 So. 215 (1938).

§ 26-8-48. Sale of property to effect removal thereof from state — Authorization.

When the property of a minor or incapacitated person is ordered to be removed from the state under any provision contained in this article, the court making the order may, on the application of the person by whom such order of removal was obtained, order a sale of any property, real or personal, of such minor or incapacitated person as may be necessary to effect such removal. (Code 1896, § 2382; Code 1907, § 4472; Code 1923, § 8245; Code 1940, T. 21, § 117; Acts 1987, No. 87-590, p. 975, § 2-333(b).)

§ 26-8-49. Sale of property to effect removal thereof from state — Application for order of sale.

The application for such order of sale must be in writing, verified by affidavit, must describe the property sought to be sold and must state the facts showing that the interest of the minor or incapacitated person would be promoted by the proposed sale. (Code 1896, § 2383; Code 1907, § 4473; Code 1923, § 8246; Code 1940, T. 21, § 118; Acts 1987, No. 87-590, p. 975, § 2-333(b).)

§ 26-8-50. Sale of property to effect removal thereof from state — Proceedings under application; appointment, powers, etc., of commissioner for conduct of sale.

The court, in the order of sale, must appoint a suitable person commissioner to make the sale and, except as otherwise provided in this article, the authority and duty of such commissioner is the same as that of a conservator authorized to sell property of a minor or ward for reinvestment. If the commissioner so appointed fails to act or to complete the sale, another may be appointed at any time by an order of the court. (Code 1896, § 2384; Code 1907, § 4474; Code 1923, § 8247; Code 1940, T. 21, § 119; Acts 1987, No. 87-590, p. 975, § 2-333(b).)

§ 26-8-51. Sale of property to effect removal thereof from state — Disposition of proceeds from sale; compensation of commissioner.

The commissioner must, as soon as practicable after the receipt of the purchase money for the property sold by him, pay the same to the judge of probate or register or clerk, as the case may be, of the court ordering the sale, and such money must be retained and safely kept by such judge or register or clerk until the sale has been duly confirmed or vacated. If the sale is vacated, the purchase money must be, by such judge or register or clerk, returned to the purchaser. If the sale is confirmed, such money must be by such officer paid over to the foreign conservator entitled to receive the same, after deducting therefrom the costs and expenses attending the sale, including compensation to the commissioner in the amount of two and one-half percent upon the proceeds of such sale, but in no case more than $100.00. (Code 1896, § 2385; Code 1907, § 4475; Code 1923, § 8248; Code 1940, T. 21, § 120; Acts 1987, No. 87-590, p. 975, § 2-333(b).)

§ 26-8-52. Foreign conservator to execute and deliver receipts for money or property removed from state.

When a foreign conservator receives any money or property to be removed to another state under any of the provisions of this article, he shall execute and deliver to the person or officer from whom he receives such money or property receipts therefor, in duplicate, one of which must be by such person or officer duly forwarded by mail to the presiding officer of the court from which such conservator received his appointment. (Code 1896, § 2386; Code 1907, § 4476; Code 1923, § 8249; Code 1940, T. 21, § 121; Acts 1987, No. 87-590, p. 975, § 2-333(b).)

CHAPTER 9.

GUARDIANSHIP AND COMMITMENT OF INCOMPETENT VETERANS AND DEPENDENTS.

Cross references. — As to the appointment of a curator of property for persons who are mentally or physically incapacitated, see chapter 7A of this title.

U.S. Code. — As to guardianship, commitment, payment of benefits, etc., to veterans who are minors, incompetents and other wards, see 38 U.S.C., § 3201 et seq.

Collateral references. — 77 Am. Jur. 2d, Veterans & Veterans' Laws, §§ 57-67.

§ 26-9-1. Short title.

This chapter may be cited as the "Uniform Veterans' Guardianship Act." (Acts 1931, No. 240, p. 280.)

§ 26-9-2. Definitions.

When used in this chapter, the following words and phrases shall have the following meanings, respectively, unless the context clearly indicates otherwise:

(1) PERSON. A partnership, corporation or an association.

(2) ADMINISTRATION. The United States Veterans' Administration or its successor.

(3) ESTATE and INCOME. Such terms include only moneys received by the guardian from the Veterans' Administration and all earnings, interest and profits derived therefrom.

(4) BENEFITS. All moneys payable by the United States through the Veterans' Administration.

(5) ADMINISTRATOR. The Administrator of Veterans' Affairs of the United States Veterans' Administration.

(6) WARD. A beneficiary of the administration.

(7) GUARDIAN. Any person acting as a fiduciary for a ward and includes a conservator appointed under Alabama Uniform Guardianship and Protective Proceedings Act. (Acts 1931, No. 240, p. 280; Code 1940, T. 21, § 160; Acts 1987, No. 87-590, p. 975, § 2-333(b).)

Cited in Shores v. Sanders, 271 Ala. 552, 126 So. 2d 201 (1961).

§ 26-9-3. When guardian to be appointed for ward.

Whenever, pursuant to any law of the United States or regulations of the administration, the administrator requires, prior to payment of benefits, that a guardian be appointed for a ward, such appointment shall be made in the manner provided in this chapter. (Acts 1931, No. 240, p. 280; Code 1940, T. 21, § 161.)

Collateral references. — Parent's or relative's rights of visitation of adult against latter's wishes. 40 ALR4th 846.

§ 26-9-4. Limitations as to appointment of guardians.

Except as provided in this chapter, it shall be unlawful for any person to accept appointment as guardian of any ward if such proposed guardian shall at that time be acting as guardian for five wards. In any case, upon presentation of a petition by an attorney of the administration under this section alleging that a guardian is acting in a fiduciary capacity for more than five wards and requesting his discharge for that reason, the court, upon proof substantiating the petition, shall require a final accounting forthwith from such guardian and shall discharge such guardian in said case. The limitations of this section shall not apply where the guardian is a bank or trust company acting for the wards' estates only. An individual may be guardian of more than five wards if they are all members of the same family. (Acts 1931, No. 240, p. 280; Code 1940, T. 21, § 162.)

§ 26-9-5. Procedure for appointment of guardian — Filing of petition; contents thereof.

A petition for the appointment of a guardian may be filed in any court of competent jurisdiction by or on behalf of any person who under existing law is entitled to priority of appointment. If there is no person so entitled or if the person so entitled shall neglect or refuse to file such a petition within 30 days after mailing of notice by the administration to the last known address of such person indicating the necessity for the same, a petition for such appointment

141

may be filed in any court of competent jurisdiction by or on behalf of any responsible person residing in this state.

The petition for appointment shall set forth the name, age, place of residence of the ward, the names and places of residence of the nearest relative, if known, and the fact that such ward is entitled to receive moneys payable by or through the administration and shall set forth the amount of moneys then due and the amount of probable future payments. The petition shall also set forth the name and address of the person or institution, if any, having actual custody of the ward.

In the case of a mentally incompetent ward, the petition shall show that such ward has been rated incompetent on examination by the administration in accordance with the laws and regulations governing the administration. (Acts 1931, No. 240, p. 280; Code 1940, T. 21, § 163.)

§ 26-9-6. Procedure for appointment of guardian — Certification as to age, etc., of minor ward.

Where a petition is filed for the appointment of a guardian of a minor ward, a certificate of the administrator or his representative setting forth the age of such minor as shown by the records of the administration and the fact that the appointment of a guardian is a condition precedent to the payment of any moneys due the minor by the administration shall be prima facie evidence of the necessity for such appointment. (Acts 1931, No. 240, p. 280; Code 1940, T. 21, § 164.)

§ 26-9-7. Procedure for appointment of guardian — Certification as to incompetence, etc., of mentally incompetent ward.

Where a petition is filed for the appointment of a guardian of a mentally incompetent ward, a certificate of the administrator or his representative setting forth the fact that such person has been rated incompetent by the administration on examination in accordance with the laws and regulations governing such administration and that the appointment of a guardian is a condition precedent to the payment of any moneys due such persons by the administration shall be prima facie evidence of the necessity for such appointment. (Acts 1931, No. 240, p. 280; Code 1940, T. 21, § 165.)

§ 26-9-8. Procedure for appointment of guardian — Notice of filing of petition.

Upon the filing of a petition for the appointment of a guardian under the provisions of this chapter, the court shall cause such notice to be given as provided by law. (Acts 1931, No. 240, p. 280; Code 1940, T. 21, § 166.)

§ 26-9-9. Procedure for appointment of guardian — Appointment of guardian; execution and filing of bonds by guardian; filing of certificate by personal sureties.

Before making an appointment under the provisions of this chapter the court shall be satisfied that the guardian whose appointment is sought is a fit and proper person to be appointed.

Upon the appointment being made, the guardian shall execute and file a bond to be approved by the court in an amount not less than the sum then due and estimated to become payable during the ensuing year. The said bond shall be in the form and be conditioned as required of a guardian appointed under the guardianship laws of this state and it shall be the duty of the court having jurisdiction of the cause, upon the application by any party in interest, to require the filing of an individual bond in accordance with the provisions of this section without regard to the provisions of any preexisting general or local statute or charter provision of any corporation exempting the fiduciary from the posting of an individual guardianship bond. The court shall have power from time to time to require the guardian to file an additional bond.

Where a bond is tendered by a guardian with personal sureties, such sureties shall file with the court a certificate under oath which shall describe the property owned, both real and personal, and that they are each worth the sum named in the bond as the penalty thereof over and above all their debts and liabilities and exclusive of property exempt from execution. (Acts 1936-37, Ex. Sess., No. 227, p. 270; Code 1940, T. 21, § 167.)

Collateral references. — Eligibility for appointment as guardian under Uniform Veterans' Guardianship Act. 173 ALR 1061.

§ 26-9-10. Investment of funds of estate by guardian; limitation as to loans of funds of ward.

(a) Every guardian shall invest the funds of the estate in one or more of the following forms in which the guardian has no interest and not otherwise:

(1) Interest-bearing obligations of the State of Alabama or of the United States or as to which the State of Alabama or the United States has guaranteed the payment of both principal and interest.

(2) Loans secured by direct first mortgage on improved real estate located within the State of Alabama. Such loans shall not exceed 50 percent of the actual value fixed by a competent appraiser or of the value for which such real estate, with improvements, was assessed for taxation for the last preceding tax year, whichever is the lower, except as provided in subdivision (3) of this section.

(3) Purchase of indebtedness secured by first real estate mortgages which have been accepted for insurance by the Secretary of Housing and Urban Development or his successor in office pursuant to Title Two of the National Housing Act; provided, that only the entire indebtedness as a unit is purchased and before maturity.

(4) Purchase of a home or farm for the sole use of the ward or his dependents if the ward does not already own real estate suitable for a home, such real estate to be located in the State of Alabama and to be of area and location suitable to the station in life and prospects of the ward and his dependents. Title thereto must be conveyed to the ward, but the property must be managed by the guardian for the ward and the guardian must account for any rents and profits derived therefrom. Before investing funds of the ward in real estate, the guardian must require an abstract of title to be examined by a reputable attorney and secure from such attorney a certificate in writing showing title thereto to be clear and free from any incumbrance. The guardian, acting in good faith, shall not be individually responsible for any depreciation in value of land so purchased when such depreciation results from causes which cannot be prevented by the guardian.

(5) Deposit in the savings department of any banking institution in the state which bank is a member of the Federal Deposit Insurance Corporation; provided, that the total amount deposited in any such bank, with interest, must not at any time exceed the amount by which such funds so deposited are insured by the Federal Deposit Insurance Corporation. In the event the fiduciary is a banking institution, it may likewise deposit the funds in its own savings department, subject to the same regulations as other savings depositors therein and shall be liable for interest thereon, but only at the same rate as that paid other savings account depositors.

(b) No fiduciary shall make any loan of the funds of the ward for any period in excess of one calendar year from the date of such loan without prior written approval of the court of appointment, which written approval shall not be granted except upon the filing with the court of an application verified by the oath of the guardian setting forth the identity of the proposed borrower, the amount proposed to be loaned, the terms of repayment, the interest rate, a complete description of the real estate and improvements, a statement that the guardian has no interest therein and the facts upon which the guardian deems it proper to negotiate a loan for a period longer than one year, which application must also be accompanied by a written appraisal of the proposed security by a competent, disinterested appraiser. (Acts 1931, No. 240, p. 280; Acts 1936-37, Ex. Sess., No. 227, p. 270; Code 1940, T. 21, § 172.)

§ 26-9-11. Application of estate for support and maintenance of person other than ward.

A guardian shall not apply any portion of the estate of his ward for the support and maintenance of any person other than his ward, except upon order of the court after a hearing, notice of which has been given the proper office of the administration in the manner provided in Section 26-9-14. (Acts 1931, No. 240, p. 280; Code 1940, T. 21, § 173.)

§ 26-9-12. Furnishing of copy of public record used to determine eligibility for benefits to applicant for benefits.

Whenever a copy of any public record is required by the administration to be used in determining the eligibility of any person to participate in benefits made available by such administration, the official charged with the custody of such public record shall without charge provide the applicant for such benefits or any person acting on his behalf or the representative of such administration with a certified copy of such record. (Acts 1931, No. 240, p. 280; Code 1940, T. 21, § 174.)

§ 26-9-13. Commitment of incompetent veteran to veterans' hospital.

Whenever it appears that an incompetent veteran of any war, military occupation or expedition is eligible for treatment in a United States veterans' hospital and commitment to such hospital is necessary for the proper care and treatment of such veteran, the courts of this state are hereby authorized to communicate with the administration with reference to available facilities and eligibility and, upon receipt of a certificate from the administration stating that there are facilities available in a United States veterans' hospital and that the veteran is entitled to hospitalization therein, the court may then direct such veteran's commitment to such United States veterans' hospital. Thereafter such veteran upon admission shall be subject to the rules and regulations of such hospital and the officials of such hospital shall be vested with the same powers now exercised by superintendents of state hospitals for mental diseases within this state with reference to the retention of custody of the veteran so committed. Notice of such pending proceedings shall be furnished the person so committed, and his right to appear and defend shall not be denied. (Acts 1931, No. 240, p. 280; Code 1940, T. 21, § 175.)

Exhaustion of state remedies prerequisite to invoking jurisdiction of federal court. — A veteran committed to a United States veteran's hospital by virtue of an order entered by a court of the state of Alabama under this section has state remedies available for the purpose of testing the legality of his commitment. He is not being held in custody pursuant to any order of any federal agency or court. Under such circumstances, the hospital holds him as an agent for the state of Alabama and not as an agent of the federal government. His status by reason of his commitment to this federal facility is no different than if he had been committed to a state institution. For this reason, the remedies provided by the state of Alabama must be exhausted as a prerequisite to the right to invoke the jurisdiction of a federal court. Lee v. Giles, 271 F. Supp. 785 (M.D. Ala. 1967).

Right to apply for writ of habeas corpus in federal court. — An individual committed to a facility of the United States pursuant to a judgment of a state court under this section, may not, without attempting to avail himself of state habeas corpus remedies, proceed on his application for a writ of habeas corpus in the United States district courts. Lee v. Giles, 271 F. Supp. 785 (M.D. Ala. 1967).

§ 26-9-14. Filing of account of receipts and disbursements for settlement by guardian; certification of copy thereof to veterans' administration; notice of hearing thereon.

Every guardian who shall receive on account of his ward any moneys from the administration shall file with the court annually on the anniversary date of the appointment, in addition to such other accounts as may be required by the court, a full, true and accurate account under oath of all moneys so received by him and of all disbursements thereof, showing the balance thereof in his hands at the date of such account and how invested, including a complete descriptive itemization of all investments, and must submit to the court for its examination all securities and evidences of debt belonging to the ward, and the decree of the court passing the settlement must recite that all securities and evidences of debt due the ward have been presented to and examined by the court; provided, that in the absence of objection by any party in interest, the court may in its discretion and without formal proceedings extend from time to time the time for the filing of the accounts for annual or partial settlement, but no such continuance shall be granted so as to extend the time for filing such settlements to a period beyond three calendar years from the date of the appointment or the date of the last partial settlement, whichever is the later, and upon the termination of the guardianship from any cause a like account must be filed for final settlement.

A certified copy of each of such accounts filed with the court shall be sent by the guardian to the office of the administration having jurisdiction over the area in which such court is located. The court shall fix a time and place for the hearing on such account not less than 15 days nor more than 30 days from the date of filing same, and notice thereof shall be given by the court to the aforesaid administration office not less than 15 days prior to the date fixed for the hearing. Notice of such hearing shall in like manner be given to the guardian; provided, that notice as required in this section may be given by registered or certified mail, addressed to the principal office of the administration located in the State of Alabama as such address appears on record in the probate office. (Acts 1936-37, Ex. Sess., No. 227, p. 270; Code 1940, T. 21, § 168.)

Cited in Maddox v. Elliott, 248 Ala. 271, 27 So. 2d 498 (1946).

§ 26-9-15. Removal of guardian for failure to file account of moneys received for ward, etc.

If any guardian shall fail to file any account of the moneys received by him from the administration on account of his ward within 30 days after such account is required by either the court or the administration or shall fail to furnish the administration a copy of his accounts as required by this chapter, such failure shall be grounds for removal. (Acts 1931, No. 240, p. 280; Code 1940, T. 21, § 170.)

§ 26-9-16. Discharge of guardian.

When a minor ward for whom a guardian has been appointed shall have attained his majority and has not been found incompetent and when any incompetent ward has been rated competent by the administration, a certificate of the administrator or his duly authorized representative to that effect shall be prima facie evidence that a guardian is no longer required and the court, upon the guardian filing a satisfactory final account, may discharge such guardian upon a petition filed for that purpose. Nothing contained in this section shall be construed to prevent a ward from filing a petition for the discharge of his guardian on the ground that the ward has attained majority or is competent or the court from acting on its own motion in such cases. (Acts 1931, No. 240, p. 280; Code 1940, T. 21, § 176.)

Evidence of restoration of competency. — Decision in a subsequent guardianship proceeding in the probate court in which the court found the ward competent and discharged the guardian, which was apparently based upon the veterans' administration rating of competency, was, under the statute, prima facie evidence that a guardian was no longer required because of a restoration of competency. Therefore, when the will contestants' counsel agreed to the admission of the pertinent exhibits (documents disclosing the guardianship proceeding) "for whatever they are," he agreed to that prima facie quality, and could not complain of any error in the trial court's failure to grant his directed verdict motion. Lawrence v. First Nat'l Bank, 516 So. 2d 630 (Ala. 1987).

§ 26-9-17. Compensation of guardian generally.

Compensation payable to a guardian shall not exceed five percent of the income of the ward during any year. In the event of extraordinary services rendered by such guardian, the court may, upon petition and after hearing thereon, authorize additional compensation therefor payable from the estate of the ward. Notice of such petition and hearing shall be given the proper office of the administration in the manner provided in Section 26-9-14. No compensation shall be allowed on the corpus of an estate received from a preceding guardian. The guardian may be allowed from the estate of his ward reasonable premiums paid by him to any corporate surety upon his bond. (Acts 1931, No. 240, p. 280; Code 1940, T. 21, § 171.)

Excessive charges. — Five hundred dollars allowed guardian for extraordinary services performed in securing repayment of $5,000.00 invested by guardian's predecessor in company which became insolvent after guardian's appointment, and in investing funds of the ward to advantage, was excessive by $250.00, notwithstanding that services allegedly consumed approximately one year's time, and resulted in enhancing the value of the ward's estate. Hines v. Dollar, 236 Ala. 329, 181 So. 748 (1938).

§ 26-9-18. Taxing of costs and fees of guardian.

The costs and fees, exclusive of fees of the guardian ad litem incident to any partial or final settlement by any guardian subject to the provisions of this chapter, shall be taxed in the amounts provided by the general statutes for like services, but there shall not be taxed or charged against the estate of the ward, on any partial settlement, any amount in excess of one half of one percent of the amount of money with which the guardian is chargeable on the settlement as having received since the last preceding settlement and with which the guardian has not previously been charged; provided, that the limitations contained in this section as to costs and fees shall not affect the commissions and fees otherwise payable to the general guardian and to guardians ad litem. (Acts 1936-37, Ex. Sess., No. 227, p. 270; Code 1940, T. 21, § 169.)

§ 26-9-19. Construction and applicability of chapter.

(a) This chapter shall be construed liberally to secure the beneficial intents and purposes thereof and shall apply only to beneficiaries of the administration.

(b) This chapter shall be so interpreted and construed as to effectuate its general purpose to make uniform the laws of those states which enact it. (Acts 1931, No. 240, p. 280.)

CHAPTER 10.

ADOPTION OF CHILDREN.

ARTICLE 1.

GENERAL PROVISIONS.

Cross references. — For present provisions pertaining to adoption, see Chapter 26-10A.

§§ 26-10-1 through 26-10-4. Repealed by Acts 1990, No. 90-554, p. 912, § 38, effective January 1, 1991.

§ 26-10-4.1. Fee for investigation services involving adoption; disposition of moneys received.

(a) The State Department of Human Resources shall charge and collect a fee in the amount of $300.00 for investigation services they perform in cases involving adoption, provided, however, that in those adoption proceedings in which an investigation is specifically not required by statute because the petitioner is a stepfather, stepmother or closely related relative, no fee shall be charged for investigation services. This fee shall not apply to investigation services for cases in which a child was placed for adoption by the State Department of Human Resources, in cases in which a child was placed for adoption as a result of or pursuant to a court order in which parental rights in the child were terminated or in cases in which the investigative services were performed by a licensed child-placing agency.

The Department of Human Resources may waive this fee in the case of an indigent and for other good cause shown.

(b) All investigation services fees received pursuant to this section shall be received by the State Department of Human Resources and shall be deposited in the State Treasury to the credit of the state general fund. (Acts 1988, 1st Ex. Sess., No. 88-733, p. 136, §§ 1, 2; Acts 1990, No. 90-554, p. 912, § 36.)

Comment

This act (90-554) amends section 26-10-4.1 and restricts DHR's collection of this fee to only those cases in which the department itself performs the investigation. In all other cases this fee does not apply. The maximum fee allowed under this section has been reduced from $1,000 to $300. Additionally, the fee may be waived by DHR in case of indigency or for other good cause shown.

As amended, the responsibility for collecting the fees has been changed from the court to the department.

§§ 26-10-5 through 26-10-10. Repealed by Acts 1990, No. 90-554, p. 912, § 38, effective January 1, 1991.

ARTICLE 2.

SUBSIDIZED ADOPTION.

Collateral references. — 2 C.J.S., Adoption of Persons, §§ 1 to 40, 49 to 72.

2 Am. Jur. 2d, Adoption, §§ 1 to 12, 23 to 47.

§ 26-10-20. Short title.

This article should be known and may be cited as the "Alabama Subsidized Adoption Act." (Acts 1979, No. 79-691, p. 1231, § 8.)

§ 26-10-21. Purpose of article.

The purpose of this article is to supplement the Alabama adoption statutes by making possible through public financial subsidy the most appropriate adoption of each child certified by the State Department of Human Resources as requiring a subsidy to assure adoption. (Acts 1979, No. 79-691, p. 1231, § 1.)

§ 26-10-22. "Child" defined.

As used in this article, except as otherwise required by the context, "child" means a child or a minor as defined by Alabama statute, who is (a) in the permanent custody of a public or voluntary licensed child-placing agency, (b) legally free for adoption and (c) in special circumstances because he is not likely to be adopted by reason of one or more conditions, such as:

(1) Physical or mental disability,

(2) Emotional disturbance,

(3) Recognized high risk of physical or mental disease,

(4) Age,

(5) Sibling relationship,

(6) Racial or ethnic factors,

(7) Potential danger to the child in severance of his emotional ties with the prospective adoptive parents, or

150

(8) Any combination of these conditions. (Acts 1979, No. 79-691, p. 1231, § 2.)

Cross references. — As to the age of majority, see § 26-1-1.

§ 26-10-23. Administration of subsidization program; provision for funds.

The State Department of Human Resources shall establish and administer an ongoing program of subsidized adoption. Subsidies and services for children under this program shall be provided out of funds appropriated to the State Department of Human Resources for the maintenance of children in foster care or made available to it from other sources. (Acts 1979, No. 79-691, p. 1231, § 3.)

§ 26-10-24. Certification for subsidy; procedures; approval of plan.

When foster parents are the prospective adoptive parents, certification of the child's eligibility for a subsidy shall be conditioned upon his adoption by the said prospective adoptive parents under applicable Alabama adoption policies, procedures and statutes.

In all other cases, after reasonable efforts have been made and no appropriate adoptive family without the use of subsidy has been found for a child, the State Department of Human Resources shall certify the child as eligible for a subsidy in the event of adoption.

If the child is in the permanent custody of a voluntary licensed child-placing agency, that agency shall present to the State Department of Human Resources (a) evidence to support the existence of potential danger to the child in severing his emotional ties with his foster parents who are the prospective adoptive parents, or (b) evidence of inability to place the child for adoption due to any of the other conditions specified in Section 26-10-22. In the latter case, the agency shall present evidence that reasonable efforts have been made to place the child without subsidy, such as recruitment of potential parents, use of adoption resource exchanges and referral to appropriate specialized adoption agencies.

The decision concerning certification of the child for subsidy shall be made by the State Department of Human Resources. Evidence submitted by the voluntary licensed child-placing agency shall serve as a basis for the decision and the State Department of Human Resources may request and receive from the voluntary licensed child-placing agency additional information which the State Department of Human Resources considers necessary to the decision.

If the State Department of Human Resources approves the subsidy plan, it will draft and sign jointly with the adoptive parents the subsidy agreement. The State Department of Human Resources will be the administrator of the subsidy agreement according to its regulations and the terms of this article.

The voluntary licensed child-placing agency shall continue supervisory responsibility for the child and the family until after the final adoption decree has been issued. (Acts 1979, No. 79-691, p. 1231, § 4.)

§ 26-10-25. Subsidies — Agreements; type; amount; duration; limitation.

When parents are found and approved for adoption of a child certified as eligible for subsidy, and before the final decree of adoption is issued, there must be a written agreement between the State Department of Human Resources and the adopting family as to the terms and conditions of the subsidy. Adoption subsidies in individual cases may commence at any time after the adoption placement or at the appropriate time after the adoption decree, and will vary with the needs of the child as well as the availability of other resources to meet the child's needs. The subsidy may be for special services only, or for money payments, and either for a limited period, or for a long term, or for any combination of the foregoing. The amount of the time-limited or long-term subsidy may in no case exceed that which would be allowable from time to time for such child in foster care, or, in the case of special service, the reasonable fee for the service rendered. (Acts 1979, No. 79-691, p. 1231, § 5.)

§ 26-10-26. Subsidies — Annual report; termination of subsidy; modification.

When subsidies are for more than one year, the adoptive parents shall present an annual sworn certification that the adopted child remains under their care and that the condition(s) that caused the child to be certified continue(s) to exist. The subsidy agreement shall be continued in accordance with its terms but only as long as the adopted child is the legal dependent of the adoptive parents and the child's condition continues, except that, in the absence of other appropriate resources provided by law and in accordance with Alabama regulations, it may be continued after the adopted child reaches majority, provided he is in school or in training in a program, the purpose of which is to aid him toward self-support. If the child certified for subsidy was in permanent custody of a voluntary licensed child-placing agency, that agency shall, upon request, furnish the State Department of Human Resources additional information which may be needed to assure that the condition(s) that caused the child to be certified continue(s) to exist. The subsidy agreement may be modified only with approval of the State Department of Human Resources. The adoptive parents may request termination of the subsidy agreement at any time. (Acts 1979, No. 79-691, p. 1231, § 5.)

§ 26-10-27. Effect of nonresidence of adopting parents.

A child who is a resident of Alabama when eligibility for subsidy is certified shall remain eligible and receive subsidy, if necessary for adoption, regardless of the domicile or residence of the adopting parents at the time of application for adoption, placement, legal decree of adoption or thereafter. (Acts 1979, No. 79-691, p. 1231, § 5.)

§ 26-10-28. Records confidential.

All records regarding subsidized adoption shall be confidential and may be disclosed only in accordance with Sections 26-10A-31, 26-10A-32, 38-2-6(8) and 38-7-13. (Acts 1979, No. 79-691, p. 1231, § 5.)

§ 26-10-29. Review of subsidy decision.

Any subsidy decision by the State Department of Human Resources which the placement agency or the adoptive parents deem adverse to the child is reviewable by the State Department of Human Resources. (Acts 1979, No. 79-691, p. 1231, § 6.)

Collateral references. — Validity and construction of surrogate parenting agreement. 77 ALR4th 70.

§ 26-10-30. Promulgation of regulations.

The State Department of Human Resources shall promulgate regulations consistent with this article within 120 days of its enactment. (Acts 1979, No. 79-691, p. 1231, § 7.)

CHAPTER 10A.

ALABAMA ADOPTION CODE.

Effective date. — The act which added this chapter became effective January 1, 1991.

§ 26-10A-1. Short title.

This chapter shall be known as and may be cited as the Alabama Adoption Code. (Acts 1990, No. 90-554, p. 912, § 1.)

Code commissioner's note. — In addition to the provisions of this chapter, the juvenile court has jurisdiction of adoption proceedings when such proceedings have been removed from the probate court on motion of any party to the proceedings. See § 12-15-30(b)(5).

Cross references. — As to adoption of adults for purposes of inheritance, see § 26-10A-6.

Editor's note. — The cases annotated below were decided under prior law.

For legislative history of adoption statutes in Alabama, see Doby v. Carroll, 274 Ala. 273, 147 So. 2d 803 (1962).

Law devolves custody of infant children upon their parents, not so much upon the ground of natural right in the latter, as because the interests of the children, and the good of the public, will, as a general rule, be thereby promoted. The law recognizes that a higher authority ordains natural parenthood, and a fallible judge should disturb the relationship thus established only where circumstances compel human intervention. Hanlon v. Mooney, 407 So. 2d 559 (Ala. 1981).

Adoption is purely statutory right. — The right of adoption is purely statutory and was never recognized by the rules of the common law. And prior to the Code of 1852 the right was limited to the legitimation of bastard children by their father. Abney v. De Loach, 84 Ala. 393, 4 So. 757 (1888).

While statutes authorizing adoption are in derogation of the common law, and for this reason are, in some respects, to be strictly construed, their construction cannot be narrowed so closely as to defeat the legislative intent which may be made obvious by their terms, and by the mischief to be remedied by their enactment. Abney v. De Loach, 84 Ala. 393, 4 So. 757 (1888). But they must be substantially complied with. See Prince v. Prince, 188 Ala. 559, 66 So. 27 (1914).

The right of adoption is purely statutory, and in derogation of the common law. Franklin v. White, 263 Ala. 223, 82 So. 2d 247 (1955).

In Alabama, the right of adoption is purely statutory and in derogation of the common law. Doby v. Carroll, 274 Ala. 273, 147 So. 2d 803 (1962); Evans v. Rosser, 280 Ala. 163, 190 So. 2d 716 (1966); Davis v. Turner, 55 Ala. App. 366, 315 So. 2d 602 (1975).

Unless a statute by express provision or necessary implication confers the right to adoption, such right does not exist. Doby v. Carroll, 274 Ala. 273, 147 So. 2d 803 (1962); Evans v. Rosser, 280 Ala. 163, 190 So. 2d 716 (1966); Taylor v. McCormick, 48 Ala. App. 76, 261 So. 2d 907 (1972).

Any proceedings had relating to the adoption of children must conform to the statutes authorizing such proceedings. Davis v. Turner, 55 Ala. App. 366, 315 So. 2d 602 (1975).

Adoption is purely a statutory right and the adoption statutes must in most instances be strictly construed. Straszewicz v. Gallman, 342 So. 2d 1322 (Ala. Civ. App. 1977); Holcomb v. Bomar, 392 So. 2d 1204 (Ala. Civ. App. 1981).

Adoption is purely statutory. It was unknown to the common law. The courts of this state have always required strict adherence to statutory requirements in adoption proceedings. Hanlon v. Mooney, 407 So. 2d 559 (Ala. 1981).

Because adoption is strictly statutory and involves the curtailment of the fundamental rights of the natural parents, the adoption statute must be closely adhered to. Vice v. May, 441 So. 2d 942 (Ala. Civ. App. 1983).

Adoption is the permanent termination of all legal parental rights and may not be accomplished without strict compliance with the statute. Vice v. May, 441 So. 2d 942 (Ala. Civ. App. 1983).

Adoption proceedings are purely statutory and the requirements of these statutes must be closely adhered to. McCombs v. Shields, 497 So. 2d 149 (Ala. Civ. App. 1986).

Strict adherence to statutory require-ments is required. — In order to adopt a child in Alabama, one must follow the statutory adoption procedures set out by the legislature, and adoption is purely statutory and is in derogation of the common law. Strict adherence to the statutory requirements in adoption proceedings is required. McCoy v. McCoy, 549 So. 2d 53 (Ala. 1989).

Procedures must be complied with to establish parent-child relationship. — The provisions of Alabama Uniform Parentage Act cannot be used to create a "common law adoption," and without compliance with the adoption procedures as set out in former § 26-10-1 et seq., there can be no parent-child relationship created by adoption. McCoy v. McCoy, 549 So. 2d 53 (Ala. 1989).

Probate court is primary forum for adoption cases. — Petitions for adoption must be filed in the probate court; therefore, that court has been made the primary forum for deciding adoption cases. It is only after a motion to transfer has been granted that the other courts have jurisdiction to decide adoption cases. Hicks v. Crosslin, 451 So. 2d 324 (Ala. Civ. App. 1984).

Probate courts have jurisdiction. — Alabama's adoption statutes provide that general jurisdiction over adoption proceedings rests with the probate courts. Holcomb v. Bomar, 392 So. 2d 1204 (Ala. Civ. App. 1981).

Probate court acts as court of limited jurisdiction. — In entertaining adoption proceedings the probate court acts as a court of limited jurisdiction. Claunch v. Entrekin, 272 Ala. 35, 128 So. 2d 100 (1961); Doby v. Carroll, 274 Ala. 273, 147 So. 2d 803 (1962); Taylor v. McCormick, 48 Ala. App. 76, 261 So. 2d 907 (1972).

And no presumption of jurisdiction will be indulged. — Where the court acts as one of limited jurisdiction, no presumption of jurisdiction will be indulged. Claunch v. Entrekin, 272 Ala. 35, 128 So. 2d 100 (1961).

It is the taking into one's family the child of another as son and heir; conferring on it "a title to the privileges and rights of a child" — an act, in other words, "which a person appoints as his heir and child of another." Russell v. Russell, 84 Ala. 48, 3 So. 900 (1888); Abney v. De Loach, 84 Ala. 393, 4 So. 757 (1888).

Which creates a status. — Adoption creates the status of parent and child, with the duty of care, maintenance, training and education, along with the right to the custody, control and services of the child. Buttrey v. West, 212 Ala. 321, 102 So. 456 (1924). And the adoptive parent is entitled to the earnings of the child, against all persons unless it may be the true parents when they have not consented to the adoption. Tilley v. Harrison, 91 Ala. 295, 8 So. 802 (1891).

Adoption of adult. — Under former statutes the word "child" was used in the sense of relationship, and not of infancy, and one 25 years of age was subject to adoption. Sheffield v. Franklin, 151 Ala. 492, 44 So. 373 (1907).

This chapter does not authorize the adoption of an adult. Doby v. Carroll, 274 Ala. 273, 147 So. 2d 803 (1962).

There is no procedure of any kind provided in the statutes for the adoption of an adult. Doby v. Carroll, 274 Ala. 273, 147 So. 2d 803 (1962).

Exact age of child is not essential. — It was held in Abney v. De Loach, 84 Ala. 393, 4 So. 757 (1888), that the exact age of the child was not an indispensable element of the validity of the written declaration.

Adopted child may claim exemptions out of adoptive parent's estate. — Upon adoption the status of the parties is fixed, and all the incidents usually attendant or flowing out of the relations so established attach to both the adoptive parent and child. For this reason the supreme court has held that an adopted child is entitled, during minority, to claim exemptions out of his adoptive parent's estate. Cofer v. Scroggins, 98 Ala. 342, 13 So. 115 (1893); Prince v. Prince, 188 Ala. 559, 66 So. 27 (1914).

Effect of noncompliance. — Person taken into home of foster parents while child, under common understanding with foster parents that she would inherit property at their death, held not entitled to be declared sole legatee and heir, where no attempt was made to comply with adoption statutes, and there was no contract in writing nor evidence of anything in form of contractual engagement. Marietta v. Faulkner, 220 Ala. 561, 126 So. 635 (1930).

Evidence insufficient to prove agreement to adopt. — Evidence that mother of unborn infant said that she would give infant to married couple upon birth of infant and that after child was five or six months old the mother stated that she would and did consent to adoption, and that one of the proposed adoptive parents stated that he hated to die without the baby being cared for and that he wanted to adopt the baby before he died so that it would get what he had, was insufficient to prove agreement to adopt so that child would be able to inherit enforceable by specific performance where proposed adoptive parent petitioning for adoption died before consummation of such proceeding. Rivers v. Rivers, 240 Ala. 648, 200 So. 764 (1941).

Estoppel to deny validity of adoption. — Heirs of deceased who had applied for adoption of infant but died before consummation of

proceedings were not "estopped" to deny the validity of adoption of infant. Rivers v. Rivers, 240 Ala. 648, 200 So. 764 (1948).

Adopted children treated same as natural unless clearly excluded by testator. — In will made in 1952 dividing estate among three nephews of testator upon termination of testamentary trust and providing that, if one or more nephews died without leaving descendants, his share would go to the descendants of the other nephew or nephews, testator intended to include one nephew's adopted children, and they were entitled to take upon death of life income beneficiary who survived the three nephews, because it is the public policy of this state that adopted children are treated the same as natural children, unless a desire to exclude them is clearly indicated by the testator. Gotlieb v. Kolotzman, 369 So. 2d 798 (Ala. 1979).

Stepfather held resident of Marshall county although in Germany on military duty. — Authorities generally agree that a person inducted into military service retains his domicile or residence in the state from which he entered the military service. A person who is inducted into military service retains residence in the state from which he is inducted until a new residence is established or initial residence is abandoned. Since there is no evidence that the stepfather has established a new residence, nor has he had any intent to abandon his Marshall county residence, as required by statute, the stepfather was a resident of Marshall county at the time he filed the petition for adoption even though he was stationed in Germany under military orders. McCombs v. Shields, 497 So. 2d 149 (Ala. Civ. App. 1986).

Collateral references. — 2 C.J.S., Adoption of Persons, § 77.

2 Am. Jur. 2d, Adoption, §§ 53, 54.

Adoption of adult. 21 ALR3d 1012.

Residence or domicile: requirements as to residence or domicile of adoptee or adoptive parent for purposes of adoption. 33 ALR3d 176.

Modern status of law as to equitable adoption or adoption by estoppel. 97 ALR3d 347.

Validity and application of statute authorizing change in record of birthplace of adopted child. 14 ALR4th 739.

Race as factor in adoption proceedings. 34 ALR4th 167.

Right of parent to regain custody of child after temporary conditional relinquishment of custody. 35 ALR4th 61.

Natural parent's parental rights as affected by consent to child's adoption by other natural parent. 37 ALR4th 724.

Necessity and sufficiency of consent to adoption by spouse of adopting parent. 38 ALR4th 768.

Adoption as precluding testamentary gift under natural relative's will. 71 ALR4th 374.

Marital or sexual relationship between parties as affecting right to adopt. 42 ALR4th 776.

Action for wrongful adoption based on misrepresentation of child's mental or physical condition or parentage. 56 ALR4th 375.

Postadoption visitation by natural parent. 78 ALR4th 218.

§ 26-10A-2. Definitions.

The following words and phrases shall have the following meaning whenever used in this chapter except where the context clearly indicates a different meaning:

(1) ABANDONMENT. A voluntary and intentional relinquishment of the custody of a minor by parent, or a withholding from the minor, without good cause or excuse, by the parent, of his presence, care, love, protection, maintenance, or the opportunity for the display of filial affection, or the failure to claim the rights of a parent, or the failure to perform the duties of a parent.

(2) ADOPTEE. The person being adopted.

(3) ADULT. A person who is 19 years of age or older or who by statute is otherwise deemed an adult.

(4) CONSENT. Voluntarily agreeing to adoption.

(5) FATHER. A male person who is the biological father of the minor or is treated by law as the father.

(6) LICENSED CHILD PLACING AGENCY. Any adoption agency that is licensed under the provisions of the Alabama Child Care Act of 1971 or any adoption agency approved by the Department of Human Resources.

(7) MINOR. A person under the age of 19.

(8) MOTHER. A female person who is the biological mother of the minor or is treated by law as the mother.

(9) PARENT. Natural or legal father or mother.

(10) PARTIES IN INTEREST. The adoptive parents and the natural parents unless the rights of the natural parents have been terminated or relinquished for purposes of adoption then the agency that has custody becomes a party in interest. This phrase does not include the adoptee.

(11) PRESUMED FATHER. Any male person as defined in the Alabama Uniform Parentage Act.

(12) PUTATIVE FATHER. The alleged or reputed father.

(13) RELINQUISHMENT. Giving up the physical custody of a minor for purpose of placement for adoption to a licensed child placing agency or the Department of Human Resources.

(14) SPECIAL NEEDS CHILD. A child as defined by the Federal Adoption Assistance and Child Welfare Act of 1980. (Acts 1990, No. 90-554, p. 912, § 2.)

Comment

The definition of "abandonment" in subdivision (1) is derived from Ala. Code § 26-18-3 (1975).

The definition of "adult" in subdivision (3) is derived from Ala. Code § 26-1-1 which designates the age of majority. An adult is any person who is not a minor as defined in this section.

The Alabama Child Care Act of 1971 as referred to in subdivision (6) is located in Ala. Code §§ 38-7-1 through 38-7-10 (1975).

The definition of "minor" in subdivision (7) is derived from Ala. Code § 26-1-1 (1975).

The definition of "parties in interest" in subdivision (10) is generally derived from the informal opinion of Alabama Attorney General to Honorable Lynda Knight, March 26, 1979.

The Alabama Uniform Parentage Act as referred to in subdivision (11) is located in Ala. Code §§ 26-17-1 through 26-17-21 (1975).

The Adoption Assistance and Child Welfare Act of 1980 as referred to in subdivision (14) is located at Pub L. 96-272, 94 Stat. 501 (1980).

§ 26-10A-3. Jurisdiction.

The probate court shall have original jurisdiction over proceedings brought under the chapter. If any party whose consent is required fails to consent or is unable to consent, the proceeding will be transferred to the court having jurisdiction over juvenile matters for the limited purpose of termination of parental rights. The provisions of this chapter shall be applicable to proceedings in the court having jurisdiction over juvenile matters. (Acts 1990, No. 90-554, p. 912, § 3.)

Comment

This section is generally derived from section 1 of the ABA Model State Adoption Act. It is generally consistent with former section 26-10-1, Code of Alabama, which was repealed and further consistent with section 12-12-35 of the Code of Alabama. If a party whose consent is required under the act fails to consent or is unable to consent, the proceeding is transferred to the court having jurisdiction over juvenile matters for the limited purpose of termination of parental rights. Section 12-12-35 permits a transfer from probate court on the motion of the parties at the discretion of the probate court but does not have this mandatory transfer provision in the absence of the proper consent. The petition for investigation under section 26-10A-19 shall be within the jurisdiction of the probate court.

§ 26-10A-4. Venue.

All petitions may be filed in the probate court in the county in which:

(1) The minor resides or has a legal residence;

(2) A petitioner resides, or is in military service; or

(3) An office of any agency or institution operating under the laws of this state having guardianship or custody of the minor is located. (Acts 1990, No. 90-554, p. 912, § 4.)

Comment

Broad venue provisions facilitate access to the court. Section 26-10A-4(2) relating to military service is new to the act. This section is consistent with former section 26-10-1, Code of Alabama, which is repealed.

§ 26-10A-5. Who may adopt.

Any adult person or husband and wife jointly who are adults may petition the court to adopt a minor.

(1) No rule or regulation of the Department of Human Resources shall prevent an adoption by a person/persons solely because the person/persons is employed outside the home, provided however, the Department of Human Resources may exercise sound discretion in requiring person/persons to remain in the home with a minor for a reasonable period of time when a particular minor requires the presence of that person/persons to ensure his/her adjustment. Provided, however, said reasonable period of time shall not exceed 60 consecutive calendar days.

(2) No rule or regulation of the Department of Human Resources or any agency shall prevent an adoption by a single person solely because such person is single or shall prevent an adoption solely because such person is of a certain age.

(3) Provided however, in cases, where one who purports to be the biological father marries the biological mother, on petition of the parties, the court shall order paternity tests to determine the true biological father. If the court determines by substantial evidence that the biological father is the man married to the biological mother, then the biological father shall be allowed to adopt said child without the consent of the man who was married to the biological mother at the time of the conception and/or birth of said child, when the court finds said adoption to be in the best interest of the child. (Acts 1990, No. 90-554, p. 912, § 5.)

Comment

The goal of adoption statutes is to create parent-child relationships. Just as courts, within their discretion, may refuse to grant an adoption because it is not in the best interests of the adoptee, the court should refuse to consummate an adoption when the parties seek to accomplish some goal not based on, or to create a relationship which does not result in a parent-child bond. Although the petitioner's age alone may not preclude an adoption, it may be considered by the court along with other factors.

Furthermore, no rule or regulation of any agency shall prevent an adoption solely because a person is single or solely because a person is of a certain age. Former section 26-10-1 had the same provision relating to adoption by singles but did not have any provision relating to age discrimination.

When an adoptee requires the adoptive parent/parent(s) presence in the home in order to ensure adjustment, the parent(s) may be required to temporarily forego employment outside of the home and remain with the adoptee for a reasonable period not to exceed 60 consecutive calendar days. This provision is the same as former section 26-10-2.1.

Section 26-10A-5(1) is generally consistent with former section 26-10-2.1 and also consistent with the relevant provisions of former section 26-10-1 of the Code of Alabama. This section is further consistent with section 26-18-5 of the Code of Alabama. This section is a departure from section 3 of the ABA Model State Adoption Act which permits adoptions of and by persons of any age.

Section 26-10A-5(3) was added to the Adoption Code after the Alabama Supreme Court issued its opinion in *Ex parte Presse,* 554 So. 2d 406 (Ala. 1989).

Circuit court that granted divorce could not set aside adoptions. — Where the circuit court which granted the divorce had not acquired subject matter jurisdiction over the adoptions by any statutory mechanism, the circuit court that granted the divorce could not have ratified or set aside the adoptions, because it had not acquired subject matter jurisdiction pursuant to any statute. B.W.C. v. A.N.M & K.C., 590 So. 2d 282 (Ala. Civ. App. 1991).

§ 26-10A-6. Who may be adopted.

Any minor may be adopted. (Acts 1990, No. 90-554, p. 912, § 6.)

Comment

The primary goal of this adoption code is to establish the parent-child relationship. Adult adoptions for inheritance purposes provided for in former sections 43-41-1 through 43-41-4 of the Alabama Code was repealed. Section 4 of the ABA Model State Adoption Act allows adoptions of persons of any age as long as the goal is to establish a parent-child relationship. Section 26-10A-6 is a departure from the ABA Model State Adoption Act. Only minors may be adopted which is consistent with former sections of chapter 10 of Title 26 of the Code of Alabama.

§ 26-10A-7. Persons whose consents or relinquishment are required.

Consent to the petitioner(s)' adoption or relinquishment for adoption to the Department of Human Resources or a licensed child placing agency shall be required of the following:

(1) The adoptee, if 14 years of age or older, except where the court finds that the adoptee does not have the mental capacity to give consent;

(2) The adoptee's mother;

(3) The adoptee's presumed father, regardless of paternity, if:

a. He and the adoptee's mother are or have been married to each other and the adoptee was born during the marriage, or within 300 days after the marriage was terminated by death, annulment, declaration of invalidity, or divorce, or after a decree of separation was entered by a court; or

b. Before the adoptee's birth, he and the adoptee's mother have attempted to marry each other by a marriage solemnized in apparent compliance with law, although the attempted marriage is or could be declared invalid, and,

1. If the attempted marriage could be declared invalid only by a court, the adoptee was born during the attempted marriage, or within

300 days after its termination by death, annulment, declaration or invalidity, or divorce; or

    2. If the attempted marriage is invalid without a court order, the adoptee was born within 300 days after the termination of cohabitation; or

    c. After the adoptee's birth, he and the adoptee's mother have married, or attempted to marry each other by a marriage solemnized in apparent compliance with law, although the attempted marriage is or could be declared invalid, and

    1. With his knowledge or consent, he was named as the adoptee's father on the adoptee's birth certificate; or

    2. He is obligated to support the adoptee pursuant to a written voluntary promise or agreement or by court order; or

    d. He received the adoptee into his home and openly held out the adoptee as his own child;

    (4) The agency to which the adoptee has been relinquished or which holds permanent custody and which has placed the adoptee for adoption, except that the court may grant the adoption without the consent of the agency if the adoption is in the best interests of the adoptee and there is a finding that the agency has unreasonably withheld its consent; and

    (5) The putative father if made known by the mother or is otherwise made known to the court provided he responds within 30 days to the notice he receives under Section 26-10A-17(a)(10). (Acts 1990, No. 90-554, p. 912, § 7.)

Comment

    The act separates the substantive right to consent to the adoption from the procedural due process right to notice of the adoption proceedings. Section 26-10A-7 specifies only those persons whose consent to the adoption is required; subdivisions 26-10A-17(a)(1) through (a)(10) specify those persons to whom notice of the adoption proceedings must be given.

    The relinquishment, or the actual or implied consent (see section 26-10A-9) of all persons specified in section 26-10A-5 must be obtained for the adoption to become final. In effect, the persons listed in section 26-10A-7 have an absolute veto power over the proposed adoption. Subdivision (3)(c) grants this substantive right to consent to the adoption to some individuals who claim to be the father of the adoptee. These subsections are patterned after the Uniform Parentage Act which has been enacted into law in Ala. Code § 26-17-1. It is intended that these two acts be interpreted in pari materia.

    Notice of the adoption proceedings must be given to all persons specified in subsections 26-10A-17(a)(1) through (a)(10) in order for the final decree of adoption to withstand a subsequent challenge to its legality. If they desire, the persons listed in those subsections may appear before the court and receive a contested hearing (see section 26-10A-24) on the merits of their objections to the proposed adoption. Unlike the persons specified in section 26-10A-7, however, those persons specified in subsections 26-10A-17(a)(1) through (a)(10) have the burden of persuading the court that the best interest of the adoptee would not be served by the adoption, on one of the other grounds listed in subsections 26-10A-24(a)(2) through (a)(4).

This provision is in general compatible with former section 26-10-3 except in two instances. First, consent by the presumed father is new. The language describing the adoptee's presumed father is from section 26-17-5. Second, the requirement that the putative father respond within 30 days is new. The current law concerning consent of the father of an illegitimate child remains unsettled in light of the Supreme Court's dismissal of *McNamara v. San Diego County Dep't of Social Services,* 488 U.S. 152, 109 S. Ct. 546 (1988).

Section 26-10A-7(4) which allows an agency holding permanent custody of the child to consent to an adoption is consistent with former sections 26-10-3 and 26-18-10.

I. General Consideration.
II. Decisions Under Prior Law.

I. GENERAL CONSIDERATION.

Section 26-18-8(1) must be read in pari materia with subdivision (4) of this section, which sets the perimeters of the agency's authority to withhold its consent. Ex parte R.C., 592 So. 2d 589 (Ala. 1991).

The statute authorizes the trial judge to consider, together, the best interest of the child and the reasonableness of the agency's refusal. Ex parte R.C., 592 So. 2d 589 (Ala. 1991).

The existence of bona fide agency regulations would be only one factor to be considered by the trial court in its assessment of the reasonableness of the Department of Human Resources' (DHR's) nonconsent. Ex parte R.C., 592 So. 2d 589 (Ala. 1991).

That the DHR had a bona fide policy against placing a child for adoption in the county of the child's origin was merely one fact to be considered by the juvenile court in determining the best interest of the child. Ex parte R.C., 592 So. 2d 589 (Ala. 1991).

II. DECISIONS UNDER PRIOR LAW.

Constitutionality. — See Thomas v. Culpepper, 356 So. 2d 656 (Ala. Civ. App. 1978).

Jurisdiction. — The probate court had jurisdiction where only the mother gave her consent and the petition contained an allegation that the father of the child had abandoned it, in a proceeding brought by the natural father to set aside the adoption order. Lankford v. Hollingsworth, 283 Ala. 559, 219 So. 2d 387 (1969).

The consent of the parent or, in circumstances falling under this section, the consent of the guardian or the department of pensions and security (now department of human resources) is jurisdictional. Vice v. May, 441 So. 2d 942 (Ala. Civ. App. 1983).

The giving of consent at some point is one of the prerequisites to the probate court's consideration of the subject matter. Where this jurisdictional prerequisite has been satisfied at the time of the decree, the decree consummates the adoption and a later withdrawal of consent has no effect. Where a required consent has never been given, the trial court never obtains jurisdiction to proceed to the paramount question of the child's welfare. Hicks v. Crosslin, 451 So. 2d 324 (Ala. Civ. App. 1984).

An allegation in the petition that the natural father had given his consent to the adoption was essential to the jurisdiction of the probate court, and the fact that the father had only visitation rights as a result of a divorce decree, where the mother had been given custody, did not obviate the necessity of an allegation of consent. Taylor v. McCormick, 48 Ala. App. 76, 261 So. 2d 907 (1972).

The mother's consent for adoption was sufficient where the adoptive father had lost guardianship of the child, through divorce proceedings, and his consent to the adoption was not necessary. Lankford v. Hollingsworth, 283 Ala. 559, 219 So. 2d 387 (1969).

Because adoption is strictly statutory and involves the curtailment of the fundamental rights of the natural parents, the adoption statutes must be closely adhered to. Thus, in regard to this section, it naturally follows that consent is jurisdictional and, where the required consent is never given, the court never obtains jurisdiction to proceed on the ultimate issue of adoption. Shelley v. Nowlin, 494 So. 2d 453 (Ala. Civ. App. 1986).

Adoption is a purely statutory right in Alabama, and a probate court has only limited jurisdiction in adoption proceedings and, without either express or implied statutory authority, the right of adoption is nonexistent. Meyers v. Smith, 518 So. 2d 734 (Ala. Civ. App. 1987).

The consent of the parent, the consent of the guardian or department of human resources is jurisdictional, and where a required consent is never given the trial court never obtains jurisdiction. J.L.F. v. B.E.F., 571 So. 2d 1135 (Ala. Civ. App. 1990).

Jurisdiction attaches with the initial acknowledgement of consent by the natural parent, and once the child is placed, remains despite attempts at revocation, so long as the child's welfare is thereby furthered. Davis v. Turner, 337 So. 2d 355 (Ala. Civ. App.), cert. denied, 337 So. 2d 362 (Ala. 1976).

Where a required consent has never been given, the trial court never obtains jurisdiction to proceed to the paramount question of the child's welfare. Davis v. Turner, 337 So. 2d 355 (Ala. Civ. App.), cert. denied, 337 So. 2d 362 (Ala. 1976); Vice v. May, 441 So. 2d 942 (Ala. Civ. App. 1983).

This section requires consent of both parents absent certain enumerated factors. Steele v. McDaniel, 380 So. 2d 892 (Ala. Civ. App. 1980).

And parent must be given at least reasonable notice of an adoption proceeding. Steele v. McDaniel, 380 So. 2d 892 (Ala. Civ. App. 1980).

Consent of department. — This section is construed to mean that the consent of the department is required only when the custody of the child has been awarded to that agency, or where there is no parent whose consent is required and the child has no guardian. Lankford v. Hollingsworth, 283 Ala. 559, 219 So. 2d 387 (1969); In re Roberts, 349 So. 2d 1170 (Ala. Civ. App. 1977); Walker County Dep't of Pensions & Security v. Mason, 373 So. 2d 863 (Ala. Civ. App. 1979).

Where the permanent custody of a child has not yet been placed with the department of pensions and security, (now department of human resources), the consent of the child's natural parents is sufficient to support an adoption proceeding. Walker County Dep't of Pensions & Security v. Mason, 373 So. 2d 863 (Ala. Civ. App. 1979).

The consent required of the department of pensions and security (now department of human resources) is jurisdictional, so that on its refusal to grant such consent, the court is without power to issue an adoption order unless the agency's actions are found to be arbitrary and unreasonable. In re Roberts, 349 So. 2d 1170 (Ala. Civ. App. 1977).

The department of pensions and security (now department of human resources) cannot arbitrarily withhold its consent to the adoption of a child that has been committed to its custody and care. In re Roberts, 349 So. 2d 1170 (Ala. Civ. App. 1977).

Whether the consent of the department of pensions and security (now department of human resources) is being withheld unreasonably or arbitrarily is a question of fact. In re Roberts, 349 So. 2d 1170 (Ala. Civ. App. 1977).

The burden of proof is on the party asserting that the consent of the department of pensions and security (now department of human resources) is being withheld arbitrarily or unreasonably. In re Roberts, 349 So. 2d 1170 (Ala. Civ. App. 1977).

In a case in which the parental rights of the child's natural parents have been terminated and the child's custody is with the department, the consent of the department is required in order for the trial court to proceed with the adoption. State Dep't of Human Resources v. Smith, 567 So. 2d 333 (Ala. Civ. App. 1990).

The department's refusal to consent cannot be deemed to be arbitrary or unreasonable where there is a reasonable justification for its decision or where such refusal is founded upon adequate principles or fixed standards. State Dep't of Human Resources v. Smith, 567 So. 2d 333 (Ala. Civ. App. 1990), cert. denied, 567 So. 2d 335 (Ala. 1990).

Petitioners held to have lacked good faith to comply with consent mandates. — The grandparents' admission that they never attempted to locate the child's mother prior to filing the adoption petition, coupled with the fact that they had corresponded with her shortly before doing so and that she had refused her consent to any such adoption on at least two occasions, evidenced a lack of good faith by the grandparents to comply with the consent mandates of the adoption laws. Shelley v. Nowlin, 494 So. 2d 453 (Ala. Civ. App. 1986).

Father's consent or abandonment necessary for adoption by stepfather. — In the absence of the natural father's consent as mandated by former § 26-10-7, or the obviation thereof by his abandonment of the child, the trial court was without authority to grant the adoption by the child's stepfather. Schwaiger v. Headrick, 281 Ala. 392, 203 So. 2d 114 (1967).

In order to sustain a petition for adoption, it is incumbent to show that the father has consented to the adoption or has abandoned his child. Adkison v. Adkison, 286 Ala. 306, 239 So. 2d 562 (1970).

Where the stepfather of a child petitions for adoption, and the natural father, simultaneously having visitation rights under a divorce decree, refuses to give his consent, a court has no authority to grant the petition, except where the evidence is clear that the natural father has evinced a settled purpose to forego all parental duties and relinquish all parental claims to the child. Butler v. Giles, 47 Ala. App. 543, 258 So. 2d 739 (1972).

Loss of custody of child in divorce proceeding does not obviate necessity of obtaining consent of natural parent to an adoption. Steele v. McDaniel, 380 So. 2d 892 (Ala. Civ. App. 1980).

Where no order was entered to terminate father's rights. — Where adoption proceedings were initiated by the natural mother without the consent of the natural father, although she petitioned the court to terminate his parental rights, no order was entered to that effect. Consequently, the adoption entered by the trial court fell within the purview of this section. Smith v. Jones, 554 So. 2d 1066 (Ala. Civ. App. 1989).

Collateral references. — 2 C.J.S., Adoption of Persons, §§ 51-72.

2 Am. Jur. 2d, Adoption, §§ 23 et seq., 55-57.

Consent by public authority or person other than parent having control of child, as necessary to valid adoption. 104 ALR 1464.

Necessity of consent of guardian to adoption. 104 ALR 1465.

Withdrawal of consent. 138 ALR 1038, 156 ALR 1011.

Sufficiency of parent's consent to adoption of child. 24 ALR2d 1127.

Consent of natural parents as essential to adoption where parents are divorced. 47 ALR2d 824.

Necessity of securing consent of parents of illegitimate child to its adoption. 51 ALR2d 497.

What constitutes undue influence in obtaining a parent's consent to adoption of child. 50 ALR3d 918.

Right of natural parent to withdraw valid consent to adoption of child. 74 ALR3d 421.

Mistake or want of understanding as ground for revocation of consent to adoption or of agreement releasing infant to adoption placement agency. 74 ALR3d 489.

What constitutes "duress" in obtaining parent's consent to adoption of child or surrender of child to adoption agency. 74 ALR3d 527.

Parent's involuntary confinement, or failure to care for child as result thereof, as permitting adoption without parental consent. 78 ALR3d 712.

Race as factor in adoption proceedings. 34 ALR4th 167.

Required parties in adoption proceedings, 48 ALR4th 860.

§ 26-10A-8. Consent or relinquishment by a minor parent.

(a) Prior to a minor parent giving consent a guardian ad litem must be appointed to represent the interests of a minor parent whose consent is required. Any minor, 14 years of age and beyond, can nominate a guardian ad litem either prior to the birth of the baby or thereafter.

(b) A consent or relinquishment executed by a parent who is a minor shall not be subject to revocation by reason of such minority. (Acts 1990, No. 90-554, p. 912, § 8.)

Comment

The statutory scheme of the act is underpinned by principles of contract. It is imperative to (1) allow a minor to consent, and (2) at the same time negate the normal contractual disability of a minor. Section 26-10A-8(b) is derived from section 6 of the ABA Model State Adoption Act and is new to Alabama law.

Revocation of consent. — The mere fact that the mother was a minor is not sufficient legal cause to revoke the consent once given. Anderson v. Hetherinton, 560 So. 2d 1078 (Ala. Civ. App. 1990) (decided under former § 26-10-3).

§ 26-10A-9. Implied consent or relinquishment.

A consent or relinquishment required by Section 26-10A-7 may be implied by any of the following acts of a parent:

(1) Leaving the adoptee without provision for his or her identification for a period of 30 days; or

(2) Knowingly leaving the adoptee with others without provision for support and without communication, or not otherwise maintaining a significant parental relationship with the adoptee for a period of six months; or

(3) Receiving notification of the pendency of the adoption proceedings under Section 26-10A-17 and failing to answer or otherwise respond to the petition within 30 days. (Acts 1990, No. 90-554, p. 912, § 9.)

Comment

Just as acceptance of the terms of a commercial contract can be implied from the conduct of a party, so may the consent of a person to the adoption be implied from the conduct of that individual. When it is not possible to obtain the actual consent of a person who is specified in section 26-10A-7, this section enumerates instances in which a person's consent may be implied from his or her acts or omissions with respect to his or her duty to care for the adoptee in the past.

The six (6) month time period specified in subdivision (2) is consistent with Ala. Code § 26-18-7(c) which provides a rebuttable presumption that parents are unwilling or unable to act as parents after a six (6) month period of abandonment.

This section is derived from section 7 of the ABA Model State Adoption Act.

§ 26-10A-10. Persons whose consents or relinquishments are not required.

Notwithstanding the provisions of Section 26-10A-7, the consent or relinquishment of the following persons shall not be required for an adoption:

(1) A parent whose rights with reference to the adoptee have been terminated by operation of law in accordance with the Alabama Child Protection Act, Sections 26-18-1 through 26-18-10;

(2) A parent who has been adjudged incompetent pursuant to law or a parent whom the court finds to be mentally incapable of consenting or relinquishing and whose mental disability is likely to continue for so long a period that it would be detrimental to the adoptee to delay adoption until restoration of the parent's competency or capacity. The court must appoint independent counsel or a guardian ad litem for an incompetent parent for whom there has been no such prior appointment;

(3) A parent who has relinquished his or her minor child to the department of human resources or a licensed child placing agency for an adoption;

(4) A deceased parent or one who is presumed to be deceased under Alabama law;

(5) An alleged father who has signed a written statement denying paternity; or

(6) The natural father where the natural mother indicates the natural father is unknown, unless the natural father is otherwise made known to the court. (Acts 1990, No. 90-554, p. 912, § 10.)

Comment

This section incorporates the involuntary parental termination law of Alabama which is known as the Child Protection Act. Ala. Code §§ 26-18-1 through 26-18-10 (1975).

Relinquishment is defined as giving up physical custody of a minor to a licensed child placing agency or to DHR for purposes of adoption. Therefore, once a parent has relinquished his or her child to an agency, the agency then assumes the parent's role of placing the child for adoption. Consequently, under subdivision (3) the consent of the parent who relinquished the minor is no longer required since the agency has assumed placement responsibilities.

Subdivision (4) is considered to be consistent with Ala. Code § 43-8-6(c) which directs that a person be presumed dead after a continuous absence of five (5) years.

Notice of pendency of the adoption proceedings is required to numerous parties even though their consent or relinquishment is not required. Section 26-10A-17 provides for notice requirements.

This section is derived from section 8 of the ABA Model State Adoption Act and is generally consistent with former section 26-10-3.

§ 26-10A-11. Consent or relinquishment.

A consent or relinquishment must be in writing, signed by the person consenting or relinquishing, and shall state the following:

(1) The date, place, and time of execution;

(2) The date of birth or if prior to birth expected date of birth of the adoptee and any names by which the adoptee has been known;

(3) The relationship of the person consenting or relinquishing to the adoptee;

(4) The name of each petitioner, unless (i) the document is relinquishment of the adoptee to an agency, or (ii) the consent contains a statement that the person executing the consent knows that he or she has a right to know the identity of each petitioner but voluntarily waives this right;

(5) That the person executing the document is voluntarily and unequivocally consenting to the adoption of the named adoptee;

(6) That by signing the document and subsequent court order to ratify the consent, the person executing the document understands that he or she will forfeit all rights and obligations; that he or she understands the consent or relinquishment and executes it freely and voluntarily;

(7) That the person executing the document understands that the consent may be irrevocable, and should not execute it if he or she needs or desires psychological or legal advice, guidance or counseling;

(8) The address of the court in which the petition for adoption has been or will be filed, if known, and if not known, the name and address of the agency, the petitioners or their attorney on whom notice of the withdrawal of consent may be served;

166

(9) In the case of relinquishment, the name and address of the agency to which the adoptee has been relinquished;

(10) That the person executing the same has received or been offered a copy of the consent or relinquishment;

(11) That the person executing a relinquishment waives further notice of the adoption proceeding;

(12) That the person executing a consent waives further notice of the adoption proceedings, unless there is a contest or appeal of the adoption proceeding. (Acts 1990, No. 90-554, p. 912, § 11.)

Comment

The form of the document evidencing consent to or relinquishment for adoption must comply strictly with all requirements in this section.

Subdivision (4) provides for the anonymity of the adopting parent(s) in those cases in which the parent executing the document desires it and voluntarily waives on the face of the document his or her right to know the identity of the adopting parent(s).

Subdivision (8) provides where a person is to initiate notice of withdrawal. See also section 26-10A-13 and section 26-10A-14.

Subdivisions (11) and (12) provide for the waiver of further notice of the adoption proceedings to the person executing the consent or relinquishment. Subdivision (12), however, recognizes that a person executing a consent does not waive the right to further notice if the adoption is contested in the trial court or the final decree of adoption is appealed. (See section 26-10A-26(b)). The reason for this distinction is that a person who relinquishes a minor to an agency gives the agency authority to choose suitable adopting parents, whoever they may be. But a person who consents to the adoption of a minor may condition his or her consent on the adoption of the minor by a specific person(s). If the adoption of the minor by the designated person(s) is challenged, either by a successful contested hearing in the trial court or by appeal of the final decree, the person executing the consent in reliance on that assumption has a continuing interest in the adoption proceeding, notwithstanding the waiver of the right to further notice in the consent document.

This section is derived from section 9 of the ABA Model State Adoption Act. Prior Alabama law did not specifically delineate the form of consent.

§ 26-10A-12. Persons who may take consent or relinquishments; forms.

(a) A consent of the natural mother taken prior to the birth of a child shall be signed or confirmed before a judge of probate. At the time of taking the consent the judge shall explain to the consenting parent the legal effect of signing the document and the time limits and procedures for withdrawal of the consent and shall provide the parent with a form for withdrawing the consent in accordance with the requirements of Sections 26-10A-13 and 26-10A-14.

(b) All other pre-birth or post-birth consents or relinquishments shall be signed or confirmed before:

(1) A judge or clerk of any court which has jurisdiction over adoption proceedings, or a public officer appointed by such judge for the purpose of taking consents; or

(2) A person appointed to take consents who is appointed by any agency which is authorized to conduct investigations or home studies provided by Section 26-10A-19, or, if the consent is taken out of state, by a person appointed to take consents by any agency which is authorized by that state's law to conduct investigations and home studies for adoptions; or

(3) A notary public.

(c) The form for the consent or relinquishment or the withdrawal of the consent or relinquishment shall state in substantially the same form as follows:

CONSENT OR RELINQUISHMENT OF MINOR FOR ADOPTION

THE STATE OF ALABAMA   )
_____ COUNTY)
KNOW ALL MEN BY THESE PRESENT, that:

1. I, _____
(name of person consenting or relinquishing)
the _____ of
(parents, legal guardian, agency)
(a) a minor _____
(state any names by which the minor has been known)
born _____, 19____.
(or)
(b) an unborn child whose expected date of birth is
_____, do hereby:
(a) consent to the adoption of the said minor by

_____
(name of petitioners, unless identity waived)
(or)
(b) relinquish the said minor for the purpose of adoption to

_____
(name and address of agency)
in order that said minor may have all the privileges which may be accorded to (him) (her) by the laws of Alabama upon (his) (her) legal adoption;

2. I am executing this document voluntarily and unequivocally thereby [consenting to the adoption of] [relinquishing] said minor;

3. I understand that by signing this document and the subsequent court order to ratify the consent, I will forfeit all rights and obligations and that I understand the [consent to the adoption] [relinquishment] and execute it freely and voluntarily;

4. I understand that the [consent to the adoption] [relinquishment] may be irrevocable, and I should not execute it if I need or desire psychological or legal advice, guidance or counseling;

5. I have received or been offered a copy of this document;

6. I waive the right to know the identity of each petitioner who petitions to adopt the said minor child;

7. [I waive further notice of the adoption proceedings by the execution of this relinquishment to the named agency];
(or)
[I waive further notice of the adoption proceedings by the execution of this consent, unless there is a contest or appeal of the adoption proceedings];

8. I understand that notice of withdrawal of [consent] [relinquishment] must be mailed to

[_____,

(county where consent or petition is filed if known)
Probate Court at the following address_____]
or

[_____

(name and address of agency with whom document is filed or the
_____]

petitioners or their attorney if county where petition is filed is unknown) and that such withdrawal must be mailed within five days after the birth of said minor or the execution of this document whichever comes last;

9. I do hereby request that the probate judge make all such orders and decrees as may be necessary or proper to legally effectuate said adoption.

Given under my hand at _____ o'clock, _____
day of _____, 19____, at _____

(address of filing)
_____ (SEAL)

Affiant's Signature
"I, _____, sign my name to
this instrument this _____ day
of _____, 19_____, and being first duly sworn, do hereby declare to the undersigned authority that I execute it as my free and voluntary act for the purposes therein expressed, and that I am _____ years of age or older, of sound mind, and under no constraint or undue influence."

_____ (SEAL)
Affiant's Signature

STATE OF ALABAMA   )
COUNTY OF _____   )

Subscribed, sworn to and acknowledged before me by _____
_____, this _____ day of
_____, 19____.

SEAL   (Signed) _____

_____
(Official Capacity of Officer)
I acknowledge receipt of two copies of this document.

_____ (SEAL)

Date

169

I _____, on this _____ day of _____, 19____, at
     affiant

_____ a.m./p.m. in the presence of the two witnesses
    (time of day)

whose signatures and addresses are subscribed below, hereby withdraw the adoption [consent] [relinquishment] previously signed by me.

_____   _____

Witness   Affiant's Signature

_____

Address

_____

Witness

_____

Address

(Acts 1990, No. 90-554, p. 912, § 12.)

Comment

This section provides the methods for the taking of consents or relinquishments from the mother and father. Section 26-10A-12(a) provides for pre-birth consent by the natural mother and ensures that the legal effect of consent and procedures for withdrawal are explained by a judge of probate. Subsection (b) incorporates the procedures for all other pre-birth consents as well as all post-birth consents. Special care should be taken when obtaining consents soon after the birth of the child. The mother, unlike the father, may have been sedated during labor, and, in any event, had to undergo the physical stress of delivery. Forms are provided to implement the consent or relinquishment procedure.

This section is derived from section 10 of the ABA Model State Adoption Act and contains provisions new to Alabama law.

§ 26-10A-13. Time of consent or relinquishment; filing with court.

(a) A consent or relinquishment may be taken at any time, except that once signed or confirmed, may be withdrawn within five days after birth or within five days after signing of the consent or relinquishment, whichever comes last.

(b) Consent or relinquishment can be withdrawn if the court finds that the withdrawal is reasonable under the circumstances and consistent with the best interest of the child within 14 days after the birth of the child or within 14 days after signing of the consent or relinquishment, whichever comes last.

(c) All consents or relinquishments required by this act shall be filed with the court in which the petition for adoption is pending before the final decree of adoption is entered. (Acts 1990, No. 90-554, p. 912, § 13.)

Comment

It is desirable that the consent or relinquishment be taken before mother and infant are discharged from the hospital in order that a stable environment be available for the infant. However, certain conditions may make it desirable to withdraw consent or relinquishment within five (5) days on motion of the party or within fourteen (14) days if the court finds it to be reasonable and consistent with the best interest of the child.

Unlike the provision, former adoption statutory law did not require written consent. See, e.g., *Davis v. Turner,* 337 So. 2d 355 (Ala. Civ. App.), *cert. denied,* 337 So. 2d 362 (Ala. 1976).

The consent or relinquishment must be filed with the probate court before the final decree of adoption is entered.

§ 26-10A-14. Withdrawal of consent or relinquishment.

(a) The consent or relinquishment, once signed or confirmed, may not be withdrawn except:

(1) As provided in Section 26-10A-13; or

(2) At any time until the final decree upon a showing that the consent or relinquishment was obtained by fraud, duress, mistake, or undue influence on the part of a petitioner or his agent or the agency to whom or for whose benefit it was given. After one year from the date of final decree of adoption is entered, a consent or relinquishment may not be challenged on any ground, except in cases where the adoptee has been kidnapped.

(b) The withdrawal of consent or relinquishment as provided in Section 26-10A-13(a) shall be effected by the affiant signing and dating the withdrawal form provided pursuant to Section 26-10A-12(c) or other written withdrawal of consent containing the information set forth in Section 26-10A-12(c), and by delivering the withdrawal to the court or having the withdrawal postmarked within five days of the child's birth or of signing the consent or relinquishment, whichever comes last.

(c) The petition to withdraw consent or relinquishment must be in writing, signed by the person seeking to withdraw the consent or relinquishment, dated, and signed by two witnesses.

(d) In adjudicating a petition to withdraw a consent or relinquishment, the person seeking to withdraw the consent or relinquishment shall establish the facts necessary to withdraw the consent or relinquishment by a preponderance of the evidence. The court shall not apply any presumption or preference in favor of the natural parents in reviewing an action brought under this section.

(e) If the court directs that the consent or relinquishment be withdrawn, the court shall order the minor restored to the custody of his or her parent, the department of human resources or a licensed child placing agency; otherwise, the court shall deny the withdrawal and declare that the consent or relinquishment is final and binding. Any order made by the court upon a petition to withdraw consent or relinquishment under this section shall be deemed a final order for the purpose of filing an appeal under section 26-10A-26. (Acts 1990, No. 90-554, p. 912, § 14.)

Comment

Subsection 26-10A-14(a) establishes the time periods within which a consent or relinquishment may be withdrawn. The difference between the right to withdraw the consent or relinquishment during the time periods is the burden of the party seeking withdrawal. The consenting party has the absolute right to withdraw his or her consent or relinquishment up to five (5) days after the signing or five (5) days after the birth whichever comes last. It is not uncommon for some parents to change their minds about giving up their child for adoption once the child has been born.

Furthermore, the consenting party has an additional nine (9) days in which consent or relinquishment may be withdrawn if the court finds it is reasonable under the circumstances and in the best interest of the child. A higher burden is required since in many instances the child would already be placed with the petitioner and bonding occurred.

Additionally, under the enumerated circumstances such as fraud, duress, etc., the consenting parties may withdraw their consent at any time until the final decree. Under prior case law, generally a parent could not withdraw his or her consent once the child had been placed with the petitioners. *Kelly v. Licensed Foster Parents,* 429 So. 2d 265 (Ala. 1982).

It was determined that a decree of adoption should always be subject to challenges when a minor was kidnapped. Otherwise, the wrongful act would be given protection.

After one year from the date of the final decree of adoption the consent may not be challenged on any ground except when the adoptee was kidnapped. This differs from former section 26-10-5(c) which provided that a final order of adoption would not be set aside after five years because of any irregularities, infirmity or defect in the adoption proceedings.

This provision providing for a formalized withdrawing of a consent or relinquishment is new to Alabama law and was derived from section 12 of the ABA Model State Adoption Act.

§ 26-10A-15. Surrender of custody of minor under age of majority.

(a) No health facility shall surrender the physical custody of an adoptee to any person other than the Department of Human Resources, a licensed child placing agency, parent, relative by blood or marriage, or person having legal custody, unless such surrender is authorized in a writing executed after the birth of the adoptee by one of the adoptee's parents or agency or the person having legal custody of the adoptee.

(b) A health facility shall report to the Department of Human Resources on forms supplied by the department, the name and address of any person and, in the case of a person acting as an agent for an organization, the name and address of the organization to whose physical custody an adoptee is surrendered. Such report shall be transmitted to the department within 48 hours from the surrendering of custody.

(c) No adoptee shall be placed with the petitioners prior to the completion of a pre-placement investigation except for good cause shown and with written notice immediately given to the court, and to the county department of human resources. (Acts 1990, No. 90-554, p. 912, § 15.)

Comment

If a child is released to someone other than the biological parent, or certain specified individuals or agencies, notice must be given by the health facility in order that children are not placed in homes of unrelated persons prior to a pre-placement investigation. Pre-placement investigation assists in ensuring a stable environment for the adoptee and expedites the adoption process.

This section is derived from section 13 of the ABA Model State Adoption Act and is new to Alabama law.

§ 26-10A-16. Petition.

(a) A petition for adoption shall be filed with the clerk of the court within 30 days after the minor is placed with the prospective adoptive parent or parents for purposes of adoption unless the minor is in custody of the Department of Human Resources or a licensed child placing agency except that a petition for good cause shown may be filed beyond the 30-day period. The petition shall be signed, and verified by each petitioner, and shall allege:

(1) The full name, age, and place of residence of each petitioner and, if married, the place and date of marriage;

(2) The date and place of birth of the adoptee, except in the case of abandonment;

(3) The birth name of the adoptee, any other names by which the adoptee has been known, and the adoptee's proposed new name;

(4) Where the adoptee is residing at the time of the filing of the petition, and if the minor is not in the custody of a petitioner, when he, she, or they intend to acquire custody;

(5) That each petitioner desires to establish a parent and child relationship between himself or herself and the adoptee and that he or she is a fit and proper person able to care for and provide for the adoptee's welfare;

(6) The existence and nature of any prior court orders known to the petitioner which affect the custody, visitation, or access to the adoptee;

(7) The relationship, if any, of each petitioner to the adoptee;

(8) The name and address of the placing agency, if any; and

(9) The names and addresses of all persons known to the petitioner at the time of filing from whom consents or relinquishment to the adoption are required;

(b) The caption of a petition for adoption shall be styled "In the Matter of the Adoption Petition of _____." Each petitioner shall be designated in the caption.

(c) The petition shall be accompanied by a copy of the child's birth certificate or affidavit stating that application for a birth certificate has been made except in cases where the child has been abandoned. (Acts 1990, No. 90-554, p. 912, § 16.)

Comment

Recognizing the need to encourage the prompt filing of petitions led to the conclusion that general guidelines were needed. The investigator's role is especially important with the type of petition required. The investigation will determine the validity of the petitioner's information and generally use the petition as a basis for the investigatory stage. It is impractical to require petitioners to ascertain certain information prior to filing of the petition, and therefore the language, "known to petitioner," in subdivisions (a)(6) and (a)(9) was selected.

Subdivision (a)(9) requires that the petition list all persons specified in section 26-10A-7 from whom consents must be obtained who are known to the petitioners at the time of filing the petition.

Subsection (b) seeks to ensure confidentiality by requiring that the petitioner's name be designated in the caption of the petition for adoption rather than the name of the adoptee.

This section is derived from section 14(a) and (b) of the ABA Model State Adoption Act and is generally consistent with former section 26-10-1 of the Code of Alabama. The requirement, however, that the petition must be filed within 30 days after placement is new to Alabama law.

§ 26-10A-17. Notice of petition; form of service; waiver.

(a) Unless service has been previously waived, notice of pendency of the adoption proceeding shall be served by the petitioner on:

(1) Any person, agency, or institution whose consent or relinquishment is required by Section 26-10A-7, unless service has been previously waived;

(2) The legally appointed custodian or guardian of the adoptee;

(3) The spouse of any petitioner who has not joined in the petition;

(4) The spouse of the adoptee;

(5) The surviving parent or parents of a deceased parent of the adoptee;

(6) Any person known to the petitioners as having physical custody, excluding licensed foster care or other private licensed agencies or having visitation rights with the adoptee under an existing court order;

(7) The agency or individual authorized to investigate the adoption under Section 26-10A-19;

(8) Any other person designated by the court;

(9) Department of Human Resources; and

(10) The father and putative father of the adoptee if made known by the mother or otherwise known by the court.

(b) The notice shall specifically state that the person served must respond to the petitioner within 30 days if he or she intends to contest the adoption. A copy of the petition for adoption shall be delivered to those individuals or agencies in subdivisions (a)(2) through (a)(10).

(c) Service of the notice shall be made in the following manner:

(1) Service of process shall be made in accordance with the Alabama Rules of Civil Procedure except as otherwise provided by the Alabama Rules of Juvenile Procedure. If the identity or whereabouts of the parent is unknown, or if the one parent fails or refuses to disclose the identity or

whereabouts of the other parent, the court shall then issue an order providing for service by publication, by posting, or by any other substituted service.

(2) As to the agency or individual referred to in subdivisions (a)(7) and (a)(9) above, notice shall be by certified mail.

(3) As to any other person for whom notice is required under subsection (a) of this section, service by certified mail, return receipt requested, shall be sufficient. If such service cannot be completed after two attempts, the court shall issue an order providing for service by publication, by posting, or by any other substituted service.

(d) The notice required by this section may be waived in writing by the person entitled to receive notice.

(e) Proof of service of the notice on all persons for whom notice is required by this section must be filed with the court before the adjudicational hearing, provided in Section 26-10A-24. (Acts 1990, No. 90-554, p. 912, § 17.)

Comment

This section specifies the persons who are entitled to notice of the adoption proceedings. According to the Supreme Court in *Lehr v. Robertson,* 463 U.S. 248 (1983), due process requires that notice be sent only to "responsible" fathers who have come forward prior to the adoption proceedings to participate in the rearing of the minor. The category of person listed in subdivisions 26-10A-17(a)(1) through (a)(10) is broader than the minimum requirements of the due process clause as interpreted by the Supreme Court in *Lehr.* A person who is merely alleged by the mother to be the father of the adoptee is given the right to notice, even if he has never developed a relationship with the minor. However, a putative father does not have an absolute veto power over the adoption. If the putative father receives notice of the adoption and fails to respond within thirty days, his consent is no longer required under § 26-10A-7. Furthermore, under § 26-10A-10(6), the consent of the natural father is not required when the mother indicates that the natural father is unknown, unless the natural father is otherwise made known to the court.

This section is derived from section 15 of the ABA Model State Adoption Act and is generally consistent with former section 26-10-3 of the Code of Alabama. This provision, however, is much more detailed concerning what type of service is effective than was provided under former section 26-10-2. Furthermore, section 26-10A-17 broadens the class of individuals that must be given notice of the adoption proceeding from those enumerated in former section 26-10-3.

§ 26-10A-18. Custody pending final decree.

Once a petitioner has received the adoptee into his or her home for the purposes of adoption and a petition for adoption has been filed, an interlocutory decree shall be entered delegating to the petitioner (1) custody, except custody shall be retained by the Department of Human Resources or the licensed child placing agency which held custody at the time of the placement until the entry of the final decree and (2) the responsibility for the care, maintenance, and support of the adoptee, including any necessary medical or surgical treatment, pending further order of the court. (Acts 1990, No. 90-554, p. 912, § 18.)

Comment

There is a need to establish the legality of the custody of the prospective adopting parents quickly to enable them to authorize any emergency medical care for the minor. However, adopting parents may not obtain legal custody of the minor until the minor is physically present in the home and a petition for adoption has been filed and an interlocutory decree entered. The reason for this requirement is to encourage prompt filing of petitions for adoption. Section 26-10A-16(a) generally requires petitioner to file within thirty (30) days of the date adoptee is placed in home except for good cause shown. It is not desirable to have a minor in the care of persons who do not have legal custody of the minor and who are not under the supervision of the court. Prompt filing of the petition for adoption brings the child's situation to the attention of the court and gives the court jurisdiction over the parties.

The final language, "pending further order of the court", makes it clear that the adopting parents' custody of the minor is subject to the continuing supervision of the court until a final decree of adoption is entered. As provided for in section 26-10A-24, a proper person at any time before a final decree of adoption is entered may petition the court for a contested hearing. If the contesting party is successful, the court shall dismiss the adoption proceedings.

Section 26-10A-18 is derived from section 16 of the ABA Model State Adoption Act. This section differs from former section 26-10-4 which provided for the entry of an interlocutory order after the judge had determined the merits of the adoption. The purpose of this change is to encourage parents having physical custody of a child to notify the court of their intent to adopt the child and to secure for the child a legal custodian to be responsible for the care and support of that child. The existence of an interlocutory order will enable the petitioners to make necessary medical and other decisions concerning the welfare of the child.

§ 26-10A-19. Investigation.

(a) A pre-placement investigation shall be made to determine the suitability of each petitioner and the home in which the adoptee will be placed. The investigation shall include a criminal background investigation and any other circumstances which might be relevant to the placement of an adoptee with the petitioners. A copy of the pre-placement investigation shall be filed with the court when the petition for adoption is filed.

(b) An individual or couple may initiate a pre-placement investigation by request directly through the Department of Human Resources or a licensed child placing agency or by filing a request with the probate court. The court may appoint any agency or individual qualified under subsection (d) to perform the pre-placement investigation. Upon completion of the investigation, a copy of the report shall be sent to the petitioners. The report is to be filed with the court at the time of the filing of the petition for adoption.

(c) Unless a pre-placement investigation has been performed within 24 months of the petition or an investigation is dispensed with by court order for good cause shown on the record, no decree for the adoption of any adoptee shall be entered until a full post-placement investigation ordered by the court has been made concerning:

(1) The suitability of each petitioner, and his, her, or their home for the adoptee;

(2) Why the natural parents, if living, desire to be relieved of the care, support and guardianship of such minor;

(3) Whether the natural parents have abandoned such minor or are otherwise unsuited to have its custody;

(4) Any orders, judgments, or decrees affecting the adoptee or any children of the petitioner;

(5) Any property owned by the adoptee;

(6) The medical histories, both physical and mental, of the adoptee and the biological parents. This history shall be provided to the petitioner in writing before the decree is entered;

(7) Criminal background investigations;

(8) The costs and expenses connected with the adoption; and

(9) Any other circumstances which may be relevant to the placement of the adoptee with the petitioners.

(d)(1) A pre-placement investigation or a post-placement investigation must be performed by one of the following:

a. The Department of Human Resources;

b. A licensed child placing agency;

c. An individual or agency licensed by the department to perform investigations; or

d. An individual appointed by the court who is a social worker licensed by the State Board of Social Work Examiners or a social worker II or above who is under the state merit system who is also certified by the State Board of Social Work Examiners for private independent practice in the social casework specialty, as provided for in Section 34-30-3.

(2) Notwithstanding subdivision (d)(1), the court on its own motion may order the post-placement investigation be performed by an agency or individual other than the agency placing the adoptee, when the court has cause to believe the investigation is insufficient.

(e) In every adoption proceeding, after a child has been placed in the home, in the post-placement investigation an investigator must observe the adoptee and interview the petitioner in their home as soon as possible after notice of the placement but in any event within 45 days after the placement.

(f) The investigator shall complete and file his or her written report with the court within 60 days from receipt of notice of the proceeding and shall deliver a copy of the report to the petitioner's attorney or to each petitioner if he or she is appearing pro se. The investigation shall include a verification of all allegations of the petition. The report shall include sufficient facts for the court to determine whether there has been compliance with consent or relinquishment provisions of this chapter. The post-placement investigation shall include all of the information enumerated within subdivisions (c)(1) through (c)(9) that was not obtained in the pre-placement investigation required under subsection (a).

(g) Upon a showing of a good cause and after notice to the petitioners, the court may grant extensions of time to the investigator to file his or her investigation.

(h) Notwithstanding this section no investigations shall be required for those adoptions under Sections 26-10A-27 and 26-10A-28.

(i) When the investigation has been conducted, the investigatory report shall not be conclusive but may be considered along with other evidence. (Acts 1990, No. 90-554, p. 912, § 19.)

Comment

Pre-placement investigation by parties enumerated in subsection (d) is generally required in order to facilitate the adoption process and ensure the protection of the child. It is important that adoption proceedings be expeditious, therefore the post-placement investigation report must be filed within sixty (60) days. In addition, it is imperative that the investigating officer visit the adoptee in the home of the petitioners as soon as possible to ensure the safety and health of the adoptee.

No investigations are required for those adoptions under sections 26-10A-27 and 26-10A-28 which deal with stepparent adoptions and adoption by other relatives unless directed by the court. This is consistent with former sections 26-10-2 and 26-10-7 which did not require investigations in similar cases.

Pre-placement or post-placement investigations may be performed by the Department of Human Resources, licensed agencies or individuals, or a court appointee. This section broadens the categories of people who may investigate to include licensed individuals and court appointees. Former section 26-10-2 provided for the investigation to be completed by DHR or other agencies licensed through DHR.

Under section 26-10A-19 there must be a post-placement in which the investigator must observe the adoptee in the home within 45 days of notice of petition and make a report to the court within 60 days. This differs from former section 26-10-4 which required that after an interlocutory decree had been entered there were to be at least two visits in the home.

This section is derived from section 17 of the ABA Model State Adoption Act.

Cross references. — As to case notes relating to conduct of investigation as to petition and report of findings, see §§ 26-10A-16 and 26-10A-17.

Editor's note. — The cases annotated below were decided under prior law.

The report and recommendations of the department of human resources is admissible and is not a private matter of consultation between the trial court and agents of the department. Williams v. Pope, 281 Ala. 416, 203 So. 2d 271 (1967); Lawson v. Jennings, 52 Ala. App. 582, 296 So. 2d 176 (1974).

And agents of the department are subject to cross-examination as to their recommendations. Williams v. Pope, 281 Ala. 416, 203 So. 2d 271 (1967); Lawson v. Jennings, 52 Ala. App. 582, 296 So. 2d 176 (1974).

Report is analogous to master's report. — The report of the authorities made under this section is analogous to a master's report, which is a matter of record and is accorded the weight of the verdict of a jury. Claunch v. Entrekin, 272 Ala. 35, 128 So. 2d 100 (1961); Williams v. Pope, 281 Ala. 416, 203 So. 2d 271 (1967).

Report of Catholic Social Services is analogous to report of a master and is due to be accorded the weight of a jury verdict. In re Morrison, 388 So. 2d 1014 (Ala. Civ. App. 1980).

Report is not confidential as between litigants, trial court and supreme court. — While the source of the information may remain confidential, the report by the department of human resources is not confidential as between the litigants, the trial court or the supreme court on appeal. Williams v. Pope, 281 Ala. 416, 203 So. 2d 271 (1967).

All the litigants in an adoption proceeding are entitled to know all the evidence that is considered by a court in arriving at a judicial determination. Williams v. Pope, 281 Ala. 416, 203 So. 2d 271 (1967).

Trial judge can recess hearing to his chambers to hear evidence which possibly should not be made public. Williams v. Pope, 281 Ala. 416, 203 So. 2d 271 (1967).

Cited in Williams v. Pope, 284 Ala. 456, 225 So. 2d 861 (1969); Davis v. Turner, 55 Ala. App. 366, 315 So. 2d 602 (1975); McLeod v. United States, 276 F. Supp. 213 (S.D. Ala. 1967).

Collateral references. — 2 C.J.S., Adoption of Persons, § 49.

2 Am. Jur. 2d, Adoption, § 58 et seq.

What constitutes abandonment or desertion of child by its parent or parents within purview of adoption laws. 35 ALR2d 662, 78 ALR3d 712.

Mental illness and the like of parents as ground for adoption of their children. 45 ALR2d 1379.

Religion as factor in adoption proceedings. 48 ALR3d 383.

Adoption of child in absence of statutorily required consent of public or private agency or institution. 83 ALR3d 373.

Age of prospective adoptive parent as factor. 84 ALR3d 665.

Marital status of prospective adopting parents as factor in adoption proceedings. 2 ALR4th 555.

Race as factor in adoption proceedings. 34 ALR4th 167.

Marital or sexual relationship between parties as affecting right to adopt. 42 ALR4th 776.

§ 26-10A-20. Removal of adoptee from county.

After the petitioner has received the adoptee into his or her home, the adoptee shall not be removed from the county in which the petitioner resides until the final decree has been issued for a period of longer than 15 consecutive days unless notice is given to the investigating agency or person. (Acts 1990, No. 90-554, p. 912, § 20.)

Comment

The adoptee should be readily accessible to the court and to any investigating officers. The period between filing the petition and obtaining the final decree is so short that removal of the minor for longer than fifteen (15) days without notice could interfere with timely completion of the adoption process. The removal of the minor without notice could indicate a lack of responsibility on part of the potential adoptive parent.

This section is derived from section 18 of the ABA Model State Adoption Act and is new to Alabama law.

§ 26-10A-21. Related proceedings.

If, at any time during the pendency of the adoption proceeding, it is determined that any other custody action concerning the adoptee is pending in the courts of this state or any other state or country, any party to the adoption proceeding, or the court on its own motion, shall move to stay such adoption proceeding until a determination has been made by an appropriate court with jurisdiction pursuant to the provisions of the Uniform Child Custody Jurisdiction Act (UCCJA) or the Parental Kidnapping Prevention Act (PKPA). (Acts 1990, No. 90-554, p. 912, § 21.)

Comment

Multiple proceedings, in one state or in several states, affecting the adoptee, should be discouraged. A single proceeding, or a consolidation of proceedings, is to be encouraged. The philosophies of the Interstate Compact on Juveniles, Alabama Code § 44-2-1, the Uniform Child Custody Jurisdiction Act, Alabama Code § 30-3-22 and the Parental Kidnapping Prevention Act, 28 USC § 1738A are to be encouraged.

The circuit court is the proper forum for the initial determination of jurisdictional questions.

This section is consistent with section 19 of the ABA Model State Adoption Act and is new to Alabama law.

§ 26-10A-22. Attorney participation and appointment of attorney for the adoptee or other party.

(a) In making adoption arrangements, potential adopting parents and birth parents may obtain counsel to provide legal advice and assistance.

(b) Upon the motion of any party, or upon the court's own motion, before or after the filing of petition for adoption the court may appoint a guardian ad litem for the adoptee, or for any incompetent or minor who is a party to the proceeding or who would be a party to the proceeding. In the event of a contested adoption, a guardian ad litem shall be appointed. The fees of a guardian ad litem shall be assessed as court costs. (Acts 1990, No. 90-554, p. 912, § 22.)

Comment

The typical uncontested adoption does not require that an attorney or guardian ad litem be appointed for the adoptee. The minor is in the custody of the adopting parents and the parties are under the supervision of the court as soon as a petition for adoption is filed. See section 26-10A-18. The primary responsibility for assessing the suitability of the adopting parents' home for permanent placement of the adoptee is placed on the investigating agency and ultimately the court. See section 26-10A-19. If the court determines there are special circumstances which make it advisable that an attorney be appointed for the minor, or any other party, the court on its motion may do so. In a contested adoption, appointment of an independent attorney is mandated to ensure the best interest of the minor is protected.

This section is an expansion of section 20 of the ABA Model State Adoption Act and is new to Alabama law.

§ 26-10A-23. Fees and charges.

(a) No person, organization, group, agency or any legal entity may accept any fee whatsoever for bringing the adopting parent or parents together with the adoptee or the natural parents. A violation of this section shall be punished under Section 26-10A-33.

(b) Prior to payment, the petitioners must file with the court a full accounting of all charges for expenses, fees or services they or persons acting on their behalf will be paying relating to the adoption. Payment may be made only with court approval except that fees may be placed in an escrow account prior to court approval. The court may not refuse to approve a fee for documented services on the sole basis that a child has not been placed. The court shall approve all reasonable fees and expenses unless determined by the court to be unreasonable based upon specific written findings of fact.

(c) The petitioner must file a sworn statement that is a full accounting of all disbursements paid in the adoption.

(d) Under penalty of perjury, the adoptive parents and the parent or parents surrendering the minor for adoption shall, prior to the entry of the final adoption order, sign affidavits stating that no moneys or other things of value have been paid or received for giving the minor up for adoption. In addition to any penalties for perjury, the payment or receipt of money as referred to herein shall be punished as set forth in section 26-10A-33. (Acts 1990, No. 90-554, p. 912, § 23.)

Comment

Parties to an adoption are emotionally vulnerable. Therefore, the petitioners and the natural parent(s) are required to submit affidavits which state that they have not paid or received money in exchange for the minor being given up for adoption. The adoptive parents, however, may pay reasonable maternity-connected medical expenses as provided in section 26-10A-34. To underscore the prohibition against "baby selling" and to ensure that only appropriate fees and expenses are paid in connection with the adoption, all payments must receive prior approval from the court or be placed in escrow.

Penalties for violations of this provision are: (1) the penalty for perjury; and (2) the misdemeanor and felony penalty provided for in section 26-10A-34.

Although substantially different from former section 26-10-8, this section does embody the concept that financial inducements should not be used to entice parents to part from their children. The penalty revisions in this section are substantially greater than those provided for in former section 26-10-9.

This section is an expansion of section 21 of the ABA Model State Adoption Act.

§ 26-10A-24. Contested hearing.

(a) Whenever a motion contesting the adoption is filed, the court shall set the matter for a contested hearing to determine:

(1) Whether the best interests of the adoptee will be served by the adoption;

(2) Whether the adoptee is a person capable of being adopted by the petitioner in accordance with the requirements of this chapter;

(3) Whether an actual or implied consent or relinquishment to the adoption is valid; or

(4) Whether a consent or relinquishment may be withdrawn.

(b) The court shall give notice of the contested hearing by certified mail to all parties who have appeared before the court. The moving party and each petitioner shall be present at the contested hearing. The guardian ad litem shall appear and represent the interests of the adoptee.

(c) The court may continue the hearing from time to time to permit notice to all parties, or to permit further discovery, observation, investigation, or consideration of any fact or circumstances affecting the granting of the adoption petition. The court may order the investigating officer, appointed under Section 26-10A-19, to investigate the allegations set forth in the motion for a contested hearing or the whereabouts of any person entitled to notice of the proceeding.

(d) After hearing evidence at a contested hearing, the court shall dismiss the adoption proceeding if the court finds:

(1) That the adoption is not in the best interests of the adoptee;

(2) That a petitioner is not capable of adopting the adoptee;

(3) That a necessary consent cannot be obtained or is invalid; or

(4) That a necessary consent may be withdrawn. Otherwise the court shall deny the motion of the contesting party.

(e) On motion of either party or of the court, a contested adoption hearing may be transferred to the court having jurisdiction over juvenile matters.

(f) All references to the names of the parties in the proceedings shall be by initial only.

(g) Where the contested hearing is held in the probate court the judge may, upon completion of the contested hearing, immediately proceed with the dispositional hearing as provided in Section 26-10A-25. (Acts 1990, No. 90-554, p. 912, § 24.)

Comment

This section establishes the procedure for handling a contested adoption. All references to the names of the parties in the proceedings are to be by initial only.

On motion of either party or the court's own motion a contested adoption hearing may be transferred to the court having jurisdiction over juvenile matters. This is similar to current law section 12-12-35 which provides for the transfer of adoption proceedings to district court on the motion of a party.

The right to notice of the persons specified in section 26-10A-17 is meaningless if they are not provided with an opportunity to be heard by the court. The contested hearing, prior to the dispositional hearing, provides an opportunity for those persons who have received notice to present evidence that the adoption is not in the best interests of the adoptee or that any of the other grounds specified in subdivisions 26-10A-24 (a)(1) through (a)(4) are true. A contested hearing is initiated by filing a motion and serving notice upon the parties in accordance with subdivisions 26-10A-24 (a) and (b). The form of the motion and burden of proof as to establishing the allegations in subdivisions 26-10A-24(a)(1) through (a)(3) should be determined by the rules of procedure applicable in all civil proceedings. As to a petition to withdraw a consent or relinquishment (subdivision 26-10A-24(a)(4)), see sections 26-10A-13(a) and (b) and section 26-10A-14. If the contesting party is successful, the court must dismiss the adoption proceedings and determine custody according to the best interests of the minor. If the contesting party is unsuccessful, the court must deny the motion and set the matter for a dispositional hearing.

This section is derived from section 22 of the ABA Model State Adoption Act and is new to Alabama law.

§ 26-10A-25. Final decree; dispositional hearing.

(a) When the pre-placement investigation has been completed and approved or the investigation has been waived for good cause shown, the petition for adoption shall be set for a dispositional hearing as soon as possible or no later than 90 days after the filing of the petition. When there has not been a pre-placement investigation or the investigation has not been waived for good cause shown or when the adoptee is a special needs child, the petition for adoption shall be set for a dispositional hearing as soon as possible or no later than 120 days after the filing of the petition. Upon good cause shown, the court may extend the time for the dispositional hearing and entry of the final decree.

(b) At the dispositional hearing, the court shall grant a final decree of adoption if it finds on clear and convincing evidence that:

(1) The adoptee has been in the actual physical custody of the petitioners for a period of 60 days, unless for good cause shown, this requirement is waived by the court;

(2) All necessary consents, relinquishments, terminations or waivers have been obtained and, if appropriate, have been filed with the court;

(3) Service of the notice of pendency of the adoption proceeding has been made or dispensed with as to all persons entitled to receive notice under Section 26-10A-17;

(4) All contests brought under Section 26-10A-24 have been resolved in favor of the petitioner;

(5) That each petitioner is a suitable adopting parent and desires to establish a parent and child relationship between himself or herself and the adoptee;

(6) That the best interests of the adoptee are served by the adoption; and

(7) All other requirements of this chapter have been met.

(c) The court shall enter its finding in a written decree which shall also include the new name of the adoptee, and shall not include any other name by which the adoptee has been known or the names of the natural or presumed parents. The final decree shall further order that from the date of the decree, the adoptee shall be the child of the petitioners, and that the adoptee shall be accorded the status set forth in Section 26-10A-29.

(d) A final decree of adoption may not be collaterally attacked, except in cases of fraud or where the adoptee has been kidnapped, after the expiration of one year from the entry of the final decree and after all appeals, if any. (Acts 1990, No. 90-554, p. 912, § 25.)

Comment

The dispositional hearing is the only one necessary to complete the adoption if there is no motion for a contested hearing. A timely disposition of the proceedings is provided in section 26-10A-25(a). The requirements for the granting of a final decree of adoption by the court are delineated in section 26-10A-25(b)(1) through (b)(7). Section 26-10A-25(c) facilitates the confidentality of the adoption process.

This section decreases the length of time that an adoptee must live with the petitioners from six months as was required in former section 26-10-4 to 60 days.

When the final order is entered, the adoptee shall have a new name and the decree shall not include any other name by which the adoptee had been known or the names of the natural or presumed parents. The final decree of adoption may not be collaterally attacked after the expiration of one year from the entry of the filed decree after all appeals except for fraud, or when the adoptee has been kidnapped because it is imperative that the adoptee be assured a secure and stable environment without an untimely and unfounded interruption (see section 26-10A-25(d)). This section differs from former section 26-10-5(c) which provided for a five year statute of limitations to set aside an adoption because of any irregularity, infirmity or defect in the adoption proceedings.

This section is derived from section 23 of the ABA Model State Adoption Act.

Cross references. — As to rights of adopted child under will of adoptive parents made prior to adoption, see § 43-8-91.

I. General Consideration.
II. Decisions Under Prior Law.

I. GENERAL CONSIDERATION.

Key to retaining right to set aside adoption is commencement of action within specified time period. — The instant revisions in this section evidence the legislative intent that the key to retaining the right to set aside the final order of adoption is the commencement of the action within the specified time period. Ex parte B.W.C., 590 So. 2d 279 (Ala. 1991).

II. DECISIONS UNDER PRIOR LAW.

Weight of adoption proceeding. — In an action to restore an adopted child to its natural parents, it was held that the adoption proceedings, though not conclusive, were entitled to weighty consideration, especially where they were had with the consent and at the request of the parents of the child. McClure v. Williams, 201 Ala. 499, 78 So. 853 (1918).

Alabama courts are always open to consider any matter which may affect the welfare or best interest of a child. Of course, legal relationships, whether natural or established by law, are of primary consideration in any case. However they are not preemptive. The paramount consideration is the welfare of the child, and all other rules pertaining to child custody are subservient to this main principle. Murphy v. Bronstein, 434 So. 2d 778 (Ala. Civ. App. 1982).

The authority of the Alabama circuit court to hear matters which may involve the welfare of children, particularly those already under its protection, is not limited to so-called legal or bloodline relationships. Murphy v. Bronstein, 434 So. 2d 778 (Ala. Civ. App. 1982).

The probate court is a court of limited jurisdiction. Skipper v. Skipper, 283 Ala. 286, 215 So. 2d 885 (1968).

Jurisdictional facts must affirmatively appear on face of record. — The existence of facts necessary to confer jurisdiction on the probate court must affirmatively appear on the face of the record. Skipper v. Skipper, 283 Ala. 286, 215 So. 2d 885 (1968).

And nothing is presumed. — It must appear from the face of the petition before probate court that its action is within the scope of its special or limited jurisdiction, and nothing is presumed. Skipper v. Skipper, 283 Ala. 286, 215 So. 2d 885 (1968).

Court has jurisdiction to withdraw custody from adoptive parent. — In view of former § 26-10-5 it is clear that the adoptive parent stands in the right of the natural parent and it does not determine his right to custody against the claims of others and the interests of the child. The act of adoption merely carries the prima facie right to custody such as a natural parent has. A court has jurisdiction to withdraw custody from a natural parent, and a fortiori from an adoptive parent. Adoption proceedings cannot defeat that power, and do not judicially determine the right to custody as against the natural parent. Praytor v. Cole, 247 Ala. 259, 23 So. 2d 713 (1945).

Right of inheritance depends upon statute. — Unless the statute by express provision or necessary implication confers upon an adoptive relative the right to inherit the property of an adoptive relative who dies intestate, such right does not exist. Franklin v. White, 263 Ala. 223, 82 So. 2d 247 (1955).

Statute in effect at time of death is

controlling. — The rights of an adoptive parent in the estate of the adopted child are to be determined by the law in effect at the time of the child's death rather than the law in effect at the time of the adoption. Franklin v. White, 263 Ala. 223, 82 So. 2d 247 (1955).

The law providing for inheritance by an adopted child, or by the adoptive parent as an heir of the child, in effect at the time of the death of the person whose estate is involved, is controlling. Gamble v. Cloud, 263 Ala. 336, 82 So. 2d 526 (1955).

Adopted children may inherit from adoptive parents. — In the absence of a contrary intent clearly appearing, adopted children may inherit from their adoptive parents. Sellers v. Blackwell, 378 So. 2d 1106 (Ala. 1979).

But not from natural parents. — The 1984 amendment to this section removed from the statute the language which allowed an adopted child to inherit property from its natural parents. Barnett ex rel. Barnett v. Beck, 481 So. 2d 348 (Ala. 1985).

Child could not inherit from adoptive parent within one-year period. — Where by express terms of former section no child could have legal status of an adopted child until it had lived one year in home of adoptive parent, and until court entered its final decree of adoption, child could not during such period inherit from its adoptive parent. Rivers v. Rivers, 240 Ala. 648, 200 So. 764 (1941).

Adopted child's natural brothers and sisters not divested of rights in his estate. — Former section did not operate to divest the children of the natural parents, that is, the adopted child's natural brothers and sisters, of any rights which they might otherwise have had in the adopted child's estate. Franklin v. White, 263 Ala. 223, 82 So. 2d 247 (1955).

Adopted child did not inherit from collaterals. — There was no provision in this section for the adopted child to inherit from collaterals or others than the adoptive parent or parents. Gamble v. Cloud, 263 Ala. 336, 82 So. 2d 526 (1955).

An adopted daughter of a deceased brother of testatrix has no such interest in the estate, nor is she so related to testatrix, as to have a right to contest the probate of the will. Gamble v. Cloud, 263 Ala. 336, 82 So. 2d 526 (1955).

Presumption that "lawful issue" includes adopted children. — For case holding that, unless there clearly appears language or circumstances by which the testator foreclosed operation of the presumption, adopted children are included within the term "lawful issue," see Southside Baptist Church v. Drennen, 362 So. 2d 854 (Ala. 1978).

Presumption that adopted child is de- scendant of adopting parent so as to take remainder estate. — For case holding that, consistent with the adoption statute which creates a parent-child relationship bewteen the adopter and the adoptee, the latter is presumptively within the designation of the adopter's descendants, so as to take remainder estates created by deeds unless the context or circumstances clearly establish a contrary intention, see McCaleb v. Brown, 344 So. 2d 485 (Ala. 1977).

Previously adopted child not entitled to share in fund established for children of deceased police officers. — Child who had previously been adopted by her mother's second husband was not entitled to a distributive share in a private trust funded by public donations, which had been established for the benefit of the widows and children of two police officers killed in the line of duty, one of whom was the child's natural father, as she had not been intended by the settlers to be included. Barnett ex rel. Barnett v. Beck, 481 So. 2d 348 (Ala. 1985).

Adoption was not void although adoptive father's marriage was void. — Probate court did not err in failing to set aside the adoption of H.D. due to the fact that, at the time of the adoptive father's marriage to the child's natural mother, she remained married to a previous husband. In re Adoption of H.D.M., 568 So. 2d 828 (Ala. Civ. App. 1990).

Collateral references. — 2 C.J.S., Adoption of Persons, §§ 57, 98-102, 145-151.

2 Am. Jur. 2d, Adoption, § 65 et seq.

"Issue" as including adopted children. 2 ALR 974, 117 ALR 714.

Validity and effect of preadoption agreements derogating from the status or rights of an adopted child as fixed by statute. 9 ALR 1627.

Presumptive heir's right to object to adoption. 16 ALR 1020.

Amendment or vacation of adoption decree by adopting parent or natural parent consenting to adoption. 2 ALR2d 887.

Adoption as affecting right of inheritance through or from natural parents or other natural kin. 37 ALR2d 333.

Right of adopted child to inherit from kindred of adoptive parent. 43 ALR2d 1183.

Applicability of res judicata to decrees or judgments in adoption proceedings. 52 ALR2d 406.

What law, in point of time, governs inheritance from or through adopted person. 52 ALR2d 1228.

Change of child's name in adoption proceedings. 53 ALR2d 927.

Law governing effect, with respect to inheritance, of foreign contract to adopt. 81 ALR2d 1128.

Testamentary gift, adopted child as within class. 86 ALR2d 12.

Conflict of laws as to adoption, as affecting descent and distribution of decedent's estate. 87 ALR2d 1240.

Right of children of adopted child to inherit from adopting parent. 94 ALR2d 1200.

Adoption by third person as excluding one who otherwise answers to the description of a testamentary beneficiary. 96 ALR2d 639.

Restricting access to judicial records of concluded adoption proceedings. 83 ALR3d 800.

Restricting access to judicial records of pending adoption proceedings. 83 ALR3d 824.

Postadoption visitation by natural parent. 78 ALR4th 218.

§ 26-10A-26. Appeals.

(a) Appeals from any final decree of adoption shall be taken to the Alabama Court of Civil Appeals and filed within 14 days from the final decree.

(b) An appeal from any final order or decree rendered under this chapter shall have priority in all courts and shall have precedence over all other matters, except for other matters which have been given priority by specific statutory provision or rule of court. The trial court may enter further orders concerning the custody of the adoptee pending appeal.

(c) If an order, judgment, or decree rendered under this chapter is appealed, the party who files the appeal shall cause notice of the appeal to be transmitted to all persons entitled to receive notice pursuant to Section 26-10A-17, except for persons for whom consent or relinquishment has been implied under Section 26-10A-9 or whose consent or relinquishment is not required under Section 26-10A-10. Such notice of appeal shall set forth the pendency of the appeal and the right of interested parties to be heard. The notice shall not identify by name the party filing such appeal, unless the appellant is unrepresented, but shall specify the identity of the court in which the appeal is pending, the docket number of the petition, the general nature of the appeal, and the name, address and telephone number of the attorney who has filed the petition. The caption of an appeal shall show only the initials of the adoptee's birthname. Only the initials of the natural parents and the petitioner shall be indicated in all pleadings and briefs. (Acts 1990, No. 90-554, p. 912, § 26.)

Comment

Appeals from the final decree of the probate court shall be taken to the Alabama Court of Civil Appeals and are given priority since the question of where an adoptee lives is at stake and resolution of the appeal will mean stability to the adoptee.

Appealing directly to the Alabama Court of Civil Appeals is consistent with former section 12-3-10 and section 12-22-20.

The use of initials for the names of the adoptee, the natural parents and the petitioner will assist in ensuring the privacy of the parties and confidentiality of the adoption process.

This section is derived from section 24 of the ABA Model State Adoption Act.

§ 26-10A-27. Stepparent adoptions.

Any person may adopt his or her spouse's child according to the provisions of this chapter, except that:

(1) Before the filing of the petition for adoption, the adoptee must have resided for a period of one year with the petitioner, unless this filing provision is waived by the court for good cause shown;

(2) No investigation under Section 26-10A-19 shall occur unless otherwise directed by the court, and

(3) No report of fees and charges under Section 26-10A-23 shall be made unless ordered by the court. (Acts 1990, No. 90-554, p. 912, § 27.)

Comment

Stepparent adoptions are the most frequent type of adoptions. Subdivision (1) seeks to prevent the occurrence of an adoption before the new marriage has had a chance to stabilize. The adoptee must have resided with the petitioners for one (1) year; however, this requirement may be waived by the court for good cause. Generally, there is a de facto family unit in stepparent adoption situations, and the adoption proceedings may safely be streamlined by waiving the requirement of the investigation. If, however, the court learns of any extraordinary facts, an investigation may be ordered. The "baby-buying" situation does not ordinarily apply to stepparent adoptions; therefore, this subsection waives the report as to fees and charges as required by section 26-10A-23, unless facts called to the attention of the court suggest the necessity of such a report.

This section is similar to former section 26-10-7 except that the child must reside with the petitioner for a period of one year rather than six months as was previously required. Also, this section is consistent with former section 26-10-2 in that an investigation is not required in a stepparent adoption.

This section is derived from section 26 of the ABA Model State Adoption Act.

Subject matter jurisdiction of probate court. — Probate court had subject matter jurisdiction when it annulled a stepfather's adoption. C.C.K. v. M.R.K., 579 So. 2d 1368 (Ala. Civ. App. 1991) (decided under prior law).

Stepfather held resident of Marshall county although in Germany on military duty. — Authorities generally agree that a person inducted into military service retains his domicile or residence in the state from which he entered the military service. A person who is inducted into military service retains residence in the state from which he is inducted until a new residence is established or initital residence is abandoned. Since there is no evidence that the stepfather has established a new residence, nor has he had any intent to abandon his Marshall county residence, as required by statute, the stepfather was a resident of Marshall county at the time he filed the petition for adoption even though he was stationed in Germany under military orders. McCombs v. Shields, 497 So. 2d 149 (Ala. Civ. App. 1986) (decided under prior law).

§ 26-10A-28. Adoption by other relatives.

A grandfather, a grandmother, great-grandfather, great-grandmother, great-uncle, great-aunt, a brother, or a half-brother, a sister, a half-sister, an aunt or an uncle of the first degree and their respective spouses, if any may adopt a minor grandchild, a minor brother, a minor half-brother, a minor sister, a minor half-sister, a minor nephew, a minor niece, a minor great-grandchild, a minor great niece or a minor great nephew, according to the provisions of this chapter, except that:

(1) Before the filing of the petition for adoption, the adoptee must have resided for a period of one year with the petitioner, unless this filing provision is waived by the court for good cause shown;

(2) No investigation under Section 26-10A-19 shall occur unless otherwise directed by the court; and

(3) No report of fees and charges under Section 26-10A-23 shall be made unless ordered by the court. (Acts 1990, No. 90-554, p. 912, § 28.)

Comment

It is important to provide for adoption procedures by legally related individuals other than stepparents. The parties named in former section 26-10-7 were incorporated into this section and expanded to include great grandfather, great grandmother, great uncle, and great aunt. A similar provision is not in the ABA Model State Adoption Act. Less restrictive provisions are applicable where adoptions are of this type. Former section 26-10-7 provided, as does section 26-10A-28, that the adoptee must live with the petitioner for one year before a final decree of adoption can be entered. Under the new act, however, this provision may be waived by the court for good cause.

§ 26-10A-29. Name and status of adoptee.

(a) The adoptee shall take the name designated by the petitioner. After adoption, the adoptee shall be treated as the natural child of the adopting parent or parents and shall have all rights and be subject to all of the duties arising from that relation, including the right of inheritance.

(b) Upon the final decree of adoption, the natural parents of the adoptee, except for a natural parent who is the spouse of the adopting parent are relieved of all parental responsibility for the adoptee and will have no parental rights over the adoptee. (Acts 1990, No. 90-554, p. 912, § 29.)

Comment

The petitioners have freedom to designate the name of the minor. In some instances, for example, in a stepparent adoption of an older child, the petitioners may decide that it is in the best interest of the minor to retain the former surname. Subsection (a) also addresses the situation in which a husband and wife are known by different surnames. Subsection (b) is traditional in adoption acts, that is, the termination of all rights of the natural parents. All adoption acts, however, do not relieve the natural parents of all obligations for the adopted minor. This statute makes it clear that both the rights and responsibilities of the natural parents are terminated by the adoption which is consistent with former section 26-10-5. The right of inheritance of the adoptee is determined by the Probate Code, Ala. Code § 43-8-48.

This section is derived from section 27 of the ABA Model State Adoption Act.

§ 26-10A-30. Grandparent visitation.

Post-adoption visitation rights for the natural grandparents of the adoptee may be granted when the adoptee is adopted by a stepparent, a grandfather, a grandmother, a brother, a half-brother, a sister, a half-sister, an aunt or an uncle and their respective spouses, if any. Such visitation rights may be maintained or granted at the discretion of the court at any time prior to or after the final order of adoption is entered upon petition by the natural grandparents, if it is in the best interest of the child. (Acts 1990, No. 90-554, p. 912, § 29.1.)

Comment

The best interest of the child is the controlling factor in determining visitation rights. Grandparent visitation rights have been expanded by this section. The court may grant to the natural grandparents post-adoption visitation rights if it is in the best interest of the child. *Snipes v. Carr,* 526 So. 2d 591 (Ala. Civ. App. 1988). *See also Clark v. Leslie,* 537 So. 2d 25 (Ala. Civ. App. 1988) (visitation disallowed). This is in line with emerging case law concerning this area and goes beyond former section 26-10-5. See, Grandparental Rights to Visitation and Custody: A Trend in the Right Direction, 15 Cumberland Law Review 161 (1984).

Association with grandparents. — A child not only needs the love, care and attention of his or her parents or parent, but if fortunate enough to have living grandparents, deserves to have the love and association with its grandparents. Graves v. Graves, 51 Ala. App. 601, 288 So. 2d 142 (1973) (decided under former § 26-10-4).

Circuit court jurisdiction permitted for post-adoption grandparent visitation action. — The word "court" in § 30-3-4 was intended by the legislature to be the circuit court. Matters affecting the best interests of the child, as well as parental rights relating to the child, have essentially been within the jurisdiction of the circuit court; thus, grandmother seeking visitation rights was not limited to the probate court jurisdiction provided under former § 26-10-5. Ex parte Palmer, 574 So. 2d 44 (Ala. 1990).

Visitation rights for natural grandparents of adopted children. — Although at one time in this state adoption automatically cut off the grandparents' visitation rights, such has not been the case since 1984 when the legislature enacted former § 26-10-5. Under former § 26-10-5, following a final order of adoption, at the discretion of the court, visitation rights for the natural grandparents of the minor grandchildren may be maintained, or allowed upon petition of modification at any time after the final order of adoption is entered. Snipes v. Carr, 526 So. 2d 591 (Ala. Civ. App. 1988).

Collateral references. — Postadoption visitation by natural parent. 78 ALR4th 218.

§ 26-10A-31. Confidentiality of records, hearing; parties.

(a) After the petition is filed and prior to the entry of the final decree, the records in adoption proceedings shall be open to inspection only by the petitioner or his or her attorney, the investigator appointed under Section 26-10A-19, any attorney appointed for the adoptee under Section 26-10A-22, and any attorney retained by or appointed to represent the adoptee. Such records shall be open to other persons only upon order of court for good cause shown.

(b) All hearings in adoption proceedings shall be confidential and shall be held in closed court without admittance of any person other than interested parties and their counsel, except with leave of court.

(c) After the final decree of adoption has been entered, all papers, pleadings, and other documents pertaining to the adoption shall be sealed, kept as a permanent record of the court, and withheld from inspection except as otherwise provided in this section. No person shall have access to such records except upon order of the court in which the decree of adoption was entered for good cause shown. Identifying information should not be given except with the consent of the parties in interest.

(d) When the court issues the adoption order, all licensed agencies or individuals shall send a sealed information summary sheet and the non-identifying information referred to in subsection (g) in a separate summary sheet to the State Department of Human Resources. The following information shall be included:

(1) Birthname and adoptive name;

(2) Date and place of birth of person adopted, except in the case of abandonment;

(3) Circumstances under which the child came to be placed for adoption;

(4) Physical and mental condition of the person adopted, insofar as this can be determined by the aid of competent medical authority;

(5) Name and last known address of natural parents, dates of birth and social security numbers, if known;

(6) Age of the natural parents at child's birth;

(7) Nationality, ethnic background, race, and religious preference of the natural parents;

(8) Educational level of the natural parents;

(9) Pre-adoptive brother/sister relationships;

(10) Whether the identity and location of the natural father is known or ascertainable.

(e) The State Department of Human Resources and the investigating agency's adoption records must be kept for a minimum term of 75 years. If a licensed child placing agency ceases to operate in Alabama, all adoption records of the agency, including those of the child, the natural family and the adoptive family, shall be transferred to the Department of Human Resources.

(f) All files of the investigating office or agency appointed by the court under Section 26-10A-19 shall be confidential and shall be withheld from inspection except upon order of the court for good cause shown.

(g) Notwithstanding subsection (f) of this section, the State Department of Human Resources or the licensed investigating agency appointed by the court pursuant to Section 26-10A-19(b) and (c), shall furnish, upon request, to the petitioners, natural parents or an adoptee 19 years of age or older, nonidentifying information which shall be limited to the following:

(1) Health and medical histories of the adoptee's natural parents;

(2) The health and medical history of the adoptee;

(3) The adoptee's general family background, including ancestral information, without name references or geographical designations;

(4) Physical descriptions;

(5) The length of time the adoptee was in the care and custody of one other than the petitioner; and

(6) Circumstances under which child comes to be placed for adoption.

(h) Notwithstanding subsection (f) if either the natural mother or the natural or presumed father have given consent in writing under oath to disclosure of identifying information, the State Department of Human Resources or a licensed child placing agency shall release such identifying information including a copy of the birth certificate as it relates to the consenting parent to an adult adoptee when that adoptee reaches the age of 19.

(i) If the court finds that any person has a compelling need for nonidentifying information not otherwise available under subsection (e) of this section which only can be obtained through contact with the adoptee, the adoptee's parents, an alleged or presumed father of the adoptee, or the adoptee's adoptive parents, the court shall direct the agency or a mutually agreed upon intermediary, to furnish such information or to establish contact with the adoptee, the adoptee's natural parents, the alleged or presumed father of the adoptee, or the adoptive parents of the adoptee in order to obtain the information needed without disclosure of identifying information to or about the applicant. Said information then shall be filed with the court and released to the applicant within the discretion of the court. However, the identity and whereabouts of the person or persons contacted shall remain confidential.

(j) Notwithstanding any subsection of this section to the contrary, when an adult adoptee reaches the age of 19, the adoptee may petition the court for the disclosure of identifying information if a natural or presumed parent has not previously given consent under subsection (h). The court shall direct an intermediary to contact the natural parents to determine if the natural parents will consent to the release of their identity. If the natural parents consent to the release of their identity the court shall so direct. If the natural parents are deceased, cannot be found or do not consent to the release of the information then the court shall weigh the interest and rights of all of the parties and determine if the identifying information should be released without the consent of the natural parents. Moreover, if the court releases the identifying information without the consent of the natural parents, the court may restrict the distribution and use of that information and may restrict or prohibit contact between the parties as the court determines to be fair and equitable. (Acts 1990, No. 90-554, p. 912, § 30.)

Comment

The records and court proceedings in connection with an adoption should be confidential, unless the court otherwise directs. Release of identifying information is discretionary. A substantial increase in nonidentifying information will be made available to the parties under subsection (g).

Subsection (a) is similar to former section 26-10-5 which provided that the adoption records were open only to the parties in interest and DHR. This section is more restrictive and limits accessibility of records to the adult adoptee than did former section 26-10-5 and section 26-10-4. Former section 26-10-4 provided that the original birth certificate would be open to an adult adoptee or the adoptee's parents or by court order. While providing for greater accessibility to non-identifying information, identifying information will be available only upon consent or through court order. Limiting access to identifying information to primarily those cases in which the natural parent(s) consent is consistent with the policy encompassed within section 38-7-13.

If the natural mother and the natural or presumed father have given consent, a mature adoptee of nineteen should have access to identifying information under subsection (h). At the time of adoption, the natural parent should be given the option of giving consent to the release of identifying information. If the natural parents have not consented, an adult adoptee may petition the Court for the appointment of an intermediary to contact the natural parents to determine if they object to the release of identifying information under subsection (j). If they do object, the courts will weigh the interests and rights of all the parties to determine if such information should be released. Moreover, the court may restrict the use of information and contact between the parties as may be equitable.

This section is derived in part from section 28 of the ABA Model State Adoption Act.

§ 26-10A-32. Birth certificates.

(a) Within 10 days of the final decree being entered the judge or the clerk of the court shall send a copy of the final order to the Department of Human Resources and shall send a certificate of the final order of adoption to the State Registrar of Vital Statistics of the State Board of Health upon the form supplied by the state registrar for that purpose.

(b) Upon receipt of copy of any final order of adoption the State Registrar of Vital Statistics shall cause to be made a new record of the birth in the new name and with the name or names of the adopting parent or parents as contained in the final decree. The state registrar shall then cause to be sealed and filed the original certificate of birth with the decree of the court.

(c) After the new birth certificate has been issued, the original birth certificate and the evidence of adoption are not subject to inspection except upon order of the court for good cause shown. (Acts 1990, No. 90-554, p. 912, § 31.)

Comment

The confidentiality of adoption records is to be preserved. The right of privacy of the natural parent(s) is to be protected thereby ensuring an orderly adoption process. After the new birth certificate is issued, the original birth certificate is sealed and not subject to inspection except upon order of the court for good cause. See section 26-10A-31 for guidelines relative to the inspection of adoption records.

This section is derived from section 29 of the ABA Model State Adoption Act and is similar to former section 26-10-4 except that under prior law the adult adoptee, adopting parents or others through court order could have inspected the original birth certificate.

§ 26-10A-33. Crime to place children for adoption.

Only a parent, a parent of a deceased parent, or a relative of the degree of relationship specified in Section 26-10A-28, the Department of Human Resources or a licensed child placing agency, or an agency approved by the Department of Human Resources may place a minor for adoption. No person or entity other than the Department of Human Resources or a licensed child placing agency shall engage in the business of placing minors for adoption. Any person or entity making more than two unrelated placements of minors for adoption within the preceding twelve month period shall be deemed to be in the business of placing minors for adoption. Any other person who places a minor for adoption is guilty, upon the first conviction, of a Class A misdemeanor and upon subsequent convictions is guilty of a Class C felony. This section does not intend to make it unlawful for any person not engaged in the business of placing minors for adoption to give advice and assistance to a natural parent in an adoption. In making adoption arrangements, potential adopting parents and birth parents are entitled to the advice and assistance of legal counsel. Surrogate motherhood is not intended to be covered by this section. (Acts 1990, No. 90-554, p. 912, § 32.)

Comment

This section is penal in nature and limits who may place a child for adoption and prohibits any person or entity other than DHR or a licensed child placing agency from engaging in the business of placing minors for adoption. It retains the rights of the natural parents to make independent placements of their child and extends the same authorization to other close relatives who might naturally be expected to have a special interest in the child and have a special relationship with one or more of the natural parents.

This section also preserves the rights of the natural and adoptive parents to obtain legal counsel. Moreover, it preserves the right of any person who is not engaged in the business of placing minors for adoptions to offer advice and assistance to the natural parent(s) who are contemplating placing their child for adoption. These detailed rights were included to ensure that this section would not have a chilling effect on anyone who was attempting to help natural parent(s) in their decision relating to the adoption of their child. Consequently, the limitations are directed only at those who are engaged in the business of placing children.

Placing children is intended to be more than merely assisting a natural parent in identifying potential adoptive parents. It contemplates the assumption of the natural parents' role of selecting the adoptive parents. Consequently, doctors, ministers, lawyers and others who merely assist a natural parent by identifying potential adoptive parents as an incidental part of their professional roles are not deemed to be placing children. On the other hand, anyone who essentially steps in the shoes of the natural parent and assumes the responsibility of selecting the adoptive parents is placing children. Accordingly, when any unauthorized person or entity makes more than two unrelated placements within a twelve-month period, they will be deemed to be in the business of placing minors for adoption.

Other indicia of being in the business of placing children is when it occupies or engages the time and labor of persons as a principal concern, interest or for profit. The unauthorized placement of children is prohibited because it is generally recognized that it is in the best interest of the child to be placed by a parent or relative who has a special interest in the child or by individuals who are specially trained in that field.

Additional safeguards are provided in other sections of the bill to ensure that the placement occurs because it is in the best interest of the minor and not because of any potential monetary benefit either to the parents or to any party assisting in the adoption.

This section did not have a comparable provision under prior law. However, former section 26-10-8 made the advertisement of certain conduct unlawful.

§ 26-10A-34. Payments to parent for placing minor for adoption; maternity expenses; receipt of financial benefits by father.

(a) It shall be a Class A misdemeanor for any person or agency to offer to pay money or anything of value to a parent for the placement for adoption, for the consent to an adoption, or for cooperation in the completion of an adoption of his or her minor. It shall be a Class C felony for any person or agency to pay money or anything of value to a parent for the placement of a child for adoption, for the consent to an adoption, or for cooperation in the completion of an adoption of his or her minor. This section does not make it unlawful to pay the maternity-connected medical or hospital and necessary living expenses of the mother preceding and during pregnancy-related incapacity as an act of charity, as long as the payment is not contingent upon placement of the minor for adoption, consent to the adoption, or cooperation in the completion of the adoption.

(b) It shall be a Class C felony for any person or agency to receive any money or other thing of value for placing, assisting or arranging a minor placement. This section is not intended to prohibit legitimate charges for medical, legal, prenatal or other professional services.

(c) Surrogate motherhood is not intended to be covered by this section. (Acts 1990, No. 90-554, p. 912, § 33.)

Comment

This section is penal in nature. If an individual is found guilty of committing an act which is prohibited by this section, he or she shall be punished in accordance with the sentencing provisions for misdemeanors and felonies in the State of Alabama.

Subsection (a) permits adopting parents or other persons to pay the maternity-connected medical or hospital and necessary living expenses of the mother, but it prohibits any other payments to the parents as an inducement for the adoption. The purpose of this subsection is to make it illegal to engage in "baby-buying". It invokes the sanctions of the criminal law to protect the integrity of the adoption proceedings and to safeguard the best interests of the child.

Subsection (b) prohibits any person or agency from receiving money or thing of value for involvement in the placement process except as specified in the Code. This section is not intended to prohibit licensed CPA from charging fees for legitimate professional adoption services.

Subsection (c) underscores the fact that surrogate motherhood is not covered in this Code. It was determined that this matter should be addressed in separate legislation.

This section is derived from section 32 of the ABA Model State Adoption Act and increases the penalties provided for in former section 26-10-9 for violations under the prior Code. Sanctions under former section 26-10-9 were limited to a fine of not more than $100 or imprisonment in the county jail for not more than three months or both.

§ 26-10A-35. Bringing child into state for adoption purposes.

Children may be brought into Alabama for purposes of adoption as provided in Section 38-7-15 except that investigations shall be made as provided in Section 26-10A-19(c). (Acts 1990, No. 90-554, p. 912, § 34.)

Comment

This section incorporates section 38-7-15 of the Code of Alabama and is not found in the ABA Model State Adoption Act. See also Interstate Compact on Placement of Children, Ala. Code § 44-2-20 et seq.

§ 26-10A-36. Advertisement as to adoption by persons, organizations, etc., not licensed by Department of Human Resources.

It shall be unlawful for any person or persons, organizations, corporation, partnership, hospital, association, or any agency to advertise verbally, through print, electronic media, or otherwise that they will:

(1) Adopt children; or assist in the adoption of children in violation of this chapter;

(2) Place or assist in the placement of children in foster homes, group homes, or institutions in violation of this chapter; or

(3) Pay or offer money or anything of value to the parents of a child in violation of Section 26-10A-34. Any violation of this subsection shall be punished as a Class A misdemeanor. (Acts 1990, No. 90-554, p. 912, § 35.)

Comment

Advertisements by individuals or organizations concerning the placement or adoption of children in violation of this act are unlawful and constitute a Class A misdemeanor. An advertisement containing an offer to pay money or give anything of value to the parents of the child in violation of section 26-10A-34 is also punishable under this section. Any monetary benefit or value given to the parent of the child or to a party assisting in the adoption process has the potential for negating the best interest of the child which is of primary concern.

This provision is not intended to prohibit an attorney from listing in an otherwise proper advertisement that he or she represents persons in adoption proceedings. See *Bates v. O'Steen*, 433 U.S. 350 (1977).

Furthermore, this provision does not prohibit licensed child placing agencies or DHR from advertising that they place or assist in the placement of minors for adoption consistent with this act.

This substantially differs from former section 26-10-8 which had been judicially determined to be unconstitutionally vague. *State of Alabama v. Gooden*, No. 89-2072, No. 89-2119, No. 89-2120 (Ala. 15 Cir. Jan. 17, 1990).

I, § 6, of the Alabama Constitution. State v.
Gooden, 570 So. 2d 865 (Ala. Crim. App. 1990).

§ 26-10A-37. Rules of procedure and rules of evidence.

The Rules of Civil Procedure and the Rules of Evidence apply to the probate court in adoption proceedings to the extent they apply under Section 12-13-12. (Acts 1990, No. 90-554, p. 912, § 37.)

§ 26-10A-38. Application to existing adoptions.

Final orders of adoptions entered prior to January 1, 1991, remain in effect on January 1, 1991, even though the statute under which the adoption was made may be repealed or modified by this chapter. Those adoptions continue in effect as they existed prior to this chapter except that proceedings after final orders of adoption previously entered will be governed under this chapter. (Acts 1990, No. 90-554, p. 912, § 39.)

CHAPTER 10B.

INTERSTATE ADOPTION ASSISTANCE COMPACTS.

Effective date. — The act which enacted this chapter became effective August 8, 1991.

§ 26-10B-1. Legislative findings.

The legislature finds that:

(1) Finding adoptive families for children, for whom adoption assistance is desirable, and assuring the protection of the interests of the children affected during the entire assistance period requires special measures when the adoptive parents move to other states or are residents of another state; and

(2) The provision of medical and other necessary services for children, with state assistance, encounters special difficulties when the provision of services takes place in other states. (Acts 1991, No. 91-662, p. 1267, § 1.)

§ 26-10B-2. Purpose.

The purpose of this chapter is to authorize the State Department of Human Resources to enter into interstate agreements with agencies of other states for the protection of children for whom adoption assistance is being provided by the State Department of Human Resources, and to provide procedures for interstate adoption assistance payments for children, including medical payments. (Acts 1991, No. 91-662, p. 1267, § 2.)

§ 26-10B-3. Definitions.

As used in this chapter, the following terms shall have the following meanings, respectively, unless the context clearly indicates otherwise:

(1) STATE. A state of the United States, the District of Columbia, the Commonwealth of Puerto Rico, the Virgin Islands, Guam, the Commonwealth of the Northern Mariana Islands, or a territory or possession of or administered by the United States.

(2) ADOPTION ASSISTANCE STATE. The state that is signatory to an adoption assistance agreement in a particular case.

197

(3) RESIDENCE STATE. The state of which the child is a resident by virtue of the residence of the adoptive parents. (Acts 1991, No. 91-662, p. 1267, § 3.)

§ 26-10B-4. Department of Human Resources authorized to enter into interstate compacts.

The State Department of Human Resources, by and through its commissioner, is authorized to develop, negotiate and enter into one or more interstate compacts on behalf of this state with other states to implement one or more of the purposes set forth in this chapter. When so entered into, and for so long as it shall remain in force, such a compact shall have the force and effect of law. (Acts 1991, No. 91-662, p. 1267, § 4.)

§ 26-10B-5. Provisions required to be included in compact.

A compact entered into pursuant to the authority conferred by this chapter shall include:

(1) A provision making the compact available for joinder by all states;

(2) A provision or provisions allowing withdrawal from the compact upon written notice to the parties, but requiring a period of one year between the date of the notice and the effective date of the withdrawal;

(3) A requirement that the protections afforded by or pursuant to the compact continue in force for the duration of the adoption assistance and be applicable to all children and their adoptive parents who, on the effective date of the withdrawal, are receiving adoption assistance from a party state other than the one in which they are residents and have their principal place of abode;

(4) A requirement that each instance of adoption assistance to which the compact applies be covered by an adoption assistance agreement in writing between the adoptive parents and the state child welfare agency of the state which undertakes to provide the adoption assistance, and further, that any such agreement be expressly for the benefit of the adopted child and enforceable by the adoptive parents and the state agency providing the adoption assistance;

(5) Such other provisions as may be appropriate to implement the proper administration of the compact. (Acts 1991, No. 91-662, p. 1267, § 5.)

§ 26-10B-6. Provisions which may be included in compact.

A compact entered into pursuant to the authority conferred by this chapter may contain provisions in addition to those required pursuant to Section 26-10B-5, as follows:

(1) Provisions establishing procedures and entitlements to medical, developmental, child care or other social services for the child in accordance with applicable laws, even though the child and the adoptive parents are in

a state other than the one responsible for providing the services or the funds to defray part or all of the costs thereof; and

(2) Such other provisions as may be appropriate or incidental to the proper administration of the compact. (Acts 1991, No. 91-662, p. 1267, § 6.)

§ 26-10B-7. Medical assistance; applicability.

(a) A child with special needs residing in this state who is the subject of an adoption assistance agreement with another state shall be entitled to receive a medical assistance identification from this state upon the filing in the medicaid office of a certified copy of the adoption assistance agreement obtained from the adoption assistance state. The adoptive parents shall be required at least annually to show that the agreement is still in force or has been renewed.

(b) The terms of the compact entered into by the department and addressed in this statute will apply to children who are the subject of a federal adoption assistance agreement. At the department's option, and in concurrence with the Alabama Medicaid Agency, the state may elect to provide the benefits described in this statute to children who are the subject of a state adoption assistance agreement, in which case the Department of Human Resources will pay the state's share of the cost of Medicaid coverage for children who are the subject of a state adoption assistance agreement and who are also eligible for Medicaid according to applicable federal and state laws and regulations.

(c) The state medicaid office shall consider the holder of a medical assistance identification pursuant to this section as any other holder of a medical assistance identification under the laws of this state and shall process and make payment on claims on account of such holder in the same manner and pursuant to the same conditions and procedures as for other recipients of medical assistance.

(d) The provisions of this section shall apply only to medical assistance for children under adoption assistance agreements from states that have entered into a compact with this state under which the other state provides medical assistance to children with special needs under adoption assistance agreements made by this state. (Acts 1991, No. 91-662, p. 1267, § 7.)

§ 26-10B-8. Department to provide coverage and benefits not provided by residence state; procedure for reimbursement.

The State Department of Human Resources shall provide coverage and benefits for a child who is in another state and who is covered by an adoption assistance agreement made by the State Department of Human Resources for coverage or benefits, if any, not provided by the residence state. To this end, the adoptive parents acting for the child must obtain prior approval from the State Department of Human Resources and may submit evidence of payment for services or benefit amounts not payable in the residence state and shall be reimbursed therefor. However, there shall be no reimbursement for services or benefit amounts covered under any insurance or other third party medical contract or arrangement held by the child or the adoptive parents. The State Department of Human Resources shall make regulations implementing this section. Among other things, such regulations shall include procedures to be followed in obtaining prior approvals for service in those instances where required for the assistance. (Acts 1991, No. 91-662, p. 1267, § 8.)

§ 26-10B-9. Penalty for false, misleading, or fraudulent claim or statement.

The submission of any claim for payment or reimbursement for services or benefits pursuant to Section 26-10B-7 or 26-10B-8 of this chapter or the making of any statement in connection therewith, which claim or statement the maker knows or should know to be false, misleading or fraudulent shall be punishable as perjury. (Acts 1991, No. 91-662, p. 1267, § 9.)

§ 26-10B-10. Provision required to be included in state plan made pursuant to federal laws.

Consistent with federal law, the State Department of Human Resources and the Alabama Medicaid Agency, in connection with the administration of this chapter and any compact pursuant hereto, shall include in any state plan made pursuant to the Adoption Assistance and Child Welfare Act of 1980 (P.L. 96-272), Title IV-E, 42 U.S.C. §§ 670-676 and XIX of the Social Security Act, 42 U.S.C. § 1396 and any other applicable federal laws, the provision of adoption assistance and medical assistance for which the federal government pays some or all of the cost. The aforementioned department(s) shall apply for and administer all relevant federal aid in accordance with law. (Acts 1991, No. 91-662, p. 1267, § 10.)

CHAPTER 11.

LEGITIMATION OF CHILDREN.

A married woman who conceives a child by one not her husband may institute paternity proceedings against the putative father. There is reasonable cause for debate as to whether denial of a similar right to the putative father may be contrary to the equal protection clause of the U.S. Const., amend. 14. Finkenbinder v. Burton, 452 So. 2d 880 (Ala. Civ. App. 1984), aff'd, 477 So. 2d 459 (Ala. Civ. App. 1985).

The biological father of a child born during the marriage of the mother to another man may bring an action for declaratory judgment to establish his paternity of the child. Finkenbinder v. Burton, 452 So. 2d 880 (Ala. Civ. App. 1984), aff'd, 477 So. 2d 459 (Ala. Civ. App. 1985).

If an action to establish paternity of a child born during the marriage of the mother to another man may be brought through suit for declaratory judgment, there is no basis for denying it being done by way of intervention in an already pending action relating to custody and best interest of the child. The purpose of avoiding multiple suits and speeding the determination of issues is served in both intervention and declaratory judgment actions. Finkenbinder v. Burton, 452 So. 2d 880 (Ala. Civ. App. 1984), aff'd, 477 So. 2d 459 (Ala. Civ. App. 1985).

The matter of custody of a child to which one seeks to establish paternity is a matter of such interest as to provide intervention of right under A.R.C.P., Rule 24. Finkenbinder v. Burton, 452 So. 2d 880 (Ala. Civ. App. 1984), aff'd, 477 So. 2d 459 (Ala. Civ. App. 1985).

Collateral references. — Right of illegitimate grandchildren to take under testamentary gift to "grandchildren." 17 ALR4th 1292.

Admissibility, weight and sufficiency of Human Leukocyte Antigen (HLA) tissue typing tests in paternity cases. 37 ALR4th 167.

§ 26-11-1. Legitimation by marriage of parents and recognition of child by father.

The marriage of the mother and reputed father of a bastard child renders it legitimate if the child is recognized by the father as his child. (Code 1852, § 2008; Code 1867, § 2404; Code 1876, § 2742; Code 1886, § 2364; Code 1896, § 364; Code 1907, § 5199; Code 1923, § 9299; Code 1940, T. 27, § 10.)

This section does not violate equal protection of the law by discriminating on the basis of illegitimacy. Everage v. Gibson, 372 So. 2d 829 (Ala. 1979), cert. denied, 445 U.S. 931, 100 S. Ct. 1322, 63 L. Ed. 2d 765 (1980).

The presumption of legitimacy remains one of the highest known to law and is not to be overcome except upon the highest proof. It has never been allowed just and reasonable to hold a child a bastard unless there is no judicial escape from that conclusion. Curry v. Curry, 402 So. 2d 1019 (Ala. Civ. App. 1981).

When a child is born to a married woman, a strong presumption arises that the child is the legitimate offspring of her husband, and this presumption may be rebutted only by clear and convincing evidence which tends to show that it is naturally, physically, or scientifically impossible for the husband to be the father.

Underwood v. Underwood, 460 So. 2d 1306 (Ala. Civ. App. 1984).

There are only two methods by which a bastard may be legitimated so as to inherit from one as his father. They are both provided by this section and § 26-11-2. Lingen v. Lingen, 45 Ala. 410 (1871); Moore v. Terry, 220 Ala. 47, 124 So. 80 (1929), overruled on other grounds, Everage v. Gibson, 372 So. 2d 829 (Ala. 1979).

A child is "legitimated" by the marriage of the parents and recognition of the child by the father as his own. Everage v. Gibson, 372 So. 2d 829 (Ala. 1979), cert. denied, 445 U.S. 931, 100 S. Ct. 1322, 63 L. Ed. 2d 765 (1980).

When a child is born of an illicit relationship, and the parties subsequently enter into a common-law marriage, this marriage serves to legitimate the child. But even after the common-law marriage of the parties, the father must recognize the child as his to legitimate it. Recognition must be unambiguous and clear. The essence of this recognition is treatment of the child as one's own. Underwood v. Underwood, 460 So. 2d 1306 (Ala. Civ. App. 1984).

The law embraced in this section stems from a rule of canon law. — The law embraced in this section has long been the law of Alabama. It is a rule of the canon law, the adoption of which the ecclesiastics urged in vain upon the English parliament in the reign of Henry II. Butler v. Elyton Land Co., 84 Ala. 384, 4 So. 675 (1888).

The whole object of this section is to enable parents by marrying to clothe their offspring with legitimacy. McBride v. Sullivan, 155 Ala. 166, 45 So. 902 (1908).

The use of the word "reputed" was intended merely to dispense with absolute proof of paternity so that if the child is "regarded," "deemed," "considered," by the parents themselves as their child, it is legitimate. And there is no intention to require the parents to publish their shame before marriage. McBride v. Sullivan, 155 Ala. 166, 45 So. 902 (1908).

Word "reputed," used in this section means regarded, deemed, considered or held in thought by husband and wife as their child either before or after marriage. Moore v. Terry, 220 Ala. 47, 124 So. 80 (1929).

Recognition is indispensable. — Marriage without recognition is not sufficient. Lingen v. Lingen, 45 Ala. 410 (1871); Moore v. Terry, 220 Ala. 47, 124 So. 80 (1929); Howard v. Pike, 290 Ala. 213, 275 So. 2d 645 (1973).

Recognition is essential and must be unambiguous and clear in its character. Coleman v. Sparkman, 370 So. 2d 977 (Ala. 1979).

It must be unambiguous in character. — The marriage of mother and reputed father of bastard renders such bastard legitimate, if recognized by father as his child, but recognition must be unambiguous and clear in character. Martin v. Martin, 233 Ala. 310, 171 So. 734 (1937); Howard v. Pike, 290 Ala. 213, 275 So. 2d 645 (1973).

Recognition must be unambiguous and clear in its character. Everage v. Gibson, 372 So. 2d 829 (Ala. 1979), cert. denied, 445 U.S. 931, 100 S. Ct. 1322, 63 L. Ed. 2d 765 (1980).

"Recognized" is not a thaumaturgic word to be recited every time legitimation is at issue. Coleman v. Sparkman, 370 So. 2d 977 (Ala. 1979).

Essence of recognition is treatment of child as one's own, including an acknowledgment of parenthood, meaning acquiescence in the relationship of parent and child. Coleman v. Sparkman, 370 So. 2d 977 (Ala. 1979).

Recognition is shown by the treatment of the child. — The recognition by the parents of the child as theirs is shown by their treatment of the child after marriage as well as before. McBride v. Sullivan, 155 Ala. 166, 45 So. 902 (1908).

Recognition is shown by the manner of treatment, how the child is regarded and held in thought, and does not depend upon a showing of actual parentage. Coleman v. Sparkman, 370 So. 2d 977 (Ala. 1979).

Publication of parentage of child before the marriage is unnecessary. Coleman v. Sparkman, 370 So. 2d 977 (Ala. 1979).

Legitimation in foreign country. — A bastard born in France and legitimated there, cannot inherit the estate of his father in Alabama; nor can he inherit his personalty if his father, at his death, was domiciled in this state. Lingen v. Lingen, 45 Ala. 410 (1871).

Effect of legitimation is to place bastard in same state as if he were born in wedlock. — By legitimating a bastard he is placed in the same state as if he were born in wedlock, that is, in a lawful manner. With the marriage, the product of the illicit connection is, in a legal sense, expurgated when the parents form such a union. The duties and obligations which such a child and its parents owe to each other are the same as if the marriage preceded its birth. It can inherit and transmit the inheritance in consequences of its paternity to and from relatives of the father. The father is under a legal obligation to provide for his legitimated offspring. Hunter v. Whitworth, 9 Ala. 965 (1846).

And if wife dies without issue subsequently born, husband is entitled to curtesy. — Where a child is legitimated under this section, and the wife dies without issue subsequently born, the husband becomes tenant by curtesy of the lands of which the wife was seized. Hunter v. Whitworth, 9 Ala. 965 (1846).

In order to claim right to inherit from intestate father, child born out of wedlock may (1) prove legitimation by marriage of his parents plus clear and unambiguous recognition of the child by the father; (2) introduce a written, attested, and filed declaration of legitimation; or (3) show a judicial determination of paternity made within two years of birth and during father's lifetime. Everage v. Gibson, 372 So. 2d 829 (Ala. 1979), cert. denied, 445 U.S. 931, 100 S. Ct. 1322, 63 L. Ed. 2d 765 (1980).

There are three situations in Alabama in which a child born out of wedlock may inherit from his intestate father, short of having been adopted by the father. In the first, the child is "legitimated" by the marriage of the parents and recognition of the child by the father as his own. Such recognition must be unambiguous and clear in its character. In the second, the child is "legitimated" by the father's written declaration, attested by two witnesses, which is filed in the office of the probate judge. The third situation is a "judicial determination of paternity." Murphy v. Murphy, 421 So. 2d 1285 (Ala. Civ. App. 1982).

There are three means by which an illegitimate child may inherit from an intestate father short of adoption by the father. The father may marry the mother and recognize the child as his own, the father may legitimate the child by following the statutory procedure for legitimation by written declaration or the court may make a judicial determination of paternity. Handley ex rel. Herron v. Schweiker, 697 F.2d 999 (11th Cir. 1983).

Evidence. — In action by youngest son of woman, who had not married until after birth of her three sons, against older sons to quiet title to land of woman's deceased husband, evidence held sufficient to justify judgment for plaintiff on ground that plaintiff was heir and son of deceased husband and that woman's older sons were not. Martin v. Martin, 233 Ala. 310, 171 So. 734 (1937).

Cited in Fairclough v. St. Amend, 217 Ala. 19, 114 So. 472 (1927); Law v. State, 238 Ala. 428, 191 So. 803 (1939); Gilbreath v. Lewis, 242 Ala. 510, 7 So. 2d 485 (1942); Hunter v. Lynn, 256 Ala. 501, 55 So. 2d 849 (1951); Foster v. Anderson, 287 Ala. 111, 248 So. 2d 707 (1971); Foster v. Martin, 286 Ala. 709, 246 So. 2d 435 (1971); Rudolph v. Bradley, 295 Ala. 19, 321 So. 2d 659 (1975); Walton v. Lindsey, 349 So. 2d 41 (Ala. 1977); King v. King, 437 So. 2d 565 (Ala. Civ. App. 1983); Thomaston v. Thomaston, 468 So. 2d 116 (Ala. 1985); Hart ex rel. Morse v. Bowen, 802 F.2d 1334 (11th Cir. 1986).

Collateral references. — 10 C.J.S., Bastards, § 12.

10 Am. Jur. 2d, Bastards, § 49.

What amounts to recognition within statutes affecting the status or rights of illegitimates. 33 ALR2d 705.

Presumption of legitimacy, or of paternity, of child conceived or born before marriage. 57 ALR2d 729.

Legitimation by marriage to natural father of child born during mother's marriage to another. 80 ALR3d 219.

§ 26-11-2. Procedure for legitimation by written declaration of father generally; notification of mother; filing of response; appointment of guardian ad litem; hearing; issuance of order by court; certification of minutes of court to Bureau of Vital Statistics.

(a) A father of a bastard child may seek to legitimate it and render it capable of inheriting his estate by filing a notice of declaration of legitimation in writing attested by two witnesses, setting forth the name of the child proposed to be legitimated, its sex, supposed age and the name of mother and that he thereby recognizes it as his child and capable of inheriting his estate, real and personal, as if born in wedlock. The declaration, being acknowledged by the maker before the judge of probate of the county of the father's residence or the child's residence or its execution proved by the attesting witnesses, shall be filed in the office of the judge of probate of the father's residence or the child's residence.

(b) Upon the filing of the declaration of legitimation, notice shall be given to the child's mother and to the child as provided by the Alabama Rules of

Civil Procedure. Notice may be waived as provided by the Alabama Rules of Civil Procedure. The child's mother shall, within 30 days after receiving notice, file her objection or consent to the legitimation with the probate court. The probate court shall appoint a guardian ad litem to represent the child if the mother files a timely objection or if the court determines such appointment to be in the best interest of the child. Following receipt of the mother's response or upon expiration of the time for her response, the probate court shall conduct an informal hearing at which all interested parties may present evidence for determination of whether legitimation is in the best interest of the child. The court shall issue an order of legitimation or denial of declaration of legitimation.

(c) Upon legitimation of the child, a certified copy of the minutes of the court shall be sent by the judge of probate to the Bureau of Vital Statistics, State Board of Health and to the Registrar of Vital Statistics of the county where the petition was filed within 30 days after the minutes are recorded. (Code 1852, § 2009; Code 1867, § 2405; Code 1876, § 2743; Code 1886, § 2365; Code 1896, § 365; Code 1907, § 5200; Code 1923, § 9300; Code 1940, T. 27, § 11; Acts 1959, No. 640, p. 1555; Acts 1961, No. 802, p. 1165; Acts 1961, Ex. Sess., No. 175, p. 2136; Acts 1981, No. 81-800, p. 1407, § 1.)

This section does not violate equal protection of the law by discriminating on the basis of illegitimacy. Everage v. Gibson, 372 So. 2d 829 (Ala. 1979), cert. denied, 445 U.S. 931, 100 S. Ct. 1322, 63 L. Ed. 2d 765 (1980).

Sole method of legitimation by father. — The mode provided in this section is the only way by which the father of a bastard child can legitimate it by his own act, and make it capable of inheriting his property in this state. Lingen v. Lingen, 45 Ala. 410 (1871).

This section contemplates a deliberate act by the father, done for the purpose of legitimizing a bastard. Johnson v. Barnett, 240 Ala. 413, 199 So. 804 (1941).

A will describing devisee as testator's son, but not naming the mother nor stating explicitly that testator thereby recognized devisee as his child and capable of inheriting as if born in wedlock, was held not sufficient to meet the requirements of this section. Johnson v. Barnett, 240 Ala. 413, 199 So. 804 (1941).

There are only two procedures which serve to legitimate a bastard and make him capable of inheriting from his father. They are § 26-11-1, by putative father marrying the mother and recognizing his paternity of the child, and pursuing the course provided for in this section. Bagwell v. Powell, 267 Ala. 19, 99 So. 2d 195 (1957).

Putative father puts himself in attitude of legitimate parent. — When this section is complied with the child not only is capable of inheriting as a legitimate child would, but the putative father puts himself in the attitude of a legitimate parent with respect to the child's maintenance and support. Bagwell v. Powell, 267 Ala. 19, 99 So. 2d 195 (1957).

Right of father to visit children in custody of mother. — A father who had legitimated his bastard children as provided in this section was entitled to visit the children, who were in the custody of their mother and her husband, but the father should not be the judge of the details incident thereto. There should be an order of court fixing reasonable and regular intervals and other details for such visitation. Bagwell v. Powell, 267 Ala. 19, 99 So. 2d 195 (1957).

The formal acknowledgment requisite under this section ends bastardy. Residing in a sort of semantic limbo, there can be in legal parlance acknowledged (as well as unacknowledged) bastards. Ward v. State, 42 Ala. App. 529, 170 So. 2d 500 (1964).

In order to claim right to inherit from intestate father, child born out of wedlock may (1) prove legitimation by marriage of his parents plus clear and unambiguous recognition of the child by the father; (2) introduce a written, attested, and filed declaration of legitimation; or (3) show a judicial determination of paternity made within two years of birth and during father's lifetime. Everage v. Gibson, 372 So. 2d 829 (Ala. 1979), cert. denied, 445 U.S. 931, 100 S. Ct. 1322, 63 L. Ed. 2d 765 (1980).

There are three means by which an illegitimate child may inherit from an intestate father short of adoption by the father. The father may marry the mother and recognize the child as his own, the father may legitimate the child by following the statutory procedure for legitimation by written declaration or the court may make a judicial determination of paternity. Handley ex rel. Herron v. Schweiker, 697 F.2d 999 (11th Cir. 1983).

As a result of a declaration under this section, the man can claim the rights of a natural father, which includes the right to withhold consent to the adoption of the child by any person, including a future stepfather. Roe v. Conn, 417 F. Supp. 769 (M.D. Ala. 1976).

Burden of proof. — One asserting that a bastard child has been legitimized by its father has burden of proving it. Johnson v. Barnett, 240 Ala. 413, 199 So. 804 (1941).

Cited in Law v. State, 238 Ala. 428, 191 So. 803 (1939); Denney v. State, 249 Ala. 459, 31 So. 2d 328 (1947); Walton v. Lindsey, 349 So. 2d 41 (Ala. 1977); Leonard v. Leonard, 360 So. 2d 710 (Ala. 1978); Murphy v. Murphy, 421 So. 2d 1285 (Ala. Civ. App. 1982); Hart ex rel. Morse v. Bowen, 802 F.2d 1334 (11th Cir. 1986).

Collateral references. — 10 C.J.S., Bastards, §§ 7-14.

10 Am. Jur. 2d, Bastards, § 51.

What amounts to recognition within statutes affecting the status or rights of illegitimates. 33 ALR2d 705.

Conflict of laws as to legitimacy or legitimation or as to rights of illegimates, as affecting descent and distribution of decedent's estate. 87 ALR2d 1274.

Right of putative father to custody of illegitimate child. 45 ALR3d 216.

§ 26-11-3. Procedure for change of name of child upon petition by father generally; notification of mother and child; filing of response; appointment of guardian ad litem; hearing; issuance of order by court; certification of minutes of court to Bureau of Vital Statistics, etc.

(a) The father may petition at the time of filing the declaration of legitimation or at any time subsequent to the determination of legitimation to change the name of such child, stating in his declaration the name it is then known by and the name he wishes it afterwards to have. Such petition shall be filed in the office of the judge of probate of the father's residence or the child's residence.

(b) Upon the filing of the petition for name change, notice shall be given to the child's mother and to the child as provided by the Alabama Rules of Civil Procedure. Notice may be waived as provided by the Alabama Rules of Civil Procedure. The child's mother shall, within 30 days after receiving notice, file her objection or consent to the name change with the probate court. The probate court shall appoint a guardian ad litem to represent the child if the mother files a timely objection or if the court determines such appointment to be in the best interest of the child. Following receipt of the mother's response or upon expiration of the time for her response, the probate court shall conduct an informal hearing at which all interested parties may present evidence for determination of whether the name change is in the best interest of the child. The court shall issue an order of name change or denial of name change.

Upon change of the name of the child, a certified copy of the minutes of the court shall be sent by the judge of probate to the Bureau of Vital Statistics, State Board of Health and to the Registrar of Vital Statistics of the county where the petition was filed within 30 days after the minutes are recorded. (Code 1852, § 2010; Code 1867, § 2406; Code 1876, § 2744; Code 1886,

§ 2366; Code 1896, § 366; Code 1907, § 5201; Code 1923, § 9301; Code 1940, T. 27, § 12; Acts 1981, No. 81-800, p. 1407, § 2.)

Due process requires an individual determination as to the appropriateness of the name change. Roe v. Conn, 417 F. Supp. 769 (M.D. Ala. 1976).

Thus notice to mother and opportunity to be heard before name change takes effect required. — To enable the probate judge to determine the appropriateness of the name change, notice and an opportunity to be heard must be given to the mother and to the child before a name change takes effect. Roe v. Conn, 417 F. Supp. 769 (M.D. Ala. 1976).

Standard as to appropriateness of name change. — In changing a child's name pursuant to a declaration of the father, the state should be directed not by the desires of the father but by the best interest of the child. Roe v. Conn, 417 F. Supp. 769 (M.D. Ala. 1976).

CHAPTER 12.

DETERMINATION OF PATERNITY OF ILLEGITIMATE CHILDREN.

REPEALED.

§§ 26-12-1 through 26-12-9. Repealed by Acts 1984, No. 84-244, p. 375, § 22, effective May 7, 1984.

Cross references. — For the Alabama Uniform Parentage Act, see now § 26-17-1 et seq.

CHAPTER 13.

RELIEF OF MINOR CHILDREN FROM DISABILITIES OF NONAGE.

Cross references. — As to age of majority, see § 6-1-1.

Collateral references. — 43 C.J.S., Infants, § 30.

§ 26-13-1. When authorized; procedure generally.

The several juvenile courts of the state are authorized to relieve minors over 18 years of age from the disabilities of nonage in the following cases and none other:

(1) Whenever the father or the mother of such minor shall file a petition with the court, in writing, requesting that such minor be relieved from the disabilities of nonage, and the court shall be satisfied that it is to the best interest of such minor. The parent filing such petition shall aver whether he is the guardian of such minor.

(2) Whenever any such minor, having no father, mother or guardian, or if a parent is living but is insane or has abandoned such minor for one year, shall file a petition with the court to be relieved of the disabilities of nonage, and the court shall be satisfied that it is to the interest of such minor.

(3) Whenever any such minor, having no father or mother, or if a parent is living but is insane or has abandoned such minor for one year, but having a guardian, shall file a petition with the juvenile court to be relieved from the disabilities and the guardian shall join in such petition and the court shall be satisfied that it is to the interest of such minor. (Code 1876, § 2735; Code 1886, § 2357; Code 1896, § 829; Code 1907, § 4505; Acts 1923, No. 562, p. 735; Code 1923, § 8280; Acts 1936-37, Ex. Sess., No. 95, p. 110; Code 1940, T. 27, § 13.)

Cross references. — As to jurisdiction of juvenile court in proceedings to remove disabilities of nonage, see § 12-15-30. As to relief from disabilities of minority for married persons over 18 years of age, see §§ 30-4-15, 30-4-16.

Common-law rule. — By the common law persons become sui juris at the age of 21, but the legislature has full power to prescribe a different age. Hutchinson v. Till, 212 Ala. 64, 101 So. 676 (1924).

Infants are incompetent to make express contracts without permission and decree of court. — Without the permission and judgment of the court under this section, infants are incompetent to become parties to an express contract; their contracts generally are avoidable. Commercial Credit Co. v. Ward

& Son Auto Co., 215 Ala. 31, 109 So. 574 (1926). And they may, upon arriving at majority, repudiate or avoid them. Bell v. Burkhalter, 176 Ala. 62, 57 So. 460 (1912).

The jurisdiction exercised under this section is statutory and limited, and the jurisdictional facts must affirmatively appear. Hutchinson v. Till, 212 Ala. 64, 101 So. 676 (1924).

If jurisdiction is shown, irregularities do not render proceeding void. — The general rule is that if the jurisdiction of the person and subject matter is shown, irregularities thereafter do not render the proceeding void. Hutchinson v. Till, 212 Ala. 64, 101 So. 676 (1924). Therefore, where an infant obtains a judgment removing disability, the court finding as a fact that he was 18 years of age, he cannot thereafter obtain a judgment vacating the former judgment on the ground that he was mistaken as to his age, in order that he may have the disability removed and enable him to sell land to another. Hutchinson v. Till, supra. But where a guardian presents the petition under this section and signs the ward's name without authority, the judgment is subject to collateral attack. Cox v. Johnson, 80 Ala. 22 (1885).

The judgment is not considered void on collateral attack for failure to give the statutory notice required by § 26-13-3. Such failure would affect the propriety but not the power of entering a judgment on the merits. Boykin v. Collins, 140 Ala. 407, 37 So. 248 (1904).

Allegation of best interest of infant is a nonjurisdictional fact. — The petition need not allege that the relief therein sought would be to the best interest of the minor. Such an allegation would not be a jurisdictional fact. Boykin v. Collins, 140 Ala. 407, 37 So. 248 (1904).

Contents of judgment. — Judgment relieving minors of such disabilities need not set out all the evidence which induced the court to enter the judgment, nor recite in express terms that the court was satisfied by the evidence of all the facts averred, which were necessary to support the judgment; the fact that the court so found as the judgment recited it found being sufficient. Ex parte Price, 192 Ala. 158, 68 So. 866 (1915).

Infant no right to file petition where father resides outside state. — A minor whose father is living at the time, though in another state, has no right to file a petition under this section, and § 26-13-2 gives no aid in this connection. Ex parte Singleton, 192 Ala. 117, 68 So. 253 (1915).

A minor is not entitled, after spending inheritance, to avoid judgment, not shown to have been obtained by fraud, removing disabilities of nonage, and compel mother's estate to account for his expenditures. McGathey v. Thompson, 224 Ala. 163, 138 So. 841 (1931).

Mismanagement of guardian's estate is proper matter to be litigated in petition to annul judgment. — In petition to annul judgment removing disabilities of nonage, questions regarding mismanagement of guardian's estate are matters to be litigated in court having jurisdiction of final settlement. McGathey v. Thompson, 224 Ala. 163, 138 So. 841 (1931).

Cited in Hinson v. Williamson, 74 Ala. 180 (1883).

Collateral references. — 42 Am. Jur. 2d, Infants, §§ 3, 5.

§ 26-13-2. Filing of petition.

The petition must be filed in the county in which the parent or guardian of such minor resides or in the county in which the guardianship of such minor is pending when the petition is filed by the parent or guardian and in the county where the minor resides when the petition is filed by a minor who has no parents or guardian or whose parents reside beyond the limits of the state and such minor resides in this state. In the event that the parent, guardian or minor filing such petition resides beyond the limits of the State of Alabama, then the petition may be filed in the county in which the guardianship of such minor is pending or in the county where the minor owns any real or personal property. (Code 1876, § 2736; Code 1886, § 2358; Code 1896, § 830; Code 1907, § 4506; Code 1923, § 8281; Acts 1936, Ex. Sess., No. 189, p. 222; Code 1940, T. 27, § 14.)

This section only serves to establish the venue wherein the petition must be filed, and does not state when or when not the infant himself can file the petition for removal of disability. Ex parte Singleton, 192 Ala. 117, 68 So. 253 (1915).

§ 26-13-3. Notice of filing of petition.

Whenever the petition is filed by the minor and the guardian it shall be the duty of the clerk to give notice of the filing of such petition in some newspaper published in the county or, if no newspaper is published in such county, then in such manner as may be prescribed by the judge. Such notice shall be given once a week for three successive weeks before the time of hearing such petition. Whenever the petition is filed under subdivision (1) of Section 26-13-1, a copy of the petition must be served on the minor by the sheriff if the minor resides in this state or, if a nonresident or absent from the state, by registered or certified mail. (Code 1876, § 2737; Code 1886, § 2359; Code 1896, § 831; Code 1907, § 4507; Code 1923, § 8282; Acts 1936, Ex. Sess., No. 191, p. 225; Code 1940, T. 27, § 15.)

Purpose of notice. — The duty of publishing notice enjoined on the clerk by this section is created to the end of affording opportunity for contests under § 26-13-4. Boykin v. Collins, 140 Ala. 407, 37 So. 248 (1904).

Failure of compliance and effect on judgment. — See Boykin v. Collins, 140 Ala. 407, 37 So. 248 (1904).

Cited in Willis v. Rummage, 214 Ala. 313, 107 So. 864 (1926).

§ 26-13-4. Contests of petition; receipt of evidence as to petition.

Upon the hearing of such petition, any person may contest the granting of same upon giving security for costs of such contest. All evidence touching such petition shall be taken in such manner as may be directed by the court. (Code 1876, § 2738; Code 1886, § 2360; Code 1896, § 832; Code 1907, § 4508; Code 1923, § 8283; Code 1940, T. 27, § 16.)

Cited in Fort v. State, 1 Ala. App. 195, 55 So. 434 (1911).

§ 26-13-5. Entry of judgment relieving minor from disabilities of nonage and effect thereof generally.

If on the hearing of the evidence adduced and upon such other evidence as may be required by the court, the court shall be satisfied that it will be to the interest of such minor to be relieved from the disabilities of nonage, the court shall thereupon enter judgment accordingly, and such judgment shall have the effect of investing such minor with the right to sue and be sued, to contract, to buy, sell and convey real estate and generally to do and perform all acts which such minor could lawfully do if 19 years of age, except as provided in this chapter. (Code 1876, § 2739; Code 1886, § 2361; Code 1896, § 833; Code 1907, § 4509; Code 1923, § 8284; Code 1940, T. 27, § 17.)

Operation and effect of section. — After obtaining a judgment under this section, an infant cannot get a valid judgment vacating the former judgment on the ground that he was not in fact 18 years old. Hutchinson v. Till, 212 Ala. 64, 101 So. 676 (1924).

Averments on information and belief that minor has been relieved of disabilities of nonage by proceeding under this section and § 26-13-6, so as to authorize an action against minor, are not permissible. Garth v. Ewing, 218 Ala. 143, 117 So. 665 (1928).

Sufficiency of judgment. — A judgment declaring that the minor is authorized to sue and be sued, contract and be contracted with, etc., following the words of the section, is sufficient, and it is not necessary that it specifically state that the minor is relieved of the disabilities of nonage. Ketchum v. Faircloth-Segrest Co., 155 Ala. 256, 46 So. 476 (1908).

Cited in Grayson v. Deal, 85 F. Supp. 431 (N.D. Ala. 1949); Thornton v. Badger Northland, Inc., 346 So. 2d 944 (Ala. 1977).

§ 26-13-6. Restriction of rights of minor by judgment of court.

The court, in its judgment, may, if it deems it advisable, restrict and qualify the rights of a minor relieved from the disabilities of nonage, as to acquittances to and contracts with guardians, executors, administrators, trustees and other persons indebted to such minor, to such an extent as to the court may seem proper in each particular case. Such restrictions shall be fully set forth in the judgment relieving such minor from the disabilities of nonage. (Code 1876, § 2740; Code 1886, § 2362; Code 1896, § 834; Code 1907, § 4510; Code 1923, § 8285; Code 1940, T. 27, § 18.)

§ 26-13-7. Filing of copy of judgment with probate court; recordation, etc., of judgment by probate judge.

Every minor relieved of the disabilities of nonage under the provisions of this chapter must file a certified copy of the judgment relieving him from such disabilities in the office of the judge of probate in each of the counties in which such minor shall thereafter reside and in the office of the judge of probate of each county in the state where such minor shall do any business or make any contracts. It shall be the duty of the judge of probate to record the judgment and keep the same for the inspection of the public. (Code 1876, § 2741; Code 1886, § 2363; Code 1896, § 835; Code 1907, § 4511; Code 1923, § 8286; Code 1940, T. 27, § 19.)

Effect of filing. — This section does not provide that the judgment shall not go into effect until the copy is filed, but, on the contrary, it is the "minor relieved of the disabilities" who files it. In other words, it is not until he is relieved of the disabilities by the judgment that he can file it. Whenever the judgment is entered he is relieved. Ketchum v. Faircloth-Segrest Co., 155 Ala. 256, 46 So. 476 (1908), impliedly overruling Wilkinson v. Buster, 124 Ala. 574, 26 So. 940 (1899).

§ 26-13-8. Recordation of foreign judgments relieving minors of disabilities of nonage and effect thereof.

A copy of a judgment entered by a court of competent jurisdiction of another state of the United States, duly certified according to the acts of Congress of the United States, relieving a minor nonresident of this state of the disabilities of nonage may be recorded in the probate office of any county in this state where such minor owns property, and when so recorded the said judgment shall have the same force and effect throughout this state as in the state where entered. (Acts 1909, No. 74, p. 228; Code 1923, § 8287; Code 1940, T. 27, § 20.)

U.S. Constitution. — As to requirement that each state give full faith and credit to judicial proceedings of other states, see U.S. Const., art. IV, § 1.

U.S. Code. — For act of congress requiring courts of all states, territories and possessions to give full faith and credit to records and judicial proceedings of other states, territories and possessions, see 28 U.S.C., § 1738.

CHAPTER 14.

REPORTING OF CHILD ABUSE OR NEGLECT.

Constitutionality. — The Child Abuse Reporting Act clearly survives constitutional scrutiny under the established rule that legislation which alters a common-law or statutory cause of action is not automatically invalid under Ala. Const., art. I, § 13. Harris v. City of Montgomery, 435 So. 2d 1207 (Ala. 1983).

Legislation attacked as violating Ala. Const., art. I, § 13 is upheld if one of two conditions is satisfied: (1) The right is voluntarily relinquished in exchange for equivalent benefits or protection, or (2) The legislation eradicates or ameliorates a perceived social evil and is thus a valid exercise of the police power. Clearly, this act meets the requirements of the second condition in that there has been a valid exercise of the police power to eradicate child abuse. That society receives a great benefit in having children protected from abuse and neglect needs no amplification. It is equally clear that the legislature could conclude that the immunity provision helps accomplish this goal and is thus specifically justifiable as an exercise of the police power. Harris v. City of Montgomery, 435 So. 2d 1207 (Ala. 1983).

§ 26-14-1. Definitions.

For the purposes of this chapter, the following terms shall have the meanings respectively ascribed to them by this section:

(1) ABUSE. Harm or threatened harm to a child's health or welfare. Harm or threatened harm to a child's health or welfare can occur through nonaccidental physical or mental injury, sexual abuse or attempted sexual abuse or sexual exploitation or attempted sexual exploitation. "Sexual abuse" includes rape, incest and sexual molestation as those acts are defined by Alabama law. "Sexual exploitation" includes allowing, permitting or encouraging a child to engage in prostitution and allowing, permitting, encouraging or engaging in the obscene or pornographic photographing, filming or depicting of a child for commercial purposes.

(2) NEGLECT. Negligent treatment or maltreatment of a child, including the failure to provide adequate food, medical treatment, clothing or shelter; provided, that a parent or guardian legitimately practicing his religious beliefs who thereby does not provide specified medical treatment for a child, for that reason alone, shall not be considered a negligent parent or guardian; however, such an exception shall not preclude a court from ordering that medical services be provided to the child, where his health requires it.

(3) CHILD. A person under the age of 18 years.

(4) DULY CONSTITUTED AUTHORITY. The chief of police of a municipality or municipality and county; or the sheriff, if the observation of child abuse or neglect is made in an unincorporated territory; or the Department of Human Resources; or any person, organization, corporation, group or agency authorized and designated by the Department of Human Resources to receive reports of child abuse and neglect; provided, that a "duly constituted authority" shall not include an agency involved in the acts or omissions of the reported child abuse or neglect. (Acts 1975, No. 1124, p. 2213, § 1; Acts 1981, No. 81-615, p. 1031; Acts 1981, No. 81-789, p. 1387.)

DHR required to make investigation and not required to make proceedings recommendation. — This chapter does not require that the Department of Human Resources (DHR) make any type of recommendation concerning judicial proceedings. Section 26-14-7 requires only that DHR make an investigation as to the protection of the child. Brown v. State, 588 So. 2d 551 (Ala. Crim. App. 1991).

Collateral references. — Admissibility at criminal prosecution of expert testimony on battering parent syndrome. 43 ALR4th 1203.

Tort liability of public authority for failure to remove parentally abused or neglected children from parents' custody. 60 ALR4th 942.

Denial or restriction of visitation rights to parent charged with sexually abusing child. 1 ALR5th 776.

§ 26-14-2. Purpose of chapter.

In order to protect children whose health and welfare may be adversely affected through abuse and neglect, the legislature hereby provides for the reporting of such cases to the appropriate authorities. It is the intent of the legislature that, as a result of such efforts, and through the cooperation of state, county, local agencies and divisions of government, protective services shall be made available in an effort to prevent further abuses and neglect, to safeguard and enforce the general welfare of such children, and to encourage cooperation among the states in dealing with the problems of child abuse. (Acts 1975, No. 1124, p. 2213, § 1.)

Legislative intent. — The child abuse statute clearly indicates the legislative intent to protect children from child abuse to give Department of Human Resources (DHR) the power to act as necessary to carry out its responsibility within the parameters established. Protection of children is in the child's best interest and is an overriding concern of the public. Decatur City Bd. of Educ. v. Aycock, 562 So. 2d 1331 (Ala. Civ. App. 1990).

Child abuse statutes are exceptions to powers of school boards. — Where the boards of education claim that §§ 16-8-8 and 16-11-9 give them the power to control all activities occurring at schools and involving school children, the court finds this to be a general statute and that the specific statutory provisions regarding child abuse are exceptions to the general statute and, therefore, are controlling. Decatur City Bd. of Educ. v. Aycock, 562 So. 2d 1331 (Ala. Civ. App. 1990).

Thorough investigation determined. — The statute directs Department of Human Resources (DHR) to conduct a thorough investigation, and implicit with the mandate is the authority of DHR to determine what is thorough. Expert testimony has shown the importance of private interviews of alleged victims of child abuse by those trained in special techniques, and, in fact, private interviews have been granted by court order in 170 cases filed to date of trial. Considering the reasons given by experts in support of private interviews and a likely need for prompt action to protect a child, the court finds that the boards' of education continued requirement of the presence of a representative in all instances impedes the intent of the child abuse statute and in emergency instances may render it inoperable and ineffective. Decatur City Bd. of Educ. v. Aycock, 562 So. 2d 1331 (Ala. Civ. App. 1990).

Presence of school official not necessary during abused child's interview. — There is no reasonable justification for, or right to, the boards' of education policy requiring that an official school representative be present at all alleged child abuse interviews, and, therefore,

the trial court's findings were supported by the evidence. Decatur City Bd. of Educ. v. Aycock, 562 So. 2d 1331 (Ala. Civ. App. 1990).

Cited in Burkett v. State, 439 So. 2d 737 (Ala. Crim. App. 1983).

Collateral references. — Sexual abuse of child by parent as ground for termination of parent's right to child. 58 ALR3d 1074.

§ 26-14-3. Mandatory reporting.

(a) All hospitals, clinics, sanitariums, doctors, physicians, surgeons, medical examiners, coroners, dentists, osteopaths, optometrists, chiropractors, podiatrists, nurses, school teachers and officials, peace officers, law enforcement officials, pharmacists, social workers, day care workers or employees, mental health professionals or any other person called upon to render aid or medical assistance to any child, when such child is known or suspected to be a victim of child abuse or neglect, shall be required to report, or cause a report to be made of the same, orally, either by telephone or direct communication immediately, followed by a written report, to a duly constituted authority.

(b) When a report is made to a law enforcement official, such official subsequently shall inform the Department of Human Resources of the report so that the department can carry out its responsibility to provide protective services to the respective child or children. (Acts 1965, No. 563, p. 1049, § 1; Acts 1967, No. 725, p. 1560; Acts 1975, No. 1124, p. 2213, § 1.)

Legislative intent. — The child abuse statute clearly indicates the legislative intent to protect children from child abuse to give Department of Human Resources (DHR) the power to act as necessary to carry out its responsibility within the parameters established. Protection of children is in the child's best interest and an overriding concern of the public. Decatur City Bd. of Educ. v. Aycock, 562 So. 2d 1331 (Ala. Civ. App. 1990).

Cited in Harrison v. State, 384 So. 2d 641 (Ala. Crim. App. 1980); Harris v. City of Montgomery, 435 So. 2d 1207 (Ala. 1983).

Collateral references. — Civil liability of physician for failure to diagnose or report battered child syndrome. 73 ALR4th 782.

Validity, construction, and application of state statute requiring doctor or other person to report child abuse. 73 ALR4th 782.

§ 26-14-4. Permissive reporting.

In addition to those persons, firms, corporations and officials required by Section 26-14-3 to report child abuse and neglect, any person may make such a report if such person has reasonable cause to suspect that a child is being abused or neglected. (Acts 1975, No. 1124, p. 2213, § 1.)

§ 26-14-5. Contents of reports.

The reports provided for in this chapter shall state, if known, the name of the child, his whereabouts, the names and addresses of the parents, guardian or caretaker and the character and extent of his injuries. The written report shall also contain, if known, any evidence of previous injuries to said child and any other pertinent information which might establish the cause of such injury or injuries, and the identity of the person or persons responsible for the same. (Acts 1965, No. 563, p. 1049, § 2; Acts 1975, No. 1124, p. 2213, § 1.)

§ 26-14-6. Temporary protective custody.

A police officer, a law enforcement official or a designated employee of the State or County Department of Human Resources may take a child into protective custody, or any person in charge of a hospital or similar institution or any physician treating a child may keep that child in his custody, without the consent of the parent or guardian, whether or not additional medical treatment is required, if the circumstances or conditions of the child are such that continuing in his place of residence or in the care and custody of the parent, guardian, custodian or other person responsible for the child's care presents an imminent danger to that child's life or health. However, such official shall immediately notify the court having jurisdiction over juveniles of such actions in taking the child into protective custody; provided, that such custody shall not exceed 72 hours and that a court of competent jurisdiction and the Department of Human Resources shall be notified immediately in order that child-protective proceedings may be initiated. During such period of temporary custody, the director of the county department of human resources may give or cause to be given effective consent for medical, dental, health and hospital services for any abused or neglected child. (Acts 1975, No. 1124, p. 2213, § 1.)

Legislative intent. — The child abuse statute clearly indicates the legislative intent to protect children from child abuse to give Department of Human Resources (DHR) the power to act as necessary to carry out its responsibility within the parameters established. Protection of children is in the child's best interest and an overriding concern of the public. Decatur City Bd. of Educ. v. Aycock, 562 So. 2d 1331 (Ala. Civ. App. 1990).

Cited in Murphy v. State, 355 So. 2d 1153 (Ala. Crim. App. 1978).

Collateral references. — Validity and application of statute allowing endangered child to be temporarily removed from parental custody. 38 ALR4th 756.

Tort liability of public authority for failure to remove parentally abused or neglected children from parents' custody. 60 ALR4th 942.

§ 26-14-7. Duties of Department of Human Resources.

(a) The State or County Department of Human Resources shall make a thorough investigation promptly upon either the oral or written report. The primary purpose of such an investigation shall be the protection of the child.

(b) The investigation, to the extent that is reasonably possible, shall include:

(1) The nature, extent and cause of the child abuse or neglect;

(2) The identity of the person responsible therefor;

(3) The names and conditions of other children in the home;

(4) An evaluation of the parents or person responsible for the care of the child;

(5) The home environment and the relationship of the child or children to the parents or other persons responsible for their care; and

(6) All other data deemed pertinent.

(c) The investigation may include a visit to the child's home, an interview with the subject child, and may include a physical, psychological or psychiatric examination of any child or children in that home. If the admission to the home, school or any other place that the child may be, or permission of the parent or other persons responsible for the child or children, for the physical, psychological or psychiatric examination, cannot be obtained, then a court of competent jurisdiction, upon cause shown, shall order the parents or persons responsible and in charge of any place where the child may be to allow the interview, examinations and investigation. If, before the examination is complete, the opinion of the investigators is that immediate removal is necessary to protect a child or children from further abuse or neglect, a court of competent jurisdiction, on petition by the investigators and with good cause being shown, shall issue an order for temporary removal and custody.

(d) The county department of human resources shall make a complete written report of the investigation, together with its recommendations. Such reports may be made available to the appropriate court, the district attorney and the appropriate law enforcement agency upon request. The county department of human resources shall make a written report or case summary, together with services offered and accepted to the state's central registry on forms supplied by the registry for that purpose. (Acts 1975, No. 1124, p. 2213, § 1.)

Legislative intent. — The child abuse statute clearly indicates the legislative intent to protect children from child abuse to give Department of Human Resources (DHR) the power to act as necessary to carry out its responsibility within the parameters established. Protection of children is in the child's best interest and an overriding concern of the public. Decatur City Bd. of Educ. v. Aycock, 562 So. 2d 1331 (Ala. Civ. App. 1990).

DHR required to make investigation and not required to make proceedings recommendation. — This chapter does not require that the Department of Human Resources (DHR) make any type of recommendation concerning judicial proceedings. This section requires only that DHR make an investigation as to the protection of the child. Brown v. State, 588 So. 2d 551 (Ala. Crim. App. 1991).

DHR recommendation concerns need for protective services. — The recommendation to be made by the Department of Human Resources (DHR) concerns the need for protec-

tive services. Brown v. State, 588 So. 2d 551 (Ala. Crim. App. 1991).

Thorough investigation. — This section directs Department of Human Resources (DHR) to conduct a thorough investigation, and implicit with the mandate is the authority of DHR to determine what is thorough. Expert testimony has shown the importance of private interviews of alleged victims of child abuse by those trained in special techniques, and, in fact, private interviews have been granted by court order in 170 cases filed to date of trial. Considering the reasons given by experts in support of private interviews and a likely need for prompt action to protect a child, the court finds that the boards' of education continued requirement of the presence of a representative in all instances impedes the intent of the child abuse statute and in emergency instances may render it inoperable and ineffective. Decatur City Bd. of Educ. v. Aycock, 562 So. 2d 1331 (Ala. Civ. App. 1990).

§ 26-14-8. Establishment of central registry; confidentiality of records and reports.

(a) The State Department of Human Resources shall establish a statewide central registry for reports of child abuse and neglect made pursuant to this chapter. The central registry shall contain, but shall not be limited to:

(1) All information in the written report;

(2) Record of the final disposition of the report, including services offered and services accepted;

(3) The names and identifying data, dates and circumstances of any persons requesting or receiving information from the registry;

(4) The plan for rehabilitative treatment; and

(5) Any other information which might be helpful in furthering the purposes of this chapter.

(b) The State Department of Human Resources shall establish and enforce reasonable rules and regulations governing the custody, use and preservation of the reports and records of child abuse and neglect. The use of such reports and records shall be limited to the purposes for which they are furnished and by the provisions of law under which they may be furnished. The reports and records of child abuse and neglect shall be confidential, and shall not be used or disclosed for any purposes other than:

(1) To permit their use to prevent or to discover abuse or neglect of children through the information contained therein; or

(2) For investigation of child abuse or neglect by the police or other law enforcement agency; or

(3) For use by a grand jury upon its determination that access to such reports and records is necessary in the conduct of its official business; or

(4) For use by a court where it finds that such information is necessary for the determination of an issue before the court; or

(5) For use by any person engaged in bona fide research who is authorized to have access to such information by the Commissioner of the State Department of Pensions and Security; or

(6) For use by any person authorized by a court to act as a representative for an abused or neglected child who is the subject of a report; or

(7) For use by a physician who has before him a child whom he reasonably suspects may be abused or neglected; or

(8) For use by an attorney or guardian ad litem in representing or defending a child or its parents or guardians in a court proceeding related to abuse or neglect of said child.

(c) Any violation of this provision of confidentiality shall be a misdemeanor and punishable accordingly. (Acts 1975, No. 1124, p. 2213, § 1.)

Legislative intent. — The child abuse statute clearly indicates the legislative intent to protect children from child abuse to give Department of Human Resources (DHR) the power to act as necessary to carry out its responsibility within the parameters estab-lished. Protection of children is in the child's best interest and an overriding concern of the public. Decatur City Bd. of Educ. v. Aycock, 562 So. 2d 1331 (Ala. Civ. App. 1990).

This section is applicable to child dependency cases. Linnell v. Lee County Dep't of

Pensions & Sec., 484 So. 2d 451 (Ala. Civ. App. 1985), writ quashed, 484 So. 2d 455 (Ala. 1986).

Identity of informants. — The ruling of the trial court in a juvenile dependency and custody case which denied to counsel the identity of informants who instigated department investigations as to abuse or neglect was contrary to the provisions of subdivision (b)(8) of this section. Linnell v. Lee County Dep't of Pensions & Sec., 484 So. 2d 451 (Ala. Civ. App. 1985), writ quashed, 484 So. 2d 455 (Ala. 1986).

Cited in Drinkard v. Board of Sch. Comm'rs, 423 So. 2d 202 (Ala. 1982); Ex parte Smith, 555 So. 2d 1106 (Ala. Civ. App. 1989).

§ 26-14-9. Immunity from liability for actions under chapter.

Any person, firm, corporation or official participating in the making of a report or the removal of a child pursuant to this chapter, or participating in a judicial proceeding resulting therefrom, shall, in so doing, be immune from any liability, civil or criminal, that might otherwise be incurred or imposed. (Acts 1965, No. 563, p. 1049, § 3; Acts 1975, No. 1124, p. 2213, § 1.)

Constitutionality. — Immunity under this section does not violate Ala. Const., art. I, § 13. Harris v. City of Montgomery, 435 So. 2d 1207 (Ala. 1983).

Legislation attacked as violating Ala. Const., art. I, § 13 is upheld if one of two conditions is satisfied: (1) The right is voluntarily relinquished in exchange for equivalent benefits or protection, or (2) The legislation eradicates or ameliorates a perceived social evil and is thus a valid exercise of the police power. Clearly, this act meets the requirements of the second condition in that there has been a valid exercise of the police power to eradicate child abuse. That society receives a great benefit in having children protected from abuse and neglect needs no amplification. It is equally clear that the legislature could conclude that the immunity provision helps accomplish this goal and is thus specifically justifiable as an exercise of the police power. Harris v. City of Montgomery, 435 So. 2d 1207 (Ala. 1983). Harris v. City of Montgomery, 435 So. 2d 1207 (Ala. 1983).

Absolute immunity where action within requirements of Child Abuse Reporting Act. — While mere compliance with the statute is not an automatic grant of immunity, where case did not present any allegations of injury or damage not related to the reporting of suspected child abuse, the case was properly dismissed. Because action of doctor and center were within requirements of the Child Abuse Reporting Act, this section provided them with absolute immunity. Brown v. Pound, 585 So. 2d 885 (Ala. 1991).

Collateral references. — Tort liability of public authority for failure to remove parentally abused or neglected children from parents' custody. 60 ALR4th 942.

§ 26-14-10. Doctrine of privileged communications not grounds for exclusion of evidence as to child's injuries.

The doctrine of privileged communication, with the exception of the attorney-client privilege, shall not be a ground for excluding any evidence regarding a child's injuries or the cause thereof in any judicial proceeding resulting from a report pursuant to this chapter. (Acts 1965, No. 563, p. 1049, § 4; Acts 1975, No. 1124, p. 2213, § 1.)

Acts of violence perpetrated by defendant on his stepdaughter were not confidential communications which fell within the marital privilege. Brown v. State, 588 So. 2d 551 (Ala. Crim. App. 1991).

Collateral references. — Validity, construction, and application of statute limiting physician-patient privilege in judicial proceedings relating to child abuse or neglect. 44 ALR4th 649.

§ 26-14-11. Appointment of attorney to represent child.

In every case involving an abused or neglected child which results in a judicial proceeding, an attorney shall be appointed to represent the child in such proceedings. Such attorney will represent the rights, interests, welfare and well-being of the child, and serve as guardian ad litem for said child. (Acts 1975, No. 1124, p. 2213, § 1.)

Applicability of section. — While this section appears to have carte blanche application to all judicial proceedings involving an abused child, it is directed primarily at protecting the interests of the child in a civil proceeding instituted against the child or in those proceedings attendant to a criminal prosecution for child abuse where the interests of the child conflict with those of the original guardian and/or cannot be adequately represented or protected by the state. Such a conclusion gains support from the nature of the chapter in which the above section appears and the expressed purpose stated therein by the legislature. Burkett v. State, 439 So. 2d 737 (Ala. Crim. App. 1983).

Cited in Murphy v. State, 355 So. 2d 1153 (Ala. Crim. App. 1978).

§ 26-14-12. Establishment of regulations by department of human resources.

The State Department of Human Resources may establish such regulations as may be necessary to implement this chapter and to encourage cooperation with other states in exchanging reports to effect a national registration system. (Acts 1975, No. 1124, p. 2213, § 1.)

Legislative intent. — The child abuse statute clearly indicates the legislative intent to protect children from child abuse to give Department of Human Resources (DHR) the power to act as necessary to carry out its responsibility within the parameters established. Protection of children is in the child's best interest and an overriding concern of the public. Decatur City Bd. of Educ. v. Aycock, 562 So. 2d 1331 (Ala. Civ. App. 1990).

§ 26-14-13. Penalty for failure to make required report.

Any person who shall knowingly fail to make the report required by this chapter shall be guilty of a misdemeanor and shall be punished by a sentence of not more than six months' imprisonment or a fine of not more than $500.00. (Acts 1965, No. 563, p. 1049, § 5; Acts 1975, No. 1124, p. 2213, § 1.)

Cited in Harris v. City of Montgomery, 435 So. 2d 1207 (Ala. 1983).

Collateral references. — Tort liability of public authority for failure to remove parentally abused or neglected children from parents' custody. 60 ALR4th 942.

CHAPTER 15.

CHILD ABUSE GENERALLY.

Cross references. — As to reporting of child abuse and neglect, see § 26-14-1 et seq.

Chapter constitutional. — The new Alabama Child Abuse Act defines the crime of child abuse with appropriate certainty and definiteness and conveys sufficiently definite warnings as to the proscribed conduct when measured by common understanding and practices so as to pass constitutional muster. Chambers v. State, 364 So. 2d 416 (Ala. Crim. App.), cert. denied, 364 So. 2d 420 (Ala. 1978).

Sufficient statement of facts in indictment. — Where, under the indictment for child abuse, defendant is charged with torturing, willfully abusing, cruelly beating, or otherwise willfully maltreating her daughter by "beating said child with a belt and hand," the indictment states sufficient facts, in ordinary and concise language, to enable the appellant to understand both the nature of the crime charged and the particular acts against which she must prepare her defense. Chambers v. State, 364 So. 2d 416 (Ala. Crim. App.), cert. denied, 364 So. 2d 420 (Ala. 1978).

§ 26-15-1. Short title.

This chapter shall be known and may be cited as The Alabama Child Abuse Act. (Acts 1977, No. 502, p. 658, § 1.)

Victim's testimony does not require corroboration. — Where victim testified to the effect that the defendant repeatedly burned him with a cigarette on his legs, the Alabama Child Abuse Act does not require the corroboration of the victim's testimony; his testimony alone presented a jury question on the issue of the defendant's guilt or innocence. Wilburn v. State, 545 So. 2d 231 (Ala. Crim. App. 1989).

Cited in State Auto Mut. Ins. Co. v. McIntyre, 652 F. Supp. 1177 (N.D. Ala. 1987).

Collateral references. — Admissibility at criminal prosecution of expert testimony on battering parent syndrome. 43 ALR4th 1203.

Sexual child abuser's civil liability to child's parent. 54 ALR4th 93.

§ 26-15-2. "Responsible person" defined.

For the purposes of this chapter, wherever used, "responsible person" means a child's natural parent, stepparent, adoptive parent, legal guardian, custodian or any other person who has the permanent or temporary care or custody or responsibility for the supervision of a child. (Acts 1977, No. 502, p. 658, § 2.)

Whether appellant was "responsible person" under statute was question for jury. Dabbs v. State, 518 So. 2d 825 (Ala. Crim. App. 1987).

Cited in Burkett v. State, 439 So. 2d 737 (Ala. Crim. App. 1983); Payne v. State, 487 So. 2d 256 (Ala. Crim. App. 1986).

Collateral references. — Who has custody or control of child within terms of penal statute punishing cruelty or neglect by one having custody or control. 75 ALR3d 933.

§ 26-15-3. Torture, willful abuse, etc., of child under 18 years of age by responsible person.

A responsible person, as defined in Section 26-15-2, who shall torture, willfully abuse, cruelly beat or otherwise willfully maltreat any child under the age of 18 years shall, on conviction, be punished by imprisonment in the penitentiary for not less than one year nor more than 10 years. (Acts 1977, No. 502, p. 658, § 3.)

Whether appellant was "responsible person" under statute was question for jury. Dabbs v. State, 518 So. 2d 825 (Ala. Crim. App. 1987).

The words "torture" and "willfully abuse" in defining what constitutes child abuse are not so vague and indefinite as to destroy the constitutional validity of the statute. Chambers v. State, 364 So. 2d 416 (Ala. Crim. App.), cert. denied, 364 So. 2d 420 (Ala. 1978).

For discussion of the term "willfully," see Phelps v. State, 439 So. 2d 727 (Ala. Crim. App. 1983).

The child abuse statute does encompass acts of omission as well as those of commission. Phelps v. State, 439 So. 2d 727 (Ala. Crim. App. 1983).

Assault in third degree not designated as lesser offense of child abuse. — It is clear from the language of this section that subdivision (a)(3) of § 13A-1-9 does not apply, as assault in the third degree is not specifically designated by this statute as a lesser degree of the offense of child abuse; neither is assault in the third degree an attempt or solicitation to commit the offense of child abuse. Updyke v. State, 501 So. 2d 566 (Ala. Crim. App. 1986).

But is lesser included offense thereof where evidence shows child beaten. — Defendant was entitled to a jury charge on third degree assault as lesser included offense in a prosecution for child abuse despite the fact that this section, unlike third degree assault statute, does not require a showing of physical injury, where the evidence showed that the child had been beaten. Updyke v. State, 501 So. 2d 566 (Ala. Crim. App. 1986).

Victim's testimony does not require corroboration. — Where victim testified to the effect that the defendant repeatedly burned him with a cigarette on his legs, the Alabama Child Abuse Act does not require the corroboration of the victim's testimony; his testimony alone presented a jury question on the issue of the defendant's guilt or innocence. Wilburn v. State, 545 So. 2d 231 (Ala. Crim. App. 1989).

There was sufficient evidence for a jury to conclude that burns on an infant which were caused by a hand held dryer were willfully inflicted rather than self-inflicted, where a doctor testified that the burns exhibited a symmetrical pattern and that if the burns were self-inflicted the infant would have pulled to one side or the other, negating any possibility of a symmetrical pattern, and where the doctor also noted that the infant received "full thickness" burns caused by exposure to intense heat over an extended period of time. Brandon v. State, 542 So. 2d 1316 (Ala. Crim. App. 1989).

Trial judge did not err in denying defendant's motion to introduce into evidence a photograph depicting scratches on the victim's face since the photograph of the victim's self-inflicted scratches to his face did not tend to prove that the child inflicted different type wounds to his legs and thighs; there was no evidence that the child physically abused himself in the same, or a similar, manner at any other time and the connection between the self-inflicted scratches on the child's face and the issues of who burned the child's legs and whether the lesions on the legs were actually burns or merely insect bites was tenuous and remote. Wilburn v. State, 545 So. 2d 231 (Ala. Crim. App. 1989).

Indictment was sufficient where it closely paralleled the language of this section, the indictment informed the defendant that the nature of the crime he was charged with was child abuse, and the particular act or means by which defendant committed the child abuse was alleged to be beating the victim about her head, torso, and arms. Hewlett v. State, 520 So. 2d 200 (Ala. Crim. App. 1987).

Circumstantial evidence is not inferior evidence, and will support a conviction of child abuse as strongly as direct evidence provided it points to the guilt of the accused. The jury is under a duty to draw whatever permissible inferences it may from circumstantial evidence and to base its verdict on whatever permissible inferences it chooses to draw. Gullatt v. State, 409 So. 2d 466 (Ala. Crim. App. 1981).

Evidence of mental condition of the mother of appellant does not appear to be in any way determinative of the issue of appellant's guilt where the mother had no contact with appellant. Gullat v. State, 409 So. 2d 466 (Ala. Crim. App. 1981).

Admissibility of evidence generally. — A trial court properly allowed an expert witness to testify that in her examination and treatment of the abused children, they complained of being deprived of food, being beaten and eating out of garbage cans. Gullatt v. State, 409 So. 2d 466 (Ala. Crim. App. 1981).

Child not allowed to testify. — Four-year-old victim of physical abuse was not allowed to testify under the authority of this section where the accused was indicted under this section, and not the sexual abuse statute, § 15-25-3. Price v. State, 590 So. 2d 381 (Ala. Crim. App. 1991), cert. denied, 590 So. 2d 383 (Ala. 1991).

Mother's knowledge of abuse. — Evidence sustained defendant's conviction, where there was sufficient evidence from which the jury could lawfully infer that defendant knew that her child was being abused by her live-in boyfriend, and that she was also trying to conceal this fact from others. P.S. v. State, 565 So. 2d 1209 (Ala. Crim. App. 1990).

Cited in Harrison v. State, 384 So. 2d 641 (Ala. Crim. App. 1980); Poe v. State, 389 So. 2d 154 (Ala. Crim. App. 1980); Miller v. State, 565 So. 2d 275 (Ala. Civ. App. 1989).

Collateral references. — 22A C.J.S., Criminal Law, § 691 (4); 67 C.J.S., Parent and Child, §§ 7, 61.

Admissibility of expert medical testimony on battered child syndrome. 98 ALR3d 306.

Validity and construction of penal statute prohibiting child abuse. 1 ALR4th 38.

Tort liability of public authority for failure to remove parentally abused or neglected children from parents' custody. 60 ALR4th 942.

§ 26-15-4. Effect of chapter upon existing rights or liabilities, pending prosecutions, etc.

All proceedings pending and all rights and liabilities existing, acquired or incurred on May 11, 1977 are hereby saved and may be consummated according to the law in force when they were commenced. This chapter shall not be construed to affect any prosecution pending or begun before May 11, 1977. (Acts 1977, No. 502, p. 658, § 5.)

Collateral references. — Tort liability of public authority for failure to remove parentally abused or neglected children from parents' custody. 60 ALR4th 942.

CHAPTER 16.

CHILD ABUSE AND NEGLECT.

ARTICLE 1.

CHILD ABUSE AND NEGLECT PREVENTION.

Code commissioner's note. — Acts 1983, No. 83-789 designated the act which added this article as the "Martin-Aldridge Act."

§ 26-16-1. Short title.

This article shall be known and may be cited as the "Child Abuse and Neglect Prevention Act." (Acts 1983, No. 83-736, p. 1198, § 1.)

Cited in Mitchell v. State Child Abuse & Neglect Prevention Bd., 512 So. 2d 778 (Ala. Civ. App. 1987).

Collateral references. — Admissibility at criminal prosecution of expert testimony on battering parent syndrome. 43 ALR4th 1203.

Tort liability of public authority for failure to remove parentally abused or neglected children from parents' custody. 60 ALR4th 942.

§ 26-16-2. Definitions.

(a) As used in this article, the following words and phrases shall have the meanings herein ascribed to them:

(1) CHILD. A person under 18 years of age.

(2) CHILD ABUSE. Harm or threatened harm to a child's health or welfare by a person responsible for the child's health or welfare, which harm occurs or is threatened through nonaccidental physical or mental injury; sexual abuse, which includes a violation of any provision of Chapter 6, Article 4, Title 13A.

(3) LOCAL COUNCIL. An organization which meets the criteria described in Section 26-16-10.

(4) NEGLECT. Harm to a child's health or welfare by a person responsible for the child's health or welfare which occurs through negligent treatment, including the failure to provide adequate food, clothing, shelter, or medical care.

(5) STATE BOARD. The State Child Abuse and Neglect Prevention Board created in Section 26-16-3.

(6) PREVENTION PROGRAM. A system of direct provision of child abuse and neglect prevention services to a child, parent, or guardian.

(7) TRUST FUND. The children's trust fund established in the state treasury. (Acts 1983, No. 83-736, p. 1198, § 2.)

§ 26-16-3. Child Abuse and Neglect Prevention Board — Creation; executive director; staff.

(a) The State Child Abuse and Neglect Prevention Board is created as an autonomous agency of the state government.

(b) There shall be an executive director of the state board, appointed by the Governor from a list of candidates submitted under Section 26-16-6(a)(2) of this article. The executive director shall not be a member of the state classified civil service. The executive director shall be compensated by a salary payable out of the state treasury at the times and in the manner that the salary of other state officials is paid. The exact amount of the executive director's salary shall be set by the board, but in no event shall said salary exceed 75 percent of amount set as the standard compensation for cabinet level officials of the state.

(c) The executive director shall hire all staff required to exercise the powers and carry out the duties of the state board. In carrying out the duties provided in subdivisions (a)(3), (a)(4), (a)(5), (a)(6), (a)(7), and subsection (b) of Section 26-16-6, the executive director shall coordinate these activities with the State Department of Human Resources. The executive director with the approval of the state board shall have the authority to hire outside the state classified civil service an executive assistant who shall serve at the pleasure of the executive director. The state board shall approve the number of staff members hired and their job descriptions and further shall set the rate of pay or compensation due the executive assistant. Each staff member except the executive director and his executive assistant shall be a member of the state classified civil service. (Acts 1983, No. 83-736, p. 1198, § 3; Acts 1985, No. 85-698, p. 1138.)

§ 26-16-4. Child Abuse and Neglect Prevention Board — Composition; terms of office; officers and committees; compensation.

(a) The state board shall be composed of the following 14 members:

(1) The Commissioner of the State Department of Human Resources, the State Mental Health Officer, the State Health Officer, the State Superintendent of Education, and the Director of Public Safety or designees authorized to speak on their behalf.

(2) Nine public members appointed by the Governor, one from each of the seven congressional districts into which the state is divided for the purpose of electing representatives in the United States Congress, and two from the state at large. As a group, the public members shall demonstrate knowledge in the area of child abuse and neglect prevention; shall be representative of the demographic composition of this state; and, to the extent practicable, shall be representative of all of the following categories: organized labor, the business community, the religious community, the legal community, professional providers of child abuse and neglect prevention services, and volunteers in child abuse and neglect prevention services.

(b) The term of each public member shall be three years, except that of the public members first appointed, three shall serve for three years, three for two years, and three for one year. The Governor shall designate the term which each of the members first appointed shall serve when he makes such appointments. A public member shall not serve more than two consecutive terms whether partial or full. A vacancy shall be filled for the balance of the unexpired term in the same manner as the original appointment.

(c) The Governor shall designate a chairperson of the state board from among the public members, which chairperson shall serve in that position at the pleasure of the Governor. The state board may elect other officers and committees as it considers appropriate.

(d) The actual and necessary per diem compensation and the schedule for reimbursement of expenses for the public members of the state board shall be the same as prescribed by law for state employees when traveling on state business. The compensation and reimbursement, the salaries of the executive director and staff, and all actual and necessary operating expenses of the state board shall be paid from the trust fund, pursuant to an authorization as provided in Section 26-16-9. (Acts 1983, No. 83-736, p. 1198, § 4.)

§ 26-16-5. Child Abuse and Neglect Prevention Board — Public biannual meetings required; notice; books, records, etc., to be public records.

(a) The business of the state board shall be conducted at public meetings held in compliance with Section 13A-14-2. The board shall hold two regular public meetings each year and may hold such special meetings as in the opinion of the chairman or a majority of the board are needed to transact the business of the board. Notice of the time, date, and place of each meeting shall be given in the manner and for the time prescribed therefor by the board.

(b) All books, records and documents pertaining to the board or the performance of any official function of the board shall be public records and open to the public at all reasonable times. (Acts 1983, No. 83-736, p. 1198, § 5; Acts 1988, 1st Ex. Sess., No. 88-882, p. 427, § 1.)

§ 26-16-6. Child Abuse and Neglect Prevention Board — Duties and functions.

(a) The state board shall do all of the following:

(1) Meet not less than twice annually at the times prescribed in Section 26-16-5(a), above.

(2) Transmit to the Governor a list of individuals recommended to fill the position of executive director.

(3) One year after the original appointment of the state board, and annually thereafter, develop a state plan for the distribution of funds from the trust fund. The plan shall assure that an equal opportunity exists for establishment of prevention programs and receipt of trust fund money among all geographic areas in this state. The plan shall be transmitted to the Speaker of the House, the President Pro Tempore of the Senate, to the Governor, and to the ways and means committee of the house of representatives and the finance and taxation committee of the senate.

(4) Provide for the coordination and exchange of information on the establishment and maintenance of local councils and prevention programs.

(5) Develop and publicize criteria for the receipt of trust fund money by eligible local councils and eligible prevention programs.

(6) Review, approve, and monitor the expenditure of trust fund money by local councils and prevention programs.

227

(7) Provide statewide educational and public informational seminars for the purpose of developing appropriate public awareness regarding the problems of child abuse and neglect; encourage professional persons and groups to recognize and deal with problems of child abuse and neglect; make information about the problems of child abuse and neglect available to the public and organizations and agencies which deal with problems of child abuse and neglect; and encourage the development of community prevention programs.

(8) Establish a procedure for the annual, internal evaluation of the functions, responsibilities, and performance of the state board, and coordinate the evaluation with the state plan.

(b) The state board shall enter into contracts with public or private agencies to fulfill the requirements of subdivision (a)(7) and may contract to fulfill the other requirements of subsection (a). (Acts 1983, No. 83-736, p. 1198, § 6.)

Cited in Mitchell v. State Child Abuse & Neglect Prevention Bd., 512 So. 2d 778 (Ala. Civ. App. 1987).
Collateral references. — Tort liability of public authority for failure to remove parentally abused or neglected children from parents' custody. 60 ALR4th 942.

§ 26-16-7. Child Abuse and Neglect Prevention Board — Recommendation to Governor, etc., of changes in state programs which will reduce problem of child abuse, etc.

The state board may recommend to the Governor and the legislature changes in state programs, statutes, policies, budgets, and standards which will reduce the problem of child abuse and neglect, improve coordination among state agencies that provide prevention services, and improve the condition of children and parents or guardians who are in need of prevention program services. (Acts 1983, No. 83-736, p. 1198, § 7.)

§ 26-16-8. Child Abuse and Neglect Prevention Board — Acceptance of federal funds; authorized; conditions; disposition of funds.

The state board may accept federal funds granted by Congress or executive order for the purposes of this article as well as gifts and donations from individuals, private organizations, or foundations. The acceptance and use of federal funds does not commit state funds and does not place an obligation upon the legislature to continue the purposes for which the federal funds are made available. All funds received in the manner described in this section shall be transmitted to the State Treasurer for deposit in the trust fund. (Acts 1983, No. 83-736, p. 1198, § 8.)

§ 26-16-9. Child Abuse and Neglect Prevention Board — Disbursement generally.

(a) The state board may authorize the disbursement of available money from the trust fund exclusively for the following purposes, which are listed in the order of preference for expenditure:

(1) To fund a private nonprofit or public organization in the development or operation of a program if at least all of the following conditions are met:

a. The appropriate local council has reviewed and approved the program. This paragraph does not apply if a local council does not exist for the geographic area to be served by the program.

b. The organization demonstrates an ability to match, through money or in-kind services, 50 percent of the amount of any trust fund money received. Not more than 50 percent of the local match shall be in in-kind services. In-kind services are subject to the approval of the state board.

c. The organization demonstrates a willingness and ability to provide program models and consultation to organizations and communities regarding program development and maintenance.

d. Other conditions that the state board may deem appropriate.

(2) To fund local councils.

(3) To fund the state board created in Section 26-16-3 for the actual and necessary expenses that the board incurs in performing its duties.

(b) Authorizations for disbursement of trust fund money under subdivision (a)(3) shall be kept at a minimum in furtherance of the primary purpose of the trust fund which is to disburse money under subdivisions (a)(1) and (2) to encourage the direct provision of services to prevent child abuse and neglect. (Acts 1983, No. 83-736, p. 1198, § 9.)

§ 26-16-10. Child Abuse and Neglect Prevention Board — Criteria for making grants to local councils.

In making grants to a local council, the state board shall consider the degree to which the local council meets the following criteria:

(1) Has as its primary purpose the development and facilitation of a collaborative community prevention program in a specific geographical area. The prevention program shall utilize trained volunteers and existing community resources wherever practicable.

(2) Is administered by a board of directors composed of an equal number of members from the following two groups:

a. A representative from each of the following local agencies: the county department of human resources, the county public health department, the probate court, the office of the prosecuting attorney, a local law enforcement agency, a school district, and a number of private, local agencies that provide treatment or prevention services for abused and neglected children and their parents or guardians. The number of private agencies to be represented on the local council shall be designated in the bylaws of the local council by the remaining members.

b. Members of the local council elected by the membership. The elected members shall represent the demographic composition of the community served, as far as practicable.

(3) Does not provide direct services except on a demonstration project basis, or as a facilitator of interagency projects.

(4) Demonstrates a willingness and ability to provide prevention program models and consultation organizations and communities regarding prevention program development and maintenance.

(5) Demonstrates an ability to match, through money or in-kind services, 50 percent of the amount of any trust fund money received. Not more than 50 percent of the local match shall be in in-kind services. In-kind services are subject to the approval of the board.

(6) Other criteria that the state board deems appropriate. (Acts 1983, No. 83-736, p. 1198, § 10.)

§ 26-16-11. Child Abuse and Neglect Prevention Board — Promulgation of rules.

Not later than two years after August 8, 1983, the state board shall promulgate rules pursuant to the Alabama Administrative Procedures Act, Act No. 81-855 of 1981, now codified as Chapter 22 of Title 41. (Acts 1983, No. 83-736, p. 1198, § 11.)

§ 26-16-12. Review of board conducted every five years.

A thorough, independent review of the functions, responsibilities, and performance of the state board shall be completed each five years after August 8, 1983, and transmitted to the individuals listed in Section 26-16-6(a)(3). (Acts 1983, No. 83-736, p. 1198, § 12.)

§ 26-16-13. State agencies to share information concerning investigations of child abuse or neglect.

Law enforcement agencies of this state, social service agencies of this state, and state and local departments of human resources shall share information concerning investigations of suspected or actual child abuse or neglect when the sharing of such information is necessary to prevent or discover abuse or neglect of children. (Acts 1985, No. 85-699, p. 1140.)

Collateral references. — Tort liability of public authority for failure to remove paren- tally abused or neglected children from parents' custody. 60 ALR4th 942.

ARTICLE 2.

CHILDREN'S TRUST FUND.

Code commissioner's note. — Acts 1983, No. 83-789 designated the act which added this article as the "Martin-Aldridge Act."

§ 26-16-30. Creation of fund; purpose; investment; disposition.

(a) The children's trust fund is created as a separate fund in the state treasury. The function of the children's trust fund shall be to serve as a permanent trust pursuant to Section 26-16-8, and as an investment account for the earnings and funds received by the Child Abuse and Neglect Prevention Board pursuant to Sections 26-16-8, 26-16-31, and 26-16-30(e).

(b) The State Treasurer shall credit to the trust fund all amounts appropriated for this purpose under this article and any amounts received under Section 26-16-8.

(c) The State Treasurer shall invest trust fund money in the same manner as funds are invested pursuant to Section 16-33C-6. Earnings shall be credited to the trust fund.

(d) A separate revenue trust account in the State Treasury is created to be known as the "child abuse and neglect prevention board operations fund" which shall serve as the administrative fund for the children's trust fund and the Child Abuse and Neglect Prevention Board. All state general fund or special educational trust fund appropriations designated for the trust fund or board shall be deposited directly into this fund. The fund shall be disbursed only by warrant of the State Comptroller, upon itemized vouchers, approved by the executive director or the chairman of the board. No funds shall be withdrawn or expended except as budgeted and allotted according to Sections 41-4-80 to 41-4-96, inclusive, and only in the amounts as appropriated by the legislature.

(e) One half of the funds received each year through the income tax refund designation program established in Section 26-16-31, and other amounts specified by motions passed by the board, are not available for transfer into the operations fund and shall become a permanent part of the trust fund. All other funds received by the trust fund after September 30, 1988, including earnings credited after September 30, 1987, and one half of the funds received each year through the income tax refund designation program shall be transferred to the operations fund. The executive director or chairman of the board is authorized to transfer all eligible funds from the trust fund into the operations fund for the purpose of disbursing the funds in accordance with this chapter.

(f) The primary purpose of the trust fund and the operations fund is to encourage professional persons and groups to recognize and deal with problems of child abuse and neglect; to make information about the problems of child abuse and neglect available to the public and organizations and agencies which deal with problems of child abuse and neglect; and to encourage the development of community prevention programs. To these ends the fund shall be expended only as provided in this chapter, Sections 26-16-1 to 26-16-13, inclusive, or other laws specifically regulating those expenditures. (Acts 1983, No. 83-735, p. 1195, § 1; Acts 1985, No. 85-698, p. 1138; Acts 1989, No. 89-656, p. 1300, § 1; Acts 1992, No. 92-606, § 1.)

The 1992 amendment, effective May 21, 1992, substituted "shall" for "will" in the second sentence of subsection (a); deleted "of the Child Abuse and Neglect Prevention Act" following "Section 26-16-8" in subsection (b); in subsection (c) deleted "surplus" preceding "funds" and substituted "Section 16-33C-6" for "section 36-17-18"; in subsection (d) substituted "shall serve" for "will serve" in the first sentence, in the second sentence deleted "children's" preceding "trust fund or board," and deleted "child abuse and neglect prevention" preceding "board," divided the former third sentence into the present third and fourth sentences by deleting "provided, however that" at the end of the present third sentence, substituted "The fund" for "Such fund" in the present third sentence, and in the present last sentence, substituted "according to Sections 41-4-80 to 41-4-96, inclusive" for "according to the provisions of sections 41-4-80 through 41-4-96," and substituted "the amount" for "such amounts"; in subsection (e), in the first sentence deleted "as" preceding "specified," deleted "child abuse and neglect prevention" preceding "board," and deleted "children's"

preceding "trust fund," in the second sentence deleted "the children's trust fund" preceding "after September 30, 1987," and substituted "shall be transferred" for "shall be available for transfer," and in the last sentence deleted "children's" preceding "trust fund," substituted "the funds" for "such funds," and deleted "the provisions of" preceding "this chapter"; and in subsection (f) in the first sentence deleted "children's" preceding "trust fund," and deleted "child abuse and neglect prevention board" preceding "operations fund," and in the second sentence, substituted "Sections 26-16-1 to 26-16-13, inclusive" for "the Child Abuse and Neglect Prevention Act," substituted "other laws" for "other law," inserted "those," and deleted "therefrom" following "expenditures."

No legislative intent to exempt fund from reversion under § 41-4-93. — Sections 26-16-30 through 26-16-33 do not evidence a legislative intent to exempt the children's trust fund from the general reversion requirements of § 41-4-93. Mitchell v. State Child Abuse & Neglect Prevention Bd., 512 So. 2d 778 (Ala. Civ. App. 1987).

§ 26-16-31. State income tax refund designation program — Authorization; procedure.

(a) For the tax year beginning October 1, 1983, and until the state treasurer certifies that the assets in the children's trust fund exceed $10,000,000.00, a resident individual taxpayer who files an Alabama income tax return and who is entitled to an income tax refund from the State Department of Revenue sufficient to make a designation under this section may designate that $5.00, $10.00, $25.00 or other sum of his or her refund be credited to the children's trust fund. In the case of a joint return of husband and wife who are entitled to a tax refund sufficient to make a designation under this section, a designation may be made in the same denominations or sums of their refund to be credited to the children's trust fund. Such designation shall be made by marking the appropriate box, printed on the return pursuant to subsection (b) of this section.

(b) The State Department of Revenue shall print on the face of the state income tax form for residents a space for taxpayers to designate that a contribution be made to the children's trust fund from their income tax refund due. The space for designating the contribution shall provide for checkoff boxes in the stated amounts or other dollar amount, commencing for the tax year 1989 and thereafter.

(c) The State Child Abuse and Neglect Prevention Board, created pursuant to Section 26-16-3, may, from time to time, change the designated checkoff sums upon resolution passed, in accordance with the provisions of the administrative procedure laws, and upon proper notification to the Department of Revenue. (Acts 1983, No. 83-735, p. 1195, § 2; Acts 1988, No. 88-544, p. 843.)

No legislative intent to exempt fund from reversion under § 41-4-93. — Sections 26-16-30 through 26-16-33 do not evidence a legislative intent to exempt the children's trust fund from the general reversion requirements of § 41-4-93. Mitchell v. State Child Abuse & Neglect Prevention Bd., 512 So. 2d 778 (Ala. Civ. App. 1987).

§ 26-16-32. State income tax refund designation program — Disposition of contributions.

(a) Each year that the refund designation program established in Section 26-16-31(a), above, is in effect, the Commissioner of the Department of Revenue shall transfer to the children's trust fund an amount equal to the total amount designated by individuals to be paid to the fund under this article, less an amount, equal to not more than three percent of the total of such funds then collected, for the additional cost incurred by the Department of Revenue in collecting and handling such funds which shall be deposited in the general fund of the State Treasury for the use of the revenue department. Such deposits shall be made not less than quarterly commencing with the first day such funds are collected from the taxpayer.

(b) Moneys contained in the children's trust fund are continuously appropriated to the Child Abuse and Neglect Prevention Board for the purposes set out in Section 26-16-30(f) of this article. Such funds shall be supplemental to any and all other appropriations heretofore or hereafter made to the Child Abuse and Neglect Prevention Board. No provision of this article shall be construed to be in lieu of annual appropriations.

(c) The Child Abuse and Neglect Prevention Board shall have access to and control of the moneys in said fund and shall be authorized to distribute such funds only for the purposes of this article and Section 26-16-9 of the Child Abuse and Neglect Prevention Act (the Act proposed by House Bill No. 57 of the 1983 Regular Session of the Alabama Legislature). (Acts 1983, No. 83-735, p. 1195, § 3; Acts 1989, No. 89-656, p. 1300, § 1.)

No legislative intent to exempt fund from reversion under § 41-4-93. — Sections 26-16-30 through 26-16-33 do not evidence a legislative intent to exempt the children's trust fund from the general reversion requirements of § 41-4-93. Mitchell v. State Child Abuse & Neglect Prevention Bd., 512 So. 2d 778 (Ala. Civ. App. 1987).

Appropriations not used during year appropriated revert to general fund. — The language used by the legislature in the second and third sentences of subsection (b) indicates its intent, if not anticipation, that the children's trust fund could also be composed of legislatively appropriated funds — funds subject to reversion to the state's general fund if not used during the fiscal year in which they were appropriated. The balance of the $250,000 appropriated to the children's trust fund for the 1984-85 fiscal year was, therefore, not part of the monies continuously appropriated to the board. Rather, like all appropriations by the legislature, if not used, it must revert to the state's general fund. Mitchell v. State Child Abuse & Neglect Prevention Bd., 512 So. 2d 778 (Ala. Civ. App. 1987).

Funds derived from income tax refund

designation program do not revert to general fund. — The "moneys" referred to in the first sentence of subsection (b) must be interpreted to refer to that part of the trust fund derived from the income tax refund designation program. Since such funds are not appropriated by the legislature, it only makes sense that they should not revert to the state's general fund, but should remain in the trust fund "continuously appropriated" to the board. Mitchell v. State Child Abuse & Neglect Prevention Bd., 512 So. 2d 778 (Ala. Civ. App. 1987).

§ 26-16-33. General repealer; construction of article.

All laws or parts of laws which conflict with this article are hereby repealed except that no part of this article shall be construed to authorize any board, person, or entity to assume the duties and responsibilities of any other state agencies or to repeal or preempt or take precedence over any part of Title 26, Chapter 14, Sections 26-14-1 through 26-14-13. (Acts 1983, No. 83-735, p. 1195, § 5.)

No legislative intent to exempt fund from reversion under § 41-4-93. — Sections 26-16-30 through 26-16-33 do not evidence a legislative intent to exempt the children's trust fund from the general reversion requirements of § 41-4-93. Mitchell v. State Child Abuse & Neglect Prevention Bd., 512 So. 2d 778 (Ala. Civ. App. 1987).

ARTICLE 3.

MULTI-DISCIPLINARY CHILD PROTECTION TEAMS.

Code commissioner's note. — Pursuant to Acts 1986, No. 86-432, the name of the Department of Pensions and Security was changed to the Department of Human Resources. See the Code commissioner's note under ch. 2, T. 38.

§ 26-16-50. Department of Human Resources to provide for teams; composition of teams.

The Department of Human Resources shall provide for the development and coordination of the multi-disciplinary child protection teams created by this article and for the services to be provided by such teams throughout the state. Such teams shall be composed of representatives from the local departments of human resources, the local law enforcement agencies, the local district attorneys' offices, and the local educational agencies. The teams may also include representatives from the local health field, mental health services, local social service agencies, and local members of the legal profession. Representatives of other professions or disciplines may be included if the local team as established deems them useful or necessary. (Acts 1985, No. 85-682, p. 1078, § 1.)

§ 26-16-51. Department of Human Resources to adopt guidelines and criteria; general role and functions of teams.

The Department of Human Resources shall adopt guidelines and criteria relating to the operations and functions of the team as promulgated by the advisory committee created pursuant to Section 26-16-52. The guidelines will be supplemental to the existing protective service activities of the children, youth, and family programs of the State of Alabama. Nothing in this section shall be construed to remove or reduce the duty and responsibility of any person to report all suspected or actual cases of child abuse or neglect or sexual abuse of a child pursuant to law. The general role of the teams shall be to support activities of the program and to provide services to abused and neglected children upon referral by the county departments of human resources, or any other agency as set forth in the guidelines and criteria established.

To the extent that resources are available to each of the various teams throughout the state, the functions of the teams shall include, but not be limited to, the following specific functions:

    (1) To provide comprehensive medical and psychological programs for the identification and diagnosis of child abuse and for treatment and rehabilitation programs for abused children and their family members.

    (2) To provide case service coordination and assistance, including the types and locations of services available to abused children and their family members from other public or private agencies in the community in an effort to provide the fullest range of services while avoiding the duplication of services.

    (3) To provide for educational and community awareness campaigns on child abuse and neglect in an effort to enable citizens more successfully to prevent, identify, and report and treat child abuse and neglect victims in the community. (Acts 1985, No. 85-682, p. 1078, § 2.)

§ 26-16-52. Ad hoc child abuse protection team advisory committee created; composition, duties, etc.; annual report.

Upon October 1, 1985, an ad hoc child abuse protection team advisory committee shall be created and shall consist of the following members: the Governor of the State of Alabama or his designated representative; the Director of the Department of Human Resources; the executive director of the child abuse trust fund; the president of the State Parents Teachers Association; two judges in the State of Alabama that preside over courts exercising juvenile jurisdiction to be selected by the Chief Justice of the Alabama Supreme Court; one representative from the Association of County Department of Human Resources county directors to be selected by the Governor; the executive director of the Office of Prosecution Services; the chairman of the Victims Compensation Commission; and two other members selected by the president of the child abuse trust fund.

The committee shall study the operational aspects of multi-disciplinary child protection teams, hereinafter referred to as teams, including both existing teams and those teams to be created pursuant to this article, and shall promulgate guidelines for the reporting or referral of child abuse or neglect cases to the teams. The committee shall present their guidelines within three months after the committee is formed to the Governor.

Upon final approval of such guidelines by the Governor, the teams shall begin organizing and as soon as it is practicable shall begin to carry out their functions.

In order to ensure the effective implementation of these teams, the Director of the Department of Human Resources shall submit a report on the overall operation of these teams to the joint legislative committee on children and youth within 30 days of the beginning of each annual regular session of the Alabama Legislature. (Acts 1985, No. 85-682, p. 1078, § 3.)

§ 26-16-53. Existing child abuse prevention teams preserved and exempted from article.

Child abuse prevention teams in existence as of October 1, 1985, shall not be replaced by the provisions of this article. Such existing teams are hereby expressly preserved and shall be exempt from the provisions of this article. (Acts 1985, No. 85-682, p. 1078, § 4.)

ARTICLE 4.

ALABAMA NETWORK OF CHILDREN'S ADVOCACY CENTERS.

Effective date. — The act which added this article became effective May 21, 1992.

§ 26-16-70. Membership; eligibility.

In order to become eligible for a full membership in the Alabama Network of Children's Advocacy Centers, Incorporated, child advocacy centers in this state shall:

(1) Be a private, non-profit incorporated agency.

(2) Have a neutral, child-focused facility where joint Department of Human Resources and law enforcement interviews take place with children in appropriate cases of suspected child sexual and physical abuse. All multidisciplinary agencies shall have a place to interact with the child as investigative or treatment needs require.

(3) Have a minimum designated staff that is supervised and approved by the local board of directors.

(4) Having a Multidisciplinary Case Review Team that meets on a regularly scheduled basis or as the case load of the community requires. The team shall consist of representatives from the District Attorney, the Department of Human Resources, mental health, law enforcement, and the

Child Advocacy Center staff. Medical personnel and a victim's advocate may be part of the team.

(5) Provide case tracking of child abuse cases seen through the center. A center shall also collect data on: the number of child abuse cases seen at the center by sex, race, age, and other relevant data; the number of cases referred for prosecution; and the number of cases referred for mental health therapy.

(6) Provide referrals for medical exams and mental health therapy. The center shall provide follow-up on cases referred for mental health therapy.

(7) Provide training for various disciplines in the community that deal with child abuse.

(8) Have an interagency commitment covering those aspects of agency participation in a multidisciplinary approach to the handling of child sexual and serious physical abuse cases.

(9) Provide assurance that volunteers at the center are trained and screened by appropriate resources. (Acts 1992, No. 92-558, § 1.)

§ 26-16-71. Certification; eligibility for funds.

Any child advocacy center within the State of Alabama that meets the standards of Section 26-16-70 and is certified by the Alabama Network of Children's Advocacy Centers, Incorporated as being a full member in that organization shall be eligible to receive funds that are appropriated from the State of Alabama to the Alabama Network of Children's Advocacy Centers, Incorporated. (Acts 1992, No. 92-558, § 2.)

§ 26-16-72. Initial funding; failure to meet standards.

Any new child advocacy center within the State of Alabama that desires to become certified by the network may request and receive initial funding if approved by the board of directors of the network. Any center failing to meet the standards established in Section 26-16-70 for a period of one year or longer shall not be eligible to receive state funding. (Acts 1992, No. 92-558, § 3.)

§ 26-16-73. Allocation of funds.

The network board of directors shall be responsible for allocating state appropriated funds to existing and new child advocacy centers which meet the standards of Section 26-16-70. (Acts 1992, No. 92-558, § 4.)

CHAPTER 17.

ALABAMA UNIFORM PARENTAGE ACT.

I. In General.
II. Decisions Under Prior Law.

I. IN GENERAL.

The statute of limitations provisions in this chapter do not violate the equal protection clause. Thomas v. State ex rel. Williams, 523 So. 2d 434 (Ala. Civ. App. 1988).

A married woman who conceives a child by one not her husband may institute paternity proceedings against the putative father. There is reasonable cause for debate as to whether denial of a similar right to the putative father may be contrary to the equal protection clause of the U.S. Const., amend. 14. Finkenbinder v. Burton, 452 So. 2d 880 (Ala. Civ. App. 1984), aff'd, 477 So. 2d 459 (Ala. Civ. App. 1985).

Notwithstanding the fact of her marital status, mother could properly bring action under § 26-17-9(b) against putative father even though marriage was to another man.

State ex rel. Goodno v. Cobb, 567 So. 2d 376 (Ala. Civ. App. 1990).

The biological father of a child born during the marriage of the mother to another man may bring an action for declaratory judgment to establish his paternity of the child. Finkenbinder v. Burton, 452 So. 2d 880 (Ala. Civ. App. 1984), aff'd, 477 So. 2d 459 (Ala. Civ. App. 1985).

If an action to establish paternity of a child born during the marriage of the mother to another may be brought through suit for declaratory judgment, there is no basis for denying it being done by way of intervention in an already pending action relating to custody and best interest of the child. The purpose of avoiding multiple suits and speeding the determination of issues is served in both intervention and declaratory judgment actions. Finkenbinder v. Burton, 452 So. 2d 880 (Ala. Civ.

App. 1984), aff'd, 477 So. 2d 459 (Ala. Civ. App. 1985).

The matter of custody of a child to which one seeks to establish paternity is a matter of such interest as to provide intervention of right under A.R.C.P., Rule 24. Finkenbinder v. Burton, 452 So. 2d 880 (Ala. Civ. App. 1984), aff'd, 477 So. 2d 459 (Ala. Civ. App. 1985).

The "college education exception" to the general rule that a "parent has no duty to contribute to the support of his or her child after that child has reached the legislatively prescribed age of majority," applies as well where the parents were not married at the time of the birth of the child and were not married thereafter. Ex parte Jones, 592 So. 2d 608 (Ala. 1991).

The factors for the trial court to consider in awarding child support set forth in Bayliss v. Bayliss, 550 So. 2d at 986 (Ala. 1989), aside from the reference to the dissolution of marriage, are applicable in the situation where the parents have never married. Ex parte Jones, 592 So. 2d 608 (Ala. 1991).

Cited in State ex rel. Huguley v. Samuels, 457 So. 2d 977 (Ala. Civ. App. 1984).

Collateral references. — 10 C.J.S., Bastards, § 16.

10 Am. Jur. 2d, Bastards, § 74 et seq.

Death of putative father as precluding action for determination of paternity or for child support. 58 ALR3d 188.

Standing to dispute the presumption of legitimacy of a child conceived or born during wedlock. 90 ALR3d 1032.

Right of indigent defendant in paternity suit to have assistance of counsel at state expense. 4 ALR4th 363.

Prosecutor's reference in opening statement to matters not provable or which he does not attempt to prove as ground for relief. 16 ALR4th 810.

Right of illegitimate grandchildren to take under testamentary gift to "grandchildren." 17 ALR4th 1292.

Right of illegitimate child to maintain action to determine paternity. 19 ALR4th 1082.

Admissibility or compellability of blood test to establish testee's nonpaternity for purpose of challenging testee's parental rights. 87 ALR4th 572.

II. DECISIONS UNDER PRIOR LAW.

This chapter is no ex post facto law within the meaning of either the state or federal Constitutions. Ward v. State, 42 Ala. App. 529, 170 So. 2d 500 (1964).

The general purpose of this chapter is to set up a procedure whereby the paternity of an illegitimate child can be judicially determined. State ex rel. Moore v. Strickland, 289 Ala. 488, 268 So. 2d 766 (1972); Everage v. Gibson, 372 So. 2d 829 (Ala. 1979), cert. denied, 445 U.S. 931, 100 S. Ct. 1322, 63 L. Ed. 2d 765 (1980).

One of the purposes of this chapter was to make provision for children born out of wedlock. Moore v. LeFlore, 288 Ala. 315, 260 So. 2d 585 (1972); Keener v. State, 347 So. 2d 398 (Ala. 1977).

Paternity is only matter which becomes res judicata under desertion statute. — The only matter cognizable under this chapter which becomes res judicata under former § 30-4-51 is that of paternity of the child. Ward v. State, 42 Ala. App. 529, 170 So. 2d 500 (1964); Moore v. LeFlore, 288 Ala. 315, 260 So. 2d 585 (1972).

The legislature has provided for blood grouping tests in proceedings for determining the paternity of illegitimates, that is, where one is charged with being the father of an illegitimate child, but it has not seen fit to provide for the tests in a divorce proceeding wherein the legitimacy of a child born to a married mother, who is living with her husband, is brought into question. Mason v. Mason, 276 Ala. 265, 160 So. 2d 881 (1964).

Requirement that paternity proceeding be maintained during lifetime of father does not appear in the Alabama Code at all. It is an aspect of judge-made law which was first formally stated in Everage v. Gibson, 372 So. 2d 829 (Ala. 1979), which concerned a challenge to the Alabama intestacy laws based upon the fact that the language of former § 43-3-1, which governed intestate inheritance, provided no avenue for inheritance by illegitimate children. The court was able to sustain the constitutionality of the statute by holding that a paternity proceeding, pursuant to this chapter, serves the same state purpose as legitimation in establishing the right to intestate succession. Handley ex rel. Herron v. Schweiker, 697 F.2d 999 (11th Cir. 1983).

This chapter does not violate equal protection of the law by discriminating on the basis of illegitimacy. Everage v. Gibson, 372 So. 2d 829 (Ala. 1979), cert. denied, 445 U.S. 931, 100 S. Ct. 1322, 63 L. Ed. 2d 765 (1980).

Adjudication under chapter enables child to inherit from intestate father. — Under Alabama law, there are three means by which an illegitimate child may inherit from an intestate father short of adoption by the father. The father may marry the mother and recognize the child as his own, the father may legitimate the child by following the statutory procedure for legitimation by written declaration or the court may make a judicial determination of paternity. Handley ex rel. Herron v. Schweiker, 697 F.2d 999 (11th Cir. 1983).

Adjudication of paternity in a proceeding

under this chapter is sufficient state expression by which to obtain legitimation of an illegitimate child in order that it may inherit from intestate father's estate in the same manner as a legitimate child. Everage v. Gibson, 372 So. 2d 829 (Ala. 1979), cert. denied, 445 U.S. 931, 100 S. Ct. 1322, 63 L. Ed. 2d 765 (1980).

§ 26-17-1. Short title.

This chapter shall be known and may be cited as the Alabama Uniform Parentage Act. (Acts 1984, No. 84-244, p. 375, § 1.)

Purpose. — The ultimate objective of the Alabama Uniform Parentage Act (UPA) is to promote full equality for all children, be they legitimate or illegitimate. Ex parte Presse, 554 So. 2d 406 (Ala. 1989).

Judgment under former statute held not void for lack of jurisdiction. — The Alabama Uniform Parentage Act is clearly remedial in nature, as it impairs no vested right, and does not disturb past transactions but rather heals what may have been perceived as defects in the original paternity statute. Moreover, its principal function is to provide a procedure for establishing the paternity of a child. Therefore, a circuit court's judgment in a paternity action instituted under the former paternity statute was not void for lack of jurisdiction. Ritter v. State, 494 So. 2d 76 (Ala. Civ. App. 1986).

Human leukocyte antigen (HLA) test results were admissible evidence in paternity action even before passage of this chapter. Lyle v. Eddy, 481 So. 2d 395 (Ala. Civ. App. 1985).

Inheritance from father where child legitimated by paternity decree. — Child legitimated by means of a paternity decree before the death of her father could not be barred from inheriting from her father's estate based upon the application of the invalidated and unconstitutional statute of limitations in former § 26-12-7. Abrams v. Wheeler, 468 So. 2d 126 (Ala. 1985) (decided under law prior to § 43-8-48).

Cited in State v. Washington, 467 So. 2d 253 (Ala. Civ. App. 1985).

§ 26-17-2. Parent and child relationship — Defined.

As used in this chapter, the term "parent and child relationship" shall mean the legal relationship existing between a child and his natural or adoptive parents incident to which the law confers or imposes rights, privileges, duties and obligations. It shall include the mother and child relationship and the father and child relationship. (Acts 1984, No. 84-244, p. 375, § 2.)

The provisions of Alabama Uniform Parentage Act cannot be used to create a "common law adoption," and without compliance with the adoption procedures as set out in former § 26-10-1 et seq., there can be no parent-child relationship created by adoption. McCoy v. McCoy, 549 So. 2d 53 (Ala. 1989).

Section is inapplicable where finding that person is not natural child of another. — Upon a trial court's finding that, as an established fact, a person is not the natural child of another, it logically follows that the legitimation provisions contained in the Alabama Uniform Parentage Act are inapplicable to create a presumption of legitimacy since the act expressly applies to natural or adoptive parent-child relationships. McCoy v. McCoy, 549 So. 2d 53 (Ala. 1989).

It is firmly established in this state that

parental obligations do not differ with regard to whether the parents of the child are married. Ex parte Jones, 592 So. 2d 608 (Ala. 1991).

The "college education exception" to the general rule that a "parent has no duty to contribute to the support of his or her child after that child has reached the legislatively prescribed age of majority," applies as well where the parents were not married at the time of the birth of the child and were not married thereafter. Ex parte Jones, 592 So. 2d 608 (Ala. 1991).

The absence of restrictive language in § 26-17-15 provides the trial court with jurisdiction to require the father of a child born out of wedlock to provide to the child post-minority support for a college education in a manner and to the extent of the requisites established in Bayliss v. Bayliss, 550 So. 2d 986 (Ala. 1989). Jones v. Williams, 592 So. 2d 605 (Ala. Civ. App. 1991), aff'd, 592 So. 2d 608 (Ala. 1991).

The factors for the trial court to consider in awarding child support set forth in Bayliss v. Bayliss, 550 So. 2d at 986 (Ala.

1989), aside from the reference to the dissolution of marriage, are applicable in the situation where the parents have never married. Ex parte Jones, 592 So. 2d 608 (Ala. 1991).

Cited in Ex parte Presse, 554 So. 2d 406 (Ala. 1989).

§ 26-17-3. Parent and child relationship — Relationship not dependent upon marriage.

The parent and child relationship shall extend equally to every child and to every parent, regardless of the marital status of the parents. (Acts 1984, No. 84-244, p. 375, § 3.)

It is firmly established in this state that parental obligations do not differ with regard to whether the parents of the child are married. Ex parte Jones, 592 So. 2d 608 (Ala. 1991).

The "college education exception" to the general rule that a "parent has no duty to contribute to the support of his or her child after that child has reached the legislatively prescribed age of majority," applies as well where the parents were not married at the time of the birth of the child and were not married thereafter. Ex parte Jones, 592 So. 2d 608 (Ala. 1991).

The absence of restrictive language in § 26-17-15 provides the trial court with juris-

diction to require the father of a child born out of wedlock to provide to the child post-minority support for a college education in a manner and to the extent of the requisites established in Bayliss v. Bayliss, 550 So. 2d 986 (Ala. 1989); Jones v. Williams, 592 So. 2d 605 (Ala. Civ. App. 1991), aff'd, 592 So. 2d 608 (Ala. 1991).

The factors for the trial court to consider in awarding child support set forth in Bayliss v. Bayliss, 550 So. 2d at 986 (Ala. 1989), aside from the reference to the dissolution of marriage, are applicable in the situation where the parents have never married. Ex parte Jones, 592 So. 2d 608 (Ala. 1991).

§ 26-17-4. Parent and child relationship — How established.

The parent and child relationship may be established between a child and:

(1) The natural mother by proof of her having given birth to the child, or pursuant to the provisions of this chapter;

(2) The natural father pursuant to this chapter;

(3) An adoptive parent by proof of adoption or pursuant to the Revised Uniform Adoption Act. (Acts 1984, No. 84-244, p. 375, § 4.)

§ 26-17-5. Presumption of paternity; rebuttal.

(a) A man is presumed to be the natural father of a child if:

(1) He and the child's natural mother are or have been married to each other and the child is born during the marriage, or within 300 days after the marriage is terminated by death, annulment, declaration of invalidity, or divorce, or after a decree of separation is entered by a court;

(2) Before the child's birth he and the child's natural mother have attempted to marry each other by a marriage solemnized in apparent compliance with law, although the attempted marriage is or could be declared invalid, and

a. If the attempted marriage may be declared invalid only by a court, the child is born during the attempted marriage, or within 300 days after the termination of the attempted marriage by death, annulment, declaration of invalidity, or divorce; or

b. If the attempted marriage is invalid without a court order, the child is born within 300 days after the termination of cohabitation;

(3) After the child's birth, he and the child's natural mother have married, or attempted to marry, each other by a marriage solemnized in apparent compliance with the law although the attempted marriage is or could be declared invalid, and

a. He has acknowledged his paternity of the child in writing, such writing being filed with the appropriate court or the Bureau of Vital Statistics; or

b. With his consent, he is named as the child's father on the child's birth certificate; or

c. He is otherwise obligated to support the child either under a written voluntary promise or by court order;

(4) While the child is under the age of majority, he receives the child into his home or otherwise openly holds out the child as his natural child; or

(5) He acknowledges his paternity of the child in a writing filed in accordance with provisions of the legitimation statute.

(b) A presumption of paternity under this section may be rebutted in an appropriate action only by clear and convincing evidence. In the event two or more conflicting presumptions arise, that which is founded upon the weightier considerations of public policy and logic, as evidenced by the facts, shall control. The presumption of paternity is rebutted by a court decree establishing paternity of the child by another man. (Acts 1984, No. 84-244, p. 375, § 5.)

The language of subsection (a) (1) of this section and § 26-17-11 is clear and unambiguous and applicable where mother of child brought paternity action against the putative father and therefore the husband, because he was the presumed father pursuant to this section, was required to be made a party to the action. State ex rel. Goodno v. Cobb, 567 So. 2d 376 (Ala. Civ. App. 1990).

Subdivision (a)(4) reserved for man not married to child's mother. — A reading of all the categories together makes it clear that subdivision (a)(4) is reserved for a man not married to the mother of the child and does not include married persons since the result otherwise would allow a man the opportunity to circumvent the statute of limitations by choosing the presumptive category under which he wishes to proceed and would be unreasonable to assume that the legislature intended to include such married persons. Ex parte Presse, 554 So. 2d 406 (Ala. 1989).

Standing to bring paternity action. — A man claiming to be the father of a child conceived and born during the marriage of its mother to another man does not have standing under the Alabama Uniform Parentage Act (UPA) to initiate an action to establish that he is the father of the child where the presumed father persists in the presumption that he is the father. Ex parte Presse, 554 So. 2d 406 (Ala. 1989).

A man does not have standing to bring an action seeking to declare a child illegitimate and to have himself declared the father of that child, as long as there is a presumed father, pursuant to subdivision (a)(1), who has not disclaimed his status as the child's father; consequently, another man, though he later marries the mother and lives with the mother and child, has no standing to challenge the presumed paternity of that child since so long as the presumed father persists in maintaining his paternal status, not even the subsequent marriage of the child's mother to another man can create standing in the other man to challenge the presumed father's parental relationship. Ex parte Presse, 554 So. 2d 406 (Ala. 1989).

The legislature, in adopting the Alabama Uniform Parentage Act (UPA), did not intend for a third party to be able to assert his paternity, to the exclusion of a man who was married to the child's mother when the child was conceived and born, simply because the third party has since married the man's divorced wife and, in so doing, allowed the child into his home. Ex parte Presse, 554 So. 2d 406 (Ala. 1989).

Putative father who intervened in a divorce action to establish his paternity of a child lacked standing to bring a petition for paternity, where the husband in the divorce action was married to the mother at the time of the birth. Foster v. Whitley, 564 So. 2d 990 (Ala. Civ. App. 1990).

Presumption created by section rebuttable. — Trial court erred in concluding that presumption of paternity that attached to the husband by virtue of his marriage to the mother is "irrefutable"; Alabama law clearly allows one to rebut this strong presumption of paternity in disputed cases. S.T. v. C.T.T., 571 So. 2d 1168 (Ala. Civ. App. 1990).

Trial court did not have jurisdiction. — Where child was born during marriage, husband was listed as child's father on birth certificate, husband alleged that child was not his in divorce complaint, and husband was deceased, the trial court did not have jurisdiction to determine paternity of a child who was not a party to action and did not have an appointed guardian ad litem; clearly, the case fell within the purview of the Uniform Parentage Act and this case included a strong presumption of paternity; any finding contrary to the presumed paternity was to be made by the court most adept at making that determination. S.T. v. C.T.T., 571 So. 2d 1168 (Ala. Civ. App. 1990).

How presumption may be rebutted. — The extremely heavy burden of rebutting the presumption that a child born during marriage of husband and wife is the legitimate son of the husband may only be carried by clear and convincing evidence which tends to show that it was naturally, physically, or scientifically impossible for the husband to be the father. Finkenbinder v. Burton, 477 So. 2d 459 (Ala. Civ. App. 1985).

Although the child was born only one month after the parties' marriage, Alabama law presumes that a man is the natural father of a child if he and the child's natural mother are or have been married to each other and the child is born during the marriage. Clear and convincing evidence tending to establish that the husband cannot be the father, either physically

or biologically, is required to overcome this presumption. Bishop v. Robinson, 516 So. 2d 723 (Ala. Civ. App. 1987).

This section places a strong presumption of paternity upon a husband when a child is born during his marriage. The husband's presumption of paternity could only be rebutted by clear and convincing evidence which tends to show that it is naturally, physically, or scientifically impossible for the husband to be the father. J.J.O. v. K.O., 591 So. 2d 92 (Ala. Civ. App. 1991).

Divorce judgment provided ex-husband was not child's father rebutted any presumption he was father under this section. — Where the mother in a paternity case argued that, since she was married to exhusband at the time of the birth of her daughter, ex-husband is legally presumed to be the child's father under this section and that he should have been made a party to the action because § 26-17-11 required that each man presumed to be father be made a party if he is subject to the jurisdiction of the court. However, in their divorce judgment which provided that the minor child born during the marriage was not his child that divorce judgment effectively rebutted any presumption that he was the father of the child under subsection (b), and it eliminated the requirement of § 26-17-11 that he be made a party to the paternity proceedings. Thomas v. Callen, 521 So. 2d 1322 (Ala. Civ. App. 1987).

Wife pregnant at time of marriage without husband's knowledge or agency. — Divorce judgment entered on ground that wife was pregnant at the time of the marriage without husband's knowledge or agency did not destroy the usual presumption in a paternity case that a child born to a married woman is the child of the mother's husband, nor was the judgment binding on the child, who had not been joined as a party or represented by a guardian ad litem. Ex parte Martin ex rel. Sarris, 565 So. 2d 1 (Ala. 1989).

Wife cannot testify that parties' child was illegitimate, and if she does want to deny the child's legitimacy, the burden is on her to overcome the legitimacy presumption. Bishop v. Robinson, 516 So. 2d 723 (Ala. Civ. App. 1987).

Evidence held sufficient. — Blood test indicating that there was a 98.89 percent chance that husband was father of child who was born approximately eight months and eleven days after the parties' marriage, along with a letter written by the wife's obstetrician, which placed the date of conception between April 25 and April 30, 1984, which dates coincided with the date when the parties agreed that they first engaged in sexual intercourse, i.e., April 19 or April 20, 1984, could reasonably satisfy the court that husband was the father of the child. Threadgill v. Threadgill, 487 So. 2d 935 (Ala. Civ. App. 1986).

§ 26-17-6. Action to determine father and child relationship; who may bring action; when action may be brought; stay until birth; adopted children.

(a) A child, a child's natural mother, or a man presumed to be its father under subdivision (1), (2), or (3) of Section 26-17-5(a), may bring an action within five years of the birth of said child for the purpose of declaring the existence of the father and child relationship presumed under subdivision (1), (2), or (3) of Section 26-17-5(a); or

(b) Any interested party may bring an action at any time for the purpose of determining the existence or non-existence of the father and child relationship presumed under subdivision (4) or (5) of Section 26-17-5(a).

(c) An action to determine the existence of the father and child relationship with respect to a child who has no presumed father under Section 26-17-5 may be brought by the child, the mother, or personal representative of the child, the public authority chargeable by law with support of the child, the personal representative or a parent of the mother if the mother has died, a man alleged or alleging himself to be the father, or the personal representative or a parent of the alleged father if the alleged father has died or is a minor.

(d) If an action under this section is brought before the birth of the child, all proceedings shall be stayed until after the birth, except service of process and the taking of depositions to perpetuate testimony.

(e) If the child has been adopted, an action may not be brought. (Acts 1984, No. 84-244, p. 375, § 6.)

I. General Consideration.
II. Decisions Under Prior Law.

I. GENERAL CONSIDERATION.

Subsection (c) is a remedial statute, providing a procedure for the enforcement of an existing substantive right and may be applied retroactively. Williams v. State, 504 So. 2d 282 (Ala. Civ. App. 1986).

Statute creating new procedure to implement preexisting substantive right. — That the child was more than five years old before the effective date of the Alabama Uniform Parentage Act does not change the fact that her right to parental support existed before it. The new act merely created a procedure to implement her preexisting substantive right. The presumption against retroactive application does not obtain in such a situation. Williams v. State, 504 So. 2d 282 (Ala. Civ. App. 1986).

The statute of limitations provisions in this section do not violate the equal protec- tion clause. Thomas v. State ex rel. Williams, 523 So. 2d 434 (Ala. Civ. App. 1988).

Section 26-17-5(a)(4) reserved for man not married to child's mother. — A reading of all the categories together makes it clear that § 26-17-5(a)(4) is reserved for a man not married to the mother of the child and does not include married persons since the result otherwise would allow a man the opportunity to circumvent the statute of limitations by choosing the presumptive category under which he wishes to proceed and would be unreasonable to assume that the legislature intended to include such married persons. Ex parte Presse, 554 So. 2d 406 (Ala. 1989).

Standing to bring paternity action. — A man claiming to be the father of a child conceived and born during the marriage of its mother to another man does not have standing under the Alabama Uniform Parentage Act (UPA) to initiate an action to establish that he is the father of the child where the presumed father persists in the presumption that he is the father. Ex parte Presse, 554 So. 2d 406 (Ala. 1989).

The legislature, in adopting the Alabama Uniform Parentage Act (UPA), did not intend for a third party to be able to assert his paternity, to the exclusion of a man who was married to the child's mother when the child was conceived and born, simply because the third party has since married the man's divorced wife and, in so doing, allowed the child into his home. Ex parte Presse, 554 So. 2d 406 (Ala. 1989).

Putative father who intervened in a divorce action to establish his paternity of a child lacked standing to bring a petition for paternity, where the husband in the divorce action was married to the mother at the time of the birth. Foster v. Whitley, 564 So. 2d 990 (Ala. Civ. App. 1990).

Child's action for paternity under this chapter was not barred by res judicata, where the child's mother had brought an unsuccessful paternity action against the same defendant pursuant to the prior paternity statute. Snow v. Armstrong, 508 So. 2d 266 (Ala. 1987).

Possibility of declaratory action for support purposes does not foreclose application of subsection (c). — The legislature provided a specific procedure when it adopted the Uniform Parentage Act. The possibility that a declaratory judgment action may also lie on behalf of a child seeking a paternity determination for the purposes of establishing support does not foreclose the application of subsection (c) of this section. Williams v. State, 504 So. 2d 282 (Ala. Civ. App. 1986).

Cited in Morgan County Dep't of Pensions & Sec. ex rel. Ryan v. Kelso, 460 So. 2d 1333 (Ala. Civ. App. 1984).

Collateral references. — Statute of limitations in illegitimacy or bastardy proceedings. 59 ALR3d 685.

II. DECISIONS UNDER PRIOR LAW.

Residency. — The intention of this section was to cover residency in the state at the time of delivery of the child. Trucks v. State, 292 Ala. 63, 288 So. 2d 778 (1974).

Jurisdiction. — Where alleged father and mother resided in same county when both children whose paternity and support were in question were born and where the children were supported by the alleged father, that county had jurisdiction for a paternity action, even where mother was no longer a resident of this state. Trucks v. State, 292 Ala. 63, 288 So. 2d 778 (1974).

Nature of proceeding. — A bastardy action

has long been regarded as neither strictly civil nor strictly criminal, but as partaking of the nature of both. It is quasi-criminal in character. Hunter v. State, 293 Ala. 226, 301 So. 2d 541 (1974).

In some contexts relating to the bias or prejudice of a witness, a paternity proceeding is sufficiently analogous to a criminal proceeding to bring to bear the rule applicable in criminal cases. Hunter v. State, 293 Ala. 226, 301 So. 2d 541 (1974).

Naming of state as plaintiff in paternity suit not prejudicial. — Since the state is the plaintiff in paternity proceeding and the issue in such case is to be resolved between the state and the accused, it cannot be said that the injection of the name of the state, as plaintiff in the suit, prejudiced the defendant. Clevenger v. State, 369 So. 2d 563 (Ala. Civ. App. 1979).

For discussion as to paternity proceeding generally, see State v. Palmer, 439 So. 2d 174 (Ala. Civ. App. 1983).

Formal acknowledgment not required as proof to toll of limitations. — This section does not require as proof to toll the statute of limitations the formal acknowledgment requisite under § 26-11-2, to legitimate the child. Such formulary acts ends bastardy. Residing in a sort of semantic limbo, there can be in legal parlance acknowledged (as well as unacknowledged) bastards. Ward v. State, 42 Ala. App. 529, 170 So. 2d 500 (1964).

Evidence sufficient to toll statute. — Evidence of supporting the child before expiry of two years (now five years) from the birth of the child and within two years (now five years) before complaint, tolls the running of the statute of limitations. Ward v. State, 42 Ala. App. 529, 170 So. 2d 500 (1964).

Burden of proof. — When it affirmatively appears that an action is time barred as in this section, the plaintiff has the burden of proof to show any special circumstances existing which would prevent the running of the statute of limitations. Hunter v. State, 293 Ala. 226, 301 So. 2d 541 (1974).

Limitation period is one in effect when suit filed. — The statute of limitations in effect at the time the suit is filed, as opposed to one in effect at the time of the accrual of the cause of action, is applicable unless the later statute clearly states the contrary. Adams v. State, 428 So. 2d 117 (Ala. Civ. App. 1983).

The statute of limitations in effect at the time the suit is filed, as opposed to the one in effect at the time of the accrual of the cause of action, has been held to apply unless the later statute clearly states the contrary. However, if when the successor statute becomes effective, the cause of action has already been barred by the limitations statute in effect at accrual, then the new, longer statute cannot be applied to revive the barred cause. State v. Martin, 437 So. 2d 1311 (Ala. Civ. App. 1983).

Remedial statutes such as statutes of limitations may operate retrospectively, in the absence of language clearly showing a contrary intention. Adams v. State, 428 So. 2d 117 (Ala. Civ. App. 1983).

Ex post facto prohibition not violated since paternity action is civil proceeding. — Application of extended statute of limitations under similar facts did not violate the prohibition against ex post facto laws because paternity actions are civil under the applicable laws. Adams v. State, 428 So. 2d 117 (Ala. Civ. App. 1983).

Evidence of supporting a child before the expiration of two years (now five years) from birth of the child and within two years (now five years) before the complaint is necessary to toll the running of the statute of limitations. State v. Maddox, 358 So. 2d 461 (Ala. Civ. App. 1978); State v. Hall, 388 So. 2d 1004 (Ala. Civ. App. 1980).

In order for the statute of limitations to be tolled in a paternity proceeding under this section, there must be acknowledgment or support of the child by the reputed father within two years (now five years) of the child's birth. State v. Maddox, 358 So. 2d 461 (Ala. Civ. App. 1978).

The limitation period of this section may be tolled by showing that the reputed father either legally acknowledged paternity or supported the child within the two-year (now five year) period following the birth of the child. State v. Hall, 388 So. 2d 1004 (Ala. Civ. App. 1980).

Under this section the effect of support and legal acknowledgment is the same and either one will toll the limitation period. State v. Hall, 388 So. 2d 1004 (Ala. Civ. App. 1980).

A legal acknowledgment of paternity will toll the limitation period of this section and prevent that section from barring a suit. However, the legal acknowledgment must have been made within the two-year (now five year) period following the child's birth and the suit must be brought within the two (now five) years of the acknowledgment. Miller v. State, 403 So. 2d 247 (Ala. Civ. App. 1981).

Evidence does not prevent section from barring suit. — Evidence showing that the reputed father supported the child within the two (now five) years following its birth will also toll the limitation period and prevent this section from barring a suit. However, suit must be brought within two (now five) years of the date the reputed father last provided support. Miller v. State, 403 So. 2d 247 (Ala. Civ. App. 1981).

Evidence that the reputed father orally acknowledged paternity within two (now five) years of the child's birth does not prevent this section from barring the suit. Miller v. State, 403 So. 2d 247 (Ala. Civ. App. 1981).

This section does not specify amount of support necessary to toll the statute and it is not essential that the reputed father meet all of the child's material needs. The determinative question is whether, under the facts of the case, the payments constitute an acknowledgment of paternity. If the payments do constitute such an acknowledgment, the reputed father has supported the child within the meaning of this section. Miller v. State, 403 So. 2d 247 (Ala. Civ. App. 1981).

Tolling does not abrogate the limitation period of this section. After the reputed father has legally acknowledged paternity, suit must be brought against him within two years (now five years) of the date of the acknowledgment. State v. Hall, 388 So. 2d 1004 (Ala. Civ. App. 1980).

§ 26-17-7. Style of proceedings; prosecution of proceedings.

Actions commenced under this chapter shall be in the name of the State of Alabama on relation of the complaining witness or party against the person claimed to be the father or against the person alleged to owe a duty of support as the defendant. The district attorney, special prosecutor or attorney otherwise authorized to represent the State of Alabama shall appear and prosecute all proceedings brought under this chapter. (Acts 1984, No. 84-244, p. 375, § 7.)

I. General Consideration.
II. Decisions Under Prior Law.

I. GENERAL CONSIDERATION.

Cross references. — As to jurisdiction of juvenile court in proceedings to establish paternity of a child born out of wedlock and trial of minors or adults charged with desertion and nonsupport in violation of law, see § 12-15-31.

Cited in Ex parte Presse, 554 So. 2d 406 (Ala. 1989).

Collateral references. — Death of child prior to institution of bastardy proceedings by mother, effect. 7 ALR2d 1397.

Maintainability of bastardy proceedings by infant prosecutrix in own name and right. 50 ALR2d 1029.

Incompetency: right of mentally incompetent mother to institute bastardy proceedings. 71 ALR2d 1247.

Marriage of woman to one other than defendant as affecting her right to institute or maintain bastardy proceedings. 98 ALR2d 256.

Admissibility, in disputed paternity proceedings, of evidence to rebut mother's claim of prior chastity. 59 ALR3d 659.

II. DECISIONS UNDER PRIOR LAW.

Nature of proceeding. — While this section requires the state to prosecute paternity actions, the proceeding itself is civil in nature and is governed by the Alabama Rules of Civil Procedure. Under A.R.C.P., Rule 43(b), the plaintiff may call the defendant as a witness. Miller v. State, 403 So. 2d 247 (Ala. Civ. App. 1981).

§ 26-17-8. Limitation on liability for education and support; when action for purposes of support may be brought; rights of inheritance and succession.

(a) The father's liabilities for past education and necessary support are limited to a period of two years next preceding the commencement of an enforcement action under this chapter unless an order of support has been previously entered.

(b) An action to determine paternity for the purposes of obtaining support shall not be brought after the child attains age 19.

(c) The provisions of this section and Section 26-17-6 do not extend the time within which a right of inheritance or a right to a succession may be asserted beyond the time provided by law relating to distribution and closing of decedents' estates or to the determination of heirship, or otherwise. (Acts 1984, No. 84-244, p. 375, § 8.)

The statute of limitations provisions in this section do not violate the equal protection clause. Thomas v. State ex rel. Williams, 523 So. 2d 434 (Ala. Civ. App. 1988).

It is firmly established in this state that parental obligations do not differ with regard to whether the parents of the child are married. Ex parte Jones, 592 So. 2d 608 (Ala. 1991).

Paternity must be determined during child's minority. — All cases to determine paternity for the purpose of obtaining child support must be commenced during the child's minority, under this section, regardless of whether it is based upon a marriage presumption or otherwise. Thomas v. State ex rel. Williams, 523 So. 2d 434 (Ala. Civ. App. 1988).

The "college education exception" to the general rule that a "parent has no duty to contribute to the support of his or her child

after that child has reached the legislatively prescribed age of majority," applies as well where the parents were not married at the time of the birth of the child and were not married thereafter. Ex parte Jones, 592 So. 2d 608 (Ala. 1991).

The absence of restrictive language in § 26-17-15 provides the trial court with jurisdiction to require the father of a child born out of wedlock to provide to the child post-minority support for a college education in a manner and to the extent of the requisites established in Bayliss v. Bayliss, 550 So. 2d 986 (Ala. 1989); Jones v. Williams, 592 So. 2d 605 (Ala. Civ. App. 1991), aff'd, 592 So. 2d 608 (Ala. 1991).

Cited in Free v. Free, 507 So. 2d 930 (Ala. Civ. App. 1986); Pate v. State ex rel. Corkren, 526 So. 2d 30 (Ala. Civ. App. 1988); Ex parte Presse, 554 So. 2d 406 (Ala. 1989).

§ 26-17-9. Nature of actions; rules of procedure; who may testify; other evidence; joinder; pleadings; enforcement of support under criminal code.

(a) An action under this chapter is a civil action governed by the rules of civil procedure. The mother and child and the alleged father are competent to testify and may be compelled to testify. All of the provisions of Sections 26-17-12 and 26-17-13, including those regarding evidence, expert testimony and blood tests, shall apply in actions brought under this chapter. The action brought may be joined with an action for divorce, annulment, separate maintenance or support.

(b) An action to determine paternity may be commenced upon the complaint of any female who is pregnant with or the mother of a child.

(c) An action to determine paternity may also be commenced upon the complaint of the child, the person having legal custody of the child or the representative of the public authority chargeable by law with the support of the child.

(d) A complaint for nonsupport of a child may be commenced by complaint by any party listed in subsections (b) and (c) of this section alleging sufficient facts that the defendant owes a duty of support, provided, that support payments have not been ordered previously pursuant to a decree of divorce. Upon a showing that the child is owed a duty of support by the defendant, such duty may be established pursuant to the requirements of Section 26-17-14.

(e) In addition to the civil action for nonsupport provided by this section, applicable sections of the criminal code are available for enforcement of the child's right of support. (Acts 1984, No. 84-244, p. 375, § 9.)

Actions brought under this chapter are civil and not quasi-criminal in nature. Clark v. State ex rel. Williams, 527 So. 2d 1306 (Ala. Civ. App. 1988), overruled on other grounds, Ex parte Palmer, 556 So. 2d 396 (Ala. Civ. App. 1989); Brooks v. State Dep't of Human Resources, 526 So. 2d 593 (Ala. Civ. App. 1988).

Cited in Ex parte Presse, 554 So. 2d 406 (Ala. 1989).

Collateral references. — Admissibility and weight of blood-grouping tests in disputed paternity cases. 43 ALR4th 579.

§ 26-17-10. Jurisdiction; venue; where complaint filed; process; conduct of hearing; jury.

(a) The causes of action provided by this chapter shall be brought in the juvenile or family court division of the district or circuit court and wherever used in this chapter the word "court" shall mean the juvenile or family court division of the district or circuit court and specifically shall include any district or circuit court judge otherwise sitting in one of these divisions.

(b) A defendant who resides in this state thereby submits to the jurisdiction of the courts of this state as to an action brought under this chapter.

(c) A person who is a nonresident of this state and who has sexual intercourse in this state thereby submits to the jurisdiction of the courts of this state as to an action brought under this chapter with respect to a child who may have been conceived by that act of sexual intercourse. Jurisdiction over a nonresident may be acquired only by personal service of summons outside this state or by certified mail with proof of actual receipt.

(d) A defendant who resides in this state thereby submits to the jurisdiction of the courts of this state as to a uniform reciprocal enforcement of support action filed in this state by an initiating state for the purpose of establishing paternity. If the defendant asserts as a defense that he is not the father of the child for whom support is sought and it appears to the court that the defense is not frivolous, and if both parties are present at the hearing or if proof required in the case indicates the presence of either or both is not necessary, the court shall adjudicate the issue of paternity. The appropriate provisions of this chapter shall apply to such actions. Upon determination of paternity or nonpaternity, the appropriate sections of the Reciprocal State Enforcement of Duty to Support Act (§ 30-4-80 et seq.) shall apply.

(e) The court shall retain jurisdiction of the cause for the purpose of entering such other and further orders as changing circumstances of the parties may in justice and equity require.

(f) The complaint for paternity or nonsupport shall be filed in the county in which the child resides or the county in which the defendant resides.

(g) Process directed to the defendant shall issue forthwith requiring the defendant to file written pleadings to the complaint in the manner prescribed by appropriate court rules.

(h) The court in which the action originated shall determine both the law and the facts without the intervention of a jury. A trial by jury may be had only as provided under Section 26-17-20. (Acts 1984, No. 84-244, p. 375, § 10.)

Trial court did not have jurisdiction. — Where child was born during marriage, husband was listed as child's father on birth certificate, husband alleged that child was not his in divorce complaint, and husband was deceased, the trial court did not have jurisdiction to determine paternity of a child who was not a party to action and did not have an appointed guardian ad litem; clearly, the case fell within the purview of the Uniform Parentage Act and this case included a strong presumption of paternity; any finding contrary to the presumed paternity was to be made by the court most adept at making that determination. S.T. v. C.T.T., 571 So. 2d 1168 (Ala. Civ. App. 1990).

Venue proper. — Even though mother and child resided in county for a period of approximately 11 days before filing of action, venue was proper; the parties were not married, and thus, § 30-2-4 was inapplicable; furthermore,

the Alabama Uniform Parentage Act provides that a paternity action shall be filed in the county in which the child resides or the county in which the defendant resides, and the mother's complaint averred that the mother and child were domiciled in the county, and she also testified to that fact at trial. Ex parte Hughes, 571 So. 2d 1186 (Ala. Civ. App. 1990).

Appropriate forum for determining testator's daughter. — Juvenile division or family division of the district or circuit court, not the probate court, was the appropriate forum for determining whether a child was a testator's daughter, where the case did not deal with intestate succession and included a strong presumption of paternity. Ex parte Martin ex rel. Sarris, 565 So. 2d 1 (Ala. 1989).

Cited in B.T.D. v. T.L.C.H., 585 So. 2d 97 (Ala. Crim. App. 1989).

Collateral references. — Paternity proceedings: right to jury trial. 51 ALR4th 565.

§ 26-17-11. Parties; representation of minor child; aligning parties.

The child may be made a party to the action. If the child is a minor he shall be represented by his general guardian or a guardian ad litem appointed by the court, if not otherwise represented by counsel. The child's mother or father may not represent the child as guardian or otherwise. The court may appoint the public authority chargeable by law with the support of the child as guardian ad litem for the child. The natural mother, each man presumed to be the father under the provisions of Section 26-17-5, and each man alleged to be the natural father, shall be made parties or, if not subject to the jurisdiction of the court, shall be given notice of the action in a manner prescribed by the court and an opportunity to be heard. The court may align the parties. (Acts 1984, No. 84-244, p. 375, § 11.)

Child may be made party to action. — Unlike the Uniform Parentage Act, Alabama's version provides that the child may be made a party to the action. Thomas v. Callen, 521 So. 2d 1322 (Ala. Civ. App. 1987).

The legislature of this state in passing the Alabama Uniform Parentage Act (AUPA) provided, in substance, that it is optional, not mandatory, for a child to be made a party in proceedings which are brought under AUPA. Thomas v. Callen, 521 So. 2d 1322 (Ala. Civ. App. 1987).

The language of § 26-17-5(a)(1) and this section is clear and unambiguous and applicable where mother of child brought paternity action against the putative father and therefore the husband, because he was the presumed father pursuant to § 26-17-5, was required to be made a party to the action. State ex rel. Goodno v. Cobb, 567 So. 2d 376 (Ala. Civ. App. 1990).

Divorce judgment provided ex-husband was not child's father rebutted any presumption he was the father under § 26-17-5. — Where the mother in a paternity case argued that, since she was married to ex-husband at the time of the birth of her daughter, ex-husband is legally presumed to be the child's father under § 26-17-5 and that he should have been made a party to the action because this section required that each man presumed to be father be made a party if he is subject to the jurisdiction of the court. However, in their divorce judgment which provided that the minor child born during the marriage was not his child that divorce judgment effec-

tively rebutted any presumption that he was the father of the child under subsection (b), and it eliminated the requirement of this section that he be made a party to the paternity proceedings. Thomas v. Callen, 521 So. 2d 1322 (Ala. Civ. App. 1987).

Provisions of this section as to representation of a child by a guardian ad litem, or otherwise, in paternity litigation are clearly referable to those cases where the child has been made a party to the action. Had the child been a party in this case, those requirements of section would have applied, but since this child was not a party, the trial court was not required to comply therewith. Thomas v. Callen, 521 So. 2d 1322 (Ala. Civ. App. 1987).

Appointment of guardian ad litem other than state representative allowed. — The Alabama Uniform Parentage Act clearly allows the appointment of a guardian ad litem other than a representative of the state. W.J.W. v. State ex rel. G.J.W., 587 So. 2d 397 (Ala. Civ. App. 1991).

Mandamus granted where minor child had right to be party. — Mandamus was appropriately granted where the minor child had a clear legal right to be a party to the paternity action and to be adequately represented and the circuit court was given the opportunity to remedy this inequitable situation but it refused. Ex parte V.B.N., 587 So. 2d 420 (Ala. Civ. App. 1991).

Collateral references. — Necessity or propriety of appointment of independent guardian for child who is subject of paternity proceedings. 70 ALR4th 1033.

§ 26-17-12. Blood tests; selection and compensation of experts; admissibility.

(a) Upon application of the defendant in a paternity proceeding or any other party to the action, the court shall order the mother, child and defendant to submit to one or more blood tests to assist the court in determining paternity of the child. No such blood test shall be taken before the child reaches the age of six months. Whenever the court orders any such blood test to be taken and any of the persons whose blood is to be taken refuses to submit to the test, such fact shall be disclosed upon the trial, unless good cause is shown for not doing so.

(b) Any tests shall be made by an expert qualified as an examiner of blood types who shall be approved by the court. The expert may be called by the court or any party as a witness to testify to the blood test results and shall be subject to cross-examination by the parties. The blood test results may be admitted into evidence by the defendant. The blood test results may be admitted into evidence by the state only if the statistical probability of the alleged father's paternity is available. Blood testing methods include, but are not limited to, the human leukocyte antigen test. If more than one blood test is performed and the results are conflicting, none of the blood test results shall be admissible as evidence of paternity or nonpaternity.

(c) Compensation of each expert witness shall be paid as the court shall order. The court shall order said compensation to be paid prior to the administration of the blood test. (Acts 1984, No. 84-244, p. 375, § 12.)

I. General Consideration.
II. Decisions Under Prior Law.

I. GENERAL CONSIDERATION.

Blood tests mandatory. — The legislature has made blood tests of "the mother, child, and defendant" mandatory upon demand by the defendant "or any other party" under subsection (a) of this section, and the results may be admitted into evidence by the state if the statistical probability of the alleged father's paternity is available under subsection (b) of this section. State ex rel. Goodno v. Cobb, 567 So. 2d 376 (Ala. Civ. App. 1990).

Standing of minor child to request blood testing. — The court's mandate that the minor child has no standing to request blood testing is contrary to the finding that the child has standing to participate in the trial de novo in the circuit court; to summarily preclude the child from requesting additional testing would be unfair and unjust in that it deprives the child of statutory rights to which she is entitled under the Uniform Parentage Act. Ex parte V.B.N., 587 So. 2d 420 (Ala. Civ. App. 1991).

Human leukocyte antigen (HLA) test re-sults were admissible evidence in paternity action even before passage of this chapter. Lyle v. Eddy, 481 So. 2d 395 (Ala. Civ. App. 1985).

Foundation for human leucocyte antigen (HLA) evidence. — Certain minimal foundational requirements are necessary to insure the reliability and relevancy of the human leukocyte antigen (HLA) results. The party offering the HLA test results must show that the blood tested was in fact that of the alleged father, the mother, and the child, and that the test results were based on reliable blood samples. This minimal foundation includes the establishment of a chain of identification from the time the blood samples are taken to the time the samples are analyzed. Such testimony, of course, should be based upon the first-hand knowledge of the witness. Lyle v. Eddy, 481 So. 2d 395 (Ala. Civ. App. 1985).

Additional HLA tests denied where initial tests could not eliminate either defendant as possible father. — In a paternity action filed by mother, in which defendant filed a motion to add an additional defendant, mother was not entitled to mandamus to require the trial court to order additional Human Leukocyte Antigen tests of both defendants, after initial tests could not eliminate either defendant as a possible father of the child. Phillips v. Robinson, 500 So. 2d 1131 (Ala. Civ. App. 1986).

Blood test to calculate probability of juvenile's paternity of murder victim's unborn child. — Juvenile court properly exercised its discretion in ordering juvenile, incident to transfer hearing involving the murder of a victim who was five months pregnant, to submit to a blood test so as to calculate the probability of his paternity of the victim's unborn child. Taylor v. State, 491 So. 2d 1042 (Ala. Crim. App. 1986).

Additional testing. — Where the record revealed that the "Human Leukocyte Antigen Tests" which were performed resulted in a 98.14 percent cumulative probability that husband was the biological father of child in question, and where the husband then requested DNA blood testing, and his request was denied, since paternity had been decided in Alabama courts long before blood tests were admissible evidence, and since the trial court could have determined paternity without any blood tests, trial court did not err in not ordering any additional testing. Finney v. Eagly, 568 So. 2d 816 (Ala. Civ. App. 1990).

Results were admissible in nonpaternity proceeding. — Testimony offered for the purpose of showing motive is always admissible; thus, even though the proceeding that appellant was facing was not a paternity proceeding and no such paternity proceeding had been filed on the part of any interested party pursuant to this section, the paternity test was admissible given the testimony at trial that the appellant had been angry with the victim because she had been telling other people that she was pregnant with his child. The admission of the paternity test was further proof that the unborn child was his child, and thus, gave weight to the state's claim that appellant killed the victim. Taylor v. State, 574 So. 2d 885 (Ala. Crim. App. 1990).

Cited in Blackwell v. State, 475 So. 2d 565 (Ala. Civ. App. 1985); Scott v. State ex rel. Thirkill, 500 So. 2d 469 (Ala. Civ. App. 1986); Ex parte Presse, 554 So. 2d 406 (Ala. 1989).

Collateral references. — 10 Am. Jur. 2d, Bastards, § 118.

Blood grouping test: weight and sufficiency to show paternity or legitimacy. 46 ALR2d 1000.

Admissibility, weight and sufficiency of Human Leukocyte Antigen (HLA) tissue typing tests in paternity cases. 37 ALR4th 167.

Admissibility and weight of blood-grouping tests in disputed paternity cases. 43 ALR4th 579.

II. DECISIONS UNDER PRIOR LAW.

The legislature has made blood tests mandatory upon demand by the reputed father in a paternity proceeding under this section, — which also mandates that the trial court appoint an expert to conduct such tests. Ex parte Anonymous, 414 So. 2d 72 (Ala. 1982).

Where petition seeks distinctly different determinations: one, that petitioner is a child in need of supervision under the juvenile code, and the other, that such petitioner is the putative father under the paternity statute; until a determination is made that is a paternity case, the petitioner is not entitled to blood tests. Ex parte Anonymous, 414 So. 2d 72 (Ala. 1982).

The legislature leaves the source of payment for blood tests in a paternity proceeding to the discretion of the trial court, which may direct payment by the county or any party to the case. Ex parte Anonymous, 414 So. 2d 72 (Ala. 1982).

§ 26-17-13. Evidence relating to paternity; refusal to testify; immunity; evidence of intercourse with other men.

(a) Evidence relating to paternity may include:

(1) Evidence of sexual intercourse between the mother and alleged father at any possible time of conception;

(2) An expert's opinion concerning the statistical probability of the alleged father's paternity based upon the duration of the mother's pregnancy;

(3) Blood test results, weighed in accordance with evidence, if available, of the statistical probability of the alleged father's paternity;

(4) Medical or anthropological evidence relating to the alleged father's paternity of the child based on tests performed by experts. If a man has been identified as a possible father of the child, the court may, and upon request of a party shall, require the child, the mother, and the man to submit to appropriate tests; and,

(5) All other evidence relevant to the issue of paternity of the child.

(b) Upon refusal of any witness, including a party, to testify under oath or produce evidence, the court may order him to testify under oath and produce evidence concerning all relevant facts. If the refusal is upon the ground that his testimony or evidence might tend to incriminate him, the court shall grant him immunity from all criminal liability on account of the testimony or evidence he is required to produce. An order granting immunity bars prosecution of the witness for any offense shown in whole or in part by testimony or evidence he is required to produce, except for perjury committed in his testimony. The refusal of a witness, who has been granted immunity to obey an order to testify or produce evidence shall be punishable as a civil contempt of the court.

(c) In an action against an alleged father, evidence offered by the alleged father with respect to another man who is not subject to the jurisdiction of the court concerning his sexual intercouse with the mother at or about the probable time of conception of the child is admissible in evidence only if the alleged father has undergone and made available to the court blood tests the results of which do not exclude the possibility of the alleged father's paternity of the child. A man who is identified and is subject to the jurisdiction of the court shall be made a defendant in the action. (Acts 1984, No. 84-244, p. 375, § 13.)

The pertinent statutory language is that for the other man to be named as a defendant, evidence must be offered concerning his sexual intercourse with the mother "at or about the probable time of the conception of the child." J.C.S. v. A.L.C., 580 So. 2d 586 (Ala. Civ. App. 1991).

Collateral references. — Proof of husband's impotency as rebutting the presumption of legitimacy. 84 ALR3d 495.

Admissibility of DNA identification evidence. 84 ALR4th 313.

§ 26-17-14. Orders — Determinative for all purposes; provision for support; statement of jurisdiction in case of out-of-state service; new birth certificate; other provisions; how support to be paid; amount of support; proof required for support order.

(a) The order of the court determining the existence or nonexistence of the parent and child relationship is determinative for all purposes. Upon paternity being established, the court shall immediately determine support payments at the conclusion of the paternity hearing and make support payment determination a part of the order establishing paternity.

(b) The order of the court shall include a statement of fact of jurisdiction being acquired in situations of service obtained by out-of-state personal service or service obtained by out-of-state certified mail with proof of return receipt.

(c) If the order of the court is at variance with the child's birth certificate, the court shall order that a new birth certificate be issued pursuant to the provisions of Section 26-17-19.

(d) The order may contain any other provision directed against the appropriate party to the proceeding, concerning the duty of support, the custody of the child or the furnishing of bond or other security for payment under the order. The order may direct the father to pay the reasonable expenses of the mother's pregnancy and confinement.

(e) Support orders ordinarily shall be for periodic payments which may vary in amount. Support orders may be in a lump sum amount if awarded against the appropriate party as a judgment representing an accrued arrearage or reimbursement to the agency providing support.

(f) In determining the amount to be paid by the parent for support of the child and the period during which the duty of support is owed, a court enforcing the obligation of support shall consider the needs of the child and the ability of the parents to support.

(g) Proof that a person owes a duty of support and has not contributed reasonably to support his child or proof of the award of public assistance on behalf of his child shall constitute sufficient basis for entry of an order of support. (Acts 1984, No. 84-244, p. 375, § 14.)

It is firmly established in this state that parental obligations do not differ with regard to whether the parents of the child are married. Ex parte Jones, 592 So. 2d 608 (Ala. 1991).

Final judgment in a paternity suit must include an order of child support payments. Washington v. State ex rel. King, 537 So. 2d 967 (Ala. Civ. App. 1988).

The "college education exception" to the general rule that a "parent has no duty to contribute to the support of his or her child after that child has reached the legislatively prescribed age of majority," applies as well where the parents were not married at the time of the birth of the child and were not married thereafter. Ex parte Jones, 592 So. 2d 608 (Ala. 1991).

The absence of restrictive language in § 26-17-15 provides the trial court with jurisdiction to require the father of a child born out of wedlock to provide to the child post-minority support for a college education in a manner and to the extent of the requisites established in Bayliss v. Bayliss, 550 So. 2d 986 (Ala. 1989); Jones v. Williams, 592 So. 2d 605 (Ala. Civ. App. 1991), aff'd, 592 So. 2d 608 (Ala. 1991).

The factors for the trial court to consider in awarding child support set forth in Bayliss v. Bayliss, 550 So. 2d at 986 (Ala. 1989), aside from the reference to the dissolution of marriage, are applicable in the situation where the parents have never married. Ex parte Jones, 592 So. 2d 608 (Ala. 1991).

Cited in Snow v. Armstrong, 508 So. 2d 266 (Ala. 1987).

Collateral references. — Effect, in subsequent proceedings, of paternity findings or implications in divorce or annulment decree or in support or custody order made incidental thereto. 78 ALR3d 846.

§ 26-17-15. Orders — Enforcement.

(a) If the existence of the father and child relationship is declared, or paternity or a duty of support has been acknowledged or adjudicated under this chapter, prior law or applicable sections of the criminal code, the obligation of the father may be enforced in the same or other proceedings by the mother, the child, the public authorities that have furnished or may furnish the reasonable expenses of pregnancy, confinement, education, or support, or by any other person, including a private agency, to the extent these expenses have been or are being furnished.

(b) The court shall order payments to be made to a person, corporation, agency designated to administer them under the supervision of the court, or the public authority which has furnished or may furnish support for the child including but not limited to monetary and medical payments.

(c) Willful failure to obey the judgment or order of the court is a civil contempt of the court. All sanctions for enforcement of judgments apply. (Acts 1984, No. 84-244, p. 375, § 15.)

It is firmly established in this state that parental obligations do not differ with regard to whether the parents of the child are married. Ex parte Jones, 592 So. 2d 608 (Ala. 1991).

The "college education exception" to the general rule that a "parent has no duty to contribute to the support of his or her child after that child has reached the legislatively prescribed age of majority," applies as well where the parents were not married at the time of the birth of the child and were not married thereafter. Ex parte Jones, 592 So. 2d 608 (Ala. 1991).

The absence of restrictive language in this section provides the trial court with jurisdiction to require the father of a child born out of wedlock to provide to the child post-minority support for a college education in a manner and to the extent of the requisites established in Bayliss v. Bayliss, 550 So. 2d 986 (Ala. 1989); Jones v. Williams, 592 So. 2d 605 (Ala. Civ. App. 1991), aff'd, 592 So. 2d 608 (Ala. 1991).

The factors for the trial court to consider in awarding child support set forth in Bayliss v. Bayliss, 550 So. 2d at 986 (Ala. 1989), aside from the reference to the dissolution of marriage, are applicable in the situation where the parents have never married. Ex parte Jones, 592 So. 2d 608 (Ala. 1991).

Cited in Ex parte Presse, 554 So. 2d 406 (Ala. 1989).

§ 26-17-16. Promise to render support; stipulations barring paternity action.

(a) Any promise in writing to furnish support for a child, growing out of a supposed or alleged father and child relationship does not require consideration and is enforceable according to its terms in any court having jurisdiction under Section 26-17-10(a), subject to the provisions of Section 26-17-6(d).

(b) Stipulations in any agreement that seek to bar a paternity action are not enforceable. (Acts 1984, No. 84-244, p. 375, § 16.)

§ 26-17-17. Right to counsel; representation of minors; fees, expenses, and costs.

(a) In all proceedings under this chapter, any party may be represented by counsel. If the public authority chargeable by law with support of a child is a party, the appropriate attorney as provided in Section 26-17-7 shall represent the public authority. If the child receives public assistance and no conflict of interest exists, the appropriate attorney shall also represent the person having custody. If the child does not receive public assistance, the appropriate attorney may represent the person having custody at that person's request.

(b) The court shall appoint a guardian ad litem to represent a defendant who is a minor and who is not otherwise represented by counsel.

(c) It is the express intent of this chapter that parties to proceedings under the chapter should pay the fees and expenses of retained counsel, expert witnesses, guardians ad litem, the costs of appropriate tests and other costs of the trial as they may, themselves, incur. The court may order reasonable fees for attorneys, expert witnesses, guardian ad litem fees, costs of appropriate tests and other costs of the trial, including docket fees, to be paid by the parties in such proportions as the court may direct. In the event the court determines that a party is unable to pay the fees and costs as directed, it may order fees and costs, including fees and costs of appropriate tests, if such tests have been ordered by the court as provided in Section 26-17-12, to be paid from the fund entitled, "court costs not otherwise provided for." If costs and fees are ordered to be paid from said fund, claims shall be submitted by the clerk of the court to the State Comptroller for audit and allowance and, if approved by the comptroller, shall be forwarded to the State Treasurer for payment from said fund. Provided, docket fees and fees of retained counsel shall not be paid from said fund. Docket fees shall be waived if the court determines that the parties are incapable of paying them.

(d) Nothing contained in this chapter shall be construed so as to guarantee court-appointed counsel at the state's expense to any party who is not otherwise entitled to court-appointed counsel under statutory or case law. Appointment of counsel for a minor defendant or party who is entitled to counsel and the compensation of such appointed counsel shall be governed by the other applicable law.

(e) When a party bringing an action is represented by the district attorney or attorney authorized to represent the State of Alabama, no filing fee shall be paid to the clerk of the court but may be taxed as a cost of the action as provided herein. (Acts 1984, No. 84-244, p. 375, § 17.)

Collateral references. — Necessity or propriety of appointment of independent guardian for child who is subject of paternity proceedings. 70 ALR4th 1033.

§ 26-17-18. Action to declare mother and child relationship.

Any interested party may bring an action to determine the existence or nonexistence of a mother and child relationship. Insofar as practicable, the provisions of this chapter applicable to the father and child relationship apply. (Acts 1984, No. 84-244, p. 375, § 18.)

§ 26-17-19. Issuance and contents of new birth certificate; confidentiality of evidence and original birth certificate.

(a) Upon order of a court of this state or upon request of a court of another state, the Registrar of Vital Statistics shall prepare a new certificate of birth consistent with the findings of the court and shall substitute the new certificate for the original certificate of birth.

(b) The fact that the father and child relationship was declared after the child's birth shall not be ascertainable from the new certificate but the actual place and date of birth shall be shown.

(c) The evidence upon which the new certificate was made and the original birth certificate shall be kept in a sealed and confidential file and be subject to inspection only upon the consent of the court and all interested persons, or in exceptional cases only upon an order of the court for good cause shown. (Acts 1984, No. 84-244, p. 375, § 19.)

§ 26-17-20. Appeals.

(a) The State of Alabama, the person on the relation of whom the action is brought or the defendant may appeal from any final judgment rendered under the provisions of this chapter. Appeals shall be taken from the juvenile or family court division of either the district or circuit court to the circuit court for a trial de novo and for a jury trial, if demanded by the appellant or the defendant. Written notice of appeal shall be filed with the clerk of the circuit court within 14 days of the date of the order appealed from or the denial of a post trial motion. The defendant may file a supersedeas bond on appeal to stay enforcement of a support order, but a support order shall continue to accrue during the pendency of the appeal. Any party may appeal to the court of civil appeals pursuant to the Alabama Rules of Appellate Procedure and the Alabama Rules of Juvenile Procedure upon the entry of a final judgment in the circuit court on the trial de novo. If the appeal is taken by the state, no security for the cost need be given.

(b) Appeals may be taken from the juvenile or family court division of the district or circuit court directly to the court of civil appeals if there is an adequate record or stipulation of the facts by the parties and the right to a jury trial is waived by all parties entitled thereto. Provided, that this subsection shall specifically not be construed as requiring the juvenile and family court divisions of the district and circuit courts to maintain a record of the proceedings brought pursuant to the provisions of this chapter. Written notice of appeal in appeals brought pursuant to this subsection shall be filed

257

within 14 days of the entry of the judgment or order appealed from. (Acts 1984, No. 84-244, p. 375, § 20.)

I. General Consideration.
II. Decisions Under Prior Law.

I. GENERAL CONSIDERATION.

Scope of section. — Appeals from a final judgment rendered by a juvenile or family court pursuant to an action establishing paternity, child support, or enforcement and modification of support are governed by this section. Gardner v. Buycks, 479 So. 2d 59 (Ala. Civ. App. 1985).

Time for notice of appeal. — Under this section, written notice of appeal from the family court or juvenile court to the court of civil appeals must be filed within 14 days of the judgment or order appealed from. Gardner v. Buycks, 479 So. 2d 59 (Ala. Civ. App. 1985).

Because the appellant's postjudgment motions were themselves untimely filed and did not toll the time for the appeal, the appeal was untimely and was dismissed. Pitts v. Means, 571 So. 2d 1138 (Ala. Civ. App. 1990), cert. denied, — U.S. —, 111 S. Ct. 2059, 114 L. Ed. 2d 464 (1991).

Jury waiver must be part of the record on appeal for the court of civil appeals to have jurisdiction of an appeal from a final judgment in an initial proceeding under the Alabama Uniform Parentage Act (AUPA), and all parties entitled to a jury trial must have waived that right. C.L.D. ex rel. C.L.D. v. D.D., 575 So. 2d 1140 (Ala. Civ. App. 1991).

Case transferred where no waiver of rights to jury trial in record. — For case transferred to county circuit court by court of civil appeals where there was no waiver of rights to jury trial in record, see B.T.D. v. T.L.C.H., 585 So. 2d 97 (Ala. Crim. App. 1989), aff'd, 585 So. 2d 112 (Ala. 1991).

Appeal taken to wrong court will be transferred, not dismissed. — Prior to November 15, 1985 appeals in juvenile matters were taken directly to the court of civil appeals especially where an adequate record had been made in the juvenile court. Failure to appeal to the court of civil appeals within the 14 day appeal period mandated a dismissal of the appeal. However, effective November 15, 1985, appeals in juvenile matters improperly taken to the circuit court were required to be transferred to the proper appellate court rather than be dismissed. Scott v. Brown, 497 So. 2d 192 (Ala. Civ. App. 1986).

Reopening case was error where filing of notice of appeal after more than a year. — The circuit court was in error when it ordered blood tests, the effect of which was to reopen the October 1986 paternity issue since the time for filing a notice of appeal from a paternity determination is 14 days, and notice of appeal was filed more than a year after the order establishing paternity. State ex rel. Smith v. Thomas, 540 So. 2d 69 (Ala. Civ. App. 1989).

Cited in State ex rel. Huguley v. Samuels, 457 So. 2d 977 (Ala. Civ. App. 1984).

Collateral references. — Appeal: right of mother of illegitimate child to appeal from order or judgment entered in bastardy proceedings. 18 ALR2d 948.

Paternity proceedings: right to jury trial. 51 ALR4th 565.

II. DECISIONS UNDER PRIOR LAW.

Cross references. — As to rules of supreme court relative to demand for jury trial, see A.R.C.P., Rule 38.

Appeal must be perfected pursuant to requirements of section. — An appeal is not a matter of vested right, but by the grace of this section, and must be perfected pursuant to the time and manner prescribed in this section, and if the requirements of this section are not met, the appeal must be dismissed. LeFlore v. State ex rel. Moore, 288 Ala. 310, 260 So. 2d 581, cert. denied, 409 U.S. 1007, 93 S. Ct. 436, 34 L. Ed. 2d 299 (1972); Scribner v. State, 372 So. 2d 1311 (Ala. Civ. App.), cert. denied, 372 So. 2d 1312 (Ala. 1979).

Appeal does not supersede judgment unless bond posted. — The legislature did not intend to allow an appeal to supersede the judgment unless a supersedeas bond was posted. Moore v. Leflore, 288 Ala. 315, 260 So. 2d 585 (1972).

If this section has not been complied with, the circuit court is without jurisdiction to hear the appeal. State v. Higgins, 423 So. 2d 225 (Ala. Civ. App. 1981), rev'd on other grounds, 423 So. 2d 227 (Ala. 1982).

Filing cannot be complete until notice is delivered to proper filing officer. Scribner v. State, 372 So. 2d 1311 (Ala. Civ. App.), cert. denied, 372 So. 2d 1312 (Ala. 1979).

Clerk of the family court is proper filing officer for filing of notice of appeal from a decision of the family court. Scribner v. State, 372 So. 2d 1311 (Ala. Civ. App.), cert. denied, 372 So. 2d 1312 (Ala. 1979).

Mailing of letter of notice of appeal not

filing. — The mailing of a letter to the clerk of the family court is not sufficient to perfect the requirement of filing such motion with the clerk. Moutry v. State, 359 So. 2d 388 (Ala. Civ. App. 1978).

Filing of an appeal appearance bond is inadequate to replace to replace or substitute for the proper written notices of appeal. Battles v. State, 386 So. 2d 466 (Ala. Civ. App.), cert. denied, 386 So. 2d 468 (Ala. 1980).

Reading of complaint during instruction does not apprise jury of appellate status. — Where record of paternity proceeding is totally devoid of any reference before the jury of the fact that the proceeding was appealed from an adverse judgment of the family court, reading of the district attorney's complaint during the court's instruction of the jury did not apprise the jury that the trial was not de novo. Clevenger v. State, 369 So. 2d 563 (Ala. Civ. App. 1979).

§ 26-17-21. Artificial insemination.

(a) If, under the supervision of a licensed physician and with the consent of her husband, a wife is inseminated artificially with semen donated by a man not her husband, the husband is treated in law as if he were the natural father of a child thereby conceived. The husband's consent must be in writing and signed by him and his wife. The physician shall certify their signatures and the dates of the insemination, and file the husband's consent with the State Department of Health, where it shall be kept confidential and in a sealed file. However, the physician's failure to do so does not affect the father and child relationship. All papers and records pertaining to the insemination, whether part of the permanent record of a court or of a file held by the supervising physician or elsewhere, are subject to inspection only upon an order of the court for good cause shown. The supervising physician shall not be liable to any person, including the wife, the husband, or a child resulting from an artificial insemination procedure, for the release of any information pertaining to the artificial insemination which occurs through accident, error, omission, inadvertence or the intentional conduct, without malice, of the physician or his agents, servants, or employees.

(b) The donor of semen provided to a licensed physician for use in artificial insemination of a married woman other than the donor's wife is treated in law as if he were not the natural father of a child thereby conceived. (Acts 1984, No. 84-244, p. 375, § 21.)

Collateral references. — Rights and obligations resulting from human artificial insemination. 83 ALR4th 295.

CHAPTER 18.

CHILD PROTECTION.

Authority to terminate parental rights. — The 1984 Child Protection Act, effective May 8, 1984, and codified as this chapter gives the juvenile courts of this state authority to terminate parental rights in appropriate cases. Brown v. Alabama Dep't of Pensions & Sec., 473 So. 2d 533 (Ala. Civ. App. 1985).

The Child Protection Act enumerates only some of many factors court of civil appeals has long taken into consideration in making determinations concerning the termination of parental rights. Among the factors emphasized are the conduct of the parents toward the child, the parent's love or interest in the child, activities of the parents that could be detrimental to the safety and welfare of the child, and whether there are less drastic alternatives available than the permanent removal of parental custody. Brown v. Alabama Dep't of

Pensions & Sec., 473 So. 2d 533 (Ala. Civ. App. 1985).

One ground for determining dependency of child. — The Child Protection Act is a codification of only one of the grounds upon which a court can determine that a child is dependent and thus in need of a decision as to his welfare. Columbus v. State, Dep't of Human Resources, 523 So. 2d 419 (Ala. Civ. App. 1987).

Juvenile court procedures to be followed. — Under the 1984 Child Protection Act, proceedings to terminate parental rights are to be conducted much as they had been prior to the passage of the act in accordance with juvenile court procedures provided by §§ 12-15-50 to 12-15-76. Brown v. Alabama Dep't of Pensions & Sec., 473 So. 2d 533 (Ala. Civ. App. 1985).

§ 26-18-1. Short title.

This chapter shall be known as and may be cited as the "1984 Child Protection Act." (Acts 1984, No. 84-261, p. 442, § 1.)

Mother could file petition to terminate father's rights. — The examination of § 12-15-50 et seq. reveals nothing which proscribes one parent's filing of a petition to terminate the other parent's parental rights. Also there is no compelling reason for a rule mandating that only the state initiate such actions. Furthermore, the 1984 Child Protection Act, which expressly allows a parent to file the petition, and which is to be considered

in pari materia with the act sub judice, evidences legislative intent in the area. Therefore the court of civil appeals was incorrect in concluding that the mother could not file a petition to terminate the father's parental rights. Abney v. Johnson, 474 So. 2d 715 (Ala. 1985).

Collateral references. — Parent's mental deficiency as factor in termination of parental rights — modern status. 1 ALR5th 469.

§ 26-18-2. Purpose; precedence of appeals.

It is the purpose of this chapter to provide meaningful guidelines to be used by the juvenile court in cases involving the termination of parental rights in such a manner as to protect the welfare of children by providing stability and continuity in their lives, and at the same time to protect the rights of their parents. Appeals from an order terminating parental rights or refusing to terminate parental rights shall have precedence over all other cases in the court to which the appeal is taken. (Acts 1984, No. 84-261, p. 442, § 2.)

This chapter was not intended as a means for allowing a parent to abandon his child and thereby to avoid his obligation to support the child through the termination of parental rights. The courts of this State will not be used in the furtherance of such a purpose. Ex parte Brooks, 513 So. 2d 614 (Ala. 1987), overruled on other grounds, Ex parte Beasley, 564 So. 2d 954 (Ala. 1990).

Cited in D.P. v. State Dep't of Human Resources, 571 So. 2d 1140 (Ala. Civ. App. 1990).

§ 26-18-3. Definitions.

The following words and phrases shall have the following meaning whenever used in this chapter except where the context clearly indicates a different meaning:

(1) ABANDONMENT. A voluntary and intentional relinquishment of the custody of a child by a parent, or a withholding from the child, without good cause or excuse, by the parent, of his presence, care, love, protection, maintenance or the opportunity for the display of filial affection, or the failure to claim the rights of a parent, or failure to perform the duties of a parent.

(2) CHILD. The individual under the age of 18 years whose custody is in question or as to whom a petition is pending whereby the parental rights of its parents are sought to be terminated.

(3) CHILD-PLACING AGENCY. The same as the term is defined by Section 38-7-2(7).

(4) COURT. The juvenile court or the court exercising jurisdiction over juvenile cases.

(5) DEPARTMENT. The Department of Human Resources of the State of Alabama.

(6) PARENTS. The legal or biological parents of a child, inclusive of a putative father.

(7) PETITION. A petition seeking to terminate any or all of the legal rights of one or more parents with respect to a child.

(8) PETITIONER. The person who files a petition with the court. (Acts 1984, No. 84-261, p. 442, § 3.)

Code commissioner's note. — Pursuant to Acts 1986, No. 86-432, the name of the Department of Pensions and Security was changed to the Department of Human Resources. See the Code commissioner's note following ch. 2, T. 38.

Cited in In re Stephenson, 513 So. 2d 612 (Ala. Civ. App. 1986); Roden v. Colburn, 522 So. 2d 290 (Ala. Civ. App. 1988); Columbus v. State, Dep't of Human Resources, 523 So. 2d 419 (Ala. Civ. App. 1987).

§ 26-18-4. Applicability of Rules of Juvenile Procedure; allegation and proof of ability to assume custody of child.

Unless otherwise provided herein, proceedings to terminate parental rights shall be governed by Title 12, Chapter 15, Article 3 and by the Alabama Rules of Juvenile Procedure. No complaint or petition shall be filed by any party unless it alleges that the party filing the same or a public or private licensed child-placing agency is able and willing to assume custody of said child, and no such petition shall be granted except upon proof of such allegations. (Acts 1984, No. 84-261, p. 442, § 4.)

Petition for termination of parental rights was sufficient under this section, to invoke the jurisdiction of the juvenile court, where the jurisdiction of the juvenile court was invoked in behalf of the minor child by the filing of the original petition and the finding of dependency. Once such jurisdiction is invoked, it continues until the child is 21 years of age or is discharged by the court. At the time the department filed the additional petition to terminate parental rights, it had the child already in its custody by order of the court. It was certainly unnecessary to inform the court what it already knew. Valero v. State Dep't of Human Resources, 511 So. 2d 200 (Ala. Civ. App. 1987).

Jurisdiction was proper even though statutory language was absent from petition. — Although grandparents' petition did not contain a' statement alleging that they were "able and willing to assume custody" of the children as mandated by this section, jurisdiction was still present where an earlier award of temporary custody was granted in favor of the grandparents, and this fact was duly noted in their petition to terminate. Thus, it was clearly unnecessary for them to inform the court of its jurisdiction over the matter in light of the court's past recognition that it possessed such authority. Carter v. Griffin, 574 So. 2d 800 (Ala. Civ. App. 1990).

§ 26-18-5. Who may file petition.

A petition may be filed by any public or private licensed child-placing agency or parent, with permission of the court, or any interested party. (Acts 1984, No. 84-261, p. 442, § 5.)

There is no logical reason to allow only the state to file a petition to have parental rights terminated. Abney v. Johnson, 474 So. 2d 715 (Ala. 1985).

This statute clearly evidences legislature's intent to allow parents to initiate such actions. Abney v. Johnson, 474 So. 2d 715 (Ala. 1985).

§ 26-18-6. Service of process.

Service of process shall be made in accordance with the Alabama Rules of Civil Procedure except as otherwise provided by the Alabama Rules of Juvenile Procedure. (Acts 1984, No. 84-261, p. 442, § 6.)

Presence of incarcerated parent at hearing. — Where there is representation by counsel and an opportunity to present testimony through deposition, due process does not require that an incarcerated parent be allowed to attend a termination hearing. Pignolet v. State Dep't of Pensions & Sec., 489 So. 2d 588 (Ala. Civ. App. 1986).

§ 26-18-7. Grounds for termination of parental rights; factors considered; presumption arising from abandonment.

(a) If the court finds from clear and convincing evidence, competent, material and relevant in nature, that the parents of a child are unable or unwilling to discharge their responsibilities to and for the child, or that the conduct or condition of the parents is such as to render them unable to properly care for the child and that such conduct or condition is unlikely to change in the foreseeable future, it may terminate the parental rights of the parents. In determining whether or not the parents are unable or unwilling to discharge their responsibilities to and for the child, the court shall consider, and in cases of voluntary relinquishment of parental rights may consider, but not be limited to, the following:

(1) That the parents have abandoned the child, as herein defined;

(2) Emotional illness, mental illness or mental deficiency of the parent, or excessive use of alcohol or controlled substances, of such duration or nature as to render the parent unable to care for needs of the child;

(3) That the parent has tortured, abused, cruelly beaten or otherwise maltreated the child, or attempted to torture, abuse, cruelly beat or otherwise maltreat the child, or the said child is in clear and present danger of being thus tortured, abused, cruelly beaten, or otherwise maltreated as evidenced by such treatment of a sibling;

(4) Conviction of and imprisonment for a felony;

(5) Unexplained serious physical injury to the child under such circumstances as would indicate that such injuries resulted from the intentional conduct or willful neglect of the parent;

(6) That reasonable efforts by the Department of Human Resources or licensed public or private child care agencies leading toward the rehabilitation of the parents have failed.

(b) Where a child is not in the physical custody of its parent or parents appointed by the court, in addition to the foregoing, shall also consider, but is not limited to the following:

(1) Failure by the parents to provide for the material needs of the child or to pay a reasonable portion of its support, where the parent is able to do so.

(2) Failure by the parents to maintain regular visits with the child in accordance with a plan devised by the department, or any public or licensed private child care agency, and agreed to by the parent.

(3) Failure by the parents to maintain consistent contact or communication with the child.

(4) Lack of effort by the parent to adjust his circumstances to meet the needs of the child in accordance with agreements reached, including agreements reached with local departments of human resources or licensed child-placing agencies, in an administrative review or a judicial review.

(c) In any case where the parents have abandoned a child as herein defined and such abandonment continues for a period of six months next preceding the filing of the petition, such facts shall constitute a rebuttable presumption that the parents are unable or unwilling to act as parents. (Acts 1984, No. 84-261, p. 442, § 7.)

I. GENERAL CONSIDERATION.

Incarcerated party not denied due process if fully represented. — Despite a party's absence (due to incarceration) from a termination of parental rights hearing, such party is not denied due process where he or she is fully represented at the hearing by counsel and has the opportunity to present evidence, including testimony by deposition. Thornton v. Thornton, 519 So. 2d 960 (Ala. Civ. App. 1987).

Determination of dependency in sound discretion of trial court. — The determination of dependency is left to the sound discretion of the trial court, and its decision will not be set aside unless it is so contrary to the evidence as to be plainly and palpably wrong. In re T.M.A., 590 So. 2d 298 (Ala. Civ. App. 1991).

Decision to terminate parental rights presumed correct on appeal. — When a trial court decides to terminate parental rights that decision is presumed correct and will not be overturned on appeal unless it appears that there was no evidence to support that decision. Pignolet v. State Dep't of Pensions & Sec., 489 So. 2d 588 (Ala. Civ. App. 1986).

Standard of review. — Under subsection (a) of this section, there must be clear and convincing evidence, competent, material, relevant in nature, before the trial court may terminate parental rights, and if there was such evidence before the trial court, the appellate court is not authorized to disturb the trial court's decision. Ray v. State Dep't of Pensions & Sec., 485 So. 2d 349 (Ala. Civ. App. 1986).

If there is any evidence to support the trial court's judgment, the court of appeals must affirm, absent palpable error. J.C. v. Agape of Central Ala., 590 So. 2d 302 (Ala. Civ. App. 1991).

The ore tenus rule applies to termination of parental rights case. Clemons v. Alabama Dep't of Pensions & Sec., 474 So. 2d 1143 (Ala. Civ. App. 1985).

The appellate courts utilize the ore tenus rule in reviewing cases involving termination of parental rights. Jones v. Hutchins, 474 So. 2d 1152 (Ala. Civ. App. 1985).

The determination made by the trial court following an ore tenus hearing is presumed correct and will not be disturbed on appeal

unless it is so unsupported by the evidence as to be plainly and palpably wrong. Brooks v. State Dep't of Human Resources, 513 So. 2d 632 (Ala. Civ. App. 1987).

The ore tenus rule is merely a standard of review that the appellate courts use to review factual determinations of the trial court and not the burden of persuasion. The burden of proof required is clear and convincing evidence as mandated by statute in Alabama. The appellate court must find, within the record, sufficient evidence that is clear and convincing in order to affirm. Columbus v. State, Dep't of Human Resources, 523 So. 2d 419 (Ala. Civ. App. 1987).

In child custody cases where the evidence was presented to the trial court ore tenus, the judgment of the trial court is presumed correct and will not be set aside unless it is shown to be plainly and palpably wrong. J.C. v. Agape of Central Ala., 590 So. 2d 302 (Ala. Civ. App. 1991).

Cited in Clingan v. State, 471 So. 2d 435 (Ala. Civ. App. 1985); Carpenter v. State, 475 So. 2d 574 (Ala. Civ. App. 1985); Turney v. State, Dep't of Pensions & Sec., 497 So. 2d 172 (Ala. Civ. App. 1986); Wallace v. Jefferson County Dep't of Pensions & Sec., 501 So. 2d 473 (Ala. Civ. App. 1986); Heup v. State Dep't of Human Resources, 522 So. 2d 295 (Ala. Civ. App. 1988); Clark v. State, Dep't of Human Resources, 523 So. 2d 131 (Ala. Civ. App. 1988); Brooks v. State, Dep't of Human Resources, 526 So. 2d 593 (Ala. Civ. App. 1988); Smith v. Marshall, 562 So. 2d 269 (Ala. Civ. App. 1990); T.M. v. State Dep't of Human Resources, 571 So. 2d 1201 (Ala. Civ. App. 1990); D.J. v. State Dep't of Human Resources, 578 So. 2d 1351 (Ala. Civ. App. 1991); L.W. v. State Dep't of Human Resources, 591 So. 2d 872 (Ala. Civ. App. 1991).

II. RIGHT OF PARENTS TO CUSTODY; BEST INTEREST OF CHILD CONTROLS.

Presumption in favor of parents. — There is a presumption that the child's best interest will be served by placing it in the custody of the natural parents. This presumption may be overcome only where there is clear and convincing evidence that it would not be in the child's best interest to be in the natural parents' custody. Hickman v. State Dep't of Pensions & Sec., 489 So. 2d 601 (Ala. Civ. App. 1986).

Parent has prima facie right to custody of child. However, the overriding consideration is always the best interests of the child. Brooks v. State Dep't of Human Resources, 513 So. 2d 632 (Ala. Civ. App. 1987); Kelley v. State Dep't of Human Resources, 515 So. 2d 713 (Ala. Civ. App. 1987).

The parents have a prima facie right to the custody of a child. However, the overriding consideration is always the best interests of the child. In determining the child's best interests, the court must consider whether a party to a custody proceeding is physically, financially, and mentally able to care for the child. The parental rights of the parents can then be terminated if the court finds from clear and convincing evidence that the parents are unable or unwilling to discharge their responsibilities to and for the child. Mitchell v. State Dep't of Human Resources, 513 So. 2d 647 (Ala. Civ. App. 1987).

This right, however, yields to that of the best interests of the child in cases where the evidence supports the conclusion that parental custody is contrary to the child's best interests. Burroughs v. State Dep't of Human Resources, 516 So. 2d 676 (Ala. Civ. App. 1987).

A parent has a prima facie right to custody of his or her natural child; however, this right may be overcome where such custody is shown to be contrary to the child's best interests and welfare. In re T.M.A., 590 So. 2d 298 (Ala. Civ. App. 1991).

Best interest of child controlling. — Although the natural parents have a prima facie right to the custody of their child, the best interest of the child is controlling. Clemons v. Alabama Dep't of Pensions & Sec., 474 So. 2d 1143 (Ala. Civ. App. 1985); Schalk v. Alabama Dep't of Pensions & Sec., 479 So. 2d 1254 (Ala. Civ. App. 1985); Brooks v. State Dep't of Human Resources, 513 So. 2d 632 (Ala. Civ. App. 1987).

The primary consideration in a proceeding to terminate parental rights is always the best interest of the child. Fitzgerald v. Fitzgerald, 490 So. 2d 4 (Ala. Civ. App. 1986).

It is well-settled that a parent has a prima facie right to the custody of his/her child; nevertheless, the overriding consideration is always the best interests of the child. J.C. v. Agape of Central Ala., 590 So. 2d 302 (Ala. Civ. App. 1991).

In determining best interest of child the court must consider whether a party to a custody proceeding is physically, financially, or mentally able to care for the child. Von Goyt v. State, Dep't of Pensions & Sec., 461 So. 2d 821 (Ala. Civ. App. 1984).

Although a child's parents have a prima facie right to custody, the paramount concern in these proceedings is the child's best interests. In determining the child's best interests, the court must examine whether the parents are physically, financially, and mentally able to provide for their child. If clear and convincing evidence reveals that the parents cannot or are unwilling to discharge these responsibilities, parental rights may be terminated. A.C. v. State Dep't of Human Resources, 587 So. 2d 346 (Ala. Civ. App. 1991); J.C. v. Agape of Central Ala., 590 So. 2d 302 (Ala. Civ. App. 1991).

It is well-settled that a parent has a prima facie right to the custody of his/her child; nevertheless, the overriding consideration is always the best interests of the child. J.C. v. Agape of Central Ala., 590 So. 2d 302 (Ala. Civ. App. 1991).

Where dispute over custody of child is between child's natural parent and party who is not child's natural parent, natural parent has prima facie right to the child's custody. However, the right is not absolute, but is subject to the equally well-settled rule that the best interest and welfare of the child are controlling in child custody cases. Smith v. Manuel, 469 So. 2d 659 (Ala. Civ. App. 1985).

Placement with relatives not viable alternative. — Where there was evidence in the record which indicated that certain relatives had been aware of the abuse of child prior to the time that the child was taken into protective custody, but that these relatives took no action to protect the child because they did not want to get involved, the trial court could correctly conclude that placing the child with relatives was not a viable alternative to termination of parents' rights. Haag v. Cherokee County Dep't of Pensions & Sec., 489 So. 2d 586 (Ala. Civ. App. 1986).

Paternal grandfather was not a viable alternative to termination of father's right to child where grandfather testified that upon father's anticipated prison release, he would expect father to resume care and control of child, in effect returning the child to the same environment from which he was removed; the past history of father's behavior, along with the uncertainty of the timing of his prison release, coupled with the return of child to the environment, supported the trial court's finding that the paternal grandfather was not a viable alternative to termination. Petersen v. State Dep't of Human Resources, 550 So. 2d 1032 (Ala. Civ. App. 1989).

Parent seeking to regain custody terminated by prior decree must prove that a change in custody will materially promote the best interests of the child; therefore, court's requirement that the parent prove only that the causes for a declaration of dependency had been removed and that she had taken required steps for rehabilitation as a parent, was an application of the wrong legal test. Shields v. State Dep't of Human Resources, 531 So. 2d 681 (Ala. Civ. App. 1988).

III. DECISION TO TERMINATE RIGHTS.

Evidence supporting termination must be clear and convincing. — Before parental rights to the custody of a child may be terminated, the evidence before the court must be clear and convincing that it would not be in the best interests of the child that the parent have custody. Brand v. Alabama Dep't of Pensions & Sec., 479 So. 2d 66 (Ala. Civ. App. 1985); Schalk v. Alabama Dep't of Pensions & Sec., 479 So. 2d 1254 (Ala. Civ. App. 1985).

Although the natural parents have a prima facie right to the custody of their child, such right can be overcome by clear and convincing evidence that removal from the parents' custody is in the child's best interest. Fitzgerald v. Fitzgerald, 490 So. 2d 4 (Ala. Civ. App. 1986).

Termination of a father's parental rights requires clear and convincing evidence that termination would be in the child's best interest. Ex parte Brooks, 513 So. 2d 614 (Ala. 1987), overruled on other grounds, Ex parte Beasley, 564 So. 2d 950 (Ala. 1990).

The parental rights of the parents can be terminated if the court finds from clear and convincing evidence that the parents are unable or unwilling to discharge their responsibilities to and for the child. Brooks v. State Dep't of Human Resources, 513 So. 2d 632 (Ala. Civ. App. 1987).

Where the mother's mental illness is a factor which may be considered by the trial court in determining whether to terminate the mother's parental rights, the trial court may admit into evidence and consider the mother's medical records, despite the fact that such records are ordinarily protected from disclosure by the psychologist-patient privilege. Thornton v. Thornton, 519 So. 2d 960 (Ala. Civ. App. 1987).

In order to terminate parental rights, court must apply what is essentially a two-prong test. First, the court must find from clear and convincing evidence that the child is dependent. Once dependency is found, the trial court must determine whether less drastic measures than termination of parental rights would best serve the interest of the child. Clemons v. Alabama Dep't of Pensions & Sec., 474 So. 2d 1143 (Ala. Civ. App. 1985);

Fortenberry v. Alabama Dep't of Pensions & Sec., 479 So. 2d 54 (Ala. Civ. App. 1985).

If termination of parental rights is sought, the court is called upon to apply a two-pronged test, which first requires a finding of dependency. Once dependency is established, all viable alternatives to termination of parental rights must be examined to insure that there is no less drastic measure available. Brand v. Alabama Dep't of Pensions & Sec., 479 So. 2d 66 (Ala. Civ. App. 1985).

Two-pronged test. — In making a decision to terminate parental rights, the court should apply a two-pronged test. First, the court must decide from clear and convincing evidence whether the child is dependent under subsection (a). Second, after determination that the child is a dependent, the court must then decide whether there are viable alternatives to termination of parental rights. Burroughs v. State Dep't of Human Resources, 516 So. 2d 676 (Ala. Civ. App. 1987).

The two-prong test that a court must apply in a parental rights termination case brought by a custodial parent consists of the following: First, the court must find that there are grounds for the termination of parental rights, including, but not limited to, those specifically set forth in this section. Second, after the court has found that there exist grounds to order the termination of parental rights, the court must inquire as to whether all viable alternatives to a termination of parental rights have been considered. Ex parte Beasley, 564 So. 2d 950 (Ala. 1990).

Once the court has complied with the two-prong test — that is, once it has determined that the petitioner has met the statutory burden of proof and that, having considered and rejected other alternatives, a termination of parental rights is in the best interest of the child — it can order the termination of parental rights. Ex parte Beasley, 564 So. 2d 950 (Ala. 1990).

In cases where a nonparent is the petitioner, the trial court's determination is governed by the application of a two-pronged test. First, the court must conclude, from clear and convincing evidence, that the child is dependent. Second, the court must consider and reject all other viable alternatives to termination of parental rights so that it can conclude that termination is in the child's best interest. N.A. v. J.H., 571 So. 2d 1130 (Ala. Civ. App. 1990).

Where termination is sought by a nonparent, a two-pronged test must be applied. First, the trial court must find that the child is dependent, based upon clear and convincing legal evidence. The trial court must next determine that all viable alternatives to termination have been considered and rejected. R.K. v.

State Dep't of Human Resources, 577 So. 2d 466 (Ala. Civ. App. 1990).

Findings required for termination of rights. — In order to terminate parental rights, the court must first find that the child is dependent, based on clear and convincing evidence, pursuant to § 12-15-65(e). If the court finds that the child is dependent, it must then find that there exists no viable alternative to termination of the parents' custodial rights. Hickman v. State Dep't of Pensions & Sec., 489 So. 2d 601 (Ala. Civ. App. 1986).

In order to terminate parental rights, the court must first find from clear and convincing evidence that the child is dependent. If such dependency is found, the court must then determine if measures less drastic than termination of parental rights exist. In re T.M.A., 590 So. 2d 298 (Ala. Civ. App. 1991).

Finding of unfitness unnecessary where juvenile court has found dependency and need for supervision. — Whether the parents are unfit or not is a determination necessary for termination of their parental rights. Such a determination, however, is not necessary where the juvenile court makes a disposition following a finding that the child is dependent, as well as in need of supervision. Anonymous v. Anonymous, 504 So. 2d 289 (Ala. Civ. App. 1986), appeal dismissed, 484 U.S. 805, 108 S. Ct. 52, 98 L. Ed. 2d 16 (1987).

Finding of dependency applies to the state. — Where the state seeks to terminate parental rights, the "finding of dependency" necessarily applies to the state to protect against an unwarranted intrusion into parental rights and to comply with the requirements of due process. Ex parte Beasley, 564 So. 2d 950 (Ala. 1990).

Finding of dependency not applicable to parent. — When one parent seeks to terminate the other parent's parental rights, a "finding of dependency" is not required, and the trial court should determine whether the petitioner has met the statutory burden of proof and whether that termination is in the child's best interest, in light of the surrounding circumstances. Ex parte Beasley, 564 So. 2d 950 (Ala. 1990).

Trial court did not err in determining that child was dependent where at the time of the hearing, when child came into the custody of the department of human resources, father had been imprisoned and the child had been in foster care for almost four of the six years of his life and there was the uncertainty of when father would be released from prison and what his living conditions would be at that time. Petersen v. State Dep't of Human Resources, 550 So. 2d 1032 (Ala. Civ. App. 1989).

Court is not limited to considering grounds in this section. — The court may consider the grounds listed in this section for termination but is not limited to those grounds. R.K. v. State Dep't of Human Resources, 577 So. 2d 466 (Ala. Civ. App. 1990).

This section lists several factors the court may consider in terminating parental rights; however, it is expressed that this list is neither exhaustive nor limiting. J.C. v. Agape of Central Ala., 590 So. 2d 302 (Ala. Civ. App. 1991).

The factors listed are nonexclusive, so that a court may also consider any other factors that are relevant to the child's welfare. Clemons v. Alabama Dep't of Pensions & Sec., 474 So. 2d 1143 (Ala. Civ. App. 1985).

This section is a codification of only one of the possible grounds upon which a court may find a child dependent, and thus in need of an order concerning his welfare. The statute is not intended to restrict such a determination of dependency to the circumstance in which the parents are unwilling or unable to discharge their responsibilities. As such, the basic principles for consideration for a parental rights termination case are not changed. Clemons v. Alabama Dep't of Pensions & Sec., 474 So. 2d 1143 (Ala. Civ. App. 1985).

Under this section a juvenile court may terminate parental rights if it finds from clear and convincing evidence that the parents are unwilling or unable to discharge their responsibilities to and for their child. The statute lists several factors which the court may consider, but to which it is not limited, in determining whether parental rights may be terminated. These factors include emotional or mental illness or excessive use of alcohol or drugs which render the parent unable to care for the needs of the child. Brown v. Alabama Dep't of Pensions & Sec., 473 So. 2d 533 (Ala. Civ. App. 1985).

This section does not require a showing of permanency, but rather, a showing that the condition is "of such duration or nature as to render the parent unable to care for needs of the child," and where there was evidence within the record that indicated that mother suffered a borderline psychological difficulty, this was evidence of a mental deficiency and a factor for the trial court to consider. McCulloch v. State Dep't of Human Resources, 536 So. 2d 68 (Ala. Civ. App. 1988).

Convenience of parents is not a sufficient basis for terminating parental rights. Ex parte Brooks, 513 So. 2d 614 (Ala. 1987), overruled on other grounds, Ex parte Beasley, 564 So. 2d 950 (Ala. 1990).

Factors considered in terminating parental rights. — In determining whether to terminate parental rights, the trial court may consider such factors as the excessive use of alcohol or controlled substances by the parent, the failure of reasonable efforts by the Department of Human Resources (DHR) to rehabilitate the parent, the failure of the parent to pay support of children in the custody of DHR, and the failure of the parent to adjust his circumstances to meet the needs of the child in accordance with agreements made by the parent with DHR. Wood v. State, Dep't of Human Resources, 523 So. 2d 129 (Ala. Civ. App. 1988).

Through the Child Protection Act the legislature provided a nonexclusive list of factors which the courts should consider, including emotional or mental illness or mental deficiency. McCulloch v. State Dep't of Human Resources, 536 So. 2d 68 (Ala. Civ. App. 1988).

The court may consider whether the child has been subject to physical abuse, cruelty, or neglect and whether the child is in continued danger of such abuse. In re T.M.A., 590 So. 2d 298 (Ala. Civ. App. 1991).

The court may also consider the ability of the parents to comply with Department of Human Resources (DHR)'s reasonable efforts to provide parental counseling and training. In re T.M.A., 590 So. 2d 298 (Ala. Civ. App. 1991).

When the child is not in the physical custody of the parent in question, the court may properly consider the parent's failure to provide for the child's material needs. In re T.M.A., 590 So. 2d 298 (Ala. Civ. App. 1991).

Factors where child not in parent's custody. — Under subsection (b), where the child is not in the parent's custody, the court shall consider the following: (1) The failure by the parent to maintain regular visits with the child, (2) the failure to maintain consistent contact or communication with the child, (3) the lack of efforts by the parent to adjust her circumstances to meet the needs of the child, and (4) failure by the parent to provide for the material needs of the child or to pay a reasonable portion of its support where the parent is able to do so. M.S.S. v. State, Dep't of Human Resources, 582 So. 2d 1129 (Ala. Civ. App. 1991).

Conduct and activities of parent. — Because the child's best interest is the controlling consideration, the trial court may examine the conduct and activities of the parent. Franklin v. State Dep't of Human Resources, 513 So. 2d 625 (Ala. Civ. App. 1987).

The parental rights may be terminated if the court finds, from clear and convincing evidence, that the parent is unable or unwilling to discharge her responsibilities to and for the child. M.S.S. v. State, Dep't of Human Resources, 582 So. 2d 1129 (Ala. Civ. App. 1991).

Unwilling or unable to care for child. —

The parental rights of the parents can be terminated if the court finds from clear and convincing evidence that the parents are unable or unwilling to discharge their responsibilities to and for the child. Benton v. State Dep't of Human Resources, 515 So. 2d 1263 (Ala. Civ. App. 1987).

The parental rights may be terminated if the court finds, from clear and convincing evidence, that the parent is unable or unwilling to discharge her responsibilities to and for the child. M.S.S. v. State, Dep't of Human Resources, 582 So. 2d 1129 (Ala. Civ. App. 1991).

Court consideration of mother's failure to visit or contact children. — According to this section, because the children were not in the mother's custody, the trial court was authorized to consider the evidence of the mother's failure to regularly visit the children or to maintain consistent contact with them as a factor in determining whether to terminate the mother's parental rights. Brown v. Alabama Dep't of Pensions & Sec., 473 So. 2d 533 (Ala. Civ. App. 1985).

Incarceration as evidence of unlikeliness of change of parent's conduct or condition. — In determining the unlikeliness of a change in the parent's conduct or condition, the trial court is free to consider the parent's history, as well as his or her future prospects; thus where father's incarceration was for a period of twenty-seven years, and although he may have become eligible for parole at an earlier date, the trial court could have reasonably concluded that a change in his conduct or condition was unlikely. Carter v. Griffin, 574 So. 2d 800 (Ala. Civ. App. 1990).

Lack of mental capacity. — Where testimony was presented which indicated that the parents failed to understand relatively simple matters that were told them by the department of human resources and the county department of housing, the court could conclude that the parents lacked the mental capabilities necessary to raise the child. Hayes v. State Dep't of Human Resources, 563 So. 2d 1035 (Ala. Civ. App. 1990).

Poverty and limited mentality of mother, in the absence of abuse or lack of caring, should not be the criteria for taking away a wanted child from the parents. Such should particularly be the case when there has been no apparent aid given toward keeping the family together by the agency seeking its termination. Hickman v. State Dep't of Pensions & Sec., 489 So. 2d 601 (Ala. Civ. App. 1986).

Old age is proper matter to be considered in denying custody to a relative of the parent in a termination of parental rights case.

Clemons v. Alabama Dep't of Pensions & Sec., 474 So. 2d 1143 (Ala. Civ. App. 1985).

Trial court may consider evidence of past family history, as well as evidence of present circumstances, in determining whether parental rights should be terminated. Franklin v. State Dep't of Human Resources, 513 So. 2d 625 (Ala. Civ. App. 1987).

Trial court may consider evidence of past family history. — The court was warranted in considering the past history of the child's family as well as present circumstances; the child's retention in the same type environment is also a proper factor for the trial court's consideration in determining if there is a more viable alternative to termination. S.T. v. State Dep't of Human Resources, 579 So. 2d 640 (Ala. Civ. App. 1991).

Evidence sufficient to support finding of abandonment. — Because the record clearly revealed that the mother failed to maintain any contact with the child from June 1988 until October 1989, and that the Department of Human Resources was unable, despite its efforts, to locate the mother during this period, there was clear and convincing evidence to support the juvenile court's conclusion that the mother had abandoned the child during the specific period of time in question. D.P. v. State Dep't of Human Resources, 571 So. 2d 1140 (Ala. Civ. App. 1990).

Abandonment for six months raised rebuttable presumption of inability to act as father. — Where a father abandons a child for six months before a termination petition is filed, that fact constitutes a rebuttable presumption that he was unable or unwilling to act as a father. In re Stephenson, 513 So. 2d 612 (Ala. Civ. App. 1986), rev'd on other grounds, 513 So. 2d 614 (Ala. 1987).

Evidence supported determination that father had not abandoned his child after enlisting in the navy, where he testified that he was willing to support the child and had attempted to provide complete medical and dental coverage for the child through the navy but that the mother had refused to sign the necessary papers he had mailed to her. Muncher v. Muncher, 509 So. 2d 250 (Ala. Civ. App. 1987).

Rehabilitation efforts to be considered. — One factor which the trial court must consider when making a decision whether to terminate one's parental rights is whether reasonable efforts to rehabilitate the mother were exhausted prior to terminating her rights and whether such efforts failed. Ezekiel v. State Dep't of Human Resources, 562 So. 2d 524 (Ala. Civ. App. 1990).

IV. ILLUSTRATIVE CASES.

Evidence sufficient to terminate parental rights. — In view of father's lack of concern, his prior abandonment of his children, his drug dependency problem, and the criminality and incarceration of father, the trial court was not in error in terminating the father's parental rights. Gunn v. Jefferson County Dep't of Pensions & Sec., 467 So. 2d 963 (Ala. Civ. App. 1985).

There were no viable alternatives to termination of the parental rights of the mother, where custody could not be given to the maternal grandmother, because she lived with the mother, and where custody could not be given to the father because he had provided no support for the child, had not sought custody, and had never been married to the mother. Moore v. State, Dep't of Pensions & Sec., 470 So. 2d 1269 (Ala. Civ. App. 1985).

Where the mother was diagnosed as a chronic schizophrenic with significant psychiatric disturbances, and threatened to kill herself, her mother, and the social worker, and her psychiatrist testified that she would remain at risk for potential neglect or abuse of the child, and the child had been in the temporary custody of the department of pensions and security ever since birth, such a showing by the state presented clear and convincing evidence that the child was a dependent child under § 12-15-65(e) and that his best interests would not be served by being placed in his mother's custody; thus, the trial court properly terminated the mother's parental rights, even though there was no evidence of actual abuse or neglect. Moore v. State, Dep't of Pensions & Sec., 470 So. 2d 1269 (Ala. Civ. App. 1985).

Evidence that one month old child had multiple burns and scratches on her body, including a large circular four-centimeter third-degree burn on her back, and that she was dehydrated and malnourished and had a severe ear infection and a broken arm clearly showed that the child had been subject to abuse and neglect from one or both of her parents and was a dependent child, and that her best interests would not be served by remaining in her mother's custody. Fortenberry v. Alabama Dep't of Pensions & Sec., 479 So. 2d 54 (Ala. Civ. App. 1985).

Where, prior to initial custody hearing, mother had consented to child's adoption, and where mother testified that she had also made unsuccessful attempts to abort the child, that she was a prostitute and that she was a drug addict, and further, where mother was presently incarcerated for a felony, serving a concurrent sentence for a prior offense, and the date of her release was uncertain, and in addition where the father of the child was unknown and the alleged father asserted no rights to the child, but opined that the mother was unfit to raise the child, the evidence sufficiently supported the finding that the child was dependent and that there was no better solution to serve this child than placing him in the permanent custody of the Department of Pensions and Security. Brand v. Alabama Dep't of Pensions & Sec., 479 So. 2d 66 (Ala. Civ. App. 1985).

In view of evidence that mother had a history of drug dependence, dating back to 1969, and was currently incarcerated for violation of state drug laws, that she had undergone treatment for her drug dependence at several hospitals, but with little, if any, success, that her current prison sentence was her third imprisonment related to drug usage, and that she had suffered from mental problems and was currently undergoing treatment in prison for schizophrenia and had made at least one suicide attempt, the trial court did not err in terminating the mother's parental rights in her two-year-old daughter. Rose v. Spencer, 491 So. 2d 257 (Ala. Civ. App. 1986).

Evidence that at the time he was removed from the home, three-and-one-half-year-old child was found to have multiple contusions on his head, face, forehead, arms, legs, buttocks, and genital area, caused by parents, that the child was made to stay in his bed most of the time, was not allowed to visit relatives and was seldom taken out in public, and that the wounds that the child had were extremely serious, even life-threatening, warranted termination of the parents' rights, even though there was also evidence that the situation in the home appeared to be somewhat improved at the time of the hearing. Haag v. Cherokee County Dep't of Pensions & Sec., 489 So. 2d 586 (Ala. Civ. App. 1986).

Clear and convincing evidence held to establish that it was in the best interests of two children to have parents' rights terminated, where the children had been in the custody of department of pensions and security since January 1980 and April 1981 respectively, and where the parents had made little effort toward self-rehabilitation in order to get their children back, failed to maintain regular visits and contacts with the children, never managed to establish a stable home, received their sole income from a supplemental security income check they received each month, since they suffered from mental deficiencies, and had difficulty maintaining even minimal physical existence. McCullough v. State, Dep't of Pensions & Sec., 500 So. 2d 1093 (Ala. Civ. App. 1986).

Evidence showed that termination of the mother's parental rights would be in the children's best interests, where she had an alcohol problem which caused her to be unable to adequately care for her children and all attempts at rehabilitation had been unsuccessful. McConathy v. State Dep't of Human Resources, 510 So. 2d 269 (Ala. Civ. App. 1987).

Where the department of human resources worked with the mother, but all attempts at rehabilitation were unsuccessful; when the child was not in her custody, the mother failed to maintain regular visits or consistent contact or communication with the children, she failed to adjust her circumstances to meet the needs of the children, and failed to provide for the material needs of the children or to pay a reasonable portion of their support; and the department sought less drastic alternatives other than the termination of the mother's rights, there was clear and convincing evidence that termination of the mother's parental rights would be in the children's best interests. Kelley v. State Dep't of Human Resources, 515 So. 2d 713 (Ala. Civ. App. 1987).

Where the department worked with the father in an effort for him to regain custody of his child, but these attempts at rehabilitation were unsuccessful, the father never having fulfilled the provisions of the plan set up between him and the department, even though he was given ample time to demonstrate a willingness and ability to work with the department to achieve a placement of his child in his custody, there was evidence presented to the court that the father's mental condition had been altered by the abuse of alcohol and that he was not able to sufficiently care for the child, and the court sought less drastic alternatives other than termination of parental rights and there was no other feasible alternative, there was clear and convincing evidence that termination of the father's parental rights would be in the child's best interests. Perry v. State Dep't of Human Resources, 516 So. 2d 659 (Ala. Civ. App. 1987).

Under subsections (a)(2) and (3), the evidence showing the mother's mental illness and her past cruelty to the child's brother (resulting in his death) apparently due to mental illness supports the decision by the trial court to terminate the mother's parental rights. Thornton v. Thornton, 519 So. 2d 960 (Ala. Civ. App. 1987).

Where an investigation revealed unsuitable conditions in the home, which smelled of urine and was infested with flies, and the youngest child was found to be listless and unhealthy and at the time, the family lived in a home that had a wood heater and no electricity or running water, and neither parent was employed, and the record further revealed that appropriate psychological tests were performed on the parents showing the IQ of each to be in the 70's, putting them in a category of borderline intellectual functioning, revealed sufficient evidence to support the trial court's order terminating the parents' rights in this aspect of the case. Ruffner v. State Dep't of Human Resources, 518 So. 2d 141 (Ala. Civ. App. 1987).

Termination of parental rights would be upheld where there was clear and convincing evidence in the record to support a finding that child was dependent, that there was no suitable relative who could be granted custody, and that child's adoptability was very high at the time and would decrease as she got older. Gilmore v. State Dep't of Human Resources, 531 So. 2d 913 (Ala. Civ. App. 1988).

Where the evidence was clear that mother voluntarily chose to relinquish her parental rights in order that child could be adopted, and it was undisputed that the mother knew what she was doing and was counseled by an attorney, the trial court did not err in terminating the mother's parental rights and awarding custody of the child to adoption agency to be put up for adoption. Mayer v. Agape of Cent. Ala., 536 So. 2d 86 (Ala. Civ. App. 1988).

Where mother attempted suicide, had history of impulsiveness and lack of planning, and failed objectives to stabilize her life, and where father refused to release information for determination of his stability and lived an unstable lifestyle, there was clear and convincing evidence to support trial court's decision that it was in best interests of children to terminate parental rights and locate permanent placement for them. Baker v. State Dep't of Human Resources, 533 So. 2d 633 (Ala. Civ. App. 1988).

There was clear and convincing evidence to support the trial court's decision to terminate mother's parental rights where the evidence showed that the mother had a history of chronic alcohol abuse and as a result, she suffered from numerous medical problems, where the mother also had a history of criminal activity in which she had been arrested for assault, disorderly conduct, reckless endangerment, and criminal menacing, and where the record indicated that the department had made diligent efforts to assist the mother in rehabilitating herself and the mother made little effort toward self-rehabilitation. Snipes v. State Dep't of Human Resources, 542 So. 2d 282 (Ala. Civ. App. 1989).

There was clear and convincing evidence that mother could not provide for her child where evidence was presented which established that the mother lost custody of her two older children, where testimony was also presented that indicated the mother had mental problems which would make her unable to provide for her child, and where other evidence supporting the termination included the testimony of the child's psychologist and a department of human resources foster care worker who both testified that the child's extensive knowledge of sexual behavior, her use of language with sexual connotations, and her inappropriate social behavior in kindergarten indicated that the child had been a participant in sexual activity. Polk v. State Dep't of Human Resources, 542 So. 2d 279 (Ala. Civ. App. 1988).

There was clear and convincing evidence that supported the trial court's decision to terminate the parents' parental rights where the evidence consisted primarily of testimony showing a history of the parents' mental illness and their past and present inability to adequately care for the child. Fitzgerald v. Fitzgerald, 539 So. 2d 281 (Ala. Civ. App. 1988).

Where the mother was admitted for psychiatric treatment after attempting suicide, where child was admitted to the hospital with third degree burns over 50 percent of her body, and the incident resulted in a conviction of the mother of a felony for child abuse, where the mother had been convicted of and imprisoned for a total of three felonies, where, after the dependency petition was filed in November 1986, the Department of Human Resources (DHR) made attempts to evaluate and assist the mother and after two meetings the mother failed to keep in contact with DHR, trial court did not abuse its discretion in terminating mother's parental rights. Travis v. State Dep't of Human Resources, 547 So. 2d 571 (Ala. Civ. App. 1989); Alfo v. State Dep't of Human Resources, 549 So. 2d 492 (Ala. Civ. App. 1989); Menniefield v. State Dep't of Human Resources, 549 So. 2d 496 (Ala. Civ. App. 1989).

Where the record showed that the mother had been diagnosed as schizophrenic, mildly retarded, and suffering from hallucinations and had been committed for treatment and the Department of Human Resources (DHR) made reasonable efforts to assist the mother in raising the child initially and thereafter attempted to reunite the mother and child, but the mother failed to cooperate with DHR, there was clear and convincing evidence that supported the trial court's decision to terminate the mother's parental rights. Cope v. State Dep't of Human Resources, 549 So. 2d 982 (Ala. Civ. App. 1989).

Evidence sufficient to terminate mother's rights where the child had been removed several times, once when the child was 11 months old and the mother left her in a yard, where the mother suffered from manic depression and was subject to severe mood swings and irrationality and was not faithful in taking treatment, and where the mother was at times threatening to others in several ways, such as brandishing weapons and setting fire to her family's home and her ex-husband's home. Pam v. State, 560 So. 2d 1064 (Ala. Civ. App. 1990).

Where at the time of the trial, mother had not visited her daughter for two years and the father had not seen the child in two years, and he had only made two support payments during her entire lifetime, this evidence indicated that the parents failed to maintain consistent contact and regular visits with the child, and failed to provide for her support. Hayes v. State Dep't of Human Resources, 563 So. 2d 1035 (Ala. Civ. App. 1990).

The father's incarceration, his apparent abandonment of the children during his flight from justice after murdering their mother, the fact that it was the father's own act which caused the dependency of his two children, in light of this heinous crime, the fact that his older child was four and his younger only an infant at the time of their mother's death, and the additional fact that neither child had had any significant contact with the father since that time supported the decision of the trial court to terminate the father's parental rights. Carter v. Griffin, 574 So. 2d 800 (Ala. Civ. App. 1990).

Evidence supported the termination of a mother's parental rights where child had not been in the custody of the mother since a year after its birth and had been in foster care for the preceding three years, where the mother had failed to maintain consistent contact with the child, where the mother had not made an effort to adjust her circumstances to meet the needs of the child, where there was no viable alternatives and the mother had disregarded an agreement with the department of human resources to attend a drug counseling program and parenting skills classes. R.K. v. State Dep't of Human Resources, 577 So. 2d 466 (Ala. Civ. App. 1990).

See Pilkington v. Alabama Dep't of Human Resources, 511 So. 2d 192 (Ala. Civ. App. 1987).

Evidence held insufficient. — Evidence held insufficient to meet the high standard of clear and convincing evidence that child was so dependent that parental rights should be terminated. Hickman v. State Dep't of Pensions & Sec., 489 So. 2d 601 (Ala. Civ. App. 1986), reversing and remanding for further observation and consideration of parent's ability to care for child.

Evidence was not sufficiently clear and convincing to support last and most extreme disposition permitted by law, termination of the parental rights of mother, where the record revealed that the mother and child loved each other, mother visited with her daughter as often as department allowed her to do so, and there was no evidence of neglect other than mother's inability to buy food and pay utility bills at times due to her lack of stable employment. Bowman v. State Dep't of Human Resources, 534 So. 2d 304 (Ala. Civ. App. 1988).

§ 26-18-8. Transfer of custody.

If the court determines that the parents of a child are incapable to act as parents and terminates their parental rights, it may:

(1) Transfer the permanent legal custody of the child to the department or to any public or private licensed child-placing agency able and willing to assume the care and maintenance of the child, with or without an order to proceed with plans for the adoptive placement of the child. A court order which terminates parental rights and awards permanent custody to the Department of Human Resources or to a licensed child-placing agency shall mean that the said department or said licensed child-placing agency shall have authority to make permanent plans for the child, including the authority to place for adoption and consent to adoption.

(2) Transfer the permanent legal custody of the child to a relative or other individual who, after study by the department, is found to be able to properly receive and care for the child. (Acts 1984, No. 84-261, p. 442, § 8.)

Termination of rights and granting temporary custody inconsistent with section. — The trial court's termination of mother's parental rights and granting only temporary custody of child to department of human resources was inconsistent with this section; the Child Protection Act does not provide for temporary placement of the child following termination of parental rights, and placement following termination proceedings involves permanent placement and permanent custody. State Dep't of Human Resources v. Thomas, 554 So. 2d 1063 (Ala. Civ. App. 1989).

Grandmother and her husband erroneously denied custody. — Evidence held insufficient to support the trial court's denial of petition of grandmother and her husband for custody of her granddaughters, even though petitioners already had a 14-year-old adopted son, who was blind and mentally retarded. Shackelford v. State, Dep't of Human Resources, 527 So. 2d 1329 (Ala. Civ. App. 1988).

This section must be read in pari materia with § 26-10A-7(4), which sets the perimeters of the agency's authority to withhold its consent. Ex parte R.C., 592 So. 2d 589 (Ala. 1991).

Cited in Clingan v. State, 471 So. 2d 435 (Ala. Civ. App. 1985); Kennedy v. State Dep't of Human Resources, 535 So. 2d 168 (Ala. Civ. App. 1988).

§ 26-18-9. Periodic review of efforts to achieve adoption of child in custody of another after parental rights terminated.

Where the court has terminated the rights and responsibilities of the parents and has placed custody of the child with the department or with a public or private licensed child-placing agency, or with an individual, the court shall, at least yearly, review the circumstances of the child to determine what efforts have been made to achieve the adoption of the child. (Acts 1984, No. 84-261, p. 442, § 9.)

§ 26-18-10. Authority of one in custody to place child for adoption or consent to adoption.

Upon the court's termination of parental rights and placement of custody of a child with any agency, person or department, any such agency, person or department shall have the authority to place said child for adoption or to consent to said adoption. (Acts 1984, No. 84-261, p. 442, § 10.)

Collateral references. — Marital or sexual relationship between parties as affecting right to adopt. 42 ALR4th 776.

Required parties in adoption proceedings. 48 ALR4th 860.

Natural parent's indigence as precluding finding that failure to support child waived requirement of consent to adoption. 71 ALR4th 305.

CHAPTER 19.

BUREAU FOR INFORMATION ON MISSING PERSONS.

§ 26-19-1. Definitions.

For purposes of this chapter, the following words shall have the meanings ascribed, unless the context clearly indicates otherwise:

(1) DEPARTMENT. The Alabama Department of Public Safety.

(2) DIRECTOR. The Director of the Department of Public Safety.

(3) BUREAU. The Missing Children Bureau created by this chapter within the department.

(4) LAW ENFORCEMENT AGENCIES. Federal, state and local law enforcement agencies of this state primarily, and of other states generally.

(5) NCIC. The National Crime Information Center and its computer system of reported missing persons and unidentified deceased persons maintained by the Federal Bureau of Investigation.

(6) CJIC. The Criminal Justice Information Center of the state. (Acts 1985, No. 85-538, p. 653, § 1.)

§ 26-19-2. Missing Children Bureau created; general purpose.

There is hereby created within the Department of Public Safety a statewide information and investigation center for the reporting by law enforcement agencies and other agencies and persons of missing persons and unidentified deceased persons. The bureau shall be known as the Missing Children Bureau, hereinafter referred to simply as "the bureau." (Acts 1985, No. 85-538, p. 653, § 2.)

§ 26-19-3. Authority to transfer, hire, etc., personnel.

The Director of the Department of Public Safety is hereby required to establish the Missing Children Bureau within the department, and for such purposes, is authorized to transfer or assign existing personnel within the department and to hire such additional technical, legal, clerical, investigative and other persons as are necessary to implement the provisions of this chapter. (Acts 1985, No. 85-538, p. 653, § 3.)

§ 26-19-4. Specific functions of bureau.

The bureau shall be responsible for the following specific functions:

(1) To receive and promptly enter into the state's computer system all reports of law enforcement agencies, and other persons and agencies, of missing children and adults, and of unidentified deceased persons, and all pertinent information submitted by the person or agency reporting which is contained in any investigation or investigations conducted pursuant to the report. The bureau shall also promptly enter such information in the NCIC computer network. If a missing person is subsequently found or if an unidentified deceased person is subsequently identified, and such information is reported to the bureau, the bureau shall immediately retrieve and cancel such data from the state computer system and from the NCIC computer system.

(2) To coordinate with other states and with the federal government in investigating cases of missing persons and unidentified bodies and to conduct appropriate investigations.

(3) To provide special training to law enforcement officers and medical examiners, when available, to help them handle cases of missing persons and unidentified bodies.

(4) To compile annual statistics on the number of missing persons and unidentified deceased persons in this state.

(5) To develop recommendations for better reporting and use of computer systems.

(6) To establish a toll free telephone number to assist agencies and individuals in the reporting of missing persons and unidentified deceased persons.

(7) To provide periodic lists, including photographs if available, to the State Board of Education, of all missing school children in this state, grades K-12.

(8) To assist local law enforcement agencies and other agencies to set up direct computer access to the state's computer system.

(9) To solicit and collect from the agencies of other states and the national government dealing with missing persons all available lists of missing children grades K-12 for dissemination to the State Board of Education.

(10) To provide all agencies of other states or the national government dealing with missing persons a list of all missing Alabama school children grades K-12, with photographs, if available, for dissemination to the school systems of such other states to locate such children.

(11) To act as liaison between private citizens and law enforcement agencies regarding the appropriate procedures for handling and responding to missing person cases.

(12) To assist local law enforcement agencies and community organizations who sponsor programs to fingerprint children by enabling parents to

retain a permanent fingerprint record of their children for identification purposes. (Acts 1985, No. 85-538, p. 653, § 4.)

§ 26-19-5. Law enforcement agencies to report missing persons to bureau; contents of report.

Any law enforcement agency in this state in which a complaint of a missing person has been filed shall prepare and send a report to the bureau within 72 hours on any missing person or unidentified deceased person. That report shall include, but is not limited to, the following:

(1) All information contained in the complaint on a missing person.

(2) All information or evidence gathered by a preliminary investigation, if one was made.

(3) A statement, by the law enforcement officer in charge, setting forth that officer's assessment of the case based upon all evidence and information received.

(4) An explanation of the next steps to be taken by the law enforcement agency filing the report. (Acts 1985, No. 85-538, p. 653, § 5.)

§ 26-19-6. Forwarding report to other law enforcement agencies.

Upon completion of the report, a copy of the teletype message with pertinent information shall be forwarded to:

(1) All law enforcement agencies having jurisdiction of the location in which the missing person lives or was last seen.

(2) All law enforcement agencies considered to be potentially involved by the law enforcement agency filing the report.

(3) All law enforcement agencies which the complainant requests the report to be sent to, if the request is reasonable in light of the information contained in the report.

(4) Any law enforcement agency requesting a copy of the missing person report. (Acts 1985, No. 85-538, p. 653, § 6.)

§ 26-19-7. Duties of law enforcement agencies upon receiving report of missing person.

Upon receiving a report of a person believed to be missing, the law enforcement agency shall conduct a preliminary investigation to determine whether the person is missing. If the person is determined to be missing, the agency shall immediately enter identifying and descriptive information about the person to the bureau and to the National Crime Information Center (NCIC) through the Criminal Justice Information Center (CJIC). Law enforcement agencies having direct access to the CJIC and the NCIC computer shall enter and retrieve the data directly and shall cooperate in the entry and retrieval of data on behalf of law enforcement agencies which do not have direct access to the systems. Law enforcement agencies shall likewise report or enter data to the bureau relating to unidentified deceased persons. (Acts 1985, No. 85-538, p. 653, § 7.)

§ 26-19-8. Duties of law enforcement agencies upon locating missing person.

Immediately after a missing person is located, or an unidentified deceased person is subsequently identified, the law enforcement agency which locates or returns the missing person, or which identifies a previously unidentified deceased person, shall notify the law enforcement agency having jurisdiction over the investigation, and that agency shall cancel the entry from the state CJIC, the NCIC computer, and from the state bureau. (Acts 1985, No. 85-538, p. 653, § 8.)

§ 26-19-9. Board of Education to compile and distribute list of missing school children.

The State Board of Education shall perform the following functions:

(1) Collect each month a list of missing Alabama school children, with a photograph, if available, as provided by the missing children bureau. A missing Alabama school child shall be defined for the purposes of this section as a child under 18 years whose whereabouts are unknown. The list shall be designed to include such information as the board deems necessary for the identification of the missing school child; and

(2) Compile from the information collected pursuant to subdivision (1) a list of missing school children, to be distributed monthly to all public school systems admitting children to kindergarten through grade 12. The list shall include the names of all such missing children, together with such other information, with photographs, when available. The school systems shall distribute this information to the public schools in the system by whatever manner each system deems appropriate. (Acts 1985, No. 85-538, p. 653, § 9.)

§ 26-19-10. Public school systems to notify Department of Education and bureau when missing school child found.

Every public school system in this state shall notify the Department of Education and the bureau immediately with respect to any child whose name appears on the department's list of missing school children who is subsequently found. (Acts 1985, No. 85-538, p. 653, § 10.)

CHAPTER 20.

SEX CRIME RECORDS OF EMPLOYEES SUPERVISING CHILDREN.

§ 26-20-1. Certain employers to check sex crime records of applicants who would supervise minors; limitations.

Certain prospective employers enumerated herein shall request from the Department of Public Safety records of all available convictions involving any sex crimes of a person who applies for employment or volunteers for a position in which he or she would have supervisory or disciplinary power over a minor under 18 years of age.

(1) The following employers shall request such a check upon hiring a person or otherwise selecting an applicant to be employed:

a. Any public or private school or school system with grades kindergarten through the twelfth grade;

b. Any day care or child care facility whether public or private;

c. Any person who cares for children in his home, in the home of the child or other places, on a regular day-to-day basis;

d. Any public or private domiciliary home for children or orphanages;

e. Any public or private intermediate or long-term care facilities providing care or treatment for mental, physical, emotional or rehabilitative conditions or diseases for a child or children; and

f. Any correctional or detentional facility operated by any state or local governmental agency.

(2) The Department of Public Safety shall furnish the information to the requesting employer and shall also send a copy of the information to the applicant, and the Department of Public Safety may charge a fee to be paid by the employer for the actual cost of processing the request.

(3) The Department of Public Safety shall adopt such regulations as are necessary to implement the provisions of this chapter.

(4) No check of an employee's record for prior sex crime convictions shall be required of any employee who was employed prior to September 1, 1985, except as provided in Section 26-20-2. No one may be hired by any licensed child care facility in Alabama who has been convicted of murder, rape in the first degree, assault in the first degree, kidnapping in the first degree, arson in the first degree or of a crime dealing with abuse of children. (Acts 1985, No. 85-681, p. 1074, § 1.)

§ 26-20-2. Other employers to obtain statement from employees disclosing sex crimes; required information; disposition of form statement; verification process.

Every employer, other than those enumerated in Section 26-20-1, which employs or uses the services of volunteers or paid employees in positions in which the volunteer or employee has supervisory or disciplinary power over a child or children, shall obtain from the volunteer or employee a statement signed by the volunteer or employee whether he or she has ever been convicted of a sex crime, and if so to fully disclose all such convictions.

(1) The Department of Public Safety shall furnish to employers on request form copies of the required statement to be signed and marked appropriately by the prospective employee or volunteer. The form statement shall contain the following information:

a. A list of the sex crimes brought within the contemplation of this law;

b. A notation that the statement may be verified by a check of the records of the department of public safety including the information contained in the National Crime Information Center (NCIC) computer;

c. A statement of the penalty for failure to provide accurate and truthful information;

d. Such other information as the Department of Public Safety deems appropriate to fulfill the requirement and intent of this chapter.

(2) Within 10 days from the hiring of the employee or initiation of services of the volunteer, the employer shall forward a copy of the completed statement to the Department of Public Safety and the employer shall maintain the original of the employee's or volunteer's statement for a period of three years after the employee or volunteer has discontinued employment or service with the employer. The Department of Public Safety shall maintain the copy of the statement for a period of one year if it states the employee or volunteer has no prior conviction of sex crimes. Statements which state the employee or volunteer has a prior conviction of sex crimes shall be maintained by the Department of Public Safety indefinitely.

(3) The Department of Public Safety shall provide a procedure to periodically randomly verify a sample of statements submitted by performing complete checks for prior convictions of sex crimes, to include a search of the information contained in the National Crime Information Center (NCIC) computer. In addition, employers or prospective employers may request a complete check of their employee or prospective employee. Should a request for a complete check by an employer or prospective employer or should a random verification process reveal that an employee has submitted false information, the Department of Public Safety shall immediately notify the employer and an appropriate local law enforcement agency for investigation and possible prosecution. (Acts 1985, No. 85-681, p. 1074, § 2.)

§ 26-20-3. Penalty for false statements by employees.

Any employee or prospective employee who falsely makes a statement or intentionally withholds information mandated by this chapter shall be fined not less than $500.00 nor more than $1,000.00, and may be incarcerated in the county jail for not more than six months. (Acts 1985, No. 85-681, p. 1074, § 3.)

§ 26-20-4. Exempt employees required to submit statement.

Any employee or volunteer in subdivisions (1)(a) through (1)(e) of Section 26-20-1, who is exempt from a complete check of prior convictions of sex crimes by virtue of subdivision (4) of Section 26-20-1, shall be required to submit a statement regarding prior sex crime convictions to his or her employer as described in Section 26-20-2 within 90 days of September 1, 1985. The employer shall be required to meet the requirements of Section 26-20-2 with regard to maintaining the original statement and forwarding a copy to the Department of Public Safety. (Acts 1985, No. 85-681, p. 1074, § 4.)

§ 26-20-5. "Sex crime" defined.

As used in this chapter the term "sex crimes" includes sexual abuse or exploitation as defined in subdivision (1) of Section 26-14-1, incest as defined in Section 13A-13-3 and those enumerated sexual offenses in Sections 13A-6-60 through 13A-6-70, and exploitation as defined in Section 13A-12-196. Conviction for a violation or attempted violation of an offense committed outside the State of Alabama is a sex crime if such offense would have been a crime in Alabama under one of the above sections if committed in Alabama. (Acts 1985, No. 85-681, p. 1074, § 5.)

§ 26-20-6. Records, statements, etc., required by chapter to be confidential.

The Department of Public Safety and employers who are under the requirements of this chapter shall insure that all reports, records and statements required by this chapter shall be confidential and shall not be made available for public inspection. (Acts 1985, No. 85-681, p. 1074, § 6.)

CHAPTER 21.

PARENTAL CONSENT TO PERFORMING ABORTION UPON MINOR.

§ 26-21-1. Legislative purpose and findings.

(a) It is the intent of the legislature in enacting this parental consent provision to further the important and compelling state interests of: (1) protecting minors against their own immaturity, (2) fostering the family structure and preserving it as a viable social unit, and (3) protecting the rights of parents to rear children who are members of their household.

(b) The legislature finds as fact that: (1) immature minors often lack the ability to make fully informed choices that take account of both immediate and long-range consequences, (2) the medical, emotional and psychological consequences of abortion are serious and can be lasting, particularly when the patient is immature, (3) the capacity to become pregnant and the capacity for mature judgment concerning the wisdom of an abortion are not necessarily related, (4) parents ordinarily possess information essential to a physician's exercise of his best medical judgment concerning the child, and (5) parents who are aware that their minor daughter has had an abortion may better insure that she receives adequate medical attention after her abortion. The legislature further finds that parental consultation is usually desirable and in the best interests of the minor. (Acts 1987, No. 87-286, p. 397, § 1.)

Cross references. — For temporary rules governing procedures for petitions by an unemancipated minor requesting waiver of parental consent for the performance of an abortion, see Appendix V to the Alabama Rules of Civil Procedure, in the cumulative supplement to Volume 23.

Constitutional sufficiency. — While in many cases, a minor who seeks an abortion will be a ward of the state or otherwise will not have a parent or legally appointed guardian to turn to for consultation, advice, and supervision, this does not mean that the Parental Consent Act is constitutionally deficient for its failure to provide another alternative to a court proceeding. The absence of a parent or guardian merely constitutes an additional circumstance justifying judicial supervision of the minor's liberty to make her own decision. In re Anonymous, 531 So. 2d 901 (Ala. 1988).

The state's legitimate interest in providing for supervision of minors allows it to place certain burdens on their exercise of their right to an abortion. In the overall scheme of the Parental Consent Act, the residuary provision for judicial inquiry into maturity and best interest, where the minor cannot otherwise obtain consent, bears a reasonable relation to the state's interest in protecting minor from harmful consequences of their immaturity. In re Anonymous, 531 So. 2d 901 (Ala. 1988).

Right to counsel for minor seeking abortion. — Minor's conditional right to exercise her constitutional choice to have an abortion is protected by her right to legal counsel, and although this Act does not specifically provide for a guardian ad litem, the prerogative of the trial court to make such an appointment is provided, e.g., in §§ 26-2A-52 and 12-15-8. In re Anonymous, 531 So. 2d 901 (Ala. 1988).

Attorney appointed under this Act is to

be a guardian ad litem, and future appointments should be so designated and shall entail the responsibilities attendant to such appointments. In re Anonymous, 531 So. 2d 901 (Ala. 1988).

Minor's misrepresentation of age does not destroy parents' standing to bring action. — A parent's right to be informed regarding a minor child's intended abortion creates a right of action on the part of the parents against any person who performs an abortion on the minor child without having obtained parental consent or the required court-ordered waiver of consent, despite the minor's intentional misrepresentation of her age. Boykin v. Magnolia Bay, Inc., 570 So. 2d 639 (Ala. 1990).

Cited in In re Anonymous, 549 So. 2d 1347 (Ala. Civ. App. 1989).

§ 26-21-2. Definitions.

For purposes of this chapter, the following definitions shall apply:

(1) MINOR. Any person under the age of 18 years;

(2) EMANCIPATED MINOR. Any minor who is or has been married or has by court order otherwise been legally freed from the care, custody and control of her parents;

(3) ABORTION. The use of any instrument, medicine, drug or any other substance or device with intent to terminate the pregnancy of a woman known to be pregnant, with intent other than to increase the probability of a live birth, to preserve the life or health of the child after live birth, or to remove a dead or dying unborn child. (Acts 1987, No. 87-286, p. 397, § 2.)

§ 26-21-3. Written consent of parent or guardian to performing abortion on unemancipated minor; written notice to minor's mother where pregnancy caused by natural father; written statement where abortion to be performed on emancipated minor; waiver of consent requirement.

(a) Except as otherwise provided in subsections (b) and (e) of this section and Sections 26-21-4 and 26-21-5 hereof, no person shall perform an abortion upon an unemancipated minor unless he or his agent first obtains the written consent of either parent or the legal guardian of the minor.

(b) If the minor's pregnancy was caused by sexual intercourse with the minor's natural father, adoptive father or stepfather or legal guardian, then written notice to the minor's mother by certified mail shall be sufficient.

(c) The person who shall perform the abortion or his agent shall obtain or be provided with the written consent from either parent or legal guardian stating the names of the minor, parent or legal guardian, that he or she is informed that the minor desires an abortion and does consent to the abortion, the date, and shall be signed by either parent or legal guardian. The unemancipated minor shall verify on the same form, by her signature and in the presence of such person who shall perform the abortion or his agent, that said signature of the parents, parent or legal guardian is authentic. The consent shall be kept as a part of the minor's patient file for four years.

(d) If the minor is emancipated, the person who shall perform the abortion or his agent shall obtain a written statement stating the name of the emancipated minor, that the minor is emancipated, the type of emancipation, the date and shall be signed by the minor. The written statement shall be signed in the presence of the person who shall perform the abortion or his agent and witnessed by him or the agent. The emancipated minor shall also provide a license or certificate of marriage, judgment or decree of divorce, order of emancipation or relieving her of the disabilities of nonage, or other court document evidencing her marriage, divorce, or emancipation. A copy of any such document shall be attached to the written statement and kept as a part of the minor's patient file for four years.

(e) A minor who elects not to seek or does not or cannot for any reason, including unavailability or refusal by either or both parents or legal guardian, obtain consent from either of her parents or legal guardian under this section, may petition, on her own behalf, the juvenile court, or court of equal standing, in the county in which the minor resides or in the county in which the abortion is to be performed for a waiver of the consent requirement of this section pursuant to the procedure of Section 26-21-4. (Acts 1987, No. 87-286, p. 397, § 3.)

Denial of waiver improper. — The Juvenile court's finding that an abortion was not in the best interest of a 12 year old ward of the state was not supported by the evidence where the prognosis for delivery was fair and the pregnancy was the result of a statutory rape, even though the pregnancy was in its second trimester. In re Anonymous, 531 So. 2d 901 (Ala. 1988).

§ 26-21-4. Procedure for waiver of consent requirement — Notice to parents or guardian prohibited; participation in proceedings; right to counsel; hearsay evidence; assistance in preparing petition; confidentiality; contents of petition; precedence of proceeding; time for court's decision; findings and conclusions; appeal; no fees or costs.

(a) A minor who elects not to seek or does not or cannot for any reason, obtain consent from either of her parents or legal guardian, may petition, on her own behalf, the juvenile court, or the court of equal standing, in the county in which the minor resides or in the county in which the abortion is to be performed for a waiver of the consent requirement of this chapter. Notice by the court to the minor's parents, parent or legal guardian shall not be required or permitted. The requirements and procedures under this chapter shall apply and are available to minors whether or not they are residents of this state.

(b) The minor may participate in proceedings in the court on her own behalf. The court shall advise her that she has a right to be represented by an attorney and that if she is unable to pay for the services of an attorney one will be appointed for her. If the court appoints an attorney to represent her such attorney shall be compensated as provided in Section 15-12-21. If the minor petitioner chooses to represent herself, such pleadings, documents or evidence that she may file with the court shall be liberally construed by the court so as to do substantial justice. Hearsay evidence shall be admissible.

(c) The court shall insure that the minor is given assistance in preparing and filing the petition and shall insure that the minor's identity is kept confidential. Such assistance may be provided by court personnel including intake personnel of juvenile probation services.

(d) The petition required in Section 26-21-3(e) shall be made under oath and shall include all of the following:

(1) A statement that the petitioner is pregnant;

(2) A statement that the petitioner is unmarried, under 18 years of age, and unemancipated;

(3) A statement that the petitioner wishes to have an abortion without the consent of either parent or legal guardian.

(4) An allegation of either or both of the following:

a. That the petitioner is sufficiently mature and well enough informed to intelligently decide whether to have an abortion without the consent of either of her parents or legal guardian.

b. That one or both of her parents or her guardian has engaged in a pattern of physical, sexual, or emotional abuse against her, or that the consent of her parents, parent or legal guardian otherwise is not in her best interest.

(5) A statement as to whether the petitioner has retained an attorney and the name, address and telephone number of her attorney.

(e) Court proceedings shall be given such precedence over other pending matters as is necessary to insure that the court may reach a decision promptly, but in no case, except as provided herein, shall the court fail to rule within 72 hours of the time the petition is filed, Saturdays, Sundays, and legal holidays excluded. Provided, however, this time requirement may be extended on the request of the minor. If a juvenile court judge is not available for the hearing provided herein, the clerk of the court in which the petition was filed shall forthwith notify the presiding circuit court judge and the presiding circuit court judge of the circuit shall immediately appoint a district or circuit court level judge to hear the petition.

(f) The required consent shall be waived if the court finds either:

(1) That the minor is mature and well-informed enough to make the abortion decision on her own; or

(2) That performance of the abortion would be in the best interest of the minor.

(g) A court that conducts proceedings under this section shall issue written and specific factual findings and legal conclusions supporting its decision and shall order that a confidential record of the evidence be maintained for at least four years. A transcript of the proceedings shall be recorded and if there is an appeal as provided in subsection (h), a transcript of the proceedings shall be prepared forthwith.

(h) An expedited confidential and anonymous appeal shall be available to any minor to whom the court denies a waiver of consent. If notice of appeal is given, the record of appeal shall be completed and the appeal shall be perfected within five days from the filing of the notice of appeal. Briefs shall not be required but may be permitted. Because time may be of the essence regarding the performance of the abortion, the Alabama Supreme Court shall issue promptly such additional rules as it deems are necessary to insure that appeals under this section are handled in an expeditious, confidential and anonymous manner.

(i) All proceedings under this chapter shall be confidential and anonymous. In all pleadings or court documents, the minor shall be identified by initials only.

(j) No fees or costs shall be required of any minor who avails herself of the procedures provided by this section. (Acts 1987, No. 87-286, p. 397, § 4.)

Subsection (g) of this section requires the court to issue written and specific factual findings and legal conclusions supporting its decision. In re Anonymous, 531 So. 2d 901 (Ala. 1988).

A number of factors are relevant in making determination of whether abortion is in minor's best interest. In a given case, alternatives to abortion, such as marriage to the father of the child, arranging for its adoption, or assuming the responsibilities of motherhood with the assured support of family, may be feasible and relevant to the best interest analysis. Ex parte Anonymous, 595 So. 2d 497 (Ala. 1992).

Discretion of court. — It was error to refuse consent where the minor was mature and well-informed. In re Anonymous, 515 So. 2d 1254 (Ala. Civ. App. 1987).

Indicia of maturity. — Minor's voluntary decision to resort to the judicial procedure, specifically requesting the advice of legal counsel, may, of itself, indicate maturity. In addition, her decision to seek advice from a group opposed to abortion in order to get a broader perspective on the issue demonstrates maturity. Ex parte Anonymous, 595 So. 2d 497 (Ala. 1992).

Minor held able to decide to have abortion. — Trial court abused its discretion in finding that the minor was not mature enough to make an informed decision regarding the abortion since the appellate court could not discern from the trial court's judgment nor from the record any grounds upon which the trial court's conclusion could be based and the only evidence presented showed that the minor was mature and well informed enough to make the decision to have the abortion. In re Anonymous, 549 So. 2d 1347 (Ala. Civ. App. 1989).

Where juvenile court failed to make a determination on issue of minor's maturity and there was nothing in the record except positive evidence that the minor was sufficiently mature to make her own decision, there was no alternative but to grant the minor the waiver of parental consent that she requested. Ex parte Anonymous, 595 So. 2d 499 (Ala. 1992).

Evidence did not support denial of waiver. — The Juvenile court's finding that an abortion was not in the best interest of a 12 year old ward of the state was not supported by the evidence where the prognosis for delivery was fair and the pregnancy was the result of a statutory rape, even though the pregnancy was in its second trimester. In re Anonymous, 531 So. 2d 901 (Ala. 1988).

Cited in Scott v. State Dep't of Human Resources, 510 So. 2d 274 (Ala. Civ. App. 1987).

§ 26-21-5. Medical emergencies.

This chapter shall not apply when, in the best clinical judgment of the attending physician on the facts of the case before him, a medical emergency exists that so compromises the health, safety or well-being of the mother as to require an immediate abortion. A physician who does not comply with Sections 26-21-3 and 26-21-4 by reason of this exception shall state in the medical record of the abortion, the medical indications on which his judgment was based. (Acts 1987, No. 87-286, p. 397, § 5.)

§ 26-21-6. Penalties for violation of chapter.

Any person who intentionally performs or causes to be performed an abortion in violation of the provisions of this chapter or intentionally fails to conform to any requirement of this chapter, shall be guilty of a Class A misdemeanor. Any person found guilty under this section shall immediately forfeit any professional license they may hold. (Acts 1987, No. 87-286, p. 397, § 6.)

Collateral references. — Medical malpractice in performance of legal abortion. 69 ALR4th 875.

§ 26-21-7. Nonliability of physician for claims arising out of disclosure of information; nondisclosure of information regarding abortion pursuant to court order; physician has no duty to secure waiver.

No physician who complies with the parental consent requirement(s) of this chapter shall be liable in any manner to the minor upon whom the abortion was performed for any claim whatsoever arising out of or based on the disclosure of any information concerning the medical condition of such minor to her parent(s) or legal guardian(s); provided that a physician who performs an abortion pursuant to a court order obtained under the provisions of this chapter, shall not disclose any information regarding same to the parent(s) or legal guardian(s) of the minor unless such disclosure is made pursuant to a court order. In no event shall the physician be under any duty to initiate proceedings in any court to secure a waiver of the parental consent requirement on behalf of any minor who has requested that an abortion be performed. (Acts 1987, No. 87-286, p. 397, § 7.)

§ 26-21-8. Confidentiality of records and information involving court proceedings; statistical records; penalty for disclosure; reports to Bureau of Vital Statistics.

(a) Records and information involving court proceedings conducted pursuant to Section 26-21-4 shall be confidential and shall not be disclosed other than to the minor, her attorney and necessary court personnel. Nothing in this subsection shall prohibit the keeping of statistical records and information as long as the anonymity of the minor is in no way compromised.

(b) Any person who shall disclose any records or information made confidential pursuant to subsection (a) of this section shall be guilty of a Class C misdemeanor.

(c) Provided, however, any person who performs abortions, or his agent, shall furnish to the Bureau of Vital Statistics, on confidential forms furnished by the bureau, the following: (1) the number of abortions performed on each unemancipated and emancipated minor with written consent; (2) the number of abortions performed on each unemancipated and emancipated minor pursuant to juvenile or other court proceedings pursuant to Section 26-21-3(e); and (3) the number of abortions performed pursuant to Section 26-21-5 on each unemancipated and emancipated minor. Such reporting shall be provided annually as prescribed by the Bureau of Vital Statistics which shall be retained by the bureau for at least seven years. Such information prescribed shall include nonconfidential statistics, including but not limited to: age, race and education level of minor. (Acts 1987, No. 87-286, p. 397, § 8.)

CODE OF ALABAMA
1975

1995 Cumulative Supplement

ANNOTATED

Prepared by

The Editorial Staff of the Publishers

Under the Direction of

D. S. Tussey, R. W. Walter, W. L. Jackson, M. A. Sancilio,
J. H. Runkle, and L. A. Burckell

VOLUME 15A
1992 REPLACEMENT VOLUME

*Including Acts through the 1995 Regular Session and
annotations taken through Southern Reporter,
Second Series, Volume 652, page 1133*

**Place in Pocket of Corresponding Volume of Main Set.
This Supersedes Previous Supplement, Which
May Be Retained for Reference Purposes.**

The Michie Company
Law Publishers
Charlottesville, Virginia
1995

Preface

The general and permanent laws of the State of Alabama, as enacted during the 1995 Regular Session of the Legislature which are contained in the 1995 Cumulative Supplement to certain volumes of the Code and in the 1995 Replacement Volumes of the Code, although operative on their effective dates, will not be adopted and incorporated into the Code of Alabama 1975 until the passage of the annual codification act. The annual codification act is usually passed the year following the current legislative session. As to previous years' codification acts, see Volume 1 of this set.

THIS SUPPLEMENT CONTAINS

Constitutions:

All amendments to the Alabama Constitution of 1901 ratified through September 1, 1995.

All amendments proposed to the Alabama Constitution of 1901 which are subject to referendum and which had not been voted upon as of September 1, 1995.

Statutes:

All laws of a general and permanent nature enacted by the Alabama Legislature through the 1995 Regular Session of the Legislature. Local laws and general laws of local application are not included in this supplement.

Rules of Alabama Supreme Court:

Rules promulgated by the Supreme Court of Alabama through September 1, 1995.

Annotations:

Annotations or constructions of Alabama statutes and the 1901 Constitution of Alabama and amendments thereto by the Alabama Supreme Court, the Alabama Courts of Appeal, the Supreme Court of the United States and other federal courts, taken from the following:

Southern Reporter, Second Series, through volume 652, p. 1133.
Federal Reporter, Third Series, through volume 51, p. 287.
Federal Supplement, through volume 879, p. 1340.
Federal Rules Decisions, through volume 160, p. 274.
Bankruptcy Reporter, through volume 179, p. 985.
Supreme Court Reporter, through volume 115, p. 1731.
Opinions of the Clerk of the Supreme Court of Alabama.

References to:

Corpus Juris Secundum.
American Jurisprudence, Second Edition.
American Law Reports, First Series.
American Law Reports, Second Series.
American Law Reports, Third Series.
American Law Reports, Fourth Series.
American Law Reports, Fifth Series.

Cross references to related provisions of the Code and the Alabama Constitution of 1901.

References to applicable or related federal statutes.

Tables:

Acts of Legislature to 1975 Code.

3

Index:

A supplement to the general index to the statutes, constitutional amendments and rules contained in this supplement and the bound volumes of the Code of Alabama.

4

User's Guide

In order to assist both the legal profession and the layman in obtaining the maximum benefit from the Code of Alabama, a User's Guide has been included in Volume 1. This guide contains comments and information on the many features found within the Code of Alabama intended to increase the usefulness of this set of laws to the user. See Volume 1 of this set for the complete User's Guide.

CODE OF ALABAMA

1995 Cumulative Supplement

TITLE 26.

INFANTS AND INCOMPETENTS.

TABLE OF CONTENTS

CHAPTER 1.

GENERAL PROVISIONS.

§ 26-1-1. Age of majority designated as 19 years.

On the 19th anniversary of her birth, a year has passed from the time that the child was 18; the child then arrives at the age of 19 and is an adult for the purposes of subsection (a) of this section. Massey v. Massey, 597 So. 2d 1375 (Ala. Civ. App. 1992).

Cited in Alred v. State ex rel. Hill, 603 So. 2d 1082 (Ala. Civ. App. 1992); Swint v. State ABC Bd., 628 So. 2d 769 (Ala. Civ. App. 1993).

Collateral references.

Liability of guardian ad litem for infant party to civil suit for negligence in connection with suit. 14 ALR5th 929.

§ 26-1-2. Creation of durable power of attorney; effect of acts performed pursuant to durable power of attorney during period of disability, etc., of principal; appointment by court of guardian, etc., subsequent to execution of durable power of attorney; effect of death of principal upon agency relationship and validity of acts of person acting under power of attorney; execution, etc., of affidavit by person exercising power of attorney as to lack of knowledge of revocation, etc., of power of attorney.

Subsection (b) does not supersede common law for determining authority conferred. — Subsection (b) merely provides that the incapacity of the donor of a durable power of attorney does not change the effect of actions of the donee taken in conformity with the authority conferred by the power of attorney. It does not supersede the common law rules for determining the authority conferred by a power of attorney. Lamb v. Scott, 643 So. 2d 972 (Ala. 1994).

§ 26-1-2.1. Gifts by power of attorney.

(a) If any power of attorney or other writing either authorizes an attorney in fact or other agent to do, execute, or perform any act that the principal might or could do, or evidences the principal's intent to give the attorney in fact or agent full power to handle the principal's affairs or deal with the principal's property, the attorney in fact or agent shall have the power and authority to make gifts of any of the principal's property to any individuals, including the attorney in fact or agent, within the limits of the annual exclusion as provided by Section 2503(b) of Title 26 of the United States Code, and taking into account the availability of Section 2513 of Title 26 of the United States Code, as the same may from time to time be amended, or to organizations described in Sections 170(c) and 2522(a) of Title 26 of the United States Code, or corresponding future provisions of federal tax law, or both, as the attorney in fact or agent shall determine: (1) to be in the principal's best interest; (2) to be in the best interest of the principal's estate; or (3) that will reduce the estate tax payable on the principal's death; and is in accordance with the principal's personal history of making or joining in the making of lifetime gifts.

(b) Subsection (a) shall not in any way impair the right or power of any principal, by express words in the power of attorney or other writing, to further authorize, expand, or limit the authority of any attorney in fact or other agent to make gifts of the principal's property.

(c) This section is declaratory of Section 26-1-2 and shall not be construed to nullify any actions taken by any attorney in fact prior to May 6, 1994. (Acts 1994, 1st Ex. Sess., No. 94-802, p. 108, §§ 1-3.)

Effective date. — The act which added this section became effective May 6, 1994.

CHAPTER 2A.

ALABAMA UNIFORM GUARDIANSHIP AND PROTECTIVE PROCEEDINGS ACT.

Article 1.

General Provisions, Definitions and Jurisdiction of Court.

DIVISION 1.

SHORT TITLE, CONSTRUCTION, GENERAL PROVISIONS.

Sec.
26-2A-9. Preservation of powers and duties of existing curators; curators become conservators on January 1, 1997.

ARTICLE 1.

GENERAL PROVISIONS, DEFINITIONS AND JURISDICTION OF COURT.

Division 1.

Short Title, Construction, General Provisions.

§ 26-2A-1. Short title.

Collateral references.
Propriety of surgically invading incompetent

or minor for benefit of third party. 4 ALR5th
1000.

§ 26-2A-9. Preservation of powers and duties of existing curators; curators become conservators on January 1, 1997.

(a) A curator appointed pursuant to Chapter 7A of this title prior to August 7, 1995 and continuing in effect on August 7, 1995, is not terminated, although the statute under which the appointment was made is repealed by Acts 95-751. The curator shall continue in effect as the curator existed prior to Acts 95-751, with all of the powers and duties of the curator on August 7, 1995.

(b) If, on January 1, 1997, a curator is in existence pursuant to subsection (a), the curator on that date shall be considered a conservator as provided in Chapter 2A (commencing with Section 26-2A-1) of this title, with all the power and duties of a conservator as provided in that chapter. If the powers of a curator are limited by a court, the powers granted in this subsection are limited to the same extent. (Acts 1995, No. 95-751, § 2.)

Effective date. — The act which added this
section became effective August 7, 1995.

ARTICLE 2.

PROTECTION OF PERSONS UNDER DISABILITY AND THEIR PROPERTY.

Division 3.

Protection of Property of Persons Under Disability and Minors.

§ 26-2A-144. Petitions for orders subsequent to appointment.

Cited in Meadows v. Meadows, 603 So. 2d
884 (Ala. 1992).

CHAPTER 7A.

APPOINTMENT OF CURATORS.

REPEALED.

§§ 26-7A-1 through 26-7A-17. Repealed by Acts 1995, No. 95-751, § 1, effective August 7, 1995.

Code Commissioner's note. — Acts 1995, No. 95-751, which repealed this chapter, provides in § 2: "(a) A curator appointed pursuant to Chapter 7A of Title 26 prior to the effective date of this act [August 7, 1995] and continuing in effect on the date this act becomes effective, is not terminated, although the statute under which the appointment was made is repealed by this act. The curator shall continue in effect as the curator existed prior to this act, with all of the powers and duties of the curator on the effective date of this act.

"(b) If, on January 1, 1997, a curator is in existence pursuant to subsection (a), the curator on that date shall be considered a conservator as provided in Chapter 2A (commencing with Section 26-2A-1) of Title 26 of the Code of Alabama 1975, with all the power and duties of a conservator as provided in that chapter. If the powers of a curator are limited by a court, the powers granted in this subsection are limited to the same extent."

CHAPTER 8.

REMOVAL OF PERSON OR PROPERTY OF MINORS AND WARDS.

ARTICLE 1.

GENERAL PROVISIONS.

§ 26-8-1. Applicability of chapter.

Collateral references. — Propriety of surgically invading incompetent or minor for benefit of third party. 4 ALR5th 1000.

CHAPTER 10A.

ALABAMA ADOPTION CODE.

Sec.
26-10A-36. Advertisement as to adoption by persons, organizations, etc., not licensed by Department of Human Resources.

§ 26-10A-1. Short title.

Collateral references.
Attorney malpractice in connection with services related to adoption of child. 18 ALR5th 892.

§ 26-10A-5. Who may adopt.

Collateral references. — Adoption of child by same-sex partners. 27 ALR5th 54.

§ 26-10A-7. Persons whose consents or relinquishment are required.

I. GENERAL CONSIDERATION.

Collateral references.
Validity of birth parent's "blanket" consent to

adoption which fails to identify adoptive parents. 15 ALR5th 1.

§ 26-10A-22. Attorney participation and appointment of attorney for the adoptee or other party.

Collateral references. — Attorney malpractice in connection with services related to adoption of child. 18 ALR5th 892.

§ 26-10A-29. Name and status of adoptee.

Cited in Kernop v. Taylor, 628 So. 2d 707 (Ala. Civ. App. 1993).

§ 26-10A-36. Advertisement as to adoption by persons, organizations, etc., not licensed by Department of Human Resources.

It shall be unlawful for any person or persons, organizations, corporation, partnership, hospital, association, or any agency to advertise verbally, through print, electronic media, or otherwise that they will:

(1) Adopt children or assist in the adoption of children in violation of this chapter;

(2) Place or assist in the placement of children in foster homes, group homes, or institutions in violation of this chapter; or

(3) Pay or offer money or anything of value to the parents of a child in violation of Section 26-10A-34.

Any violation of this section shall be punished as a Class A misdemeanor. (Acts 1990, No. 90-554, p. 912, § 35.)

Code Commissioner's note. — This section is set out above to correct an error in the replacement volume.

CHAPTER 11.

LEGITIMATION OF CHILDREN.

§ 26-11-2. Procedure for legitimation by written declaration of father generally; notification of mother; filing of response; appointment of guardian ad litem; hearing; issuance of order by court; certification of minutes of court to Bureau of Vital Statistics.

Legitimation of father cannot be repudiated. — Where order found that parties were each guilty of misrepresentation and fraud upon the court in securing the order of legiti-

mation, and where it did not find the order to be void, but held that the motion was not filed within a "reasonable time" under Rule 60(b)(4), Alabama Rules of Civil Procedure, there was no error in the judgment of the court, even though it did find the order of legitimation to be void, and even though it has always been the law in this state that a void judgment may be vacated at any time. After receiving the important and special rights of a father, that action may not now be repudiated by the party on the ground that the court was without authority to give them to him. Hughes v. Hughes, 624 So. 2d 198 (Ala. Civ. App. 1993).

CHAPTER 13.

RELIEF OF MINOR CHILDREN FROM DISABILITIES OF NONAGE.

Emancipated son's college expenses. — A minor child who has had all disabilities removed, at his own request, so that he can manage his own affairs as an adult is no longer due support from his parents. The trial court erred in ordering the parents to contribute to their emancipated son's college expenses. B.A. v. State Dep't of Human Resources, 640 So. 2d 961 (Ala. Civ. App. 1994).

CHAPTER 14.

REPORTING OF CHILD ABUSE OR NEGLECT.

§ 26-14-1. Definitions.

For the purposes of this chapter, the following terms shall have the meanings respectively ascribed to them by this section:

(1) ABUSE. Harm or threatened harm to a child's health or welfare. Harm or threatened harm to a child's health or welfare can occur through nonaccidental physical or mental injury, sexual abuse or attempted sexual abuse or sexual exploitation or attempted sexual exploitation. "Sexual abuse" includes the employment, use, persuasion, inducement, enticement, or coercion of any child to engage in, or having a child assist any other person to engage in any sexually explicit conduct or any simulation of the conduct for the purpose of producing any visual depiction of the conduct; or the rape, molestation, prostitution, or other form of sexual exploitation of children, or incest with children as those acts are defined by Alabama law. "Sexual exploitation" includes allowing, permitting, or encouraging a child to engage in prostitution and allowing, permitting, encouraging or engaging in the obscene or pornographic photographing, filming, or depicting of a child for commercial purposes.

(2) NEGLECT. Negligent treatment or maltreatment of a child, including the failure to provide adequate food, medical treatment, supervision, clothing, or shelter.

(3) CHILD. A person under the age of 18 years.

(4) DULY CONSTITUTED AUTHORITY. The chief of police of a municipality or municipality and county; or the sheriff, if the observation of child abuse or neglect is made in an unincorporated territory; or the Department of Human

Resources; or any person, organization, corporation, group, or agency authorized and designated by the Department of Human Resources to receive reports of child abuse and neglect; provided, that a "duly constituted authority" shall not include an agency involved in the acts or omissions of the reported child abuse or neglect. (Acts 1975, No. 1124, p. 2213, § 1; Acts 1981, No. 81-615, p. 1031; Acts 1981, No. 81-789, p. 1387; Acts 1993, 1st Ex. Sess., No. 93-890, p. 162, § 2.)

The 1993, 1st Ex. Sess., amendment, effective February 27, 1994, substituted the language beginning "the employment" for "rape, incest and sexual molestation as those acts are defined by Alabama law" in the next-to-last sentence in subdivision (1); and rewrote subdivision (2).

Photography studio's report to the FBI. — Because there is a great need for protecting children from child abuse, studio's report to Federal Bureau of Investigation (FBI) was based on "reasonable cause," the studio was exempt from any liability in making report about customer's photographs, even though investigation did not reveal any evidence of child pornography. Hall v. Van's Photo, Inc., 595 So. 2d 1368 (Ala. 1992).

In making its report to police of suspicion that customer was involved in child pornography, photography studio did not have a duty to include that customer explained that nude photographs of her three-year-old son were to be used by an artist to cast a bronze statue. Hall v. Van's Photo, Inc., 595 So. 2d 1368 (Ala. 1992).

Cited in State Dep't of Human Resources v. Funk, 651 So. 2d 12 (Ala. Civ. App. 1994).

§ 26-14-2. Purpose of chapter.

Cited in Cure v. State, 600 So. 2d 415 (Ala. Crim. App. 1992).

§ 26-14-3. Mandatory reporting.

(a) All hospitals, clinics, sanitariums, doctors, physicians, surgeons, medical examiners, coroners, dentists, osteopaths, optometrists, chiropractors, podiatrists, nurses, school teachers and officials, peace officers, law enforcement officials, pharmacists, social workers, day care workers or employees, mental health professionals, or any other person called upon to render aid or medical assistance to any child, when the child is known or suspected to be a victim of child abuse or neglect, shall be required to report, or cause a report to be made of the same, orally, either by telephone or direct communication immediately, followed by a written report, to a duly constituted authority.

(b) When an initial report is made to a law enforcement official, the official subsequently shall inform the Department of Human Resources of the report so that the department can carry out its responsibility to provide protective services when deemed appropriate to the respective child or children.

(c) When the Department of Human Resources receives initial reports of suspected abuse or neglect involving discipline or corporal punishment committed in a public or private school or suspected abuse or neglect in a state-operated child residential facility, the Department of Human Resources shall transmit a copy of school reports to the law enforcement agency and residential facility reports to the law enforcement agency and the operating state agency which shall conduct the investigation. When the investigation is completed, a written report of the completed investigation shall contain the information required by the State Department of Human Resources which shall be submitted by the law enforcement agency or the state agency to the county department of human resources for entry into the state's central registry.

(d) Nothing in this chapter shall preclude interagency agreements between Departments of Human Resources, law enforcement, and other state agencies on procedures for investigating reports of suspected child abuse and neglect to provide for Departments of Human Resources to assist law enforcement and other state agencies in these investigations. (Acts 1965, No. 563, p. 1049, § 1; Acts 1967, No. 725, p. 1560; Acts 1975, No. 1124, p. 2213, § 1; Acts 1993, 1st Ex. Sess., No. 93-890, p. 162, § 3.)

The 1993, 1st Ex. Sess., amendment, effective February 27, 1994, substituted "the child" for "such child" in the middle of subsection (a); in subsection (b), substituted "an initial report" for "a report," substituted "the offi-cial" for "such official," and inserted "when deemed appropriate"; and added subsections (c) and (d).

Cited in State Dep't of Human Resources v. Funk, 651 So. 2d 12 (Ala. Civ. App. 1994).

§ 26-14-6.1. Duties and responsibilities for investigation of reports.

The duty and responsibility for the investigation of reports of suspected child abuse or neglect shall be as follows:

(1) Reports of suspected child abuse or neglect involving disciplinary or corporal punishment committed in a public or private school or kindergarten shall be investigated by law enforcement agencies.

(2) Reports of suspected child abuse or neglect committed in a state-operated child residential facility shall be investigated by law enforcement agencies.

(3) All other reports of suspected child abuse and neglect shall be investigated by the Department of Human Resources. (Acts 1993, 1st Ex. Sess., No. 93-890, p. 162, § 1.)

Effective date. — The act which added this section became effective February 27, 1994.

§ 26-14-7. Duties of Department of Human Resources.

"Cause shown" defined. — The words "cause shown" in subsection (c) of this section are construed to mean reasonable or probable cause shown, i.e., reasonable or probable cause shown to believe that there is or has been an abuse of a child or that a child is then delinquent or dependent. H.R. v. State Dep't of Human Resources, 612 So. 2d 477 (Ala. Civ. App. 1992).

Evidence of "cause shown" not sufficient. — Where a petition purporting a present "cause shown" pursuant to this section merely alleged that there had been two reports telephoned in to the Department of Human Resources (DHR) by an anonymous person that certain conditions existed or certain events affecting the children had occurred at the home of the mother and the reports had come in more than a month before an investigation was begun and investigative entry into the home was denied and it was another month before the petition was filed in court and another month expired before the court entered judgment on the report of the referee, the "cause shown" was unsworn hearsay and could, at best, present a mere suspicion which was not sufficient to rise to reasonable or probable cause for the department to enter the family's home and interview the children without parent's consent in its investigation of neglect and abuse. H.R. v. State Dep't of Human Resources, 612 So. 2d 477 (Ala. Civ. App. 1992).

Cited in State Dep't of Human Resources v. Funk, 651 So. 2d 12 (Ala. Civ. App. 1994).

§ 26-14-7.1. Due process rights for persons under investigation by department.

Any person who comes under investigation by the Department of Human Resources for the abuse or neglect of a child or children and who is employed by, serves as a volunteer for, holds a license or certificate for, or is connected with any facility, agency, or home which cares for and controls any children and which is licensed, approved, or certified by the state, operated as a state facility, or any public, private, or religious facility or agency that may be exempt from licensing procedures shall be granted the following due process rights by the Department of Human Resources:

(1) The department shall notify the alleged perpetrator that an investigation has commenced against him after such investigation has officially begun in accordance with written policies established by the Department of Human Resources. The notice shall be in writing and shall state the name of the child or children allegedly abused, the date or dates that the alleged abuse is thought to have occurred, and the substance of the person's actions which are alleged to be abusive. The department shall establish and maintain written policies outlining the specifics of such notification and other policies deemed necessary and prudent by the department to inform the alleged perpetrator of his rights and the procedures utilized by the department involving child abuse and neglect investigations.

(2) If the department conducts an investigation relating to child abuse/ neglect, the alleged perpetrator shall be notified of the investigator's conclusions.

(3) If the department's investigators conclude that child abuse/neglect is indicated, an investigative hearing may be held to confirm or reject the investigators conclusions.

(4) The alleged perpetrator shall be given ten departmental working days from the receipt of the notification of the investigator's conclusions to request a hearing, and such request must be in writing. If no such request is received in the department's office within ten departmental working days, the alleged perpetrator's opportunity for a hearing shall be considered waived by the department.

(5) The employer of an alleged perpetrator shall not be notified of the investigator's conclusions prior to a hearing or its waiver unless, in the opinion of the department's investigators, a child is in danger of abuse or neglect; in such case, any person in a position to discover, prevent or protect the child from his abuse or neglect may be informed of information gathered in the investigation prior to a requested investigative hearing for the alleged perpetrator.

(6) The alleged perpetrator shall be notified of the date, time, and place of any investigative hearing. Such hearing shall not be open to the public.

(7) The alleged perpetrator shall have the following rights at any departmental investigative hearing:

a. The right to present his case himself or be represented by legal counsel or any other person.

15

b. The right to present written evidence, oral testimony, and witnesses.

c. The right to be provided by the department a short and plain written statement of the matters asserted which will be presented at the hearing.

d. The right to review and copy at cost any written or recorded statement made by the alleged perpetrator to departmental personnel in the course of the child abuse/neglect investigation. This request must be made prior to the date for the hearing.

e. The right to review and copy at cost, before or during the hearing, the written material and other evidence in possession of the department which will be placed into evidence at the hearing.

f. The right to inspect any exculpatory evidence which may be in the possession of departmental investigators, and the right to be informed of such evidence if known by departmental investigators before the hearing; provided, that a request for such evidence is made at least five working days prior to the date set for the hearing.

g. The right to review and copy at cost all non-confidential department documents pertinent to the case, including written policies and rights.

h. The right to cross-examine witnesses testifying at the hearing.

i. The right to request issuance of subpoenas to witnesses and compel attendance. This request must be received no later than ten calendar days prior to the hearing, unless a shorter time is agreed upon by the hearing officer.

j. The right to review and copy at cost all documents in the official hearing file maintained by the hearing officer.

k. The right to have a hearing officer appointed who shall be disinterested, fair, and impartial.

(8) The Department of Human Resources or its investigative hearing officers shall have the power and authority to issue subpoenas to compel attendance by and production of documents from any witness. Subpoenas may be served in the same manner as subpoenas issued out of any circuit court. Where any witness has been summoned by the Department of Human Resources, its Commissioner or any of his agents, and said witness refuses to appear, testify, or produce records or documents as requested; then any circuit court in this state, or any judge thereof, on application, may issue an attachment for such person and compel him to comply with such order and the court or judge shall have power to punish for contempt in cases of disobedience of such order.

(9) The Department of Human Resources shall establish policies and written guidelines for the conduct and procedures involved in an investigative hearing. At such hearing, the fact that there was a finding by a juvenile court judge or by a criminal court that child abuse or neglect has occurred shall be presumptive evidence that the report should be marked indicated.

(10) The hearing officer shall notify the alleged perpetrator in writing of the hearing officer's decision.

(11) Results of investigative hearings:

a. If the hearing officer concludes that child abuse and/or neglect is "indicated," such findings and evidence shall be filed with the appropriate

16

district attorney and other law enforcement officials which the department may deem necessary.

b. The alleged perpetrator's employer or licensing/certifying agency or group may also be notified of the "indicated" findings. Such notification shall be marked "Confidential" and "To Be Used Only For The Purpose Of Discovery Or Preventing Child Abuse." The department shall establish written policies for notification of employers, prospective employers and licensing/certifying agencies or groups. (Acts 1992, 2nd Ex. Sess., No. 92-704, p. 176, § 1.)

§ 26-14-7.2. Child denied medical treatment due to parents' religious beliefs.

When an investigation of child abuse or neglect by the Department of Human Resources determines that a parent or legal guardian legitimately practicing his or her religious beliefs has not provided specific medical treatment for a child, the parent or legal guardian shall not be considered a negligent parent or guardian for that reason alone. This exception shall not preclude a court from ordering that medical services be provided to the child when the child's health requires it. (Acts 1993, 1st Ex. Sess., No. 93-890, p. 162, § 4.)

Effective date. — The act which added this section became effective August 31, 1993.

§ 26-14-8. Statewide central registry.

(a) For the purposes of this section, the following words shall have the following meanings, respectively:

(1) INDICATED. When credible evidence and professional judgment substantiates that an alleged perpetrator is responsible for child abuse or neglect.

(2) NOT INDICATED. When credible evidence and professional judgment does not substantiate that an alleged perpetrator is responsible for child abuse or neglect.

(b) The State Department of Human Resources shall establish a statewide central registry for reports of child abuse and neglect made pursuant to this chapter. The central registry shall contain, but shall not be limited to:

(1) All information in the written report;

(2) Record of the final disposition of the report, including services offered and services accepted;

(3) The names and identifying data, dates and circumstances of any persons requesting or receiving information from the registry;

(4) The plan for rehabilitative treatment; and

(5) Any other information which might be helpful in furthering the purposes of this chapter.

(c) The State Department of Human Resources shall establish and enforce reasonable rules and regulations governing the custody, use and preservation of the reports and records of child abuse and neglect. The use of such reports and records shall be limited to the purposes for which they are furnished and by the provisions of law under which they may be furnished. The reports and records of child abuse and neglect shall be confidential, and shall not be used or disclosed for any purposes other than:

(1) To permit their use to prevent or to discover abuse or neglect of children through the information contained therein; or

(2) For investigation of child abuse or neglect by the police or other law enforcement agency; or

(3) For use by a grand jury upon its determination that access to such reports and records is necessary in the conduct of its official business; or

(4) For use by a court where it finds that such information is necessary for the determination of an issue before the court; or

(5) For use by any person engaged in bona fide research who is authorized to have access to such information by the Commissioner of the State Department of Human Resources; or

(6) For use by any person authorized by a court to act as a representative for an abused or neglected child who is the subject of a report; or

(7) For use by a physician who has before him a child whom he reasonably suspects may be abused or neglected; or

(8) For use by an attorney or guardian ad litem in representing or defending a child or its parents or guardians in a court proceeding related to abuse or neglect of said child.

(d) The names of person or information in the investigative report placed on the state's central registry which may be made available to the alleged perpetrator's employer, prospective employer, or others are those cases that the Department of Human Resources or the investigative hearing officer has determined child abuse or neglect to be indicated; provided, however, that in all other cases a hearing officer may make a determination or finding regarding the facts of the case and that said facts are reasonably related to whether the alleged perpetrator should be allowed to have regular and substantial contact with children and that said facts should be shared in order to protect children from abuse or neglect in residential programs and/or day care facilities as defined under the Child Care Act, Sections 38-7-1 through 38-7-18.

(e) In the case of any child abuse or neglect investigation which is determined to be "not indicated," the alleged perpetrator may request after five years from the completion of the investigation that his or her name be expunged from the central registry so long as the Department of Human Resources has received no further reports concerning the alleged perpetrator during said five years, at which time the department shall expunge said name.

(f) Any violation of this provision of confidentiality shall be a Class A misdemeanor. (Acts 1975, No. 1124, p. 2213, § 1; Acts 1992, 2nd Ex. Sess., No. 92-704, p. 176, § 2.)

Primary goal of this section, etc.
A secondary goal of this section was to conform to the mandates of federal law. Cure v.

State, 600 So. 2d 415 (Ala. Crim. App.), cert. denied, 600 So. 2d 421 (Ala. 1992).
The primary goal of this section, which estab-

lishes a central registry at Department of Human Resources for reporting child abuse, is to provide for confidentiality. Jordan v. State, 607 So. 2d 333 (Ala. Crim. App. 1992).

Purpose. — The purpose of central registry which maintains reports of child abuse and neglect is to protect children from child abuse, and the information in the registry is confidential and shall not be disclosed except for those reasons enumerated in subdivisions (c)(1)-(8) of this section. Duncan v. State Dep't of Human Resources, 627 So. 2d 427 (Ala. Civ. App. 1993).

This section should not be read as an entitlement to mandatory discovery in a criminal case. Cure v. State, 600 So. 2d 415 (Ala. Crim. App.), cert. denied, 600 So. 2d 421 (Ala. 1992).

Cited in State Dep't of Human Resources v. Funk, 651 So. 2d 12 (Ala. Civ. App. 1994).

§ 26-14-11. Appointment of attorney to represent child.

Inapplicable to custody dispute in divorce decree modification hearing. — This section does not require the appointment of a guardian ad litem for children in a custody dispute arising in a divorce decree modification hearing. D.E.S. v. J.S., 603 So. 2d 1064 (Ala. Civ. App. 1992).

CHAPTER 15.

CHILD ABUSE GENERALLY.

§ 26-15-3. Torture, willful abuse, etc., of child under 18 years of age by responsible person.

Requirement of intentional conduct. — The child abuse offense requires intentional conduct ("willfully abuse . . . or otherwise willfully maltreat"), while the endangering offense requires negligent conduct ("fails to exercise reasonable diligence"). Pearson v. State, 601 So. 2d 1119 (Ala. Crim. App. 1992).

Time is not a material element of first degree rape, first degree sodomy, or child abuse. Cure v. State, 600 So. 2d 415 (Ala. Crim. App.), cert. denied, 600 So. 2d 421 (Ala. 1992).

Cited in State Dep't of Human Resources v. Funk, 651 So. 2d 12 (Ala. Civ. App. 1994).

§ 26-15-4. Effect of chapter upon existing rights or liabilities, pending prosecutions, etc.

Collateral references.
Running of limitations against action for civil damages for sexual abuse of child. 9 ALR5th 321.

CHAPTER 17.

ALABAMA UNIFORM PARENTAGE ACT.

§ 26-17-1. Short title.

Doctrine of res judicata not applicable to child's claim. — The doctrine of res judicata does not apply to the child's claim by way of the Alabama Uniform Parentage Act where there was no evidence that the child was a party or represented at the prior proceeding, in that the mother and child are not the same parties and are not in privity. State ex rel. T.G. v. B.L.J., 627 So. 2d 449 (Ala. Civ. App. 1993).

Ordering father to provide medical insurance coverage for the minor child is discretionary with the trial court. Abdel-Ghany v. Peppers, 600 So. 2d 1017 (Ala. Civ. App. 1992).

Cited in Ex parte J.E.W., 608 So. 2d 728 (Ala. 1992).

§ 26-17-3. Parent and child relationship — Relationship not dependent upon marriage.

Phrases such as minor child of the parties in a divorce decree constitute a finding that a party is the parent of the child. Quebedeaux v. Lord, 599 So. 2d 51 (Ala. Civ. App. 1992).

§ 26-17-4. Parent and child relationship — How established.

Evidence supported existence of parent-child relationship. — Although the trial court order expressly stated that husband was not the biological father of child, it found that the parent-child relationship existed and ample evidence supported that determination and father was properly awarded custody where the husband testified that after he and wife married, he filed an affidavit in the probate court acknowledging paternity in order that the child would have the same last name as the other children, the husband received the child into his home and has openly held the child out as his own, treating the child no differently from his other two children and the husband has created a legal presumption that he is the child's father and the wife has not rebutted that presumption. Black v. Black, 625 So. 2d 450 (Ala. Civ. App. 1993).

§ 26-17-5. Presumption of paternity; rebuttal.

(a) A man is presumed to be the natural father of a child if any of the following apply:

(1) He and the child's natural mother are or have been married to each other and the child is born during the marriage, or within 300 days after the marriage is terminated by death, annulment, declaration of invalidity, or divorce, or after a decree of separation is entered by a court.

(2) Before the child's birth he and the child's natural mother have attempted to marry each other by a marriage solemnized in apparent compliance with law, although the attempted marriage is or could be declared invalid, and

a. If the attempted marriage may be declared invalid only by a court, the child is born during the attempted marriage, or within 300 days after the termination of the attempted marriage by death, annulment, declaration of invalidity, or divorce; or

b. If the attempted marriage is invalid without a court order, the child is born within 300 days after the termination of cohabitation.

(3) After the child's birth, he and the child's natural mother have married, or attempted to marry, each other by a marriage solemnized in apparent compliance with the law although the attempted marriage is or could be declared invalid, and

a. He has acknowledged his paternity of the child in writing, the writing being filed with the appropriate court or the Office of Vital Statistics; or

b. With his consent, he is named as the child's father on the child's birth certificate; or

c. He is otherwise obligated to support the child either under a written voluntary promise or by court order.

(4) While the child is under the age of majority, he receives the child into his home or otherwise openly holds out the child as his natural child.

(5) He acknowledges his paternity of the child in a writing filed in accordance with provisions of the legitimation statute.

(6) He and the child's mother have executed an affidavit of paternity in accordance with the provisions of this chapter.

(b) A presumption of paternity under this section may be rebutted in an appropriate action only by clear and convincing evidence. In the event two or more conflicting presumptions arise, that which is founded upon the weightier considerations of public policy and logic, as evidenced by the facts, shall control. The presumption of paternity is rebutted by a court decree establishing paternity of the child by another man. (Acts 1984, No. 84-244, p. 375, § 5; Acts 1994, No. 94-705, p. 1362, § 1.)

The 1994 amendment, effective July 1, 1994, in subsection (a) added "any of the following apply" in the introductory language; added subdivision (6); and made nonsubstantive changes.

Alabama law presumes a man to be the father of a child if the child is born during the marriage of the natural mother and him; this presumption may only be overcome by clear and convincing evidence which tends to show that it was naturally, physically, or scientifically impossible for the husband to be the father. M.M. v. C.M., 600 So. 2d 316 (Ala. Civ. App. 1992).

Paternity is a proper issue in a divorce action.

The matter concerning the paternity of a child born during the marriage is a proper issue in a divorce action, and the presumption that the husband is the child's father may be rebutted at that time. This is especially true because a divorce decree which designates a child to be "of the parties" is a paternity determination and precludes the parties from disputing the child's paternity in the future. D.D. v. C.L.D., 600 So. 2d 265 (Ala. Civ. App. 1991); Powers v. State, 622 So. 2d 400 (Ala. Civ. App. 1993).

In a custody or divorce action, the issue of parentage is central to the disposition of the case; thus it is proper to gather evidence which would clearly rebut the presumption of paternity afforded to the husband when the child is born during the marriage. M.M. v. C.M., 600 So. 2d 316 (Ala. Civ. App. 1992).

Adjudication of paternity not binding on child unless child is party. — A paternity adjudication in a divorce action, which is necessary for purposes of support and inheritance, is res judicata to the parties in the divorce action, but not binding on the child unless the child is a party. Powers v. State, 622 So. 2d 400 (Ala. Civ. App. 1993).

Although presumed to be child, defendant not entitled to share under will. — Although defendant was legally presumed to be the child of testator's son, it did not necessarily follow that defendant's legal status as a lineal descendant of the testator entitled him to a share of the estate under the testator's will. Testamentary intent is the polestar in the construction of wills. The evidence in this case indicated that the testator believed that it was impossible for his son to be defendant's father. The testator never acknowledged defendant as a grandson, and he excluded defendant as a beneficiary under the trust agreement that he executed on the same day that he executed his will. Tierce v. Gilliam, 652 So. 2d 254 (Ala. 1994).

Mother may rebut presumption that husband is father of child. — The mother of a child may seek to rebut the strong presumption that her husband is the father of a child born during their marriage. D.D. v. C.L.D., 600 So. 2d 265 (Ala. Civ. App. 1991).

A mother of a child may bring a paternity action to rebut the strong presumption that her husband is the father of a child born during the parties' marriage. M.M. v. C.M., 600 So. 2d 316 (Ala. Civ. App. 1992).

Evidence sufficient to rebut presumption of paternity. — There was "clear and convincing evidence" pursuant to subdivision (a)(1) to rebut the presumption of paternity regarding the mother's husband where the overwhelming evidence indicated that the mother did not see her husband after he moved to Tennessee and that she did not spend any time with him; the evidence also clearly indicated that the deceased openly held the appellees out as his children and not only did the deceased claim to family members and to members of the community that the appellees were his children, there was evidence that he continued this relationship into the appellees' adulthood. Hampton v. Hampton, 597 So. 2d 233 (Ala. Civ. App. 1992).

Divorce judgment not binding on child. — Where child was not the son of husband, the judgment divorcing mother of child and husband did not adjudicate the issue of paternity so as to destroy the usual presumption that a child born or conceived during a marriage is the child of the mother's husband; nor was the divorce judgment binding on child because he was not joined as a party or represented by a guardian ad litem during the divorce proceedings. Tierce v. Ellis, 624 So. 2d 553 (Ala. 1993).

Where husband excluded as father, he would be dismissed as party. — Where there was sufficient clear and convincing evidence supporting trial court's judgments concerning husband's nonpaternity of child, it is axiomatic that because the husband was excluded as the child's father, he would be dismissed as a party to the subsequent paternity proceeding. D.D. v. C.L.D., 600 So. 2d 265 (Ala. Civ. App. 1991).

Daughter barred from claim. — Just as father would have been barred by the rule of repose from asserting the claim that he was not the father of third party, daughter was also barred by the rule of repose from claiming that third party was not the son of father and therefore, was not an heir to the estate. Tierce v. Ellis, 624 So. 2d 553 (Ala. 1993).

§ 26-17-6. Action to determine father and child relationship; who may bring action; when action may be brought; stay until birth; adopted children.

(a) A child, a child's natural mother, or a man presumed to be the child's father under subdivision (1), (2), or (3) of Section 26-17-5(a), may bring an action within five years of the birth of the child for the purpose of declaring the existence of the father and child relationship presumed under subdivision (1), (2), or (3) of Section 26-17-5(a); or

(b) Any interested party may bring an action at any time for the purpose of determining the existence or non-existence of the father and child relationship presumed under subdivision (4) or (5) or (6) of Section 26-17-5(a).

(c) An action to determine the existence of the father and child relationship with respect to a child who has no presumed father under Section 26-17-5 may be brought by the child, the mother, or personal representative of the child, the public authority chargeable by law with support of the child, the personal representative or a parent of the mother if the mother has died, a man alleged or alleging himself to be the father, or the personal representative or a parent of the alleged father if the alleged father has died or is a minor.

(d) If an action under this section is brought before the birth of the child, all proceedings shall be stayed until after the birth, except service of process and the taking of depositions to perpetuate testimony.

(e) If the child has been adopted, an action may not be brought. (Acts 1984, No. 84-244, p. 375, § 6; Acts 1994, No. 94-705, p. 1362, § 1.)

The 1994 amendment, effective July 1, 1994, substituted "the child's father" for "its father" in subsection (a); inserted "or (6)" in subsection (b); and made nonsubstantive changes.

I. GENERAL CONSIDERATION.

Standing to bring paternity action.
A mother of a child may bring a paternity action to rebut the strong presumption that her husband is the father of a child born during the parties' marriage. M.M. v. C.M., 600 So. 2d 316 (Ala. Civ. App. 1992).

Because a paternity claim is equitable in nature and because decedent could have brought a paternity action but for his death the claim survived his death and the personal representative had standing to bring the paternity action. Ex parte L.F.B., 599 So. 2d 1179 (Ala. 1992).

The legislature could hardly be more clear in addressing when a personal representative for the father may bring an action to determine the father and child relationship, that is, when there is no presumed paternity; the legislature explicitly chose not to grant standing to a personal representative when there is a presumption of paternity. L.F.B. v. K.M.M. ex rel. Sarris, 599 So. 2d 1178 (Ala. Civ. App. 1991), rev'd on other grounds, 599 So. 2d 1179 (Ala. 1992).

State may prosecute action for any party who files claim. — Where mother of child in question claimed that because plaintiff was the person claimed to be the father or the person alleged to owe a duty of support, he should have been realigned as the defendant even though he brought the action, this section did not require that he be the defendant. The second sentence of § 26-17-7 is unambiguous and clearly allows the State of Alabama to prosecute the action for the party who filed claim. Pate v. State ex rel. Corkren, 526 So. 2d 30 (Ala. Civ. App. 1988).

Cited in S.E.B. v. J.H.B., 605 So. 2d 1230 (Ala. Civ. App. 1992).

§ 26-17-7. Style of proceedings; prosecution of proceedings.

Actions commenced under this chapter by the Department of Human Resources shall be in the name of the State of Alabama on relation of the complaining witness or party against the person claimed to be the father or against the person alleged to owe a duty of support as the defendant. In any action brought by the department, the district attorney, special prosecutor, or attorney otherwise authorized to represent the State of Alabama shall appear and prosecute the proceedings brought under this chapter. (Acts 1984, No. 84-244, p. 375, § 7; Acts 1992, 2nd Ex. Sess., No. 92-714, p. 211, § 1.)

Cross references. — As to provisions relating to right to bring an action to establish an order of retroactive support, see § 30-3-110 et seq.

I. GENERAL CONSIDERATION.

Requirements of § 26-17-7 address a "joinder" type issue rather than jurisdiction. — The general substance of this section is such that it effectively makes the state a party that must, in a manner, be "joined." On the analogous subject discussed in A.R.C.P., Rule 19, of the joinder of "persons needed for just adjudication," such a joinder issue does not relate to whether a court has the legal authority to hear a particular type of case, i.e., it is not a "subject matter" jurisdiction question. Ex parte J.E.W., 608 So. 2d 728 (Ala. 1992).

Trial court in paternity proceedings, absent action by a party to properly involve the state, should have adhered to the requirements of this section. However, the failure of the court to do so did not render its judgment void for a lack of subject matter jurisdiction; this is not a question of subject matter jurisdiction. Ex parte J.E.W., 608 So. 2d 728 (Ala. 1992).

State may prosecute action for any party who files claim. — Where mother of child in question claimed that because plaintiff was the person claimed to be the father or the person alleged to owe a duty of support, he should have been realigned as the defendant even though he brought the action, this section did not require that he be the defendant. The second sentence of § 26-17-7 is unambiguous and clearly allows the State of Alabama to prosecute the action for the party who filed the claim. Pate v. State ex rel. Corkren, 526 So. 2d 30 (Ala. Civ. App. 1988).

Cited in Ex parte W.Y., 605 So. 2d 1175 (Ala. 1992).

§ 26-17-10. Jurisdiction; venue; where complaint filed; process; conduct of hearing; jury.

(a) The causes of action provided by this chapter shall be brought in the juvenile or family court division of the district or circuit court and wherever used in this chapter the word "court" shall mean the juvenile or family court division of the district or circuit court and specifically shall include any district or circuit court judge otherwise sitting in one of these divisions.

(b) A defendant who resides in this state thereby submits to the jurisdiction of the courts of this state as to an action brought under this chapter.

(c) A person who is a nonresident of this state and who has sexual intercourse in this state thereby submits to the jurisdiction of the courts of this state as to an action brought under this chapter with respect to a child who may have been conceived by that act of sexual intercourse. Jurisdiction over a nonresident may be acquired only by personal service of summons outside this state or by certified mail with proof of actual receipt.

(d) A defendant who resides in this state thereby submits to the jurisdiction of the courts of this state as to a uniform reciprocal enforcement of support action filed in this state by an initiating state for the purpose of establishing paternity. If the defendant asserts as a defense that he is not the father of the child for whom support is sought and it appears to the court that the defense is not frivolous, and if both parties are present at the hearing or if proof required in the case indicates the presence of either or both is not necessary, the court shall adjudicate the issue of paternity. The appropriate provisions of this chapter shall apply to such actions. Upon determination of paternity or nonpaternity, the appropriate sections of the Reciprocal State Enforcement of Duty to Support Act (§ 30-4-80 et seq.) shall apply.

(e) The court shall retain jurisdiction of the cause for the purpose of entering such other and further orders as changing circumstances of the parties may in justice and equity require.

(f) The complaint for paternity or nonsupport shall be filed in the county in which the child resides or the county in which the defendant resides.

(g) Process directed to the defendant shall issue forthwith requiring the defendant to file written pleadings to the complaint in the manner prescribed by appropriate court rules. Once service of process is executed, if any defendant fails to file his or her answer or otherwise appear in an action commenced under this section within the time period prescribed by law, the Alabama Rules of Civil Procedures, or as ordered by the court, the court shall enter an order of default against him or her upon proper request and proof of the allegations.

(h) The court in which the action originated shall determine both the law and the facts without the intervention of a jury. A trial by jury may be had only as provided under Section 26-17-20. (Acts 1984, No. 84-244, p. 375, § 10; Acts 1994, No. 94-705, p. 1362, § 1.)

The 1994 amendment, effective July 1, 1994, added the last sentence in subsection (g).

An action brought under the Uniform Parentage Act is an equitable action, and the right to a jury trial thereunder is purely a statutory creation of the legislature. Ex parte L.F.B., 599 So. 2d 1179 (Ala. 1992).

As a general rule, the right to a jury trial attaches to legal issues only; by providing a right to a jury trial in paternity cases, the legislature has created an exception to this rule. Ex parte L.F.B., 599 So. 2d 1179 (Ala. 1992).

Cited in Ex parte J.E.W., 608 So. 2d 728 (Ala. 1992); Valley Forge Ins. Co. v. Alexander, 640 So. 2d 925 (Ala. 1994).

§ 26-17-11. Parties; representation of minor child; aligning parties.

Paternity suit. — The statute expressly contemplates situations in which a minor may be represented in a paternity suit without the appointment of a guardian ad litem. Ex parte W.Y., 605 So. 2d 1175 (Ala. 1992).

Determination of whether minor was represented. — The trial judge could properly consider not only the styles of the pleadings and notices, but the general conduct of the parties and counsel and the overall posture of the case in determining whether minor was represented. Ex parte W.Y., 605 So. 2d 1175 (Ala. 1992).

§ 26-17-12. Genetic tests; selection and compensation of experts; admissibility.

(a) Upon application of the defendant in a paternity proceeding or any other party to the action, the court shall order the mother, child and defendant to submit to one or more genetic tests to assist the court in determining paternity of the child. Whenever the court orders any genetic test to be performed and any of the persons whose genetic sample is to be taken and tested refuses to submit to the test, that fact shall be disclosed upon the trial, unless good cause is shown for not doing so.

(b) Any tests shall be made by an expert qualified in genetic testing who shall be approved by the court. The expert may be called by the court or any party as a witness to testify to the genetic test results and shall be subject to cross-examination by the parties. The genetic test results may be admitted into evidence by the defendant, the plaintiff, or the state. Genetic testing methods include, but are not limited to, the human leukocyte antigen test. If more than one genetic test is performed and the results are conflicting, none of the genetic test results shall be admissible as evidence of paternity or nonpaternity.

(c) Any objection to the admission into evidence or objection to the reliability of any genetic testing results performed on the parties shall be made in writing by the party contesting the admission at least 15 days prior to any hearing at which the results may be introduced into evidence. In the event the results of any genetic test are not made available in time for the party to submit a written objection as provided above, the court shall grant a request for continuance of the proceedings to allow the party adequate time to make a proper objection under this section. If the results of any test were available to a party in time for the party to object to the genetic test results within 15 days and no objection was made, or if a request for a continuance is not made prior to or at the hearing as provided in the preceding sentence, the test results shall be admissible into evidence without the need for foundation testimony or any other proof of authenticity or accuracy.

(d) Compensation of each expert witness shall be paid as the court shall order. The court shall order said compensation to be paid prior to the administration of the genetic test. (Acts 1984, No. 84-244, p. 375, § 12; Acts 1994, No. 94-705, p. 1362, § 1.)

The 1994 amendment, effective July 1, 1994, substituted "genetic test" for "blood test" throughout the section; in subsection (a) deleted the former second sentence which read "No such blood test shall be taken before the child reaches the age of six months" and in the present second sentence substituted "performed" for "taken", inserted "sample" and inserted "and tested"; added present subsection (c); and made nonsubstantive changes.

Cross references. — For subsection (b) of this section being commented on by new Rule 901, Alabama Rules of Evidence, effective January 1, 1996, see the Advisory Committee's Notes to new Rule 901 in the 1995 Cumulative Supplement to Volume 23.

I. GENERAL CONSIDERATION.

Blood tests mandatory.
Where in a divorce action the mother alleged in her pleadings that the husband was not the biological father of the child and in her amended complaint, the mother cited the Alabama Uniform Parentage Act (AUPA) and Alabama case law as grounds for a court order compelling blood testing of the husband, it was incumbent upon the trial court to order blood testing of the husband. S.E.B. v. J.H.B., 605 So. 2d 1230 (Ala. Civ. App. 1992).

Trial court properly failed to order blood tests. — The purpose of this section is to assist the court in determining paternity of the child. However, where trial court, based on the evidence before it at trial, made a determination of the paternity of the child prior to the filing of the post-trial motion and prior to the request for blood tests, there was no error or abuse of discretion in the trial court's failure to order blood tests. Price v. Shields, 599 So. 2d 1202 (Ala. Civ. App. 1992).

Cited in State ex rel. D.K. v. R.T., 599 So. 2d 627 (Ala. Civ. App. 1992); M.M. v. C.M., 600 So. 2d 316 (Ala. Civ. App. 1992).

§ 26-17-13. Evidence relating to paternity; refusal to testify; immunity; evidence of intercourse with other men.

(a) Evidence relating to paternity may include any of the following:

(1) Evidence of sexual intercourse between the mother and alleged father at any possible time of conception.

(2) An expert's opinion concerning the statistical probability of the alleged father's paternity based upon the duration of the mother's pregnancy.

(3) Genetic test results, weighed in accordance with evidence, if available, of the statistical probability of the alleged father's paternity. Genetic test results which indicate a 97 percent or greater probability that the alleged father is the biological or natural father of the minor child shall create a presumption of paternity that the alleged father is in fact the father of the child. This presumption may be rebutted only by clear and convincing evidence.

(4) Medical or anthropological evidence relating to the alleged father's paternity of the child based on tests performed by experts. If a man has been identified as a possible father of the child, the court may, and upon request of a party shall, require the child, the mother, and the man to submit to appropriate tests.

(5) All other evidence relevant to the issue of paternity of the child.

(b) Upon refusal of any witness, including a party, to testify under oath or produce evidence, or submit to genetic testing, the court may order him to testify under oath and produce evidence, including genetic testing, concerning all relevant facts. If the refusal is upon the ground that his testimony or evidence might tend to incriminate him, the court shall grant him immunity from all criminal liability on account of the testimony or evidence he is required to produce. An order granting immunity bars prosecution of the witness for any offense shown in whole or in part by testimony or evidence he is required to produce, except for perjury committed in his testimony. The refusal of a witness, who has been granted immunity to obey an order to testify or produce evidence shall be punishable as a civil contempt of the court.

(c) In an action against an alleged father, evidence offered by the alleged father with respect to another man who is not subject to the jurisdiction of the court concerning his sexual intercourse with the mother at or about the probable time of conception of the child is admissible in evidence only if the alleged father has undergone and made available to the court genetic tests the results of which do not exclude the possibility of the alleged father's paternity of the child. A man who is identified and is subject to the jurisdiction of the court shall be made a defendant in the action. (Acts 1984, No. 84-244, p. 375, § 13; Acts 1994, No. 94-705, p. 1362, § 1.)

The **1994 amendment**, effective July 1, 1994, substituted "genetic test" for "blood test" throughout; in subsection (a) added "any of the following" in the introductory language, and added the last two sentences in subdivision (3);

in subsection (b), in the first sentence inserted "or submit to genetic testing" and inserted "including genetic testing"; and made nonsubstantive changes.

§ 26-17-14. Orders — Determinative for all purposes; provision for support; statement of jurisdiction in case of out-of-state service; new birth certificate; other provisions; how support to be paid; amount of support; proof required for support order.

Final judgment in paternity suit must include order of child support payments. — A final judgment in a paternity suit must include an order of child support payments; in

the absence of a final judgment, no appeal will lie. Mitchell v. State ex rel. Wells, 617 So. 2d 684 (Ala. Civ. App. 1992).

§ 26-17-15. Orders — Enforcement.

(a) If the existence of the father and child relationship is declared, or paternity or a duty of support has been acknowledged or adjudicated under this chapter, prior law or applicable sections of the Criminal Code, the obligation of the father may be enforced in the same or other proceedings by the mother, the child, the public authorities that have furnished or may furnish the reasonable expenses of pregnancy, confinement, education, or support, or by any other person, including a private agency, to the extent these expenses have been or are being furnished.

(b) Pursuant to the Uniform Enforcement of Foreign Judgments Act, Sections 6-9-230 et seq., a court in this state shall give full faith and credit to a paternity determination of any other state whether established through voluntary acknowledgment, administrative processes, or judicial process which paternity determination shall be enforced and otherwise treated in the same manner as a paternity determination of this state.

(c) The court shall order payments to be made to a person, corporation, agency designated to administer them under the supervision of the court, or the public authority which has furnished or may furnish support for the child including but not limited to monetary and medical payments.

(d) Willful failure to obey the judgment or order of the court is a civil contempt of the court. All sanctions for enforcement of judgments apply. (Acts 1984, No. 84-244, p. 375, § 15; Acts 1994, No. 94-705, p. 1362, § 1.)

The **1994 amendment,** effective July 1, 1994, added subsection (b); and redesignated former subsections (b) and (c) as present subsections (c) and (d).

§ 26-17-20. Appeals.

I. GENERAL CONSIDERATION.

Either party may appeal. — Alabama's Uniform Parentage Act provides that either party to a paternity action may appeal from a final judgment rendered in the juvenile or family court to the circuit court for a trial de novo and for a jury trial. However, the fact that Alabama's legislature has created this right to jury trial in paternity cases does not in itself signify that paternity actions are legal in nature. Ex parte L.F.B., 599 So. 2d 1179 (Ala. 1992).

An action brought under the Uniform

Parentage Act is an equitable action, and the right to a jury trial thereunder is purely a statutory creation of the legislature. Ex parte L.F.B., 599 So. 2d 1179 (Ala. 1992).

As a general rule, the right to a jury trial attaches to legal issues only; by providing a right to a jury trial in paternity cases, the legislature has created an exception to this rule. Ex parte L.F.B., 599 So. 2d 1179 (Ala. 1992).

Cited in Abdel-Ghany v. Peppers, 600 So. 2d 1017 (Ala. Civ. App. 1992); Ex parte W.Y., 605 So. 2d 1175 (Ala. 1992).

§ 26-17-22. Hospital paternity acknowledgement program.

(a) The natural mother and father of a child born to a woman who was unmarried at the time of birth and had not been married or attempted to be married within 300 days prior to the birth may, at any time and place prior to the child's 19th birthday, state and acknowledge that they are the natural parents of the child in an affidavit of paternity signed by both parties before a notary public. The affidavit shall be on a form prescribed by rule of court and shall include the Social Security number and current address of each parent, a listing of the rights and responsibilities of acknowledging paternity, including the duty to financially support the child, and instruction for filing the affidavit with the Office of Vital Statistics.

(b) The affidavit of paternity shall be a legally sufficient basis for establishing an obligation for child support and for the expenses of the mother's pregnancy and confinement. The affidavit may be admitted as evidence of paternity in any action to establish a support order or an adjudication of paternity.

(c) Hospitals that have a licensed obstetric care unit or are licensed to provide obstetric services or licensed birthing centers associated with a hospital shall provide to the mother and alleged father, if he is present in the hospital, during the period immediately preceding or following the birth of a child to an unmarried woman in the hospital, all of the following: (1) Written materials about paternity establishment. (2) Form affidavits of paternity for the purposes of subsection (a) above. (3) A written description of the rights and responsibilities of acknowledging paternity. (4) An opportunity, prior to discharge from the hospital, to speak with a trained person made available through the Department of Human Resources, either by telephone or in person, who can clarify information and answer questions about paternity establishment. The Department of Human Resources shall make materials available without cost to the hospitals. If the mother and father complete the affidavit in the hospital, the hospital shall send the affidavit of paternity to the Office of Vital Statistics with required birth certificate information within five days of the birth of the child. Hospitals may be reimbursed by the Department of Human Resources up to the amount allowable by federal regulations for each completed affidavit. A hospital shall be immune from civil or criminal liability for actions taken pursuant to the requirements of this section.

(d) Notwithstanding any law to the contrary, the affidavit of paternity shall be accepted by the Office of Vital Statistics for purposes of listing the father's name on the child's birth certificate.

(e) If a birth certificate has been filed in the Office of Vital Statistics, listing a father of the child, no new birth certificate can be established by the Office of Vital Statistics based on an affidavit of paternity received subsequently by that office unless a determination of paternity has been made by a court of competent jurisdiction or following adoption.

(f) The affidavit of paternity shall be released by the Office of Vital Statistics to the Department of Human Resources upon request by the department and payment of any fee required by the Office of Vital Statistics for the purpose of child support enforcement or any other lawful purpose without the necessity of a court order. (Acts 1994, No. 94-705, p. 1362, § 2.)

Effective date. — The act which added this section became effective July 1, 1994.

CHAPTER 17A.

REOPENING OF PATERNITY CASE BASED ON SCIENTIFIC EVIDENCE.

Effective date. — The act which added this chapter became effective April 26, 1994.

§ 26-17A-1. Reopening of paternity case.

(a) Upon petition of the defendant in a paternity proceeding where the defendant has been declared the legal father, the case shall be reopened if there is scientific evidence presented by the defendant that he is not the father. The court shall admit into evidence any scientific test recognized by the court that has been conducted in accordance with established scientific principles or the court may order a blood test, or a Deoxyribose Nucleic Acid test of the mother, father, and child. Whenever the court orders a test and any of the persons to be tested refuse to submit to the test, the fact shall be disclosed at the trial, unless good cause is shown.

(b) The test shall be made by a qualified expert approved by the court. The expert may be called by the court or any party as a witness to testify to the test results and shall be subject to cross-examination by the parties. The test results may be admitted into evidence. If more than one test is performed and the results are conflicting, none of the test results shall be admissible as evidence of paternity or nonpaternity.

(c) Compensation of the expert witness shall be paid by the petitioner.

(d) In the event the child has been adopted the matter of paternity may not be reopened under this chapter. (Acts 1994, No. 94-633, p. 1177, § 1.)

§ 26-17A-2. Claim for damages against court rendering initial order of paternity.

In any decree setting aside an order of paternity pursuant to this chapter, there shall be no claim for damages against the court rendering the initial order of paternity nor any reimbursement or recoupment of money or damages against the mother, the State, or any employee or agent of the State. (Acts 1994, No. 94-633, p. 1177, § 2.)

CHAPTER 18.

CHILD PROTECTION.

The Child Protection Act enumerates only some of many factors, etc.

In determining whether to terminate parental rights, factors listed in the Child Protection Act of 1984 are nonexclusive; the trial court may consider any factors that are relevant to a child's welfare. E.M. v. State Dep't of Human Resources, 612 So. 2d 486 (Ala. Civ. App. 1992).

§ 26-18-7. Grounds for termination of parental rights; factors considered; presumption arising from abandonment.

I. General Consideration.
II. Right of Parents to Custody; Best Interest of Child Controls.
III. Decision to Terminate Rights.
IV. Illustrative Cases.

I. GENERAL CONSIDERATION.

Decision to terminate parental rights presumed correct on appeal.

The trial court's decision in proceedings to terminate parental rights is presumed to be correct when the decision is based upon ore tenus evidence, and such a decision based upon such evidence will be set aside only if the record shows it to be plainly and palpably wrong. Ex parte State Dep't of Human Resources, 624 So. 2d 589 (Ala. 1993).

Standard of review.

Parental rights may be terminated when a trial court finds from clear and convincing evidence, competent, material and relevant in nature, that the parents of a child are unable or unwilling to discharge their responsibilities to and for the child. B.R.M. v. State Dep't of Human Resources, 626 So. 2d 646 (Ala. Civ. App. 1993).

Constitutional issues not raised in the trial court cannot be considered for the first time on appeal. D.W.W. v. State Dep't of Human Resources, 607 So. 2d 240 (Ala. Civ. App. 1992).

Cited in D.H. v. State Dep't of Human Resources, 600 So. 2d 273 (Ala. Civ. App. 1992); N.R. v. State Dep't of Human Resources, 606 So. 2d 161 (Ala. Civ. App. 1992); J.R. v. D.A.M., 615 So. 2d 609 (Ala. Civ. App. 1992); Talley v. Oliver, 628 So. 2d 690 (Ala. Civ. App. 1993); B.O. v. Department of Human Resources, 628 So. 2d 805 (Ala. Civ. App. 1993); D.D. v. State Dep't of Human Resources, 628 So. 2d 718 (Ala. Civ. App. 1993); W.M. v. State Dep't of Human Resources, 634 So. 2d 143 (Ala. Civ. App. 1993); G.G.N. v. State Dep't of Human Resources, 634 So. 2d 552 (Ala. Civ. App. 1993); M.H.S. v. State Dep't of Human Resources, 636 So. 2d 419 (Ala. Civ. App. 1994); T.M.S. v. Elmore County Dep't of Human Resources, 647 So. 2d 746 (Ala. Civ. App. 1994); K.H. v. State Dep't of Human Resources, 648 So. 2d 612 (Ala. Civ. App. 1994).

Collateral references. — Parent's use of drugs as factor in award of custody of children, visitation rights, or termination of parental rights. 20 ALR5th 534.

II. RIGHT OF PARENTS TO CUSTODY; BEST INTEREST OF CHILD CONTROLS.

Parent has prima facie right to custody of child.

In accord with the third paragraph in the bound volume. See M.C. v. L.B., 607 So. 2d 1267 (Ala. Civ. App. 1992).

A parent has a prima facie right to custody of his or her child, and this right can be overcome only by clear and convincing evidence that the child's best interests would be served by permanently removing the child from the parent's custody. R.C.M. v. State Dep't of Human Resources, 601 So. 2d 100 (Ala. Civ. App. 1991).

Every parent has a prima facie right to the custody of his or her child; this prima facie right can be overcome only by clear and convincing evidence that the child's best interests would be served by removing the child from the parent's custody. H.M.W. v. Mobile County Dep't of Human Resources, 631 So. 2d 1049 (Ala. Civ. App. 1993).

Best interest of child controlling.

In child custody cases the overriding consideration is the best interest of the child. State Dep't of Human Resources v. L.W., 597 So. 2d 703 (Ala. Civ. App. 1992).

The best interest of the child is the primary consideration in a parental rights termination proceeding. R.C.M. v. State Dep't of Human Resources, 601 So. 2d 100 (Ala. Civ. App. 1991).

It is the consideration for the best interests of the child that lies at the heart of every proceeding to terminate parental rights. H.M.W. v. Mobile County Dep't of Human Resources, 631 So. 2d 1049 (Ala. Civ. App. 1993).

In determining best interest of child, etc.

In accord with the bound volume. See J.L.B. v. State Dep't of Human Resources, 608 So. 2d 1367 (Ala. Civ. App. 1992).

Loss of custody of other children. — Because the child's best interest is controlling in a termination proceeding, the trial court may consider a parent's loss of custody of other children. Ex parte State Dep't of Human Resources, 624 So. 2d 589 (Ala. 1993).

Effect of infanticide on rehabilitation efforts. — Whether rehabilitation of a mother who has killed a child is possible is highly problematical; under such circumstances, subdivision (a)(6) of this section would have no application. T.T. v. State Dep't of Human Resources, 625 So. 2d 808 (Ala. Civ. App. 1993).

III. DECISION TO TERMINATE RIGHTS.

Evidence supporting termination, etc.

The termination of parental rights requires clear and convincing evidence that termination would be in the child's best interest. State Dep't of Human Resources v. L.W., 597 So. 2d 703 (Ala. Civ. App. 1992).

The trial court is given the authority to terminate parental rights if it finds, from clear and convincing evidence, that the parents are unable or unwilling to discharge their responsibilities. L.F. v. Department of Human Resources, 597 So. 2d 1380 (Ala. Civ. App. 1992).

Two-pronged test.

In accord with the second paragraph of the bound volume. See M.C. v. L.B., 607 So. 2d 1267 (Ala. Civ. App. 1992).

In accord with the fourth paragraph in the bound volume. See L.G. v. State Dep't of Human Resources, 603 So. 2d 1100 (Ala. Civ. App. 1992).

Where termination is sought by a nonparent, a two-pronged test must be applied; the trial court first must find the child to be dependent and then determine that all viable alternatives to termination have been considered and rejected. State Dep't of Human Resources v. L.W., 597 So. 2d 703 (Ala. Civ. App. 1992).

When State is a party in case to terminate parental rights, the trial court must apply to a two-pronged test in determining whether to terminate parental rights: The trial court must find that the child is dependent, and, upon a finding of a dependency, the trial court must determine that there are no other viable alternatives to termination of parental rights.

B.R.M. v. State Dep't of Human Resources, 626 So. 2d 646 (Ala. Civ. App. 1993).

Two-pronged test applied where nonparent is petitioner. — When a nonparent (including the state) is the petitioner, the trial court must establish that the child is dependent; and, upon a finding of dependency, the trial court must determine that there are no other viable alternatives to termination of parental rights. B.S. v. Catholic Social Servs., 628 So. 2d 682 (Ala. Civ. App. 1993).

Where a nonparent is the petitioner to terminate parental rights, the trial court's determination is governed by the application of a two-pronged test. First, the trial court must conclude from clear and convincing evidence that the child is dependent, and second, the court must consider and reject all other viable alternatives to termination of parental rights, so that it can conclude that the termination is in the child's best interests. H.M.W. v. Mobile County Dep't of Human Resources, 631 So. 2d 1049 (Ala. Civ. App. 1993).

Findings required for termination of rights, etc.

In accord with the bound volume. See J.L.B. v. State Dep't of Human Resources, 608 So. 2d 1367 (Ala. Civ. App. 1992).

If clear and convincing evidence reveals that the parent cannot, or is unwilling to, discharge his or her responsibilities, parental rights may be terminated. A.N.S. v. K.C., 628 So. 2d 734 (Ala. Civ. App. 1993).

Detailed findings not required. — Although the Court of Civil Appeals seemed to indicate in its opinion that the trial court was required to make written findings regarding whether the conditions were proper for rearing an infant and regarding whether the conditions were likely to change in the "foreseeable future," there is no such requirement in the Child Protection Act. The Court of Civil Appeals had previously held that detailed findings in a termination order are preferable, but are not required. Ex parte State Dep't of Human Resources, 624 So. 2d 589 (Ala. 1993).

The trial court is given the authority to terminate parental rights if it finds from clear and convincing evidence that the parents are unable or unwilling to discharge their responsibilities. R.C.M. v. State Dep't of Human Resources, 601 So. 2d 100 (Ala. Civ. App. 1991).

No absolute requirement to find parent unfit. — There is no absolute requirement for a trial court to specifically find a parent to be unfit in these proceedings. M.S. v. State Dep't of Human Resources, 648 So. 2d 584 (Ala. Civ. App. 1994).

Considerations of the trial court. — Some of the considerations regarding termina-

tion which the trial court is required to use are whether the parents have abandoned the child, whether the parents have problems with drugs or alcohol, and whether reasonable efforts to rehabilitate the parents have failed. R.C.M. v. State Dep't of Human Resources, 601 So. 2d 100 (Ala. Civ. App. 1991).

Some of the considerations which the trial court is required to use in deciding whether to terminate parental rights are whether the parents have abandoned the child, whether the parents have problems with drugs or alcohol, and whether reasonable efforts to rehabilitate the parents have failed. L.F. v. Department of Human Resources, 597 So. 2d 1380 (Ala. Civ. App. 1992).

The trial court is given the authority to terminate parental rights if it finds from clear and convincing evidence that the parents are unable or unwilling to discharge their responsibilities to and for the children; the trial court shall consider whether the parents suffer from emotional illness, mental illness, or mental deficiency, whether the parents have abandoned their children, whether the parents have problems with drugs or alcohol, and whether reasonable efforts to rehabilitate the parents have failed. H.M.W. v. Mobile County Dep't of Human Resources, 631 So. 2d 1049 (Ala. Civ. App. 1993).

Factors where child not in parent's custody.

If the child is not in the physical custody of its parent or parents, the trial court may consider such circumstances as whether the parents have provided material needs for the child, whether the parents have maintained regular, scheduled visits with the child, and whether the parents have adjusted their circumstances to meet the needs of the child according to agreements reached in court. R.C.M. v. State Dep't of Human Resources, 601 So. 2d 100 (Ala. Civ. App. 1991).

If the child is not in the physical custody of its parent or parents, in deciding whether to terminate parental rights the trial court also may consider such circumstances as whether the parents have provided material needs for the child, whether the parents have maintained regular, scheduled visits with the child, and whether the parents have adjusted their circumstances to meet the needs of the child according to agreements reached in court. L.F. v. Department of Human Resources, 597 So. 2d 1380 (Ala. Civ. App. 1992).

Scheduled visits with child are not enough. — Although the Court of Civil Appeals seemed to focus on an indication of the parents' willingness to care for the infant in that they showed up for scheduled visits with the child, this alone does not defeat an effort by the Department of Human Resources to satisfy the requirements of this section. Ex parte State Dep't of Human Resources, 624 So. 2d 589 (Ala. 1993).

Mother's previous loss of custody of other children. — Where mother contended that the trial court erred in admitting evidence regarding her loss of custody of other children, and specifically, she contended that evidence regarding events from 10 years earlier was so remote as not to be relevant or material, it was not error for the trial court to consider the mother's previous loss of custody of other children. Such evidence may be properly admitted to show the mother's general inability to care for her children and her lack of ability to progress in learning parenting skills. G.L. v. State Dep't of Human Resources, 646 So. 2d 81 (Ala. Civ. App. 1994).

Placement with mother's friend not viable alternative. — Though mother's friend testified at trial that she would be willing to care for the child and house the mother temporarily, the trial court's determination that the offer did not constitute a viable alternative was upheld where the friend testified that she would help the mother "one more time," since the mother's past history indicated that her situation would not stabilize without protracted travail. L.M.P. v. State Dep't of Human Resources, 597 So. 2d 216 (Ala. Civ. App. 1992).

Presumption of correctness of trial court's ruling. — Trial court's determination on nonparent's petition to terminate parental rights is presumed correct on appeal, and Court of Civil Appeals will not reverse absent a determination that the judgment of the trial court is so unsupported by the evidence as to be plainly and palpably wrong. H.M.W. v. Mobile County Dep't of Human Resources, 631 So. 2d 1049 (Ala. Civ. App. 1993).

IV. ILLUSTRATIVE CASES.

Evidence sufficient to terminate parental rights.

Where the record revealed that since the child was placed in the temporary custody of Department of Human Resources the mother had not made any attempt to provide for the child's material needs, contributed nothing—in the way of money, clothes, or gifts—to the support of her child, visited the child only three times in approximately fourteen months, made little, if any, effort to adjust or correct her circumstances to meet the needs of the child, there was clear and convincing evidence to support finding the child dependent. L.M.P. v. State Dep't of Human Resources, 597 So. 2d 216 (Ala. Civ. App. 1992).

Where the evidence disclosed that the children had lived with their grandparents since

birth and that they received necessities such as food, clothing and shelter solely from them, and that the mother provided none of the necessities of life, the trial court did not commit reversible error by terminating the parental rights of the mother. The lack of a viable alternative was apparent from the evidence and, the trial court's order states that the conduct and condition of the mother is unlikely to change in the foreseeable future. Also, since the mother never provided any support for her children, termination of her parental rights would not create an economic disadvantage for them. R.C.M. v. State Dep't of Human Resources, 601 So. 2d 100 (Ala. Civ. App. 1991).

Where mother conceded the dependency of the children, despite her argument that there existed less drastic alternatives than the termination of her parental rights, the termination was supported by the evidence, no other viable alternative existed, and it was clearly in the best interests of the children. D.W.W. v. State Dep't of Human Resources, 607 So. 2d 240 (Ala. Civ. App. 1992).

There was clear and convincing evidence that no viable alternative to termination existed where Department of Human Resources first obtained legal custody of the child after the mother was arrested and incarcerated when the child was 21 months, where, at the time of the hearing, the child was approximately four years old and had not seen his mother in almost two years, where, the mother had been on probation for two months and was under the supervision of the Probation and Parole Services in the State of Florida and where, at the end of the proceedings, the mother was to be turned over to the sheriff of Lauderdale County. J.L.B. v. State Dep't of Human Resources, 608 So. 2d 1367 (Ala. Civ. App. 1992).

Where evidence clearly indicated that parents were unable or unwilling to discharge their responsibilities to and for their child and that the condition of the mother rendered her unable to properly care for the child, the termination of parental rights was in the best interests of the child. F.L.L. v. State Dep't of Human Resources, 612 So. 2d 501 (Ala. Civ. App. 1992).

Where the record reflected that the Department of Human Resources had been involved with minor children since January 1989 and parents left the children alone at home unsupervised, dirty, and without food, the Court of Civil Appeals could not hold that the trial court's decision in terminating parental rights was unsupported by the evidence so as to be plainly and palpably wrong and accordingly, the judgment was affirmed. R.L. v. State Dep't of Human Resources, 616 So. 2d 354 (Ala. Civ. App. 1992).

The trial court did not err in terminating the

parental rights of mother and father as to child; the record revealed that mother and father did not comply with Department of Human Resource's request that they obtain adequate housing; mother and father failed to correct their living conditions, and there was no evidence that they would have done so in the future, the record supported the allegations in the petition concerning the parents' inability to discharge their responsibilities to the child, and the conditions of the parents had not changed. Ex parte State Dep't of Human Resources, 624 So. 2d 589 (Ala. 1993).

Where relatives were not suitable for long-term placement, and the only alternative available was to maintain the child in foster care until the mother could get out of prison where she was serving 20 years for murdering her daughter and possibly rehabilitate herself sufficiently to become a fit mother; and the son was five years of age and presently adoptable, the court's decision terminating parental rights was in the best interest of the child. T.T. v. State Dep't of Human Resources, 625 So. 2d 808 (Ala. Civ. App. 1993).

Where record disclosed that mother entered several drug rehabilitation programs but never completed one, that she never attended counseling sessions, and that she failed to utilize the rehabilitative services Department of Human Resources (DHR) made available to her and that DHR's efforts to reunite the mother with her children were unsuccessful, there was no error by the trial court in its determination to terminate the parental rights of the mother. B.R.M. v. State Dep't of Human Resources, 626 So. 2d 646 (Ala. Civ. App. 1993).

Trial court's judgment was not so unsupported by the evidence as to be plainly and palpably wrong in terminating mother's parental rights where father contended in his consent to termination, that termination of parental rights was in the child's best interests, since the mother was serving a sentence for second degree robbery and the great-aunt was better able to provide a good environment for the minor child than the mother. M.H. v. E.F.E., 630 So. 2d 452 (Ala. Civ. App. 1992).

Mental illness. — Trial court's determination that termination of parental rights was in the best interests of children was supported by evidence where both the mother and the father had lengthy histories of mental illness. The mother was confined in a hospital psychiatric ward at the time of the birth of each minor child, and as of the time of the termination proceeding she had never exercised physical custody or care of the minor children. The mother was unable to care for herself and she had previously had her two eldest children removed from her care and custody; her parental rights as to her two eldest children were terminated because of her inability to care for those children or for herself. The father had never exercised care or custody of his minor child, nor had he ever requested visitation with the child. The father testified that he was unable to care for his minor child and that he has limited means of support. H.M.W. v. Mobile County Dep't of Human Resources, 631 So. 2d 1049 (Ala. Civ. App. 1993).

Father arrested for murder of mother. — Where the father was arrested for the murder of his ex-wife, the mother of the children at issue, and was sentenced to life imprisonment, termination of the father's parental rights is in the best interests of the children. A.N.S. v. K.C., 628 So. 2d 734 (Ala. Civ. App. 1993).

Evidence held insufficient.

Where there was an apparent diligent family effort to meet the needs of the children, there was a viable alternative to termination. State Dep't of Human Resources v. L.W., 597 So. 2d 703 (Ala. Civ. App. 1992).

While even the uncontradicted testimony regarding some of the mother's actions gave cause for concern about the mother's judgment and her parenting skills, the evidence was not so clear and convincing as to support the drastic measure of termination of parental rights. M.C. v. L.B., 607 So. 2d 1267 (Ala. Civ. App. 1992).

§ 26-18-8. Transfer of custody.

Instances where the parent has previously forfeited or lost custody of the child. — The Ex parte McLendon, 455 So. 2d 863 (Ala. 1984), standard, i.e., whether placing the child with the parent would materially promote the best interests of the child, is applied where the parent has previously forfeited or lost custody of the child. Ex parte T.L.L., 597 So. 2d 1363 (Ala. Civ. App. 1992).

CHAPTER 21.

PARENTAL CONSENT TO PERFORMING ABORTION UPON MINOR.

§ 26-21-1. Legislative purpose and findings.

Cited in In re Anonymous, 618 So. 2d 718 (Ala. Civ. App. 1993).

§ 26-21-4. Procedure for waiver of consent requirement — Notice to parents or guardian prohibited; participation in proceedings; right to counsel; hearsay evidence; assistance in preparing petition; confidentiality; contents of petition; precedence of proceeding; time for court's decision; findings and conclusions; appeal; no fees or costs.

Best interest of minor. — Having found that the minor met her burden of proof as to the first prong of subsection (f), the court need not address whether the performance of the abortion would be in the best interest of the minor. In re Anonymous, 628 So. 2d 854 (Ala. Civ. App. 1993).

In order to deny a waiver of parental consent, the trial court had to determine that the minor was not mature enough and not well enough informed and that the abortion was not in her best interest. Ex parte Anonymous, 618 So. 2d 722 (Ala. 1993).

Discretion of the court.
In order to deny a minor a waiver of her parents' consent to obtain an abortion, the court must specifically find two things: that the minor is not mature and well enough informed to make the abortion decision, and that the performance of the abortion is not in the best interest of the minor. In re Anonymous, 597 So. 2d 224 (Ala. Civ. App. 1992), rev'd on other grounds, 597 So. 2d 225 (Ala. Civ. App. 1992).

Ore tenus rule applicable as it pertained to child's demeanor and physical maturity. — Where the trial court specifically stated that it had considered the minor child's demeanor before it denied the request for a waiver of parental consent, the appellate courts must rely solely on the written transcript of the minor child's testimony. Consequently, the ore tenus rule was applicable in this case as it pertained to the demeanor and physical maturity of the child, and other observations the trial court was able to make, which were not before the court of appeals. In re Anonymous, 650 So. 2d 919 (Ala. Civ. App. 1994).

Ore tenus rule did not apply. — The only testimony in this case was the testimony of the minor; therefore, the testimony was undisputed and the ore tenus rule did not apply. The role of the appellate court was, therefore, to determine whether the trial court misapplied the law to the undisputed facts. In re Anonymous, 650 So. 2d 923 (Ala. Civ. App. 1994).

No need to show that parents would disapprove. — A waiver of consent is in no way contingent on her proving that her parents would disapprove or abuse her should they be consulted regarding her decision to obtain an abortion. Ex parte Anonymous, 618 So. 2d 722 (Ala. 1993).

Indicia of maturity.
The minor's decision to resort to the judicial process and request advice of legal counsel may, of itself, indicate maturity. In re Anonymous, 628 So. 2d 854 (Ala. Civ. App. 1993).

A minor's decision to resort to the judicial process and to request advice of counsel may, of itself, indicate maturity. In re Anonymous, 650 So. 2d 919 (Ala. Civ. App. 1994).

The reaction of the minor's parents is of little consequence as long as she can demonstrate to the court that she is mature enough and well enough informed to make the decision on her own or that an abortion is in her best interest. Ex parte Anonymous, 618 So. 2d 722 (Ala. 1993).

Minor held able to decide to have abortion.
Where unemancipated minor appealed the denial of a waiver of parental consent for an abortion, where she testified that she had a "pretty good relationship" with her mother and father but that they would be very disappointed with news that she was pregnant, and where evidence supporting the finding of a mature decision in this case included the minor's following up a home pregnancy test with a test at the "pregnancy test center" to confirm her pregnancy, her decision that the judicial by-pass was the best course to follow, and her testimony that she would not be able to continue with her job, cheerleading, and possibly her plans to go

to the university if she did not have an abortion, the minor met her burden and demonstrated that she was mature, informed, and capable of making her own decision regarding an abortion. Therefore, the trial court misapplied the law to the facts in this case. The trial court's order was reversed and the cause was remanded. In re Anonymous, 650 So. 2d 923 (Ala. Civ. App. 1994).

Trial court did not err in denying petition for waiver of consent. — Where minor child testified that it was her boyfriend that had taken the initiative in her obtaining a waiver of parental consent for an abortion and that she did not seek a judicial waiver on her own, where the minor presented no evidence that she had sought advice from a medical professional or a counselor concerning an abortion and other alternatives, and where it appeared from the record that the minor's primary reason for seeking a waiver of parental consent for an abortion was to avoid disappointing her mother, the trial judge in this case placed great weight on the minor child's demeanor, deportment, and carriage. The trial judge had personal contact with the minor child and was thereby afforded an opportunity for firsthand observation of her demeanor. The trial court did not err in denying the petition for a waiver of consent. In re Anonymous, 650 So. 2d 919 (Ala. Civ. App. 1994).

Cited in Ex parte Anonymous, 597 So. 2d 711 (Ala. 1992); In re Anonymous, 618 So. 2d 718 (Ala. Civ. App. 1993).